Ethics, Integrity and Aptitude

Ethics, Integrity and Aptitude

Foundational Values for Civil Service in India

Second Edition

P.D. SHARMA

RAWAT PUBLICATIONS

Jaipur • New Delhi • Bangalore • Hyderabad • Guwahati • Kolkata

ISBN 978-81-316-0701-5 (HB)
ISBN 978-81-316-0702-2 (PB)

First Edition, 2013
Second Edition, 2015

Reprinted, 2017

Published by
Prem Rawat for **Rawat Publications**
Satyam Apts, Sector 3, Jawahar Nagar, Jaipur 302 004 (India)
Phone: 0141 265 1748 / 7006 Fax: 0141 265 1748
E-mail: info@rawatbooks.com
Website: www.rawatbooks.com

New Delhi Office
4858/24, Ansari Road, Daryaganj, New Delhi 110 002
Phone: 011 2326 3290

Also at *Bangalore, Hyderabad, Guwahati* and *Kolkata*

Typeset by Rawat Computers, Jaipur
Printed at Nice Printing Press, New Delhi

Dedicated To

My Mother

who personified ethical virtues without being religious

Contents

Preface to the First Edition

As democracy matures in India, the patterns of urban dwelling create newer challenges in the lives of citizens, who refuse to change their rural values. The transformation being rapid, the transitional phase is taking a heavy toll of moral calibre and moral fibre. The family and the society are disintegrating quite fast, obliterating the older value system of religion, without replacing it by the newer values of science and technology. The citizens feel confused and the younger generation finds itself in a state of social insecurity and 'value vacuum'. Money and power are being viewed as the only cherishable ideals, which in turn breed crime and corruption.

True, the values of religion cannot stand to scientific scrutiny but the scientific temper also does not grow over night. This leaves the lay citizens and the civil servants in a state of 'ethical anarchy', generating a pessimistic debate on corruption and frustration.

The Union Public Service Commission (UPSC) has taken a commendable lead to revise its recruitment policy of civil servants. The crumbling system of education and the need of social justice policy in the government pressurize the recruiters to redefine the Weberian merit, which does not deliver the assured quality of service to the teeming millions. Naturally, therefore, the ethical aptitudes or ethical values, whatever they mean in the language of Bhagwat Geeta, or Kantian imperatives of conscience at least merit a sober debate with their epistemological or ontological nuances.

The purpose of preparing this small compendium is to assist the brilliant aspirants of civil service examinations to probe into the current scenario and explore the ethical problems which everybody confronts without any ready-made solutions.

This being a maiden attempt of its kind in the new area, the readers are invited to develop an open dialogue, so that the future administrators and citizens may identify their 'duty ethics' or 'virtue ethics' for a democratic living.

Thanks are due to Mr Pranit Rawat of Rawat Publications, whose phone calls kept me on the table. His most pleasing personality, instant response to help and an ethical concern for quality rendered this enterprise a rewarding experience. May God bless him and his family.

Preface to the Second Edition

The new edition of this book marks an anniversary of its growth and acceptance by the readers. The book received a warm response from civil services aspirants who have suggested a variety of revisions and additions in the text. Consequently, it has grown in contents, leading to a deeper analysis of ideas and materials presented.

Chapter 5 and 6 on moral philosophies and philosophers have been rewritten. A new chapter entitled 'Corporate Social Responsibility and Global Transparency: The Ethical Issues' has been additionally incorporated to highlight the ethical social responsibility of business and ethical interactions in global politics. The case study materials are totally new and include cases from the UPSC papers of 2013 and 2014. The civil services aspirants will find them useful for their study in the theoretical framework of the book.

P.D. Sharma

Chapter 1

Explorations in Ethics

Essence, Determinants, Dimensions and Consequences

The Chambers Dictionary defines 'ethics' as a science of morals … . A branch of philosophy, which is concerned with human character and conduct. These morals have been further elaborated as actions and behaviour, which are considered as 'good' or 'evil' by the society and the individual. An ethical being conforms to or is directed towards the right and the virtuous with a capability of knowing the right and the wrong, supported by evidence of reason or probability. Father Kamil Bulke has translated the term 'ethics' in Hindi as 'नीति शास्त्र' or 'आचार शास्त्र' which calls morals as 'सदाचार'. The epistemological explorations have developed ethics into a theory of knowledge, a part of metaphysics which ontologically accepts the nature and the essence of things as such. To a lay student, 'ethics' is ज्ञान मीमांसा (epistemology), an abstract form of truth which may have dependent ontological arguments (आश्रित तर्क) to render it plausible and even valid.

Human beings, as *homo sapiens*, are endowed with a distinctive faculty of pure reason. Additionally, they possess a conscience (अन्तःकरण), which is different from consciousness (चेतना). Consequently, human beings operate at two distinct levels of animality and sociability. Aristotle called human a 'social animal' just because this animal has to have a human interface, to stay in the state of sociability. The contradictory instincts of survival and domination constantly push him or her to confront the dilemma of 'selfishness' and 'selflessness' although the 'others regarding' part of Mill's liberty is not very distinctive from 'self-regarding' part.

Long before the dawn of 'religious ethics', human society thought of 'virtue ethics'. The Greeks conceived humans as 'moral beings' much before the birth of Jesus Christ. The non-Christian concept of justice in Plato was 'my station and its duties'. These duties were to be classified on a tripartite division of the soul into reason, spirit and appetite. The Greek concept that virtue is knowledge, was the view of an 'ethical man', who personified the Socratic true knowledge of the teleos.

Ethics, Religion and Morality

The first dilemma that an ethicist encounters is drawing contours or parameters between ethical precepts, religious dogmas and philosophical morality. They not only overlap, but the discussion degenerates into boundary loss, assertive emphasis and philosophical nihilism. The primitive man might have envisioned an ethical vista of a moral order enjoining upon kinship, which evolved into family relationships of varieties. This ethicized individual world would have conceived, the fatherhood of God and brotherhood of men as children of God. The ethicization of these precepts worked out the Ten Commandments of Bible or the *Nishkaam Karma* philosophy of Gita and the Quranic principles of divine fraternity of Allah. The human ethics because of its social and rational underpinnings created religious persuasions or the religious compulsions of human soul, which crystallized the ethical precepts. There may be a big theological debate about variations but together they created a moral universe of man which does not exist in the animal and vegetative kingdoms of the universe. The ethical man even today contends his superiority over the beastly beings, who do not have the qualms of conscience (धर्मेण हीना पशुभि समाना). It implies what is synonymous with violence, selfishness, cruelty and irrationality. Aristotle prefixed term 'social' to the human animal to stress upon the gregariousness of human nature, which makes the ethical being angelic and/or devilish in his/her behaviours and relationships. Aristotle was not a Christian, but his virtue ethics later developed into Christian ideals of love, pity, charity and compassion. The moral philosophers of today, in the West as well as in the East, regard ethics and theology as independent branches of moral philosophy but the boundary confusions abound in both. There is no exclusiveness. No ethical precept can be irreligious and immoral and the vice versa. Epistemologically, ethics remains the base of religion and philosophy, but ontologically speaking, religion and philosophy adopt ethical precepts selectively in their respective frameworks.

Ethics, Law and Conscience

Another confusion that touches the essence, determinants and consequences of ethics is about its manifestations at individual level called conscience and at collectivity level known as law. Ethics can only be practised but can never be legislated because of its interpretative variations. But left to individual conscience the ethical behaviours will be conflicting, anarchic and even irrational. Reason must unite the group but it divides them also hence the search of right reason must discover Rousseau's general will and establish the norms universally acceptable as 'Rule of law'. Here individual conscience and the citizens' collective conscience (i.e. law) must speak in one ethical voice. This being not so, the individual requires the right to resist the State or protect against the law itself. The juristic and moral philosophies, both uphold the ethical cravings but have their respective interpretations of sovereignty of law and the autonomy of the individual moral will. The boundaries exist, but they cannot be neat or universally acceptable in social situations. It is also called as *Hart and Fuller* controversy. Hart argued that morality is a realm of conscience. It postulates liberty. Liberty involves rights and rights demand the State. Finally the State has to enact laws to protect and enlarge freedom of conscience, which is essentially human. Fuller's argument is that law is concrete and has an enforce-ability terms of punishment. The law makes explicit, what is implicit in the ethical human action. So the two are complementary and supplementary.

The Essence and Its Determinants

Ethics, being a human science, concentrates upon the study of *human action only.* These actions result in certain consequences. Generally the human beings have knowledge about their actions and the probable consequences that will or may follow. These human actions are voluntary in nature and their performance can be ascribed to willfulness or volitions of the person performing them. The human actions is the result of the will of the person and the will in turn depends on the knowledge about the action. Human beings perform action only when there is knowledge and then they muster up the will to do it. This will further leads to action, which should be voluntary in nature. This action should be the result of free will, which means that the human being is aware of the available choices and has chosen to act in this particular manner. Thus, the determinants of an ethical action are:

1. Rational knowledge,
2. Free will, and
3. Voluntary action.

These three interrelated conditions or elements have to be present in an ethical action.

The voluntariness of the action includes anything that proceeds from the will. It includes not only direct actions but also omissions. The person should also have the knowledge about the objective or the end purpose of the action and its consequences. He or She should have 'sufficient' knowledge and not necessarily all the knowledge about the purpose and consequences of the action. Thus, the essence of ethical action comprises rationality, willfulness and voluntariness. These characteristics are essentially human and human beings can be ethical or unethical in contemplating or performing human actions.

The knowledge of the actions is an important criteria and any factor used in ethical reasoning and decision-making attempts to answer the questions of meaning. The normative ethics addresses questions such as 'What should one do?'— thus endorsing some ethical evaluations and rejecting others. The meta-ethics addresses abstract questions such as – 'What is goodness?' and 'How can we tell what is good from what is bad?' It requires an identification and evaluation of ethical properties of the action.

Normative thinkers investigate the set of questions that arise when considering how one ought to act, morally. Normative ethics is distinct from meta-ethics because it examines standards for the rightness and wrongness of actions, while meta-ethics studies the meaning of moral language and the metaphysics of moral facts.

The Indian Tradition

The orientals looked at ethical issues in terms of individual conscience which became the dictates of duty. The Indian *Rishis* equated *Dharma* with something which is right for the society and acceptable to the individual's soul (धारयति इति धर्म). The Indian *Dharma Shastras* are the cherished treasures of ethical truths. The corpus of Sanskrit literature abounds in quotable quotes (सुभाषित) which explain the deeper meaning of life, nature, society and the cosmos as interactive processes conjoining in divinity in their ultimate. The wisdom of Lao and Tao in China or Shinto philosophies in Japan underline this ethical universality of human nature and its rational frustrations. Most of the scriptures of the orient draw lines of *Marayada* (मर्यादा) or propound the doctrine of limits, which is respected as an ethical code of human relations and social behaviour even today. The *Ramayana, Mahabharata, Geeta* and the texts of Jainism and Buddhism explain the essence of ethical living to yield a qualitative life of peace, harmony, cooperation and compassion. Even the *Shanti Path* (शांति पाठ) is an ethical prayer for environmental harmony. The foundations of Indian moral system can be traced to both social and individual ethics in unison.

The entire duty as moral obligations in Indian system of moral philosophy is built on the assumption that every person, as a human being, has to discharge two types of moral obligations: (1) one related to the other members of society, and (2) the other related to one's own individual self. Under the former are included virtues or duties such as *ahimsa* (non-violence), *dana* (charity), *daya* (compassion), *paropkara* (help or service to others), etc. The idea here is that morality is the inculcation and practice of characteristic human virtues as against animal inclinations of conflicts. The question of inculcation or practice of such human virtues or duties arises not only in relation to members of society, but also in relation to oneself by virtue of being a human, and not an animal.

The Indian outlook is called spiritual and the Indian moral system is oriented towards a spiritual goal. The spiritual goal is generally known as *moksha* (salvation) and morality in all of its forms is a means to this goal. So, morality in India is generally spiritualistic. Then, there is also a materialist system of thought like Charvak philosophy in the Indian tradition, which neither believes in the spiritual foundation of the world nor has any spiritual goals. But, the tone of this system is so weak in the overall spiritualistic system that it has hardly left any impact on the moral system with a metaphysical base.

The Indian moral system has a metaphysical basis. In the West, ethics is autonomous and it does not need to have a metaphysical or religious foundation. It is a social affair and, therefore, the ought-to-questions of morality are to be decided simply on the grounds of social and rational considerations. It does not need to have any transcendental basis. This metaphysics purports to deal with factual questions and purely factual considerations cannot provide a foundation for deciding the 'ought-to-questions. Far from mere 'is', there is a non-passage to 'ought' and the Indian philosophers suggest such a passage. It creates a 'naturalistic fallacy'. The two distinguishable features of the Indian concept of morality are:

1. It refers not only to social obligations, but also to individual obligations related to one's own self.
2. It has the basis for deciding what is moral and what is immoral for the individual on the basis of social good.

The Hindu Ethics

The Hindu concept of the four moral ends of life (पुरूषार्थ चतुष्टयः) are moral law (धर्म), wealth (अर्थ), desire (काम) and salvation (मोक्ष). *Dharma* is the correct way in which a human being has to fulfil his personal, social and moral needs. The moral law is not embodied in God, but it is a moral ideal which transcends the physical world of time and space. *Artha*, in the sense of wealth stands for material means of well being. *Kama* refers to desires common to all humans living within a family fold and social situations. *Moksha* is attaining diversity where ultimate one-ness with the divine energies makes one transcend from material world to trans-material world.

The Hindu ethics subordinates happiness to *dharma* and the ultimate goal which Hinduism prescribes is that soul should be liberated form the constraints of the sensual world and its myriad problems. The salvation means that the self should live in its pure spiritual form or essence free from the encumbrances of the physical world of senses or of the material universe of space and time. It requires a *dharma* or *Varnashrama* system. Apart from the morals, there are duties which a person has to perform at different stages in life – *Brahmacharya, Grihastha, Vanaprastha* and *Sanyas*. The Bhagavat Gita is the primary religious and moral treatise of the Hindus. It prescribes that humans should perform their duty without any desire for its fruits, without attachment and aversion, and without getting distracted by selfish and baser motives. One has to control bad emotions such as attachment, aversion, illusions, fears, lust, grief, anger, hatred, malice and envy. The message of Gita is rooted in the concept of human duty. It is universal and timeless in its appeal and relevance. The law of *karma* is a matter of faith. The *karma* leads to social and economic conservatism. Though it is not the same as fatalism, and though the effects of bad deeds can be overcome, it has created a negative or a fatalistic outlook. Manu, the law giver, regarded the customary law of society as 'आचार' or the standard. It is sanctified by practice over many generations. Vedas provide the moral standard and Manu recognizes conscience as a source of law. The Indian ethics considers moderation or 'संयम' as a moral standard. It prescribes both political law and divine law as moral standards.

According to Gita, there are three paths to the realization of God (1) Action (कर्म), (2) Devotion (भक्ति) and (3) Knowledge (ज्ञान). Virtues, which the Gita mentions, are characteristic of the three principal occupational groups of society. In modern terms, they can be associated with intellectual, physical and commercial virtues. The Gita mentions about positive and negative emotions. At one level, Gita's message is addressed to those who are totally concerned with the realization of God but at another level the Hindu view preaches to be one with God. This can be called ethics rather than religion.

The Jain Buddhist Traditions

Jainism and Buddhism arose partly as a reaction to ritualism which marked the degeneration of Vedic religion. *Ahimsa* is a core moral principle of Jainism. It lays down that no existent life or the essence or potential of life should be injured or eliminated. For a Jain person, this life is a spiritual odyssey towards divine consciousness. The five common moral principles which are applicable to monks and Jain householders consist of:

1. Refraining from violence towards all living creatures,
2. Speaking the truth,
3. Refraining from theft,
4. Shunning from adultery, and
5. Eschewing greed for material wealth.

The concept of a God or the supreme being governing this universe is lacking in Jainism. The world, in Jain cosmology is governed by natural laws. Pride is one of the severe and deadly sins which needs to be shunned. It traces human pride or arrogance in sensory perceptions.

The Jain religion teaches *ahimsa* (non-violence) as the most relevant ethical virtue. The *triratnas* or three gems of Jainism prescribe the ethical framework which stress upon

1. *Right Knowledge* – A detailed cognition of the real nature of ego and non-ego, which is free from doubt, through studying the teachings of the *Tirthankaras* – teachers who have obtained liberation.
2. *Right Faith* – the right attitude of respect towards Truth without being blind followers.
3. *Right Conduct* – it means refraining from what is harmful and doing what is good. It implies that one should observe five great vows.
   a. *Ahimsa* – abstinence from all injuries to life
   b. *Satyam* – abstinence from falsehood
   c. *Asteyam* – abstinence from stealing

d. *Brahmacharyam* – abstinence from sensual pleasures

e. *Aparigraha* – abstinence from all kinds of attachment.

Lord Buddha preached *Buddhism* – meritorious deeds for humans to lead a happy and peaceful life by attaining knowledge. Such a life is possible by accepting a discipline of ten commandments. They are:

1. Charity
2. Morality
3. Mental culture
4. Reverence
5. Service in helping others
6. Sharing merits with others
7. Rejoicing in the merits of others
8. Preaching and teaching of *Dharma*
9. Listening to *Dharma*
10. Straightening one's views

Buddhism identifies the ten vicious deeds or evils which all human beings should avoid. These deeds lead to suffering or *Dukha* in this world and include; *Actions of the body* such as killing of living beings, stealing, unlawful sexual intercourse; *Verbal actions* – like lying, slander, harsh speech, meaningless talk; and *Actions of the Mind* – such as covetousness (being desirous especially of things belonging to others), ill-will, and wrong views. Buddhism judges morality of an action as good or bad based on the intentions from which it originated. Love, charity and wisdom are known as the 'three good roots'. Any action performed (मनसा वाचा कर्मणा) from these roots is considered as good action. It teaches that a person should act out of wisdom and understanding. A Buddhist performs good actions becausc he realises that it develops his moral strength which leads to spiritual growth and ultimately, liberation. The disciples of Buddha are expected to follow four precepts in their daily lives so as to live together in a civilized society with mutual trust and respect. They should:

1. abstain from taking life,
2. abstain from taking what is not given,
3. abstain from falsehood, and
4. abstain from drinking.

The essence of Buddha's teachings is contained in the four noble truths which are:

1. the truth of pain,
2. the truth of the origin of pain,
3. the truth of cessation of pain, and
4. the truth of path leading to cessation of pain.

The three types of sufferings (पीड़ा) are (1) pains of ordinary suffering; (2) pains of anxiety or stress in trying to hold on to things that are continuously changing; and (3) the pain of conditioned states. The purpose of understanding the nature of pain is to transcend it. The origin of pain is traced to craving (तृष्णा), conditioned by ignorance. Craving runs along three tracks which are linked to attachment to sensual pleasures and worldly objects. The noble truth is cessation of all the unsatisfactory experiences and the senses that generate them in the body.

According to Gautam, the Buddha, all human faculties are unified and directed towards a single object. This leads to a mental state without passions, necessary to concentrate on complete self-realization. Men need to follow three golden rules of taking shelter in (1) Buddha, (2) His Dhamma, and (3) the Sangha. Buddhism prescribes various morals for a harmonious family living and social life. It preaches that everyone should have happiness, security and peace. Buddha steers a middle course between extremes of self denial and excessive pursuit of material pleasures. His teachings have a strong streak of altruism. It advocates universal compassion, benevolence and kindness to all living forms. The Buddhist approach can be called a rational outlook to life. Cessation of pain is the objective of Buddhist spiritual practices. The noble path to end pain has been called the eight fold path (अष्ट पथ).

This eight-fold path consists of:

1. Right Understanding,
2. Right Thinking,
3. Right Speech,
4. Right Action,
5. Right Livelihood,
6. Right Effort,
7. Right Mindfulness, and
8. Right Concentration.

The first three help in understanding the nature of pain. The fourth path is a practical way to overcome pain. The right view is the intellectual aspect of wisdom. Right intention is commitment to moral and mental self improvement. The right speech is the foundation to moral discipline which sustains other virtues. The right action includes – acting kindly and compassionately; to be honest; to respect the belongings of others; and to avoid sexual misconduct. The right livelihood implies that one should follow righteous means of earning bread and that wealth has to be earned only through legal and nonviolent ways. Similarly right effort refers to harnessing psychic energy towards production of wholesome mental states. Buddha says that we should perceive the world with right concentration and must not be carried away by the working of intellectual processes. For this purpose, he recommends four foundations of right mindfulness.

(i) contemplation of body,

(ii) feeling,

(iii) state of the mind, and

(iv) the phenomena.

In the writings of Sri Aurobindo, Vivekananda and Mahatma Gandhi, this Indian ethical tradition has been revitalized and revised.

The Gandhian Ethics

The Gandhian thought is multi-dimensional and covers political, social, economic, religious and ethical aspects of human life.

Gandhi's ideas emerged partly from his inner religious convictions, partly from the exigencies of forging strategies for a mass political movement and partly from the influence of others – such as Tolstoy, Carlyle and Thoreau. Gandhi has a deep and abiding faith in God, and has written extensively about his conception of God, or what he refer to as Truth. He regards God as an impersonal force and benevolent governor of the world. God is present (or immanent) in every human soul. Gandhi considers that the ultimate goal of man is to realize the vision of God and realization of God is impossible unless one follows the path of truth, love, non-violence and service to humanity. People should emulate, (to the extent they can) the divine attributes in their conduct. He equates God with truth and love; as God is truth and love which manifests as non-violence, practicing these two virtues is the way to reach God. Gandhi designated his religion as 'religion of truth'. Truth for him is not an epistemological concept but it is a part of what we would call 'a value system'. Gandhi preached that the only way to see God is through his creation and by identifying oneself with it. This is possible only through service to humanity.

For Gandhi, human brotherhood and oneness follow from the unity of life. As a part of God's creation, people share the same life. People should be pure in heart. He insisted on cleanliness even in its physical manifestations. Gandhi believed that even for attaining noble objective, one has to adopt only good means. He constantly emphasized that the means have to be pure. This follows *ipso facto* from the conception of God as the embodiment of virtues. All humans have divine spark in them. People are reasonable, willing to see the viewpoints of others and can accommodate diverse views through rational discussions.

Ahimsa requires complete self purification. It also needs faith in the existence of soul which is distinct from body. *Ahimsa* is described as 'soul force', 'power of *Atman*', 'power of love' and 'utter selflessness'. Many prerequisites are necessary for a steadfast pursuit of non-violence. Foremost among these are truthfulness and fearlessness. Men need only fear God and no one else.

The Mahatma advocated that evil should be tackled by non-violent and non-cooperation techniques. One should hate the evil deed but not its perpetrators. He argues that non-violence can be a potent weapon in the hands of the masses. A non-violent non-cooperation by masses is not a act of rebellion. A *Satyagrahi* is the humble seeker of truth and the soldier of the passive resistance movement. He has to embody the virtues of truth and non-violence. He prescribes various virtues which a Satyagrahi needs to cultivate. Gandhi says that everyone should earn his own bread with his own hands or through manual labour. He calls it bread labour, and it alone gives man his right to eat. It is impossible for a few to amass wealth without exploiting the rest. The rich people are the trustees of wealth. Ultimately, as all property belongs to God, the excess or superfluous wealth which the rich people possess, belongs to society and should be used for supporting the poor. Gandhi was an advocate of religious tolerance. He preached equality or religions based on fundamental principles. The Gandhian emphasis on communal harmony is especially relevant to national integration. Gandhi did not pay lip sympathy to communal harmony, but considered it as a means of promoting an unbreakable bond of brotherhood between followers of different religions. Gandhi's ethical doctrines can be summed up in his *Concept of Seven Sins.* These sins are:

1. Amassing *Wealth* without Work.
2. Seeking *Pleasures* without Conscience.
3. Acquiring *Knowledge* without Character.
4. Doing *Commerce* without Morality.
5. Practising *Science* without Humanity.
6. Professing *Religion* without Sacrifice.
7. Conceiving *Politics* without Principles.

It can be called the Gandhian Code of Ethical Behaviour (गांधी के सात पाप सिद्धांत).

From *Geeta* to Gandhi there is a remarkable consistency and continuity in the Indian tradition. Maharishi Ved Vyas squeezed the essence of 18 *Puranas* and the philosophy of *Nishkam Karma* (निष्काम कर्म) and *Anasakt Karma Yoga* (अनासक्त कर्म योग) into Geeta. Despite the long stretch of time between Geeta and Gandhi, Gandhi's interpretation of The *Geeta Rahashya* crystallises into scripture of truth (*Satya*) and non-violence (*Ahimsa*). The perennial search for eternal truth continues and Gandhi calls them his experiments with truth in pursuit of God.

Vedant Sankhya and *Charvak Schools*: The Deontological debates can be gleaned from the Vedant and the sankhya philosophies of the Ancients. The seemingly teleologists vedantists believe that there is one and only one basic or ultimate right-making characteristic, namely, the non-moral value of what is intended to be brought into being. The so-called Sankhya Deontologists deny this characteristic. They insist that there are other basic or ultimate right-making characteristics also. In the teleological theory, conduciveness to some goal is the necessary criterion for the rightness of an action, whereas in deontological theory, either this is not the case or at least it is not the only and exclusive criterion for judging an action to be right. There are other considerations besides objective-conduciveness. Unlike their western counterparts, the Indian theories of moral obligation and value cannot be categorized as teleological and deontological on this basis only.

In a way, the whole Indian ethical system is spiritual, something is a *dharma* (duty, obligation or virtue) simply because it is a Vedic law or because the *Dharmasutras* prescribe it. This seems like a temperament of the entire Indian system in general. The definition of morality has been advanced in terms of what is enjoined by the *Vedas* and *Dharmashastras*. The scriptures do not say that what leads to *moksha* is morality, but it has repeatedly been said that what is enjoined by the *Vedas,* or what is willed by God or what marks the imitation of the virtues imbibed by God is morality. The *Mimamsa* clearly says that there is no duty other than what is prescribed by the *Vedas*. So, something becomes a duty because it is enjoined by the *Vedas* to be performed as the duty.

Whatever leads to prosperity and to the highest end of human life is *dharma*. So, here also, it seems clear that the obligation for *dharma* arises from the twin ends of worldly prosperity and the final liberation of the soul. According to Kumarila Bhatt, the end of *phala* (फल) may be said to determine the motive of the agent, but not the obligation. Obligation is the result of the *vidhi* (विधि) of which the actioṇ in question is an instance. Like other Indian systems, the system of Ramanuja also takes *moksha* to be the ultimate human end.

In *Sankhya* (सांख्य) and *Advaita Vedanta* (अद्वैत वेदांत), morality is neither necessary nor sufficient to attain *moksha*. So, the question of obligation of moral actions following from a non-moral end does not arise. Nevertheless, some of the systems of Indian philosophy take moral virtues and duties to be an integral part of valueness.

Human are a psychological being. They have evolved from *prakriti* (प्रकृति). Of the three *gunas* (गुण) of *prakriti, sattwa* (सत्) is the most commendable, because it is the repository of good human qualities. So, virtues following from *sattwa*, such as kindness, restraint of sense organs, etc. are to be inculcated and followed. Similarly, in *samskaras*, moral virtues do not derive their sanction from *moksha,* although they serve as auxiliaries in the attainment of *moksha*. The *Purush Prakriti* due in *sankhya* philosophy postulates that पुरुष: (pure consciousness) seemingly comes in contact with प्रकृति. The प्रकृति: is indeterminate and imperceptible. It is the equilibrium of the three constituents – *sattwa, raja* and *tama.* After getting the reflection of the पुरुष, प्रकृति becomes conscious and agitated. This agitation disturbs the equilibrium of the three constituents of *prakriti* and thereby evolution becomes operative.

Depending upon the dominance of one of the three constituents (*gunas*), people acquire three kinds of egos:

1. *Sattwika ahamkara* (सात्विक अहंकार)
2. *Rajasika ahamkara* (राजसिक अहंकार)
3. *Tamasika ahamkara* (तामसिक अहंकार)

Of the three non-orthodox Indian systems, the *Charvaka* (चारवाक), which is a Hindu system, is definitely a teleological system. Its criterion for any action to be moral is its conduciveness to worldly pleasure which is a non-moral end. The Charvak doctrine is

यावत् जीवेत सुखम् जीवेत ऋणम् कृत्वा घृतम् पिबेत,
भस्मी भूतस्य देहस्य पुरागमनम् कुतः।

The Buddhist and the Jain, are non-Hindu systems but being idealistic or spiritualistic, they also believe that performance of moral acts contributes to the attainment of *moksha*. In other words, both Jain and Buddhist systems believe that moral actions positively lead to desirable consequences with respect to worldly life and the life beyond. The Indian moral system, by and large, can be called as spiritual in nature and it is quite natural for it to be deontological.

All the schools of Indian philosophy, except the Charvak, are basically 'theists' in nature. The traditionalists and the modernists both stress upon *Moksha* or *Nirvana*. Aurobindo, Tagore and even Gandhi sought to make morality a direct route to liberation, of the soul. Some of these thinkers including Gandhi, believed that morality is relevant to the pursuit of truth and happiness. Tagore has defined *Moksha* as 'realizing one self into others and others into oneself'. This realization needs cultivation of social virtues like companionship and brotherhood. So morality becomes the highest kind of life goal.

The Hindu view of ethical living does not accept the teleological theory which rejects the ulterior judge – the right man or wrong man – of an action, by virtues of its own merit or demerit the action leads to or does not lead to. This consequential view of ethics can be called Hindu Deontological, because it asserts that there may be several considerations that make an action or a rule right or obligatory besides the good doer and the badness of the action. Certain other features of the act itself, other than the value, may also bring into existence what causes human responsibility.

In the Indian context, man's own nature furnishes a justification for his being moral. According to it, *dharma* is to be followed because it is its own justification. *Moksha* has been brought forth as a motivation in the sense that one who follows *dharma* will automatically pave his way for the *moksha.* But then salvation cannot be taken as a justification for being moral. Morality is ingrained in the nature of man and it can find its *moksha* to resolve dilemmas of ethics. All this boils down to the fact that the essence of a good moral life is *moral common sense.* It can be contented into the following ethical precepts:

1. Avoid doing harm to others.
2. Respect the basic rights of other people.
3. Do not lie or cheat.
4. Keep your promises and the contracts.
5. Obey the law of your land.
6. Help those who are in need.
7. Be fair to yourself and others.
8. Reinforce these imperatives in others also.

The tradition of ethical moral order has a remarkable continuity and consistency in India. It sounds like the ten commandments of the Bible. The commonality of these ethical precepts, like, 'Thou shall not kill' or 'Thou shall not steal', cuts across cultures and continues to be in high esteem everywhere. They indicate the 'essence' part of human ethics. In modern parlance, an Indian administrator or a civil servant can sum them up as:

1. A quest for good life and quality of life for the individual.

2. Pursuit of happiness through *dharma* which is another name of a life of virtue in social collectivity.
3. A virtue ethics which must have a concept of common good.
4. The notions of social good, social welfare and collective cooperation in accordance with laws and social morality.

The author of the *Mahabharata,* poet Ved Vyas, concluded his epic in unequivocal terms:

अष्टादस पुराणेयु व्यासस्य वचनं द्वयम्,
परोपकार: पुण्याय, पापाय पर पीड़नम्।

To help others is a good deed and to 'inflict pain' on others is a sin to be despised. Centuries later Goswami Tulsi Das repeated this essence of ethics in his *Ram-Charit Manas*:

पराहित सरिसि धर्म नहीं भाई,
पर पीड़ा सम नहीं अधमाई।

This essence of Indian way of life can inspire present-day administrators who are expected to have empathy and not mere sympathy with the weak, the disadvantaged and the deprived ones, who constitute more than half of the populace of our country.

The Western Tradition

In the western tradition of ethics and moral philosophy two distinct approaches are clearly discernible in the literature:

1. *The objectivist approach:* It is known as deontological theory. Advocates of this theory look for objective, ultimate or absolute standards or criteria for assessing the morality (rightness or wrongness) of human actions.
2. *The interpretivist approach:* It is called as teleological theory. Subscribers to this theory offer no absolute standards for assessing right or wrong. The individual's judgement, in particular cases, constitutes the only criterion for what is right and what is wrong. In reality, this is 'situation ethics'. The

teleological approach considers only the consequences of human actions and makes judgement on consequences.

The two approaches of western philosophy are based on theories in other branches of philosophy, particularly ontology and epistemology.

The *objectivist theory* maintains that there is a real, objective world external to human consciousness. There are real laws and standards that govern everything, including human behaviour. The interpretivist theory maintains that there is no real or physical world, external to human consciousness. Instead, our consciousness creates the world. The world as it exists is a product of human consciousness. The external world is an 'art fact' of consciousness; phenomena are shown to be willed into existence through intentional acts. Man is shown to live in a world created through consciousness.

Interpretivism in general, applies to the paradigm of ethics. As consciousness develops in a person from childhood, an ego gets shaped, which consists of and be presented primarily as a set of value commitments. Every ego is in some sense a code of ethics. Based on this theory, one might argue that there are as many codes of ethics as there are people, or that there are as many different and even contradicting codes of ethics as there are people. In a bureaucratic system, which is replete with rules and regulations and steeped in incrementalism, the interpretivist approach cannot receive strong support from people in higher echelons of hierarchy. However, it can be helpful in formulating ethical decisions with other criteria or standards for judging morality of public servants.

Ethics from a *deontological perspective* provides only the principles – that is; the standards of morality, how people ought to behave, but it does not explain how people actually act. Thus, ethics is similar to a professional football team's play-book, which contains the plans to carry out, but does not guarantee that the players will actually carry out the same accordingly. Only ethics from a teleological perspective provides the materials for sophisticated reflection on the meaning and consequences of human actions. In practice, the two theories come together to help apply general principles to concrete situations, or to reflect broadly on these particular situations. By showing the general principles and presenting conflicting theories, one can appreciate the difficulties involved in arriving at a consensus on moral issues in public management.

The western thinkers have not only delved deep, but have charted a vast ocean of ethical theories, schools and paradigms. Starting from the Socratic School of Teleology, they encapsulate theological perspectives of St. Augustine and St. Thomas Aquinas. The immoral practices of the 16th century history gave birth to one Niccolo Machiavelli, who is regarded as 'an evil incarnate'. The later contractualists view ethical bonds as a human phenomenon which Jeremy Bentham declared utilitarian or hedonistic. Immanuel Kant, with his more systematic approach of categorical imperatives of conscience, built a coherent theory of idealism which has its strong protagonists and ardent critics right up to the 21st century. The normative and applied ethics keep on struggling on 'one truth', 'many truths' and 'no truths' in the realm of moral philosophy. The epistemological and ontological questions are often pushed to meta-ethical limits and have been carried much beyond the boundary of moral nihilism. A brief history of evolution will make it clearer.

From Socrates to Rawls via Aquinas

Socrates was the first systematic moral thinker of the west. He led an exemplary life spending most of his time in philosophical speculations. He was accused of corrupting the minds of the youth and of impiety towards Gods and was condemned to death.

Political activists like Henry David Thoreau, Gandhi and Martin Luther King stand inspired by his philosophy. His pupil Plato, a great philosopher, outlined Socratic ideas in his famous dialogues namely *Apology, Republic, Phaedo, Protagoras, Meno,* and *Gorgias.*

The philosophic interests of Socrates, were essentially ethical. According to him the only worthwhile pursuit for men is virtue – the noble and the praiseworthy. Unjust acts signify improper behaviour towards others. As a moral intellectual, he holds that no one knowingly does what is bad. He advocates mild asceticism. He was a reflective moralist who analysed the moral categories. To Socrates, an unexamined life is not worth living. He gave a new direction to the then-prevalent moral values and shifted attention from the heroic virtues of his age. His conception of citizenship emphasizes the individual's powers of independent reason, argument and judgment necessary for the pursuit of 'true knowledge'.

Plato

The political philosophy of Plato was greatly influenced by the defeat of Athens in the Peloponnesian war and the death sentence to Socrates. He regards the external world, as given in senses, as only an appearance. The real world is an abstract realm of eternal *Ideas of Forms* which are archetypes and the objects of the material world. He rejects hedonism because pleasures are indeterminate and relative. He makes a three fold division of morals, and associates them with tripartite division of the human soul. The three virtues are prudence, valour and temperance. He associates different virtues with each part of the soul.

Justice is an architectonic or harmonious functioning of the related elements of this soul – (1) the appetitive, (2) the spirited and (3) the rational. Plato's *Republic,* is a vision of an ideal political society which can be called a political utopia. He proposes a constitution in which philosophers will be the kings or queens. Plutarch in his *Life of Lycurgus* gave a glowing, fictional account of the Spartan State and created the myth of Sparta. It also impressed Plato and he exhibits great respect for Spartan military dictatorship. The citizens of the republic have been divided into three classes: the worker, the soldiers and the guardians. The guardian or the philosopher kings alone will exercise political power and they will not be allowed to have private property and family.

These guardians will not be hereditary and will be given education for inculcating military skills and culture. He proposes strict censorship of literature, drama and music. Plato's ideas are seen as offensive to the modern democratic temper. Bertrand Russell traces the ancestry of fascism to Plato. Karl Popper puts Plato among the three intellectual enemies of open society – the other two being Hegel and Marx. The republic smacks of totalitarian and autocratic rule and the individual has been submerged in the State. Plato accepts *Rule of Law* only when the Philosopher Kings are not available.

Aristotle

He wrote the treatise *Nicomachean Ethics* and propounded the concept of the ultimate objective which men can seek. He identified it with refined intellectual pleasures and philosophical contemplation. The common sources of happiness like friendship, family bonds and creature comforts are necessary but Aristotle makes a distinction between intellectual and ethical virtues. The highest virtues according to him is the life of reason or intellect. Ethical virtues consist in the subordination of human passions and appetites to reason. He opposes the Socratic view that the knowledge of morals is sufficient to make a man virtuous. The unruly human passions can only be disciplined by constant exercise of self control. Aristotle regards passions as the matter of virtue and reason as its form. If passions are extirpated, virtue will become an empty shell. Aristotle's doctrine of virtue defines it as the mean between two extremes. The choice of a mean is not like bisecting a straight line or calculating the average. It results from the good judgment of the individual or from his good sense and tact. He mentions two kinds of justices: (1) distributive and (2) corrective. The former justice refers to rewarding people according to their merit, while the latter, i.e. corrective justice implies inflicting punishment for wrong doings. Aristotle is a champion of freedom of human will. The correct moral choices flow from the exercise of right reason. Politics is the ethics of the State and individual morality is not possible without a State. Thus Aristotelian State confines its benefits and privileges to a few aristocrats. He advocates slavery and accepts inequality which is repugnant to modern sentiment of justice. Critics label Aristotle's ethics as conventional.

Aristotle accepts slavery and takes it for granted that husbands are superior to wives and fathers to children. These views are an anathema to modern youth and feminists. Bertrand Russell criticises Aristotle of conventionality and smugness or what could be called 'petty bourgeoisie morality'. In Russell's words:

> There is something unduly smug and comfortable about Aristotle's speculations on human affairs; everything that makes men feel a passionate interest in each other seems to be forgotten. He leaves out, the whole sphere of religious experience. He has nothing to say to those who are possessed by a God or a Devil, or whom outward misfortune drives to despair.

Post-Aristotalian Thinkers

One should not expect to find characters from philosophy books in *Nicomachean Ethics.* In fact, the calmness, composure and balance found in Aristotle is a model for an average man.

Zeno (342-270 B.C.) was the founder of the School of Stoicism to which Marcus Aurelius, Seneca and Epictetus belonged. It rejected the idealism of Plato. Concepts have no existence outside human mind. The world has a purpose, and is marked by order. According to Zeno, freedom of will cannot exist in a world governed by necessity. Men should not follow their inclinations but their reason. Stoic writers push their opposition to pleasures and emphasizes the need to control human passions. They recommend rigourous asceticism which runs counter to human nature. In Stoic doctrine, virtue alone is good, and vice is an evil, and all else is a matter of absolute indifference. The wise person possesses all virtues, and is happy any where and every where. They seem to be far ahead of their times and cosmopolitan in their outlook.

The post-Aristotle history of western ethics falls into the hand of church 'Fathers' or pastors who explain Biblical morality for the believers or fidels. Augustine's doctrine of two swords ties down human ethics in his famous saying 'Render unto ceases what is ceases's and Render unto Peter what is Peter's'. This ethical dictum was developed into Sun and Moon theory of scholastic, particularly by Saint Thomas Aquinas. He has been called a Christianized Aristotle, preaching supreme rationality of eternal law, issuing into (1) natural, (2) canonical and (3) human laws. The medieval notion of European morality as a handiwork of Biblical interpretations was later challenged in the 16th century, when Nicholo Machiavelli made an attempt to distinguish between Private and Public moralities. He was universally condemned for his 'amoral' ideas, called as immoral. The social contract writers linked the concept with the notion of natural law and natural rights. John Locke talks of a 'moral order' in his state of nature. Rousseau sees Ethics in the manifestations of general will which according to Green is the basis of the State. The individualist and the Utilitarian Schools of Ethics reduce the ethical precepts into laws which Kant tried to revise as the categorical imperatives of conscience.

The Utilitarian School of Philosophy regards happiness as the guide for human actions. Individuals, institutions and governments should try to maximize happiness and minimize pain. Good life is one which aims at achieving the maximum happiness for oneself and others. Utilitarianism is neither egoism nor altruism. Mill introduced the concept of qualities or grades of pleasure to answer the critics. He proposes evidence to show that desire for pleasure is a part of human nature. Moore argued that accepting 'goodness' or 'happiness' as natural qualities lead to a naturalistic fallacy, which consists in drawing normative or moral conclusions from factual premises. Utilitarians try to explain human behaviour involving self sacrifice and heroism as pursuit of happiness. The philosophy faces problems since happiness is a subjective and non measurable mental state. Act-utilitarianism involves maximization of happiness in each action but rule-utilitarianism consists in following general rules which can maximize human happiness. Utilitarianism is a teleological theory distinct from a deontological theory. The deontological theories focus on moral rules without regard to their consequences. Teleological theories concentrate on the good or bad consequences of action which may be difficult to foresee. Utilitarianism ignores the distributional aspects of happiness or welfare. Moreover, individual rights cannot be adequately explained by utilitarianism. Hegel and Kant as idealist German thinkers add duty to ethics. Immanuel Kant (1724-1804), a great German idealist formulated a moral theory grounded in the idea of conscience. It is a deontological theory. 'Deontology' is derived from the Greek roots *deon* and when logos is added to it, it becomes reason. From these words, one can see that in deontological theories, an action which means duty is seen as a moral element in virtue and hence a duty.

The categorical imperatives of Kant conceives and abandons moral law in a world of pure thought. According to him, consequences have nothing to do with moral obligation or duty which alone counts for determining whether an action is moral or otherwise. To him, an action is moral if it is the outcome of a moral agent's sense of duty. Kant derives a universally valid moral rule of action known as the categorical imperative. It can be paraphrased as: A rational moral agent *should never act except in such a way that he can also will that the maxim of his action becomes a universal law.* Categorical imperative and rule-utilitarianism are different. Rule-utilitarianism is based on the consequences of actions, while categorical imperative is based on universal moral laws and ignores consequences of actions. For Kant, moral judgments are empirical; they are empirical in rule-utilitarianism. The categorical imperative holds that human beings are ends in themselves. Men cannot be treated as instruments for securing any supposedly higher ends. *'So act as always to treat man, both in your person and that of another, as an end and never solely as a means.'* Kant's moral philosophy sees a constant struggle between human inclinations and duties. He traces the origin of moral law to man's rationality. He rejects education, civic constitution, inner perfection and God's will etc. as sources of moral law. Kant's ethics rest on abstract laws without any regard to the results which may follow from rigid adherence to principles. His emphasis on abstract laws leads him into extreme positions.

Moore propounded three doctrines: (1) ideal utilitarianism; (2) naturalistic fallacy and (3) moral intuition. The naturalistic fallacy consists in identifying goodness with some natural property. Arguments containing factual notions of pleasure in the premises could entail logical conclusions containing ethical judgments. Moore held that we recognize good through a process of moral intuition. His utilitarianism is idealistic because he rejects hedonism. Ross calls such general principles prima facie duties. Ross holds that in such situations the actual duty of moral agents will be right for the particular situation. Another moral philosopher, Ayer, belongs to a philosophical school called logical positivism. He says that as the propositions of ethics fail to reduce themselves to statements capable of empirical verification, so they should be called mere expressions of emotions. According to C.L. Stevenson, moral judgments do not state any sort of fact, but rather express the moral emotions of the speaker and attempt to influence others. Stevenson also argues that moral judgments are simply a cover for the attempts which people make to persuade each other into adopting a particular normative attitude. He introduces the concept of a persuasive definition. R.M. Hare rejected the prevailing emotivism, which maintained that moral statements were merely expressions of individual preference. For Hare, moral statements are prescriptions or guides to conduct. They are universalizable, i.e. they apply to everyone. Hare believes that common morality, professional ethics and personal morality have their roots in intuitive beliefs.

John Rawls

Contemporary thinkers generally try to understand the institution of morality retrospectively. The recent approach explains the contemporary interest in John Rawls, whose treatise *A Theory of Justice* has strongly influenced recent moral philosophy. John Rawls does not discuss general ethics, but examines a particular species of ethics, namely justice. But the wide canvas of *A Theory of Justice* covers several ethical themes ranging from intuitionism and utilitarianism to the ethics of Kant and Aristotle. As such, it contains the central issues of ethics from within its own interest. John Rawls argues that the adoption of two fundamental principles of justice would guarantee a just and morally acceptable society. Each person is to have an equal right to the most extensive total system of equal basic liberties compatible with a similar system of liberty for all. Social and economic inequalities are to be arranged so that they are of greatest benefit to the least advantaged and attached to offices and positions open to all, under conditions of fair equality of opportunity.

He introduces a theoretical 'veil of ignorance'. It ensures that all the 'players' in the social game would be placed in a particular situation. Rawls calls it the 'original position.' In this position, everyone only has a general knowledge about the facts of 'life and society'. Therefore, each player is to make a 'rationally prudential choice' concerning the kind of social institution they would enter into contract with. As the players have no specific information about themselves, they cannot adopt a partisan or self regarding view. They are forced to adopt a generalized point of view that bears a strong resemblance to the moral point of view. 'Moral conclusions can be reached without abandoning the prudential standpoint and positing a moral outlook merely by pursuing one's own prudential reasoning under certain procedural bargaining and knowledge constraints'. This view of Rawls represents 'rational choice within a veil of ignorance'.

The Western Contribution to Ethics: A Review

Aristotle's approach combined epistemology, ontology and psychology. He was the founder of the peripatetic school of philosophy, often called as empiricism. In 17th century, John Locke modified this theory by discarding the role of the human intellect in search for knowledge. The arrival of Christianity added a new dimension to philosophy, as philosophers attempted to link theology and philosophy. The renowned philosophers during the first five centuries (c. 100–450) were St. Ambrose and St. Augustine. This period, known as the Patristic era, witnessed the dissolution of the Roman empire. It was not a time conducive to the study of philosophy. But beginning with the coronation of Charlemagne in 800 AD, there was an era of peace with emphasis on education. The Christian monks, particularly the Irish monks, had preserved the works of former philosophers, and philosophers like St. Alexander and St. Bonaventure could reintroduce the study of philosophy.

But it was St. Thomas Aquinas in the 13th century, who perhaps more than any other scholar since Aristotle, contributed most to modern philosophy. His most famous work, *Summa*

Theologica, represents a combination of philosophy and theology. St. Aquinas mapped out for all time the distinction and the relationships between philosophy and theology and shaped the known philosophical theories into one system. He added to ontology and epistemology new doctrines, which include:

1. The theory of moderate realism,
2. The unity of substantial form in every individual,
3. The doctrine of subsistent forms, and
4. The distinction between the soul and its faculties.

The 16th century renaissance turned scholars towards the study of the classics and pushed them away from pure philosophy. The reformation also caused serious doubts about the nature of people and particularly about the acquisition of social knowledge. But it was not until Rene Descartes in the 17th century that modern philosophy began. Descartes, a mathematician, approached the study of philosophy that parallelled Euclid, a Greek mathematician. He concentrated particularly on ontology and epistemology, with some initial success. About the same time, Thomas Hobbes, John Locke and Jean-Jacques Rousseau were focussing on philosophy, particularly on the nature of human beings, society and the state. Ontology and epistemology were subjects of great interest.

Hobbes subscribed to *Epicureanism* and emphasized that matter and motion constitute behaviours. Locke subscribed to the basic philosophy of Aristotle and became an advocate of empiricism. He claimed that humans were born with a *tabula rasa* and that they acquire knowledge through the senses alone. He denied any real difference between the concept and the sense image. A concept – ethical or philosophical – according to Locke, is a mental form of sensation. His version of empiricism is that the only knowledge human beings have is sense knowledge, and the things man can know are, what he learns through his five sense organs. The intellect or mind is not involved in the exercise of acquisition of knowledge. This view signified a departure from

Aristotle, who maintained that the intellect plays a vital role in acquiring knowledge.

The German idealist Immanuel Kant brought the study of epistemology to the forefront in the 18th century. An Irish philosopher Bishop George Berkeley advocated the Platonic school of philosophy, and denied the existence of any real physical world. In the 19th century, philosophers such as Hegel, Engles and Marx also contributed significantly to modern philosophy.

In the 20th century, Husserl, Schutz, Lukacs, Gramasci and the Frankfurt School, especially Habermas and Marcuse, have further expanded the German idealist philosophy of Hegel and that of younger Marx. Several thinkers have broadened this approach to include 'many aspects of philosophy and social theory in general'. They provide an excellent overview of the philosophical issues and related problems arising from ontology and epistemology of knowledge. They show that the writings of authors identified with the Frankfurt School have a philosophical basis and their views have a corresponding application to social life.

Some of them have also provided strength to the foundation for the deontological, and teleological schools of thought. Ontology and epistemology, as branches of philosophy, have significantly contributed to ethics in public administration or to ethical norms and laws for administrators.

The Ontological Issues

Ontology is the philosophical science that studies *being* as common to all things or objects. As a methodology of philosophy, it uses unaided human reason to study *beings*. The term *being* is understood in its broadest sense, and applies to both human beings and inanimate objects. It is the simplest of notions, the first idea that human beings acquire, an indeterminate notion that it can be applied to everything, including human beings, animals, the world and its contents. Ontology uses the word *being* in varied cases analogously – be it trees, animals or human beings. As a term, it is an abstract of ideas because it is the smallest in connotation and the broadest in its essence. Ontology can be called the starting point and a basic subject of philosophy. In its essence, ontology contains three parts:

1. It addresses the meaning of being.
2. It deals with the ten specific categories of being.
3. It investigates the causes of being.

Ontological enquiry proceeds to find out, what is it that constitutes a being. What are the constituent elements that go to make up a thing or a being? It lists categories or classes, applicable only to the real (not logical) and finite beings. It is also possible to group or list the ideas about beings under the categories, such as:

1. Substance
2. Quantity
3. Quality
4. Relations and similarity
5. Place
6. Time
7. Habit
8. Posture
9. Action
10. Passion can be other specific categories

These categories can be further compressed into two main categories, viz. (1) substance and (2) accidents. The non-substance items are accidents. Substance, nature and essence can be called synonymous. They provide answers to the questions: What is it? or Who is it? 'Substance' means a being whose nature is to exist in itself and not in something else. An accident, on the other hand, such as size, shape or colour, is unable to exist in itself and exists only in a substance. Substance supports accidents.

Philosophers do not agree on the meaning of substance. Some, including John Locke, held that substance is something unknown and unknowable. According to him, substance is an unchanging kernel. Rene Descartes held that substance is something earthless, and Immanuel Kant maintained that substance is something made up by human minds, or a 'subjective form'. Although these philosophers hold different kind of views on the nature of substance, all except Descartes admit that accidents such as colour, size and shape, etc. exist, or have a reality. Descartes denies that accidents have any reality. Scholastic philosophers, on the other hand, argue that it is possible for human beings to gain some knowledge of essence, although the knowledge gained may be imperfect.

Besides substance of things, ontology also deals with existence. It defines existence as the actual (as opposed to potential) presence of an object in the physical order. A great debate surrounds the distinction between essence and existence. Ontology, as a branch of knowledge, establishes the direction from which all sciences, including ethics, proceed. The arguments originating with Aristotle, supporting the existence of a real world external to human beings and the existence of causality are so compelling that most sciences proceed on the assumption that such a real world exists. Empiricists have also influenced some modern philosophers to think in terms of suspending reality and causality, and concentrate on the meaning of things as presented by the senses. When the issue of the certainty and validity of human knowledge is added to this debate, there are more compelling epistemological reasons for the existence of two different approaches to the sciences and particularly to ethics.

The Epistemological Riddles

While ontology concentrates on the study of the different kinds of beings and their causality, epistemology focuses on whether human knowledge provides us with real insight into beings or is it merely a cobweb spun by the mind with no relationship to real things. Epistemology, therefore, examines the validity and certitude of human knowledge. It concentrates on how human beings know these things and what are the faculties by which they acquire this knowledge of beings or things.

Knowledge appears to be the simplest human experience. People seem to know and take for granted that things exist and that they have knowledge of these things. To most people, all human knowledge can be summarized as: 'The world I know is objectively real and I have a genuine knowledge of it as it is'. This statement summarizes the ontology and the epistemology of the phenomenon. But it also raises difficulties because the obvious and transparent explanations do not satisfy the human mind and quest for truth. The roots of ethical behaviour, the relationship between ontology, epistemology and psychology, indicates that ethics is dependent on these sciences. At the same time, the theories indicate that there are limitations of human reason in establishing metaphysical certitude in answering the basic questions. The same can be said about ethics too. It does not provide answers to all questions nor can it advance ethical answers with metaphysical certitude to most questions. Various theorists have also provided a basis for different thoughts in ethics contemplations. Notwithstanding numerous definitions and their nuances, ethics has its roots in the basic philosophies of realism and idealism. They have been called *objectivism* and *interpretivism*. They are deontological perspectives. The Objectivist School defines ethics as 'the normative standards of conduct, derived from the philosophical and religious traditions of society'. It further calls it an attempt to state and evaluate principles by which ethical problems may be solved.

The classical and scholastic definition of ethics is similar. Scholastic philosophers see ethics as a philosophical science that directs or guides voluntary human actions according to ultimate principles discovered by human reason alone. Ethics in this view is a science that relies on human reason to discover the standards of conduct or morality that apply to all human beings. The human reason alone has limits and, therefore, it should not be surprising that these standards of morality also have their grave limitations.

The essential ingredient of deontological definitions is that real, objective standards of morality exist for human beings and that at least some of these standards can be discovered by efforts of human reason. Ethicists devote their energies to discovering such standards of conduct or codes of moral behaviour. Organizations that have developed codes of ethics for their members, such as the Indian Medical Association, or code of conduct rules for government servants or a moral code of conduct for campaigning during elections subscribe to this deontological definition of ethics.

The Scope of Ethical Universe

The interpretivist approach offers a different definition of ethics. Here, the interpretivist is an idealist who does not subscribe to the existence of a real, external world. The interpretivist would deny that human beings can have objective knowledge of the world around. For the interpretivist, a real world may or may not exist, and real, objective standards, laws or rules may or may not exist. These definitions are strictly teleological.

Ethics introduces a radical kind of doubt into the everyday world. It looks at the future. It is concerned with the goodness and rightness of man's doing and making. Ethics looks at the past for the sake of the future because it seeks to clarify the logic and the adequacy of the values that shape the world; and also assesses the moral possibilities which are projected and portrayed in the social give-and-take relationship. In fact, ethics is concerned with the intent morality in itself and also with the moral quality of its orientation to future and to relativism. The ethical tasks reflect several steps which are far removed from the actual conduct of man but they are concerned with society and with the assumptions and presumptions of man's moral life. The focus of ethics has to be human actions and their moral desirability constitutes the scope of ethical universe. This morality of human behaviour requires separation of human actions from their morality. The major focus of ethics is on human actions. This also happens to be the starting point for most legal systems. They are primarily interested in human actions and consequently pass judgments about their legality or illegality. Ethics, as such, does not concern itself with the actions of animals. Further, ethics focuses only on the *deliberate* actions of human beings and not on non-deliberate activities or actions done because of ignorance.

The moral action performed by human beings in ethical sense has a number of impediments. St. Thomas Aquinas has listed these factors in his own way under a framework of limits which delineate the *scope of ethical universe*:

1. Ignorance
2. Passion
3. Fear
4. Violence
5. Habit
6. Temperament
7. Pathological stages

The study of ethics limits this scope to human action only and non-human ethics cannot be considered from a moral perspective.

The Determinants and Dimensions

This moral perspective is the most vital determinant of ethical behaviour. To what extent the practice of an ideal action can or should be called 'ethical' or 'unethical' depends upon:

1. Individual personality values,
2. Social ethics,
3. Interactive situations, and
4. The level of knowledge and understanding.

The scholars in the area of ethical philosophies have examined the purpose of human action. The Epicureans, the Stoics, the Hedonists, the Marxists and the Humanists all have their respective arguments to distinguish moral good from moral evil. In the search for a criterion to assess the goodness or badness of human actions, the various schools of thought or moral philosophy have advanced their respective positions. They have been called institutionists, utilitarians, rationalists and scholastics. The determinants of human morality or human ethics can vaguely be conceptualized and listed as under:

1. Object of a human action.
2. Circumstances under which the human action takes place.
3. The end purpose of human action.
4. The consequences of the moral actions, singly and cumulatively producing results.
5. The double effect of human actions in which they are forced to act or respond in a willy-nilly manner.

These determinant factors of ethics have taken the scholars into various directions to examine the multiple dimensional notion of ethical behaviour in human history. They may be called 'bold moral conjectures', each presenting a data, about what can be regarded as a sound point of departure, when it comes to solving the practical problems of human intercourse. Some of these broad moral conjectures have been garbed in the following terminologies of moral philosophy. Currently, there are seven major ethical theories prevalent in western moral philosophy and their essence can be outlined or highlighted as under:

1. *Utilitarianism*: The idea that we always ought to act so as to maximize the sum total of welfare in the universe.
2. *Egoism*: The idea that we always ought to act so as to maximize the sum total of our own welfare.
3. *Deontological ethics*: According to which there are duties or prohibitions, binding upon the agent, irrespective of the consequences of following them.

4. *The ethics of rights*: According to which each moral subject has certain rights that no one is entitled to violate, no matter how urgent this may seem.
5. *Virtue ethics*: According to which the most basic question in ethics is not what we ought to do, but what kind of persons we ought to be.
6. *Feminist ethics*: According to which women and men tend to think differently about moral and practical problems and according to which an assumed female way of thinking deserves particular attention.
7. *Environmental or ecological ethics*: According to this not only human beings and other sentient beings have moral status, but also nature itself. We have duties to preserve nature irrespective of the consequences for sentient beings of doing so.

These moral theories of ethical action explore the dimensions of ethics as a criterion for judging something seemingly 'right' in contrast to what is apparently 'wrong'. A civil servant, as a person, has a moral duty to be honest, neutral, uncorruptable, sincere and self-sacrificing. He/She should have a consistent set of principles to justify his/her action to him/her self, to law and to other members of society. The moral theories can be formulated with or without any reference to God or religion. The Aristotelian virtue ethics was propounded much before the birth of Christianity or biblical ethics of the unknowable.

The virtue ethics had a renaissance in the 16th century. The other theories were articulated in modern times. Egoism, in its most attractive version, was presented by the English philosopher Thomas Hobbes (1588–1679). The most well-known advocate of deontological ethics was the great German philosopher Immanuel Kant (1724–1804). The theory of moral rights was articulated by the English philosopher John Locke (1632–1704). Utilitarianism was defended by another English philosopher and great social reformer, Jeremy Bentham (1748–1832). The feminist approach to ethics was recently developed by some women philosophers who took their point of departure in empirical studies of the moral development of males and females. One such study was conducted by an American psychologist Carol Gilligan. Even the environmental (or ecological) approach to ethics was articulated quite recently. The American thinker Aldo Leopold calls it a 'land ethics', and the Norwegian philosopher Arne Naess, uses the term 'deep ecology'. Even if some of these philosophers believed in God, they can't be called religious. God and religion play a little or no role in their moral philosophies. They believe that even if God exists, he cannot come to rescue when human beings settle their practical or moral problems.

The Ethical Dilemmas

Dimensions of ethics may mean the scope of ethics or aspects of morals. Values are abstract concepts of what is right, worthwhile or desirable. They refer to many aspects of human and social life. The 'essence of ethics' means only the fundamental nature or the core of ethics.

The philosophical doctrines of objectivism lead to a deontological theory of ethics. It holds that real, objective, moral principles can guide human conduct. It advocates universal, objective rules and a sense of duty. The other idealist school takes a teleological approach to ethics, which evaluates human actions as good or bad based on their consequences. The end of ethics is to define 'the welfare of human beings living in a society, organized through rules of conduct duly enforced.' These rules of ethics are the laws or moral codes which are not obligatory or binding. The essence of ethics cannot be singled out to a particular approach or a theme. The themes generally treated in ethical studies include standards of conduct derived form philosophy and religion; or principles by which ethical problems may be solved. The adequacy of the values that shape the world, need to be maintained. This scope may extend to moral aspects of relations between human beings; which represent a detached reflection on the assumptions and presumptions of moral life; and ethics of individual character. The criteria to speculate about the end of life are:

1. Pursuit of pleasures,
2. Living in harmony with nature,
3. Accumulation of wealth,
4. Working for social good, and
5. To realize God.

The common standards which evaluate human actions can be (1) God, (2) laws enacted by the sovereign and (3) harmony between action and occasion. Intuitions of human mind and self interest in various forms have been identified by deontological ethicists. The 'Virtue Ethics' deals with; the ingredients of virtue and how do people discover and follow virtue? The individual virtues – the personal life within family; altruistic conduct towards other members of society; explain different roles that experience feelings of hurt, injustice, grievance, neglect, disloyalty, exclusion, betrayal etc. They may not behave properly with one another. An action, can be viewed as an (1) object, (2) the circumstances and (3) the purpose.

An action, whose object by nature is bad, will always remain so. A good action can also become bad and an action that is indifferent can become good or bad. Circumstances refer to the time and place of an action, to the agent carrying out the action and to the manner of doing the act. They can be aggravating, extenuating and specifying and may place actions in their situational contexts. The purpose dimension is relevant and decisive. It should be conducive to good life.

The Aristotelian Nicomachean ethics was later christianized by St. Augustine and St. Thomas Aquinas. The latter has been called a christianized Aristotle of middle ages. The renaissance and reformation added a rationalist dimension of ethics, which later got tagged to the contractualist theory of Hobbes and Locke. It was Bentham who revised the rational thought to the basic tenets of hedonism or utilitarianism, popularly known as the theory of 'greatest good of the greatest number'. To this, Kant added his deontological perspective which was further developed by Thomas Hill Green and Bernard Bosanquet. Thus, the 20th century idealist tradition of philological morality or ethics got further fertilized by the scientific theories of socialism and welfare ethics, popularly known as gender ethics and environmental ethics of our times.

The Perspectives on Ethics

Against the backdrop of this ethical canvas a public servant must integrate his or her private and public relationships in such a way that his or her aptitude to public service remains in conformity to (1) law, (2) social morality and (3) individual conscience. He or she will have to introspect his or her moral universe and work out a problem-solving approach in the dilemmatic situations of public good and personal endeavours. It is not only a question of right or wrong. There is a whole series of choices in which ethical musings can help the public servant in balancing his or her decisional exercise and its probable consequences. The virtue ethics, egoism, the deontological speculations and the utilitarian logic have their relevance in dissecting the problem of moral rights of the oppressor and the oppressed. The feminist approach of Gilligan also known as Feminist Protection Discourse (FPD) is the most recent gender dimension added to the concept of public ethics. Aldo Leopord developed his 'land ethics' of environment to which his Norwegian counterpart Arne Naess added the 'ethics of deep ecology' quite independent of God and so-called connections between God, religion and morality.

The seven perspectives on ethics, glibly called as ethical dimensions of moral behaviour, can be elaborated to convince public servants to judge the rightness of their public action in private-public relationships in government as well as society. The debate of utilitarian ethics has been polemical. All objections to it are not true, but utilitarianism is inapplicable. The other objections are flawed, because it leads to wrong moral conclusions. These objections, when carried to their respective logical conclusions, lead to other moral theories. For instance, utilitarianism threatens close human relations and friendship. Should morality focus on traits of character or on the criterion of right action. Similarly, if utilitarianism puts too heavy a demand on human beings, then people will talk of ethical egoism. If utilitarianism gives too much moral licence and allows rulers to kill people to save others, then the government is taking resort to deontology or an ethics of moral rights, which is inconsistent. The ethical egoist can argue that this is as far as our moral obligation can take us. If the poor people in poor countries sacrifice their present-day happiness for their future generations, then let them do it. There is no room for any moral complaint.

The *ethical egoist* can try to play down the importance of the objections. Ethical egoism gives too much moral licence to the agent. We ought not to focus on the consequences of our actions, they would argue, but rather on the act itself. There are obligations and prohibitions facing a moral agent that have nothing whatsoever to do with the consequences of his or her action. For instance, the people have conflicting intuitions with respect to abortion. Some find that the sanctity of life is most urgently needed in the discussion about abortion, since it is the only moral stance that unequivocally gives the right answer – abortion is wrong. Others may find that at last we have run across a clear *reductio ad absurdum* of the sanctity of life doctrine. A utilitarian will find the retributivist view of punishment primitively atavistic. A criminal should be punished even if there is no point in the punishment. But in that case the utilitarian would ask, 'why cause unnecessary pain to a criminal' There is no point in a system of punishment without a deterrent effect.

However, the adherent of retributivist deontological ethics will argue that the pain inflicted through punishment, even if it does not deter from further crime, is far from unnecessary. From a moral point of view, it is a *necessary* kind of pain.

The retribution ethics says that murderers should always be executed, even when this means no gain from the point of view of deterrence. The Roman Catholics have been changing positions as if saying is just an expression of moral intuitions. The adherents of utilitarianism and egoism of the contractual variety need not enter into these speculations. They can adopt a pragmatic stance to the problem of abortion and infanticide, allowing infanticide in primitive societies as they lack methods of contraception and safe abortion, while prohibiting infanticide in modern societies with contraception and free access to safe abortion.

With respect to animals their ways part, the utilitarian must take the welfare of animals as seriously as the welfare of human beings. To the egoist, however, the suffering of animals is of no direct moral concern. Animals cannot take part in any social contract. Some moral rights theorists side with utilitarianism on this point, while others side with egoism.

One can find reasons to doubt that *virtue ethics* can provide plausible criterion of right action in competition with utilitarianism, egoism, deontological ethics, or the theory of moral rights. The virtues are of importance, and it may be a good idea to focus more exclusively on virtues only. It might be a good idea to try to find out what characterizes a moral expert (a wise person) who is capable of solving hard and pressing practical questions. It is important to teach people not to take part in any kind of atrocities, no matter how difficult a situation they may end up in.

However, there may be good reasons not to be overly optimistic about this kind of pedagogical moral endeavour. If we want to feel certain that the kinds of atrocities we know from the past will not be repeated in the future, we should try to identify those wrongs that go relatively unnoticed in our own time. We should then try to make society a place where we are free of these kinds of atrocities, without requiring too much virtue from the ordinary citizen. For there is always a risk in the zeal that governments put into moral education, if tempted, the children will forget all that they have learnt. This is perhaps the main moral lesson to be learnt from human history.

The Gender Ethics and Disempowerment of Women

Some ethicists argue that there is no such thing as a plausible feminist ethics of care in competition with utilitarianism, egoism, deontological ethics and the ethics of moral rights. However, a disposition to care, stressed by many feminist moral philosophers, may be a complement to other moral virtues of importance to both women and men who seek moral expertise and who want to guard themselves against certain kinds of evil action. If all this is correct, then, the situation within moral philosophy may seem promising from the point of view of gender equality. Women are taking up the subject in large numbers. They are participating in the discussion about moral principles on equal terms with male philosophers. At the same time, many male philosophers have entered the field of applied ethics, where they take part on equal terms with female philosophers. However, there exists a more radical feminist critique, which rejects the picture. A radical philosopher Herbert Marcuse calls it a situation of male 'repressive tolerance'. Women have involved themselves in moral philosophy, but they have not been allowed to enter the subject on their own terms. Only those women who have accepted the traditional male way of doing moral philosophy have been acknowledged.

Nel Noddings' objection to 'abstraction' in moral philosophy has been that thinking can take place clearly and logically, in isolation from the complicating factors of particular persons, places and circumstances and these feelings can be modified by the introduction of facts and personal histories. Gilligan also argues against too much trust in the use of hypothetical examples of the kind that appear so frequently.

According to her, the hypothetical dilemmas, in the abstraction of their presentation, divest moral actors from the history and psychology of their individual lives and separate the moral problem from the social contingencies of its possible occurrence. The reconstruction of the dilemma, in its contextual particularity, allows the understanding of cause and consequence which engages the compassion and tolerance to distinguish the moral judgement of women.

Feminist Practical Discourse (FPD) of Jagger

It is as if these authors take pride in what Rousseau claimed as the search for abstract and speculative truth, for principles and axioms of science. They tend to make wide generalizations which are beyond a woman's grasp. Hence, they argue that the female approach to moral problems is the only sound approach to take up. A general statement of this position can be seen in the position of a feminist philosopher Alison Jaggar, who defines something called Feminist Practical Discourse (FPD). This FPD typically does not begin with the articulation of general moral principles but instead begins with the creation of opportunities for participants to talk about their own lives. It requires that *socially disempowered women be heard with special respect.* It emphasizes the need to provide *a supportive environment* in which participants will feel safe enough to speak openly about their own lives. Its most striking feature is that it is nurturant rather than adversarial.

How should people respond to this radical feminist critique? People feel that the only reasonable response must be conciliatory in nature. The importance of facing moral dilemmas in all their concreteness seems to be perfectly reasonable as a *complement* to a more principled approach. The FPD of Jaggar is of importance as a manner of preparing the way for a more traditional approach. In the final analysis, there is no way to solve moral dilemmas unless one is prepared to go through hard normative ethical thinking which has its problems of social logic.

The Deep Ecology Ethics of Organic Wholes

The representatives of deep ecology have been bold. They have not hesitated to pay a price in terms of welfare (brought about, for example, through the reduction of the number of sentient beings living on the earth) for the preservation of certain natural organic wholes. Thomas Moore himself was cautious. If the sum total of welfare was held constant, he preferred a beautiful world to an ugly one. However, he was not prepared to pay any price for the preservation of organic wholes of the universe in terms of welfare.

So, the ecological question remains to be answered. Suppose a mountain has intrinsic value, what price we should pay in terms of welfare for its preservation? There is no convincing argument in defence of deep ecology. The position is no different from competing moral theories such as utilitarianism, egoism, deontological ethics, or the traditional ethics of rights. Two kinds of argument have often been brought forward against the deep ecological position: (1) the methodological and (2) the ethical.

According to the methodological objection, the idea that organic wholes have intrinsic value is ontological. Things like organic wholes or collective entities do not exist. And, if they do not exist, it will be a mistake to believe that they have intrinsic value.

It is true that collective entities such as species and complexes of species do exist. Many of the moral theories assume that human individuals exist. According to egoism, each individual ought to maximize his or her welfare. And, according to the theory of rights, each moral subject has moral rights. It is certainly true that, according to some philosophers, even individuals (persons) have a kind of fictitious existence. We are 'bundles of experiences'. But it would be wrong to argue against ethical egoism that the ego does not really exist. If egoism is a plausible moral view, then individuals *do* exist. A plausible methodological rule of thumb is to assume that those entities, to which we have to make a reference in our theories about the world, must be included as moral theories.

The deep ecological position can be defended along two different lines: First, there exists a traditional, conservative and pragmatic defence of the position. According to this line of argument, one ought to be extremely cautious when he wipes out, or creates new species. Second, there exists a line of argument taking its point of departure in the assumption that organic wholes, such as species, or the entire biosphere, may be of value in themselves. Both lines of argument are defensible but they face methodological and moral difficulties. In this sense, they are not very different from other moral theories. The practical implications of deep ecology may be very different, depending on which line of defence is adopted. If a conservative stance is taken up, one should try to protect an existing and well-established natural order, just to make sure that all that is not human is not put to jeopardy. This may tend to make suspicious of rapid technological and scientific advances. If the point of departure is rather the idea that organic wholes have intrinsic value, then, there are good reasons to *create* such wholes. If a complex and harmonious diversity of species is of great value to establish bio-diversity, then, the universe should be covered.

Is there life on the planet Mars? Perhaps not, but in that case, why not try to establish life there? Why not try to initiate an evolutionary process on Mars, leading up to a situation where the desired diversity is a fact? This may well mean that an environmental ethics can be very sympathetic to science and technology.

The Moral Perspective of Ethical Affairs

Thus, ethical studies – Eastern or Western – are creatively engaged in exploring the 'moral universe' in private and public affairs and relations. The virtue ethics is more personal but it gets reflected in public relations. The western thinkers have deeply investigated the varied dimensions of public ethics in public life by the individual practitioner. The civil servants in India have oriental orientations of ethics as *dharma* or duty. But, the educated administrators have debates and dilemmas about utility, responsibility and consequences of individual unethical practice in public life. The judgements are neither neat nor easy. But, an understanding of virtue ethics and utilitarian ethics can be of great benefit in running a democracy.

Virtue ethics believe that virtue is its own reward. Its consequences may not be visible but a man or a woman of virtue feels strengthened, confident and happy in doing what he or she believes to be right. The consequences of ethics in human actions and behaviours are natural and inevitable. A civil servant, who is honest to his or her duty and committed in his or her assignment, feels at home in his or her office and the so-called odds and challenges frighten him or her much less than they do to his/her counterparts with chaotic ethical values. This is what Immanuel Kant purports when he writes that categorical imperatives of conscience are a consequence of moral dictates of a moral man. Reason or no reason, the man with a conscience cannot help consequences and these consequences provoke him to do things worth doing. Christian ethics can be explained in terms of Christian conscience which obeys the commands given in the Bible. It is a matter of belief that Adam and Eve committed the original sin by eating the forbidden fruit. The consequence of this sin was that there came the Fall. Man was born in sin and the Lord Jesus had to shed his blood for human atonement. Hence, a true Christian should accept this consequence and do charity to lead a life of simplicity, purity and innocence. This consequential ethics is a part of religion and the church has a duty to keep the fellow Christians on their path of righteousness. In other words, church as an institution must play a guardian to human morals. It is a consequence of that unethical practice, which caused the birth of mankind in sin.

The Choice Consequences and Dilemma of Ethical Action

Every action has effects or consequences. *Who is responsible for the impact or consequences of an action?* When a person physically does the act, then he is responsible for the consequences of the action. If a person does not do the action himself, but influences or causes another person to do it, the first person is still morally responsible to the consequences to the extent he or she anticipated those consequences. The consequences of other persons can also be blamed on a person, if he or she has helped or encouraged the action. If a person knows even vaguely, that an action might lead to bad effects then he is morally responsible for the action.

The *contractualists* and *utilitarians* see the consequences of ethical and unethical practices and behaviours in human reason. They inevitably lead to 'good' or 'bad' results. Lockian state of nature was violated by some unscrupulous individuals and their unethical behaviours forced people to have two social contracts to escape the evil consequences. The ethical laws of mutuality and reciprocity were the basis of moral living in the state of nature. The social contract formalized or legalized this ethical order, now called *civil society*. Bentham's concept of 'good', measured by a Felicific calculus of pleasure and pain, was a scientific attempt to understand the consequences that issue from ethical and unethical human behaviours in a given society. The greatest good was the sum total of ethical goodness of the largest number. Thus, utilitarian ethics was conceived as a rational application of moral principles which human beings cannot avoid or escape. The moral rights theory also accepts the consequential ethics, which the determinants of ethical behaviours and relationships generate in social living. The sex relations and environment protection flow from basic ethical norms which ensure quality of life and quality of work-life in natural and human situations. Thus, the social consequences of ethics in human actions of private and public variety can be pinpointed as:

1. Creation of a support structure of norms and values which ensure a happy and healthy living in society.
2. Strengthening of laws by which the governments create coercive structures of authority for allocation of offices as a part of distributive justice system in the state.

3. Grooming of authority of moral leadership within and outside the bonds of law, which can discipline human behaviours in desirable directions.
4. Generation of a utilitarian culture, which is conducive to social living and development of harmonious relations among people, their social groupings and natural surroundings.

The Administrator as an Ethical Being

A public official – be a parliamentarian or a judge or a bureaucrat in the political system of the country – must know the essence of his or her ethical existence. He or she should have the capacity to examine the roots of his or her public behaviour in varied dimensions and manifestations. The legal implications apart, the extra-legal and human determinants of his or her public actions are the logical consequences in an ethical and social interface. An awareness of this 'ethical beingness' can be a great source of strength in interpreting the law of the land and appreciating the social injustices which the governments seek to redress. Ethical studies in public administration like ethics in business will always remain illusive and a far cry like a wild goose chase in their perfection, yet a debate and dialogue in the area is a precondition to train civil servants with social responsibility.

Human beings differ from one another in a number of ways. There are first and foremost, differences in personal characteristics such as health, age, sex and genetic endowments. Human beings also vary from one another in the types of external environment and social conditions they live in. These different elements of human diversity crucially affect the ways in which resources such as income and wealth are transformed into relevant capabilities. Weak, deprived and under-privileged people need more resources. Increasing the social and political participation of traditionally oppressed groups would demand efforts more than just providing access to resources; it might require tackling some entrenched social, economic and political practices and structures.

The ethicists argue that man is not an ethical animal but he is quite capable of being converted into an ethical being. Whatever meaning one ascribes to his or her 'ethical norms' they inhere in human personality. The personality studies by psychologists and psychiatrists indicate that there is something which Gordan Allport has called 'personality'. Gordan's 40-year-old research could not define personality, but he conclusively proves that this 'something' called as one's personality can be changed, revised or improved in certain directions to some extent. This personality development cannot neatly be theorized but can be given a direction by affectionate care and professional guidance. This human personality, which is partly biological and mostly psychological, can be examined with the study of value judgements which are an offshoot of long inculcated aptitudes and attitudes cherished by humans. These aptitudes and attitudes can be measured and scientifically tested, but they grow at different age groups as a part of one's perceptual equipment. The family, the school and the social peer groups play a decisive role in shaping these ingredients of human personality, which is basically composed of the genetic stuff of heredity, shaped by nurture or upbringing. It later gets revised by exposures of learning and/or experiences of frustrations or otherwise. In psychology, they are called primary, secondary and tertiary socializations. The family, the environment, the school and the religious values, coupled with one's own efforts to expand personality, finally create a value system of behaviours, beliefs and convictions to which the ethical studies belong. Hence, it is critically important to analyse and understand the attitudes, aptitudes and the nature of emotional intelligence of young people who are advised to practise ethical values in public life of their careers.

CHAPTER 2

The Ethical Foundation of Personality and Human Behaviour

The theories of ethical justification of human behaviours in a social setting represent an attempt to understand the rationale of occurrences which are regarded as 'good', 'bad' or 'neutral'. The dimensions of this ethical or unethical occurrence may be wide or problem-specific, but it is a consequence arising from several determinants, consciously and unconsciously rooted in ethical foundations of human personality. The vegetative and veterinary kingdoms do not have these ethical foundations. They have traits, habits or some attitudes which may generate fragile aptitudes that cause prioritization of values in behaviours. A dog may bite the thief and not the master, but he knows little about the consequences of biting and the desirability of his biting function as a habit. Human beings alone have the privilege of distinguishing between right and wrong, fair or foul, good and bad and above all what is sublimating and what is degrading and profane. They feel proud and accept the shame of their actions and relationships as individual actors and as a collectivity. It is primarily because there exists a sort of ethical foundation in human personality which gets stirred up and shaken, whenever one's value system is pampered or damaged. This ethical foundation may be strong or fragile. It may be pervious or impervious. It can sustain behaviours or may inhibit the same in the moments of crisis and dilemma. The edifice of human behaviour needs this basic ethical foundation which according to psychologists is a part of personality, broadly composed of perceptual experience, attitudinal habits, aptitudinal dispositions and value judgements operating as rational maturity and emotional intelligence.

The Morality of Social Conventions

Moral questions concerning the constitution of a society are resolved by establishing social conventions which regulate social behaviours. The fields of moral life and moral discourse, represent the two main parts of philosophical ethics. Between them lies the area of customary behaviour, which mediates between the two. It is a part of ethics, but not of philosophical ethics. The customary behaviour can only be investigated empirically but in society it is mediated through a social code of morality, which is acceptable to some and opposed by others.

Ethics is radically concrete, but the moral questions arise only in real situations and can only be dealt in relation to them. For this reason, most of the people are concerned with the general conditions of moral situations here and now. These include the historical preconditions of a given society, its cultural foundations and especially its moral culture, the stage of development of civilization and the whole area of existing social conventions, from customary behaviour through laws to fundamental and human rights.

A moral life is a matter of will and effort for each individual. Nevertheless, the structures which a mode of living must have to qualify as a moral being can be determined in general terms. The basic requirement is that one takes one's life seriously. If one's life is to conform to a project, one must take explicit responsibility for it.

In the field of social conventions, moral questions do not arise from every regulation affecting social behaviour. Social customs and conventions become morally relevant when they touch on the basic conception of a society in which one lives, and the concept of humanity implicit in it. Such questions arise with regard to the regulation of social behaviour towards externals and human nature that people themselves are and their relations with objects of world outside. The connection between the different parts pertains to ethics. While the division between questions of the moral life and questions of conventions of social behaviour is an analytical one, it characterizes a certain state of social development. It is one of the factors which marks out the state as *modern*. To understand this division, it is necessary to place ethics within the concrete framework of historical setting.

If customary behaviour and the moral realm can be distinguished, the moral questions with regard to one's own life and social life emerge and the customary behaviour becomes insufficient. Nevertheless, it is customary behaviour which places moral decisions in the forefront. Once taken, on a permanent footing, it turns them into habits and these habits, and the resulting solidity of modes of living, reliability of character and predictability of social behaviour become necessary for a moral life. Here, the social behaviour should conform to the basic social consensus without constant recourse to explicit rules. So, the realm of the customary behaviour must be paid its due. Even though it is not the area of true moral behaviour, it is the humus of that behaviour, or the ground from which it constantly arises and to which it returns in terms of its ethos.

Psychological theories conclude that human personality has traits and its development does not mean scaling a summit. It is like a plateau and men and women keep skating around its slopes and ascents. The organizational behaviour of individuals rests on the assumptions that:

1. Human personalities have differences,
2. Individual behaviours are caused,
3. People cherish dignity but the behaviours are holistic, and
4. Mutuality of interests, as perceived, contribute to the interest of collectivity.

Each employee in an administrative office can be regarded as an island unto himself or herself. Their ethical or not so ethical behaviours are influenced by several overt and covert factors. The foundations of this group behaviour can be explained as under:

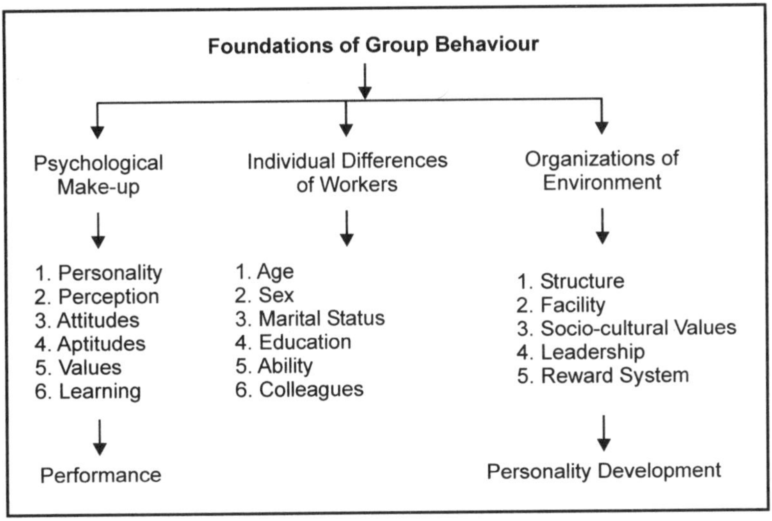

Thus, the internal and external factors, shaped by individual differences, generate behaviours. Their goodness or 'performance conduciveness' depends upon the level of personality development, which is essentially an internal matter of attitudes, aptitudes and values. Personalities can be probed and analytically broken up into specific traits, but the overall behaviour is a composite and collective response which can be seen or measured in human performance. This foundational map of human personality can help in understanding why people behave the way they do. For instance, poor people may be honest and the rich may be cheats and thieves. The female workers may be hardworking but they may exploit the male partners. The highly educated officers in government may be corrupt and the illiterate poor peons may be extra-honest or both of them may be selectively corrupt in their areas of operations. Notwithstanding all these contradictions and variations, a broad understanding of ethical relations and behaviours can be worked out by explorations in human personality.

The Ethical Character of Personality

The term 'personality' is derived from its Latin root 'persona', which means a mask, which the jokers of Greek tragedies used to wear on the stage. It means that they are not what they look like. The superficial social image of human beings does not bear out their actual self. The enemies can smile and shake hands. People play live roles in the drama of life under the garb of the respective personalities. Carl Rogers views personality in terms of an organized, permanent and subjectively perceived entity, which is at the very heart of all human experience. It is an internal something that guides and directs all human activity. Sigmund Freud, the doyen of psychologists, analysed the structure of personality into three components:

1. The id,
2. The ego, and
3. The super ego.

The Id

Id is a reflection and a primary process which the personality employs to get rid of tension. The primary process instantly attempts to form a mental image of the object that removes the tension. For instance, a hungry man experiences partial gratification of his hunger by imagining a delicious meal in his mind. In such reflex actions, the id responds automatically to sources of irritation and reduces the tension. This inbuilt reflex mechanism may cause sneezing, blinking, weeping, laughing, etc.

The Ego

The id or mental image does not satisfy physical needs. The reality persists and ego develops out of the id because of the necessity to deal with the real. Tension of hunger needs food, no matter how or what.

The Super Ego

The human beings, equipped with a system of values, norms, attitudes and ethical practices, want to have a reasonable compatibility with the prevalent values of society. The super ego represents the internalized representation of the values and morals of society as taught to the child by the parents and the peers. It judges the rightness of action from social standards.

Thus, in Freud's analysis id seeks pleasure, the ego tests reality and the super ego strives for perfection. The human organism is not born with a super ego. The children incorporate it through interactions with parents (family), teachers (school) and other peer groups in their formative years.

In the personality of a normal male or female, the three components, viz. id, ego and super ego, work as a team which produces an integrated behaviour. But in case they are at odds, the ego postpones gratification which the id wants right away, but the super ego keeps on battling with both because the behaviour falls short of the moral code of the society. Freud believed that the conflict between the id impulses of flesh, primarily sexual and aggressive instincts, and the restraining influences of the ego and the super ego, constitutes the motivating urge of personality which needs a release of energy. Much of crime, corruption, malpractices, temptations and errant unethical behaviours are caused or can be explained in this Freudian frame of psychoanalysis of personality.

The personality, conceived as some kind of a hypothetical internal structure, is somewhat similar to all the human beings, yet it can be called extremely unique also. It determines a person's adjustment to his or her environment. The traits of personality interact and bring out how one views himself or herself and others in dynamic social situations. The distinguishing characters lend identity to personality and the psycho-social adjustments determine behaviours, ethical or otherwise. The scholars have developed personality theories on the basis of this adjustment or harmony which may differ in degrees.

The Personality Theories

1. *Type Theory:* Kretschmer and Sheldon classified persons on the basis of anthropological features like height, physique, face, forehead, etc. Freud and Jung classified personalities as introverts and extroverts.
2. *Trait Theory:* A factor analysis of traits has been worked out to prepare personality inventories. Shyness, boldness, firmness, flexibility, etc. give the concept of 'job fits'. Some believe that traits give meaning to personality and are measurable.
3. *Psychoanalytic Theory*: Freud is the major exponent of this school. His concept of 'libido' gave credence to the unconscious needs and conflicts of the sub-conscious. Freud's contribution, by his study of sexuality, added several new dimensions to the areas of creative behaviour, dissatisfaction, group development and leadership influence in groups.
4. *Social Learning Theory:* This theory is credited to F. Skinner, who repudiates all explanations of behaviours based on metaphysical mass, the self, the unconscious or any other hypothetical entity that falls under it. As a social learning theorist, Skinner believes that human beings have competences by which they develop cognitive strategies, cherish

outcomes and attain subjective value performances. The reciprocal behaviour patterns heighten social learning. Abraham Maslow rejects this piecemeal approach because according to him this studies trees, not the forest.

5. *Self-actualization Theory:* Maslow's self-actualization of personality is a humanistic psychology, steeped in European existential philosophy of Kierkegard, Sartre, Camus and Binswanger. In fact, it was a humanistic school, which Carl Rogers named as 'self theory'. Rogers believes that human organism has a natural tendency to move in the direction of differentiation, self-responsibility, cooperation and maturity.
6. *Maturity Theory of Personality:* Chris Argyris of Harvard University identified a continuum from infancy to maturity of adulthood. According to him, personality evolves from immaturity to maturity and it can be measured on a seven-scale dimension. These characteristics are:

1.	From passivity	To activity
2.	From dependence	To independence
3.	From few behaviours	To diverse behaviours
4.	From shallow interests	To deep interests
5.	From short-time perspective	To long-time perspective
6.	From subordinate position	To superordinate position
7.	From lack of self-awareness	To self-awareness and control

In contrast to stage theories of Freud and Erikson, the Argyris' model assumes that personalities grow and their ossification should be discouraged. The absence of career planning in government renders the civil servants immature and even with their seniority they indulge in unethical practices in the system.

The Job Misfits in Civil Services

Human behaviour in all social groups – governmental or corporate – revolves around the personality of the worker or the employee. The HRD research confirms that wrong entries and ill-placements create job misfits and they are responsible for most of the malpractices of corruption and law breaking in bureaucracy or in open markets. Personalities can be given direction by training or discipline, but the basic stuff of attitudes and aptitudes remain active or dormant. As soon as there comes an opportunity or stimuli for immoral or illegal behaviours or relationships, they get activised and develop into habits of extortion, exploitation and domination. A deep exploration of inner personality can bring out perceptions, attitudes and aptitudinal value judgements which are too hard to be persuaded to change. Average people succumb to these allurements and worse still, their value systems start justifying them. They start feeling at home with evil practices and the undesirable behaviour gets legitimized or confirmed in their psychological estimation. It is a malaise but the erring individual takes it as a matter of triumph or achievement.

Ethical value judgements apart, the personality has a foundational base and its constituents namely perception, attitude, aptitude or value judgements, all come into play to provide a mandate to human organism. The response may be called action, reaction or interaction, which is cumulatively termed as 'behaviour'. The behaviour is a neutral term but the super ego of the 'grown up individual' dubs it as immoral or unethical. The honest and dishonest persons have a seminal role in adjusting the situations to personalities. In most cases they are helpless because the groundwork equipment of personality does not come to their rescue. They cannot create determinants of their personality but allow their unethical behaviours to obey the dictates of instable foundations of their personality. The values that inhere in human personality are an end result of a long process of aptitudinal growth and attitudinal confirmations. The early stage of childhood, i.e. first six years, according to psychologist Margret Mead, is critical and decisive. The primary socialization comes from the family, then school, religion and the secondary and tertiary socializations contribute by way of experiences, exposures and learning processes of the individual. The inculcation of values can be seen as formation, development and cementing of personality behaviours.

The Cognitive Processes

These can broadly be classified into five process categories as under:

1. Heredity,
2. Nurturing environment,
3. Family interactions,
4. Social exposures, and
5. Situational experiences.

Heredity refers to those factors that were determined at the time of conception. Physical stature, facial attractiveness, sex, temperament, muscle composition and reflexes, energy level and biological rhythms are characteristics that are generally considered to be imported either completely or substantially by one's parents. The heredity approach argues that the ultimate explanation of an individual's personality is the molecular structure of the genes, located in the chromosomes. It is said that at conception, each parent normally contributes 23 chromosomes. These chromosomes contain thousands of genes, which seem to be the transmitters of traits. Even separate children of the same parents do not have identical genetic make-ups. Only identical twins, who develop from a single fertilized ovum, possess the same pattern of genes. The role of heredity in personality development is still an unsettled area of understanding. The problem is that geneticists face a major obstacle in gathering information scientifically on the human beings. Animal scientists can conduct highly controlled breeding experiments, but geneticists studying human heredity cannot. Through research on animals, it has been shown that both physical and psychological characteristics can be transmitted through heredity. However, in the case of humans, who cannot be subjected to the necessary controls, the evidence is much less convincing.

Nevertheless, the role of heredity in personality development cannot be minimized. Physical attributes may be largely attributed to heredity. The children acquire similar traits. The following classification of these characteristics is generally inherited by humans from the personality profiles or genomes of their parents:

1. Physical structure (how tall or short one is, whether one has a long or short nose, large or small feet – briefly, how one is put together in terms of outer appearance).
2. Reflexes (direct response to stimuli, such as withdrawing from a pin prick, blinking when something approaches the eye).
3. Innate drives (impulses to act based on physiological tensions, but these must be linked through learning with activities which will reduce the tensions).
4. Intelligence (the capacity to learn, to modify responses).
5. Temperament (patterned and recurrent responses associated with basic emotional make-up, for example, phlegmatic, excitable, or lethargic).

If all personality characteristics were completely dictated by heredity, they would be fixed at birth and no amount of experience could alter them. Personality development owes much to environment rather than to mere heredity.

Environment is an omnibus term and it includes factors like culture. Culture establishes norms, attitudes and values that are passed along from one generation to another and creates consistencies overtime. Anthropologists have demonstrated the important role that culture plays in the development of human personality. The methods by which an infant is fed and toilet-trained, make the transition from adolescence to adulthood, which is culturally determined. While growing, the child learns to behave in ways expected by the culture of the family in which the baby was born. One of those expectations has to do with sex roles. Most cultures expect different behaviours from males and females. Sex roles may vary from culture to culture, but it is considered natural in any culture for boys and girls to have predictable differences in personality merely because they belong to different sex.

Every culture has its own sub-cultures, each with its own views about qualities like moral values, standards of cleanliness, styles of dress and definitions of success. The cultural sub-group exerts its influence on personality. All boys are expected to show certain personality characteristics as compared to girls, similarly, a poor boy raised in an urban slum is expected to behave differently in some respects than a well-to-do child raised in a middle-class suburb. Although this culture has significant influence on personality development, linear relationship cannot be established between personality and culture. The cultural impacts upon an individual are not uniform, because they are transmitted by parents and other kins, who are not alike in their values and practices. Thus, an individual has his or her unique experiences. Each individual reacts in his or her own way to social pressures with behavioural differences which are caused by a variety of biological factors.

The family has a decisive influence on personality development, particularly in early stages. The parents shape the identification process which is important to an individual's early development. Usually, the parents of the same sex as that of the child serve as role model for the child's identification. This process can be examined from different perspectives. For example, the identification can be viewed as the similarity of behaviour (including feelings and attitudes) between the child and the model. The identification can be looked upon as the child's motives or desires to be like that of the model. Similarly, the identification can be viewed as the process through which the child actually takes on the attributes of his or her model. From all these perspectives, the identification process is fundamental to the understanding of personality behaviour – ethical or otherwise.

The overall home environment created by the parents, in addition to their direct influence, is critical to personality inclinations and dispositions. For example, children with a markedly institutional upbringing (orphans) or children reared in cold, unstimulating home are much more likely to be socially and emotionally maladjusted than children raised by parents in a warm, loving and stimulating environment.

Siblings (brothers and sisters) also influence personality. It has been argued that sibling position is an important psychological variable because it represents a microcosm of the significant social experience of adolescence and adulthood. It is argued that those first-born are more prone to be schizophrenic, more susceptible to social pressures and more dependent than those later-born. The first-born are also more likely to experience the world as more orderly, predictable and rational than the later-born children.

Besides the heredity, environmental and family influences, there is greater realization that other relevant persons, groups and organizations exercise their due role in personality relations and interactions. This is commonly called the socialization process. It is especially relevant to official behaviour because the process is not confined to early childhood, but takes place throughout one's life. In particular, evidence is accumulating that socialization may be one of the best explanations of why employees behave the way they do, in today's public life.

This socialization involves the process by which a person acquires from the enormously wide range of behavioural potentialities that are open to him or her. It starts at birth, and the behaviour patterns that are customary become acceptable to the family, and later to the social groups and the employing organizations. Thus, socialization starts with the initial contact between a mother and her new infant. After infancy, other members of immediate family (father, brothers, sisters and close relatives or friends), followed by the social group (peers, school friends and members of the working group) play influential roles.

The Determinants of Personality

Heredity, early socialization and situational considerations pertain to the historical nature of personality development. They are no doubt important in ethical behaviour but it must be recognized that it is the immediate situation which finally predominates. The worker whose developmental history has shaped a personality that incorporates a high need for power and achievement when placed in a bureaucratized work situation, may become frustrated and behave apathetically and/or aggressively. Thus, on the surface, this worker appears to be lazy and/or a trouble maker, yet the developmental history would predict that the individual should be a very hard worker, striving to get ahead.

While it seems logical to suppose that situations will influence an individual's character, a neat classification scheme tells us that the impact of various situations always eludes prediction. However, we do know that certain situations are more relevant than others in influencing moral conduct. What is of interest taxonomically, wrote Lee Sechrest, is that situations seem to differ substantially in the constraints and they impose pressure on behaviour. The development of personality, being a complex process, reflects many influences both within and outside the individual. Personality progresses through identifiable stages and never stops changing. One can, however, examine personality at any point in time within its developmental sequence in order to compare and contrast individual personalities. One can also do this to show more effectively some of the more important components of personality.

Personality-wise Classification of Civil Servants

The civil servants can be classified personality-wise too. Some of these types express the dominant traits which determine the personality behaviour.

Authoritarian and Machiavellian

The former ones love authority and are too rigid to change, while the Machiavellians believe that the end justifies the means. They love power and wish to retain and expand it at all costs. Authoritarianism, as a concept, was developed by psychologist Theodor Adorno during World War II to measure susceptibility to autocratic, fascistic, or anti-democratic appeals. Since then, the concept has been extended to the authoritarian personality which is a generic term used to describe an individual who has a strong belief in the legitimacy of established mechanisms of formal authority. Authoritarian officials view obedience to authority as necessary, and they exhibit a negative philosophy of people that adheres to conventional and traditional value systems. Such people are intellectually rigid, and oppose the use of subjective feelings. Authoritarians tend to be rigid in their positions, place high moral value on their beliefs, and are strongly oriented towards conformity to rules and regulations. Such government officials naturally prefer stable and structured work environment which has to be governed by clean rules and procedures. Similarly, authoritarians are likely to prepare autocratic or directive leadership and they exhibit high respect for individuals in positions of authority.

Hierarchy of civil service suits to these people. The locus of control of these officials lies in outside forces. Their activities and behaviours are determined by forces beyond their own control. These personality traits are manifested in different beliefs which are significant to administrative decision. These external kind of officials are less satisfied with their jobs. They have high power assertions and are more alienated from work setting. They are less involved in their jobs in contrast to the internals who believe that events are within one's control. Internals typically have more control over their own behaviours. They are more active in seeking information to make decisions, and are more active socially than externals. The grabbing of power and its expansion and retention make them Machiavellian.

'Machiavellianism' as a term has been derived from the writings of Niccolo Machiavelli. It refers to an individual's propensity to manipulate people. Machiavellian officials are prone to participate in power politics. They are adept at interpersonal game-playing, power tactics, and in identifying influence patterns of social groups. Personality-wise, the Machiavellian employees do not believe in ethical norms. To them, the ethical considerations in evaluating job performance are irrelevant. They possess bargaining skills, such as negotiation or where there are substantial rewards for winning higher promotions these Machiavellian officers usually perform better.

Introvert and Extrovert Officials

Introversion and extroversion are common descriptions of personality traits. These terms are normally associated with an individual's sociability and interpersonal orientation. Extroverts are gregarious and sociable individuals while introverts are shy, quiet and retiring. The introverts and extroverts have significantly different career orientations and require different official environments to maximize performance in civil service. Extroverts are more suitable for positions that require high level interactions with others, whereas introverts are more inclined to excel at tasks that require thought and analytical skills. Not surprisingly, the administrative positions in India are dominated by extroverts. It suggests that extroversion trait is a factor of administrative success in civil service careers.

High and Low Self-esteem Employees

Self-esteem trait as a feeling of like or dislike of oneself is quite relevant in official behaviours. In fact, it varies from person to person. This self-esteem is directly related to the desire for success. People with high self-esteem believe that they have abilities to undertake challenging jobs. They tend to choose unconventional jobs than those with lower self-esteem. The status system of civil service affects these officers. People with low self-esteem are more susceptible to external political influence than those with high esteems. Low-esteem people like clerks and fourth-class employees are dependent on the receipt of positive evaluations from others. As a result, they are more likely to seek approval from seniors and more prone to conform to the beliefs and behaviours of those whom they respect than the senior officials. In senior administrative positions the low-esteem people tend to be concerned with pleasing others and, therefore, are less likely to take unpopular stands than the high-esteem officials in lower echelons of bureaucracy. Self-esteem is also related to job satisfaction. The high-esteem officers are more satisfied with their jobs rather than the low-esteem employees in higher positions of power.

Risk-taking and Risk-aversive Officers

People in administration differ a great deal in their willingness to take chances. Their propensity to assume or avoid risks has been shown to have an impact on how long it takes to the officials to take decisions on their files and how much information they require before making their final choice. High risk-taking officials make more rapid decisions and use less information in making their choices rather than low risk-taking administrators. The decisional accuracy for both the groups may be the same.

It is generally correct to conclude that civil servants in government are risk aversive, yet there are individual differences on this score. As a result, it makes sense to recognize these differences and even to consider risk-taking propensity as a merit. It may lead to more effective performance of the officer in the field. Some jobs demand rapid decision-making, while in others this personality characteristic might prove a major obstacle. For instance, accountants performing audit functions can be better filled by officers with a low risk-taking propensity.

High and Low Self-monitoring Civil Servants

Another personality trait more commonly found among senior officials in India is called 'self-monitoring'. It refers to the individual's ability to adjust his or her behaviour to external factors.

Individuals high in self-monitoring can show considerable adaptability in adjusting their behaviour to external situational factors. They are highly sensitive to external cues and can behave differently in different situations. High self-monitors are capable of presenting striking contradictions between their public persona and private selves. Low self-monitors cannot deviate their behaviour. They tend to display their true dispositions and attitude in every situation. Hence, there is high behavioural consistency between who they are and what they do. The high self-monitors tend to pay closer attention to the behaviour of others and are more capable of conforming than are low self-monitors. One might hypothesize that high self-monitors are more successful in senior administrative positions where individuals are required to play multiple, and even contradictory roles. The high self-monitor official is capable of putting on different 'faces' for different audiences.

Personality: The Focal Point of Integrity

Thus, personality can be understood as the focal point in determining motivation. It is impossible to give a full and comprehensive account of executive behaviour without raising questions of why they behave as they do. For example, effective executives in India spend much time on personnel matters, they concentrate lesser effort on efficiency and performance. This executive behaviour can be explained in their low motivation. This low motivation can be seen in the direction and persistence of action apparent in the unethical conduct of junior employees in India. Personality is the organizing centre around which people's motives form a unified and integrated system of ethical behaviour.

Personality characteristics of public servants influence selection of individuals to occupy various positions and government services. The traits required for a successful development officer are different from those required for an executive in charge of a municipal corporation. In this connection, a series of tests have been devised. These tests like California Test of Personality, Rorschach Ink Blot Test, Thematic Apperception Test, etc. can go a long way to help selection of right kind of officials for right jobs in government or in the corporate world.

Ethical Foundation of Personality

Although the concept of personality has an organizational context, yet there is a need to understand the human side of personality. In general, the latter is more significant than the former in the context of public service. Despite serious attempts, experts have not been able to comprehend the real nature of personality. Of all the problems that have confronted human beings since the beginning of recorded history, perhaps the most significant one has been the riddle of human nature. To the question, 'What is man', there are countless answers and a great many avenues have been explored, with an enormous variety of concepts being employed along the way. Astrology, philosophy and the life sciences are but a few of the many directions that the quest to understand human nature has taken. At this point in history, some of these avenues have proved to be dead ends, while others are just beginning to flourish. Today, the problem is more pressing than ever before, since most of the world's ills, like overpopulation, violence of wars, pollution, prejudices, etc. are brought about by the behaviour of the people. So, it may not be overstating the case to say that the quality of human life in future, nay, the very survival, and effective management will depend upon an increased understanding of human frailty inherent in human personality.

Before Second World War, studies in human psychology had a philosophical orientation. A deeper understanding of human nature bisected this into psychology into psychiatry. The practical aspects of psychic influence explained the nature of mental or neural diseases and their curses by therapeutic practices. Today a fully grown-up independent field of neurology can diagnose the mental deficiencies and disorders that cause behavioural aberrations and disruptions. At a deeper level, it can be explained in terms of personality imbalance, personality maladjustments or personality stultification. The psychiatrists explain a whole lot of abnormal human behaviours or misbehaviours of violence, aggression, irrationality and deficiency which can be cured. Obsession, schizophrenias, cruelty, sexual callousness, abnormalities are the endless sorts of undesirable behaviours which need correction. As knowledge of neural sciences improves, personality studies are being adjusted to group behaviours, which may be induced in the name of therapies and training programmes for personality development.

Chris Argyris, in his celebrated study entitled *Personality and Organization*, finds that organizations with evolution, develop organizational personalities. There is always a growing hiatus between the personalities of individual workers and the organizational personalities of government departments which the employees seek to serve. In India, the third and fourth class government servants, popularly known as non-gazetted employees suffer from the stultification of their personalities because their jobs do not grow with the age of the incumbents. The stereotype notions of work of the *babus* and the *chaprasis* deny newer opportunities of personality development and the incumbents tends to degenerate into corrupt behaviours of money and power. A *babu* personality of the civil servant dehumanises his job and the routinization of the job eats away into the very potentials of his personality.

The corporate sector employment has some awareness of this hiatus and training programmes are designed to further personality development. Here the entire area of Human Resource Development (HRD) confronts a challenge of change and changing the biological givens of the employees by induction of socialization values or job values is a delicate exercise in grafting values and consolidating them through organizational cultures. A new subject named organizational development (OD) is addressing itself to the problem areas of change management including personality change or personality growth. Merit today, is not mere intellectual ability but a suitability of employee personality traits with his job-needs or work environment. The maladjustment causes ethical decay and the meritorious employees of the past become ethical liabilities for human resource management.

Thus, ethical behaviour is a trait and an evaluation realm of human personality. These traits keep coming and going. Some stay longer and get assimilated into the fabric of personality. If the surface ground is solid in terms of values, the socially undesirable traits like dishonesty, cruelty, subjectivity, lack of empathy, exploitation and callousness cannot destabilize that ethical foundation, which has been built by the family, the school, the peer groups and the unique experiences and exposures. But then, if the case is the other way round, the desirable values of objectivity, rationality, compassion, tolerance and integrity become victims and lose reinforcements. At different age groups of biological growth, the males and females keep reformulating these aptitudes and attitudes towards work, workers and the clients. Later comes a stage when the aptitudinal values get solidified or ossified to the extent that people may turn out to be saints or criminals. But then, most of the people or government officials stay somewhere on the continuum with very few occupying any extremities. They handle their perceptions with care and discipline their aptitudes and attitudes to stay in the ambit of social morality and ethical self-discipline.

The ethics of human behaviour can be identified and improved by exploring its foundations. The public officials cannot be improved by mere training. Exposures do revise personality but the core personality persists as a determinant of ethical behaviour. Hence, it is recruitment and placement that is more crucial to ethical probity and integrity in governance. Lately, there is a growing realization that the new recruits in government jobs should be examined and screened on the basis of their aptitudes and value systems that inhere in their human personality. Though difficult, it is possible to discover the ethical foundations of an individual's personality. Public service as a career in India, cannot be a mere employment. It has to be a mission of professional variety. Explorations in a public servant's personality can explain his or her present-day money and power orientations, which are largely responsible for his or her ethical misconduct and moral degeneration. In India, the problems of ethical malpractices are so deep, so complex and so massive that no one-solution can rid the system from corruption and abuse of power. So, there has to be a multi-pronged attack and only the civil servants with solid ethical foundations can make it. Naturally, therefore, extra care has to be undertaken in screening, scanning and evaluating the aptitudinal values of personality of the new public service recruits. Once recruited, it is almost impossible to weed them out by any so-called measures of punishment. Training also stands ineffective in making these public servants ethical, because the learning process also stops in these closed personalities in their mid-life careers. Personality and ethics is a new area, besides and beyond the rules, on which the recruiters and senior officials should ponder and do research.

CHAPTER 3

The Behavioural Process

Perception, Attitude and Aptitudinal Judgement

Personality, being an internal structure, motors the positive and negative activities and behaviours of all living beings. The psychologists call them the external manifestations of inner urges which are heightened or subdued through sensory pressures of organism. The eyes, ears, nose, tongue and the skin sense the external world and convey messages to the 'Personality' which transforms them into action, reaction and interaction processes called behaviour. Thus all behaviours are caused and the consequences may be discussed as functional or dysfunctional. All human behaviours, as Thomas Hobbes discovered, are 'A moral' and his theory of scientific materialism proves that they are mechanical. It is a cause-consequence syndrome to which the human beings attribute their value systems as obtained in their attitudinal kits through perception. The formation and expression of these perceptions, attitudes and aptitudinal values is a constant and continuous process which the personality directs, motivates or depresses. Why people behave the way, they behave, cannot be neatly answered by one or few factors as they appear to the lay-outsiders.

The Perceptual Process

The studies are still engaged in demystifying the intellectual mores which pushes the individual to wade through varied perceptive notions, attitudinal barriers and aptitudinal inclinations, before one takes a plunge with his or her actions, opinions, decisions and above all the persistence or otherwise, of these personality behaviours. It is a highly complex and sensitive cognitive process and human beings have to extricate these perceptions, attitudes and value judgements in their contradictory behaviours at different points of time. But then, no human being can refuse to perceive as the phenomenon unfolds. The stimuli of the outer world are perceived by eyes, ears, touch of the body and smell of the object. The sensory organs convey messages to the mind and human beings become aware of situations by adding meaningful association to their sensations. Gilmer thinks that *perception* is a mental process which enables human beings or living beings to organize and interpret their sensory impressions to give a meaning to their environment. In fact, it is a mental process which can be comprehended by splitting it into following six stages of sensory stimulation:

1. Receiving
2. Selecting
3. Organizing
4. Interpreting
5. Checking
6. Reacting

This process is not similar in two individuals. The external factors like location, size, movement, intensity, repetition and familiarity have their own roles in perceiving selectively. But then, more complex is the internal perceptual process where the ground perception gets mixed up and evaluated by one's learning, psychic needs of personality and ambivalences, caused by age, gender and other aptitudinal dispositions. Broadly, a perception process involves:

1. Intellectual selection,
2. Cognitive acceptance or rejection, and
3. A subjective analysis of the data received.

This perceptual selectivity is automatic. The behaviour, expectations and inner-needs shape the response. The duality between internal and external factors generates perceptional defence and perceptional distortions. They have been identified as situational factors and the object perceived is often influenced by halo effect, stereotyping, etc. The psychological studies have gone too far now-a-days to build 'mindsets' which promote positive skills of perception.

The Attribution Phenomenon

The attribution theorists believe that the perceiver assigns causes to the behaviour he conceives. 'Attribution' refers to the process by which the individual strives to discover causes to his behaviour. People are interested not only in observing behaviours in social groups but in determining their causes also. Their evaluations of and reactions to other people's behaviour may be heavily influenced by their personal perception which may conclude that others are responsible for their behaviours. When office efficiency in a bank increases, the head responsible may be evaluated less favourably because the increase may be attributed to computers installed at the order of the head-office than the manager's handling of his employees. Similarly, a nurse who drops a tray of medicine can be excused if the incident is perceived as caused by a slippery floor but will be chastised if it is viewed as an incident caused by her clumsiness; and perhaps fired if it is viewed as a deliberate act of mischief.

There are critics who argue that perceptual distortion occurs because of attribution, and much credit or blame for behaviour must not be placed on persons, where environment determines perception. Nevertheless, people do seek the causes of others' behaviour, and tend to attribute behaviour to the individuals rather than to the environment. Senior officers usually evaluate or react to behaviours of juniors on the basis of their perceptions and causes attributed to the incidents.

Factors such as *status, intentions* and *consequences* influence the attribution process of public servants. One factor which strongly influences the attribution process, is the status of the senior whose behaviour is perceived by the juniors. The high-status persons are perceived to be more responsible for their actions than the low-status employees in the hierarchy. Intentions influence attribution. People are likely to attribute good intentions to high-status people than to low-status juniors. If a senior official clocks overtime on any day, it is perceived that he has done this in the interest of the government or department. If a poor worker does the same, the action is understood as being for overtime money or to finish the pending arrears. Consequences of the individual's action, whose behaviour is perceived, also influence the perceiver's attribution. If the consequences are bad, then there is a more likelihood of the individual to be viewed as responsible for the act. Disasters are a part of life, but people always tend to perceive that people are more responsible for mishaps.

The Perceptual Context

The context in which an object is placed influences perception. The visual stimuli by themselves are meaningless. Only when the doodles are placed in a verbal context they take on meaning and give value to the perceiver. The organizational culture and structure provide the primary context in which workers and administrators do their perceiving. Thus, a verbal order, a memo, a new policy, a suggestion, a raised eyebrow or a pat on the back takes on special meaning and value when placed in the context of office situation of the hierarchy. There are innumerable factors, visible and invisible, which influence human perception. In administrative situations there is a need to place perception in proper perspective to fit into cherished attitudes and value systems of the senior officials.

An employee's needs, past experience, habits, personality dispositions, values and attitudes – all influence his or her perception process. Someone with a strong need for ego satisfaction may perceive some impression and emphasize signals that either tend to satisfy or deny the desire for self-esteem. By the same token, negative attitudes towards union leaders may cause an official to look for antagonisms in even routine visits of officials. These and other personal factors will impact what a person gives attention to, in a situation and how these cues are interpreted as a basis for decision-making and action responses. The physical attributes, appearance and behaviour of other persons in the situation also influence how that situation is perceived. We tend to notice the physical attributes of a person in terms of age, sex, height, weight, etc. A person attempting to exert authority in a situation but also identified as very young, may be viewed quite differently from an older person doing exactly the same thing. Personal attire and appearance are also relevant factors. The physical, social and office settings of the situation or event in question can change perceptions. Hearing a subordinate call his or her boss by a first name may be perceived quite differently when observed in an office as opposed to an evening social reception. By the same token, a conversation with the boss may be perceived differently when taking place in a casual reception area, than when held in the office with the door closed. Such background characteristics of the situation context are additional factors that can affect how the situation is perceived by the different persons involved.

The Perceptual Analysis

A perception is a cognitive process, which can be called a unique interpretation of the situation but not an exact recording of it. It may reveal a picture of the world which is different from reality. Recognition of difference between the perceptual world and the real world is vital to the study of official behaviours. One universal assumption made by the seniors is that subordinates always want money and promotions whereas, in fact, many subordinates may not psychologically feel inclined to care about money or promotions. Administrator seldom attempts to find out whether the promotion need is a desirable situation. In other words, the perceptual world of the senior official is quite different from that of the subordinates, and both may be very different from reality. What should be done from the senior's standpoint? The best answer is to understand the perceptual process and make a perceptual analysis.

In an interview for the selection of a candidate for a government job, the interviewers' judgement about the suitability or otherwise of a candidate depends on how his or her behaviour is perceived by them. A rejected applicant might feel that he or she was wronged by the interviewer though he or she deserved selection. But, the fact is that interviewers generally form an early impression that becomes quickly entrenched. If the inadequacies of the candidate are exposed early, they weigh against him or her in the final selection.

Similarly, the hiring of new employees may cause a perceptual problem of unrealistic expectations. The applicants acquire, during the selection process, a set of expectations about the organization and the specific job he or she is hoping to be offered. It is not unusual for these expectations to be excessively inflated as a result of receiving almost uniformly positive information. There is evidence, that now demonstrates, that these inaccurate perceptions lead to premature resignations, and the realistic expectations can lead to lower turnover rates.

The realistic job expectations also need a perceptual analysis. The expectations include both favourable and unfavourable information about the job. If the candidate has been provided with both favourable and unfavourable information, the incumbent will be better equipped to cope with it and to face the frustrating elements of the job somewhat boldly. The result will be – fewer new employees will quit the jobs unexpectedly or develop hostile relations with their seniors.

Performance appraisal of government servants is another area where perception has significant relevance. Assessment of an employee's performance depends on the perception of the person who evaluates him or her. While evaluation can be objective, where assessment is quantifiable, most of the jobs in civil service are evaluated in subjective parameters. Subjective measures are easier to implement. They provide the senior officials with greater discretion, and critical jobs do not lend themselves to objective measures. Subjective measures are, by definition, judgemental. To the extent that the evaluation depends on subjective measures for assessing an employee's performance, perception of who is a 'good' or 'bad' employee greatly influences the appraisal outcome.

A civil servant's future in a government job is usually not dependent on performances alone. In many departments, the level of a junior employee's effort is given high importance. The assessment of an individual's effort is a subjective judgement susceptible to perceptual distortions and bias. If it is true, as some claim, that more workers are fired for poor attitudes and lack of discipline than for lack of ability, then the approval of an employee's effort may be a primary influence on his or her future in the public service.

The managers in corporate world make judgement about employees in terms of whether they are loyal to the organization or not. An employee in the corporate world at higher levels, who disparages the firm or looks for greener pastures outside, is generally labelled as disloyal who is risking advancement opportunities of the future. The issue is not whether organizations are right in demanding an employee's loyalty, but the fact is that many employers do, and the assessment of loyalty or commitment is highly judgemental. What is perceived as loyalty by one decision-maker may be seen as excessive conformity by another. An employee who questions his senior's decisions may be seen as disloyal by some, yet caring and concerned by others. When evaluating a person's attitude, as in loyalty assessment, one must recognize that a person's perception should not get distorted or misconstrued. Several managerial practices depend on Theory X or Theory Y assumptions in which employees are held. Theory X assumptions – that man is inherently lazy and irresponsible – create the unconscious rationale for directing and controlling authoritarian discipline. Theory Y assumptions, including the responsibility orientation of man and his potential for creativity and contributions, result in quite different practices. Both sets of assumptions incorporate many of the perceptual processes as they influence administrative behaviours.

The Perceptual Distortions

Successful officers understand the importance of perception as an influence on behaviour, and they act accordingly. They are aware of perceptual distortions, and they also know that perceptual differences are likely to exist in all situations. As a result, they try to make decisions and take action with a serious understanding of the work situation as it is viewed by other persons concerned. A senior civil servant who is skilled in the perception process will have a high level of self-awareness. Individual needs, experience, and expectations all affect perceptions. The successful senior should know this and should identify when he or she is inappropriately distorting a situation because of perceptual tendencies. The administrators should seek information from various sources to confirm or disconfirm personal impressions in a decisional situation. The official should minimize the biases of his or her personal perceptions by seeking out the viewpoints of others. These insights are used to gain additional perspectives on situations and the problems or opportunities they represent. Administration requires empathy. The senior officials should be able to see a situation as it is perceived by other people. Different people will define the same situation quite differently. The decision-maker should rise above personal impressions and understand problems as seen by other people. Perceptions of other people may distort the vision and one may draw incorrect or incomplete impression of events in the work setting. People act in terms of their perceptions. The influence of perceptions of others about events and situations has to be interpreted as accurately as possible and to the advantage of all concerned. Common perceptual distortions tend to bias administrators' views about people and situations and hence they need to be avoided. These distortions include the use of stereotypes and halo effects, as well as selective perceptions and projections. Smart civil servants have to be self-disciplined and sufficiently self-aware so that the adverse impact of these distortions can be minimized. People have a tendency to try and explain why events happened the way they did or why people behaved as they did. The effective managers have to be careful to establish the real reasons why things happen and avoid quick or inappropriate attributions of causality. Ethics and integrity of human beings need to be explored as objectively as possible. Perceptional mistakes or distortions may damage the system beyond repair.

Attitudes as Mental States

Human beings tend to evaluate environment and continuously make judgements about people, places, events, and objects. They tend to have a binary system of assessment either good or bad, either favourable or not, either like or dislike. Understanding why this happens and how it influences our behaviour and decisions requires the study of attitudes. An 'attitude is a psychological tendency that is expressed by evaluating a particular entity with some degree of favour or disfavour' (Eagly and Chaiken). It can be called, 'a learned predisposition to respond in a consistently favourable or unfavourable manner with respect to a given object' (Fishbein and Ajzen)

The objects may include people, things, events and issues. Carl Jung calls it a 'readiness of the psyche to act or react in a certain way'. Gordon Allport defines attitude as 'a mental neutral state of realism, organized through experience, exerting a directive or dynamic influence on individual regions to all objects and situations with which it is related'. It can be viewed as a tendency or a disposition to act. It represents an attempt to evaluate attribution of good or bad in a congenital and operational way in the field. Crutchfield finds attitudes – motivational, emotional, perceptual and cognitive in their organization. They are usually enduring and can be distinguished from opinions. Kolsa finds them tied to more fundamental human beliefs. Macormick dissociates attitudes from beliefs on the ground that the former can be 'all hold attitudes'. In operational terms, attitudes are evaluative statements – favourable or unfavourable – concerning objects, people, or events. They reflect how one feels about something. In fact, all attitudes are learned predispositions towards aspects of our environment. They may be positively or negatively directed towards certain people, service or institutions. By attitude, people mean the beliefs, feelings and action tendencies of an individual or group of individuals towards objects, ideas and people. Quite often persons and objects or ideas become associated in the minds of individuals and as a result, attitudes become multidimensional and complex.

Attitude as a Prejudice

In this sense, the attitudes can be called prejudices of the perceiver. An attitude may involve a prejudice in which people pre-judge an issue without giving unbiased consideration to all the evidence available. If we are prejudiced against a person, who is accused of a crime, we may regard him as a guilty person regardless of the evidence. Similarly, people can also be prejudiced in favour of anything which may be right or wrong or both. The scholars of psychology have a consensus about the six salient features of attitudes which contribute to their meaning. These are:

1. Attitudes refer to feelings and beliefs of individuals or groups of individuals.
2. These feelings and beliefs are directed towards other people, objects or ideas.
3. The attitudes tend to result in behaviour or action.
4. They can fall anywhere along a continuum from very favourable to very unfavourable.
5. Attitudes endure for long and may become lifetime dispositions.
6. People, irrespective of their status or intelligence, hold attitudes and continue to stick to them.

Thus, the significant fact is that the attitudes are acquired but not inherited. Individuals acquire attitudes from several sources. The most important among these are direct experience with the object, association, family, neighbourhood, economic and social positions, and mass communication. Attitudes can also be developed from a rewarding or punishing experience with an object. Employees form attitudes about jobs on the basis of their previous experiences. For example, if everyone holding a job was punished by a particular senior, the current job holders are likely to believe that they will also be punished even when they do their best. Attitudes formed on the basis of experience are more difficult to change. Attitude towards an object may develop from associating that object with another object about which attitudes have already been formed. A favourable or unfavourable attitude about a neighbour will often be formed by associating him or her with another neighbour, about whom an attitude has already been formed.

A person may also learn attitudes through imitation of parents. If parents have a positive attitude towards an object and the child admires his or her parents, he or she is likely to adopt a similar attitude, even without being told about the object, or even without having any direct experience. Attitudes towards the opposite sex, religion, tolerance or prejudice, education, occupations, political parties, and almost all other areas where these are capable of expression are the result of our accepting or rejecting the attitudes held by the members of our family. Similarly, attitudes are acquired from peer groups in colleges and job situations.

The neighbourhood we live in has a certain structure in terms of its having cultural facilities, religious groupings, and possibly ethnic differences. The neighbours – adults or children – tolerate, condone or deny certain attitudes and behaviours and as a result people are viewed as northerners or southerners. The people accept these moves and conform or deny them and possibly rebel. The conformity or rebellion in some respects is the evidence of the attitudes people hold very strongly.

Our economic and occupational positions also contribute to attitude formation. They determine workers' attitudes towards unions, office establishment and the belief that certain laws are 'good' or 'bad'. It is a common experience that socio-economic backgrounds influence people's attitudes in the present and also in the future.

All means of mass communication – television, radio, newspapers and magazines – feed their audiences with large quantities of information. These presentations of news or information are constructed so as to cater to the attitude of the audience. In turn, the audience also selects the specific form of mass communication that best reflects its attitudes on specific subjects. These items of interest on TV may include sex and teenagers, crime, divorce, politics, religion, pornographic literature, and the like. The material we select helps us either to substantiate our opinions or to establish new ones.

Job Attitudes and Job Joy

Individuals possess hundreds of attitudes. But, in matters of public service, work-related attitudes are mainly three, namely,

1. job satisfaction,
2. job involvement, and
3. job commitment.

Job satisfaction refers to one's feelings towards one's job. An individual having satisfaction is said to possess positive attitude towards the job. Conversely, a dissatisfied person will have negative attitude towards his or her job. When people speak of employee attitudes, they invariably refer to job joy or job satisfaction. In fact, the two terms are used interchangeably, though there are subtle differences between the two. Job involvement refers to the degree with which an individual identifies psychologically with his or her job and perceives the perceived performance level important to self-worth. High degree of job involvement results in fewer absences and lower desire of transfer rates. The job attitude fosters organizational commitment or dissatisfaction. It is understood as one's identification with his or her organization and pride of being its employee. Job involvement refers to one's attachment to the job, whereas job commitment implies an employee's identification with his or her department and its functional goals. It is possible that an individual may be attached to his or her job but may be indifferent to the public service and its objectives. When employees have high organizational commitment, they maintain ethical standards of higher variety.

Attitudes towards individuals or objects are held because these attitudes help people to respond to the individuals or objects in a meaningful manner. Allport found that without guiding attitudes the individual is confused and baffled. The attitudes (1) determine for each individual what he will see and hear or what he will think and what he will do, (2) they engender meaning upon the world, (3) they draw lines about and segregate an otherwise chaotic environment, and (4) they are our methods for finding our way in an ambiguous universe. They serve important functions, namely,

1. Utilitarian
2. Ego-defence
3. Value expression
4. Knowledge

An attitude may develop because either the attitude or the object of the attitude is instrumental in helping one to obtain rewards or avoid punishments. In some cases, the attitude is a means to an end. A worker finds that when he or she expresses a negative attitude towards his or her boss, his or her co-workers pay attention to and sympathize with him or her, but when he or she expresses a positive attitude, he or she is ignored or chastened. The negative attitude is instrumental in obtaining rewards or acceptance and avoiding punishment or rejection. In another case, the object is a means to an end, and the attitude develops from association of the object and its outcome. For example, a clerk in the public works department may develop favourable attitudes towards blue-collar labourers and negative attitude towards white-collar engineers, whom he finds searching for a bargain. He associates success and profit with blue-collar workers and failure and difficulty with engineers, and thus he develops appropriate attitudes towards those objects through association.

People often form and maintain certain attitudes to protect their own self-images. For example, the fourth-class employees may feel threatened by the employment or advancement of Scheduled Caste (SC), Scheduled Tribes (ST) or female workers in their department. The threatened workers may develop prejudices against the new workers. They may develop an attitude that such newcomers are less qualified, and they might maltreat these workers. Such an ego-defensive attitude is formed and used to cope with a feeling of guilt or threat. Unless this feeling is removed, this kind of attitude persists and remains unchanged.

Attitude as Value Reflections

Our attitudes reflect our value system and our value-expressive attitudes are closely related to our self-concept. An officer whose central value is freedom, may express very positive attitudes towards decentralization of authority in the organization, flexible work schedules, and relaxation of dress standards and other codes of behaviour. Attitude is often substituted for knowledge. In the absence of knowledge, we use our attitude to organize and make sense out of the perceived object or person. For example, people who are not familiar with nuclear energy may develop an attitude that it is dangerous and should not be used as an energy source. Stereotyping is another example. In the absence of knowledge about a person, we may use a stereotyped attitude for judging him or her.

Cognitive Dissonance

The public servants must know how an attitude functions. This knowledge can serve two purposes. It helps them to understand and predict how a certain person is likely to behave. For instance, if a senior officer is prejudiced against another junior officer, the former is less likely to be fair in judging the latter. Moreover, this knowledge helps the senior officer to see why the junior officer has developed such an attitude Secondly, it can help the senior officer to change the attitude of the junior officer by changing the conditions that sustain this attitude. The officer can also change people with low self-images by helping them increase their ability to solve their problems, or by providing them with positive feedback on what they wish to accomplish.

Attitudes of public employees can be changed and it is in the best interest of the organization to try for such a change. But change in the desirable manner is not easy because of barriers that obstruct it. One obstacle to change of attitude is the *balance and consistency theory of attitudes*. Human beings always prefer their attitudes about people and things to be in line (i.e. balanced and consistent) with their behaviours towards each other and objects. When attitudes or behaviours are not consistent, people usually seek to reduce the inconsistency. Leon Festinger offers a theory in support of attitude consistency. It is called *cognitive dissonance.* The theory states that dissonance makes an individual feel uncomfortable. This feeling makes the individual try to reduce dissonance.

The other barrier to change of attitude is prior commitments. This occurs when people feel a commitment to a particular course of action and are unwilling to change. Similarly, unanticipated barriers arise from insufficient information. People often do not find reason why should they change their attitudes. The boss may not like a subordinate's negative attitude, but the latter may be quite pleased with his or her behaviour. Unless the boss can explain the individual why a negative attitude is detrimental to his or her career progress or salary increases or some other personal objective, the subordinate will continue to have his or her negative attitude.

New information generally helps employees to change their attitudes. Negative attitudes are mainly formed owing to insufficient information. Workers in factories generally become pro-union because of the ignorance about the good intentions of the management. Once they come to know how the management cares for the welfare of the employee, they can change their attitudes and might turn pro-establishment.

In some situations, fear is also used to change attitude. However, the change depends on the degree of fear. If low levels of fear arousal are used, people often ignore them. The warnings are not strong enough to warrant attention. If moderate levels of fear arousal are used, employees often become aware of the situation and think of changing their attitudes. However, if high degrees of fear arousal are used, people often reject the message, because it is too threatening and thus not believable. Thus, high degrees of fear may prove counter-productive. On being threatened too far, people tend to become stubborn in their attitudes and may refuse to change. Change of attitude can come about through persuasion of friends or peers. Credibility of the others, especially peers, is important to effect change. Colleagues with high credibility exercise significant influence on change. The same is not true of seniors who have low credibility. Co-opting can also change attitude. This means taking people who are dissatisfied with a situation and getting them involved in improving things.

Research studies have shown that an individual is more likely to change a privately held attitude than the one he or she has stated publicly. It is, therefore, necessary that a situation is avoided where the individual makes his or her attitude public prior to the change attempt.

The individual from a culturally deprived environment and holding an array of hostile attitudes may change when he or she is given opportunities for education. Likewise, a person from a privileged sub-culture, who has always held to a democratic attitude, may become negative towards some group because of one unfortunate experience. Again, through continued association with others holding similar attitudes, one can be influenced in a positive or negative direction. Here, the attitudes of both the reference groups and the social climate are relevant and decisive.

Attitude change may be classified into congruent and incongruent change. *Congruent change* in attitude involves a movement in the same direction but with reduced intensity of feeling. A negative or positive attitude of a boss towards his or her subordinate will persist, but the degree of like or dislike may be reduced. On the contrary, *incongruent change* involves a change of direction itself from positive to negative or vice versa. It may be towards the same person. This change is observable in behavioural terms, such as change in voting for a different political candidate, divorcing a partner and resigning from a job or joining another.

The Positive Attitudes

Positive attitudes are important in public service because of their influence on behaviour, perception, job satisfaction, job involvement, and quality of organizational performance. If all employees have positive attitudes, it may result in several benefits. For instance, a positive attitude:

1. increases productivity,
2. fosters teamwork,
3. solves problems,
4. improves quality,
5. makes for congenial atmosphere,
6. breeds loyalty,
7. increases profits,
8. fosters better relationships with employees, employers and customers,
9. reduces stress, and
10. makes for a pleasing personality.

Attitudes affect employee behaviour too. However, a direct relationship between attitudes and actions is not agreeable to some since attitude does not lead to any specific action. An officer may dislike certain juniors in minority groups, but he or she may nevertheless treat them fairly and pleasantly in his or her office. This inconsistency occurs because the officer does not allow his or her attitude to interfere with his or her professional judgement. However, these attitudes may manifest themselves in other behaviours also. For example, an officer may treat the junior workers fairly on the job but does not invite them to his or her daughter's wedding.

Although the influence of attitudes on behaviour is not clearly discernible, the theories of *cognition* and *self-fulfilling prophecy* can help to understand the direction of attitudinal influences. As stated earlier, the cognitive dissonance refers to the feeling of inconsistency in feelings, beliefs and behaviour. This feeling of inconsistency makes people feel uncomfortable. They get motivated to rectify the situation by modifying the behaviours that cause the dissonance. This cognitive dissonance becomes more intense when the decision is psychologically or financially important. The foregone alternatives are many and these alternatives have several positive features. An individual usually strives to minimize the dissonance by using some of the following methods:

1. He or she may seek information that confirms the wisdom of the decision.
2. He or she may selectively perceive or distort information in a way that supports the decision.
3. He or she may like to adopt a less favourable attitude towards the foregone alternatives.
4. He or she may downplay the importance of negative aspects of the choice and magnify the positive elements.

The self-fulfilling prophecy is the process by which we try to convert our attitudes, beliefs and expectations into reality. If we predict that something is going to happen, we will try very hard to make it happen. For instance, if the employees feel that they are competent, they will undertake the challenging tasks. Consequently, people gain experience and skills that make them more competent, so that they may accomplish even more. However, if people have a negative attitude, they do not provide opportunities to juniors to become competent.

Perceptual outcomes are generally derived from past experiences and perceptions, but they also influence the way people perceive stimuli. Such sayings as 'beauty is in the eye of the beholder' and 'one person's sweet is another person's poison' emphasize the importance of attitudes in perceiving the world around us. If our attitudes are positive, things look brighter than if they are negative.

The Job Attitude as a Factor

The senior officials in government are expected to enhance job satisfaction of junior employees in their respective jobs. The job satisfaction reflects an individual's positive attitude towards his or her job. High job satisfaction generates a positive attitude in the group, while dissatisfied employees with negative attitudes cause conflicts. When people speak of employee attitudes, they usually mean job satisfaction. In fact, the two terms are used interchangeably.

The degree to which a person identifies psychologically with his or her job and considers his or her perceived performance level important, the job situation becomes involving. A high degree of involvement identifies the employee with his or her job and he or she cares about the kind of work he or she does on his or her job. Besides, such involvement in the job results in job commitment. Here, attitude is an important variable in developing job involvement.

If job involvement refers to one's identification with a particular job, job commitment means one's involvement with his or her employing organization. The positive attitudes enhance both. In fact, attitudes can be called a behavioural quality. They create relationship and make environment favourable or unfavourable. They are a sort of a bank account of the office which one can use or cash as a reserve to get things done. In this sense, they represent power. Attitudes are neither hereditary nor final. They cannot be seen as a weakness of human personality either. They may emanate from knowledge or from absolute ignorance. They are mere responses, which express this interplay of psychic forces inside. They have nothing to do with religion or God. In fact, they are rooted in aptitudinal values and can be improved by:

1. Guidance
2. Counselling
3. Introspection
4. Exposures
5. New adventures

The negative attitudes cause frustration and crime-prone behaviours, including shirking, quarrelling, strikes and sabotage. They erode:

(a) Supportive systems of officer's personality.
(b) Self-confidence of workers and lead them into a blind alley.
(c) The mental balance of the employees and ignite aggressive and destructive value systems.
(d) Rationality and weaken the base of altruism and otherliness.

On the contrary, the positive attitudes are an asset. They maintain equilibrium and sanity in the personality. They generate optimistic cravings. Bentham has called them 'pleasure maximizing and pain minimizing devices' for a happier living. Men and women derive strength from their positive attitudes and they help human beings in making themselves innovative, adventurous and original. The potentialities of positive dispositions are enormous. Their support is re-invigorating in the midst of shifting series of events.

But then, one should not forget that mere attitudes do not count for success or failures in life. Stereotype experiences may render one's capability in one field to work as a limitation on other issues. Often the context of social success binds the individual to his or her limitations. But then, people are capable to conquer the attitudinal limits of their personality. Acharya Rajneesh says that acceptance of limitations of the attitudinal universe is a triumph, a great joy, which can transform the negative attitudes into positive assets of extra support.

Attitudinal Miracles of Optimism

Positive attitudes in moral and political affairs add to one's influence patterns in his or her society. These people enhance their capacity to persuade other people to their fold. Healthy attitudes are infectious and people in society imitate and emulate their conduct as an ideal-fit category. A civil servant endowed with a positive outlook of optimistic attitudes can work wonders and accomplish miracles by a mere smile or a pat on the back. The women officers can be extra persuasive to their colleagues and juniors, if they command a social influence in their attitudinal armoury. Administration is an art of 'getting things done' and officials with wry face and horrifying disposition alienate the group and then blame the juniors for non-performance or unethical practices in their workplace. Moral and political attitudes have a persuasive role in a democratic framework of institutions. The civil servants can rule effectively with a human face for which a high Intelligence Quotient (IQ) is not a prerequisite.

Aptitudes and Values

It is said that attitudes are caught and they can never be taught. While the aptitudes are required, they cannot be acquired. In a comparative analysis the attitudes may have value contents but there are no aptitudes without a value system. Value is generally used in two different ways: as a characteristic of an object or as an attribute possessed by an individual and thought desirable. The focus in aptitudes is on the latter, and as a concept of the desirable, an internalized criterion or standard of evaluation which a person possesses. Such concepts and standards are relatively few and determine or guide an individual's evaluations of varied objects encountered in everyday life. Values are tinged with moral flavour, involving an individual's judgement of what is right, good or desirable. These values provide standards of competence and morality which are fewer in number than attitudes. They transcend specific objects, situations or persons, and tend to be relative, permanent and resistant to change. One can call them the most central to the core of a person's behaviour.

Attitudes essentially represent predispositions to respond. Values focus on the judgement of what ought to be done in given situations. This judgement can represent the specific manifestation of a determining tendency below the surface of the behaviour. Attitudes represent several beliefs focussed on a specific object or situation. Value, on the other hand, represents a single belief that transcendentally guides actions and judgements across objects and situations. A value stands in relation to some social or cultural standards or norms while attitudes are mostly personal experiences.

Aptitude and attitude are powerful instruments that influence cognitive process and behaviour of people. Both are learnt and acquired from the same sources – experience with people and objects. Values and attitudes are relatively permanent and are resistant to change. Values and attitudes influence each other and are, more often than not, used interchangeably. Similarities and differences between values and attitudes can be identified but they are difficult to be extricated or separated. Values are learnt and acquired primarily through experiences with people and institutions. Parents, for example, will have substantial influence on their children's values. A parent's reaction to everyday events demonstrates what is good and bad, acceptable and unacceptable, or important and unimportant. Values are often taught and reinforced in schools, religious organizations and social groups. As we grow and develop, each source of influence contributes to our definition of what is important in life. Cultural mores also have influence on the formation of values. In fact, basic convictions of what is good or bad are primarily derived from one's own culture. Similarities between values and attitudes can be stated as under:

1. Values and attitudes both are important variables which influence the cognitive processes and behaviours.
2. Both of them are learnt and acquired essentially from the same sources.
3. Both endure and are resistant to change.
4. Each one reciprocally influences the other and is used interchangeably.

But aptitudes and attitudes differ in their psychological meanings. Their differences can be observed in practical behavioural terms only. For example:

1. The aptitudes represent judgement of what ought to be. This judgement is a propellant to response in a given situation but the attitudes are predispositions which may hinder the aptitudes.
2. Aptitudes normally represent single belief that guides actions and judgement across objects and situations. While attitudes may contain several beliefs focussed on a specific object or situation.
3. Aptitudes in depth are derived from social and cultural mores. The attitudes generally represent personal experiences.

Another way of categorizing the aptitudinal values can be the content elements, for instance, theoretical aptitudes like interest in the discovery of truth through reasoning and systematic thinking. Economic interest may point out usefulness, practicality and the accumulation of wealth. Aesthetic aptitudes are appreciated more in females, who have interest in beauty, form and artistic harmony. These aptitudes create social interest in people and feelings of love as a human relationship. Similarly, political aptitudes generate interest in gaining power and influence over people. The saints and seers have religious aptitudes which express interest in unity and understanding of the spirit and the cosmos as a whole.

Milton Rokeach, in his study of terminal and instrumental values, lists some 18 human values as under:

	Terminal values	*Instrumental values*
1.	A comfortable life: a prosperous life	Ambitious: hard working, aspiring
2.	An exciting life: a stimulating, active life	Broad-minded: open minded
3.	A sense of accomplishment: lasting contribution	Capable: competent, effective
4.	A world at peace: free of war and conflicts	Cheerful: light hearted, joyful
5.	A world of beauty: beauty of nature and the arts	Clean: neat, tidy

Cont'd...

...Cont'd

6.	Equality: brotherhood, equal opportunity for all	Courageous: standing up for your beliefs
7.	Family security: taking care of loved ones	Forgiving: willing to pardon others
8.	Freedom: independence, free choice	Helpful: working for welfare of others
9.	Happiness: contentedness	Honest: sincere, truthful
10.	Inner harmony: freedom from inner conflict	Imaginative: daring, creative
11.	Mature love: sexual and spiritual intimacy	Independent: self-reliant, self-sufficient
12.	National security: protection from attack	Intellectual: intelligent, reflective
13.	Pleasure: an enjoyable, leisurely life	Logical: consistent, rational
14.	Salvation: saved, eternal life	Loving: affectionate, tender
15.	Self-respect: self-esteem	Obedient: dutiful, respectful
16.	Social recognition: respect, admiration	Polite: courteous, well-mannered
17.	True friendship: close companionship	Responsible: dependable, reliable
18.	Wisdom: a mature understanding of life	Self-controlled: restraint, self-disciplined

The values are important in the study of behaviour of civil servants because they lay down the foundation for the understanding of attitudes and motivations as well as influencing their perceptions. Individuals enter into careers of civil service with preconceived notions of what 'ought' to and what 'ought not' to be. Of course, these notions are not value-free. On the contrary, they contain implicit meanings of right and wrong. Further, they imply that certain behaviours or outcomes should be preferred over others. As a result, they cloud one's objectivity and rationality.

Thus, values can be called 'basic convictions', which get hardened and confirmed by the time one approaches in his or her mid-life. The aptitudes that inhere in human personality can be nurtured or damaged or even ignored in the midst of social strife. The aptitudes filter values and values nurture aptitudes. The concept of aptitude being somewhat ethical and judgemental keeps human beings struggling with cognition, dissonance of perceptions and varying beliefs and attitudes towards the jobs and the colleagues. They overlap, intermingle and change each other's contents. A brief comparison of the perception, attitude and aptitude can be attempted as under:

1. *Perceptions:* They are (a) reactive, (b) changing, (c) relative, and (d) absolutely individual.
2. *Attitudes:* They are (a) stable, (b) less enduring, (c) congenital, and (d) shared in common.
3. *Aptitudes and values:* They are (a) deep, (b) long-lasting, (c) judgemental, and even (d) plural.

Aptitudes when mature, result in confirmed value judgements. Values are values. They cannot be compared just because a comparison will require a criterion, which it self will be called a *value judgement*. To a layman, a value means something valuable. One accepts a particular value dear to his or her heart or superior to other values. Values can be found out, but a value hierarchy is not possible because the end existences are preferences that defy comparability. Normative values can be separated from empirical values, but like virtue ethics and deontological ethics, they cannot be accepted in the name of morality or goodness.

Values and assumptions are the offshoots of aptitudes and even reason can also be called a value in itself. The studies in ethics talk of higher and lower values. Higher values generally represent the 'ought content', acceptable to society in its legitimate sense. In other words, these are the aptitudes of Freud's super ego, which integrate behaviours and view them as instrument of social good. The aptitudes or the values emanating therefrom perform the following functions:

1. The aptitudes generate attitudes, relationships, commitments and behaviours.
2. They rationalize actions and operations that go on in social situations.

3. They yield assumptions, which constitute the core of legitimacy.
4. They provide moral sanction to actions by glorifying their need in society.

The values or aptitudes can be individual, societal and organizational. Allport associates and relates these aptitudinal categories with each other. He has classified aptitudinal values into six categories:

1. *Theoretical:* Truth and rationality.
2. *Economic:* Practical, functional and useful.
3. *Aesthetic:* Form of beauty and harmony.
4. *Social:* Love and welfare of people.
5. *Political:* Power, coercion and influence.
6. *Religious:* Understanding the cosmos.

The value system of human beings has an aptitudinal grounding. People may choose careers for which they have no aptitudinal disposition. Government jobs in India attract people because they offer power, social status and security. But this has very little to do with merit or job joy. The officials, once trapped, have to live and work in these jobs without any aptitude for administration or social service.

The FSS Triangle

The aptitudinal values which offer job satisfaction, job involvement and job commitment are necessary to lead an ethical life in bureaucracy. The recruiters must find out this attitudinal base from which values of honesty and sincerity get sustenance. The ground institutions that help in value inculcation and value sustenance are: (1) family, (2) school, and (3) society, popularly known as the FSS Triangle. In a democratic society striving for social justice, family backgrounds cannot be related with merit, but they are decisively linked with ethical behaviour. Mass education and right to education create another challenge to aptitudinal values. Media and the peer group behaviours do not help the youngsters to develop right kind of values. The crisis becomes deeper when merit is discovered in the FSS triangle, i.e. family, school and society. Being judgemental in their contents, the values hover around morality, ethics or the desirable 'shoulds'. They are abstracted from socio-cultural ethics by the aptitude of the individual. One can opt for absolute honesty and objectivity in the ocean of corruption and anarchic selfishness. Robert Neimbur's basic dilemma of 'a moral man in an immoral society' represents this ethical crisis of our age. Human aptitudes strive for objectivity, empathy, compassion, impartiality, dedication and other higher values of social service, while the negative or the reverse behaviours damage and distort these higher values. Selecting the right public servant is the answer, but this rightness becomes a search of people with appropriate aptitudes, which can enable him or her to stand firm in the rough and tumble of social turbulence. No wonder, our public service commissions are now-a-days engaged in sorting out able youngsters with right kind of aptitudes rather than people with high profiles of reason or IQ, called merit.

Individual aptitude as a foundational value is the most precious treasure of a civil servant to serve the country and its teeming millions. Ruling can be a service only when the ruler is imbued and inspired with a mission of social service. It is easier said than done. Such missionaries, who give more and take less, are found in missions only, where they serve the Lord or his children. Christian missionaries of charity and Ramakrishna Mission are few examples. These missionaries, with an aptitude for social service, work with dedication without adequate returns. A civil servant may not be a missionary but he or she is not a mercenary worker either. He or she needs money and facilities, but he or she does not work for them only. Merit, competence and ability are his or her strength, but all this cannot sustain him or her in his or her noble mission of public service, if he or she does not have the genuine aptitude of serving the people. Most of these public service values reflect an inner disposition and one can say that public servants are born, they cannot be made by mere training.

Civil Service as an Instrument to Combat Social Darwinism

Government service in India, or for that matter in any country, is a challenging responsibility of a very high order. Public servants may become exploiters and perpetrators of injustice, if they are devoid of that ethical foundation on which stands the entire edifice of government service. They have a legal goal and they are adequately paid for it. But it has its moral manifestation also, which converts 'ruling' into serving. The mission of any government is to keep the society together, uphold its high ethical values of fraternity and to lead the masses in their journey towards peace, harmony, development and excellence. Civil service is an instrument which translates this mission into action. This administrative capability requires objectivity, empathy, dedication and above all compassion towards those weaker sections of society, who are too weak to stand to the Social Darwinian law of struggle for existence. The governments are expected to make the misfits as more fit to survive. It presupposes the spirit of humility, self-effacement and enlightened commitment to the welfare of the community. Mere preaching or training exhortations are inadequate and they do not stir the core conscience, unless the basic aptitudinal foundation is productive enough to fertilize the seed. Law, right reason, rights to equality and information are important, but what is critical about these values is the ethical response which the public servants can ignore only at their own peril. In a modernizing society, like India, where there is massive unemployment and the so-called educated people are sadly and deeply wedded to colonial elitism, these foundational aptitudes of public service are not easy to be discovered by written examinations and interview systems. Yet, something has to be done to give credit to those who opt for these cherished values in preference to career security, social status and opportunities to exploit the unfortunates. Here, this 'black men's burden' has to be carried out by the administrators or the *black missionaries of mother India*, who feel elated in the foundational values of public service of the masses. These values are:

1. Integrity
2. Impartiality
3. Non-partisanship
4. Objectivity
5. Empathy
6. Dedication
7. Tolerance
8. Compassion

The list is just illustrative and not exhaustive. Most of these value judgements do not need any dictionary definitions also. The antonym of these service values in government are called corruption, exploitation, greediness, familialism and parochialism rooted in caste, class, religion and region. With a right kind of nurture in family and character-education in the schools, the ground work of aptitudinal values can be prepared and their availability and future growth can be stressed in the policies of recruitment and training of civil servants at all levels of public services. This can generate a chain of aptitudinal values of public service. The closed personalities with fossilised attitudes cannot polish these rational aptitudes, so very essential to recruit, train and inspire civil servants in all spheres of a democratic society.

The English rule in India built a civil service steel frame which imitated the rule-values and imbibed the elitist attitudes and aptitudes, oblivious to social justice and popular welfare. The younger generation of civil servants, in free India, could not perceive their fellow citizens as equals but proved to be the prisoners of status attitude. Their aptitudinal value system, being elitist, is a great obstacle in the percolation of constitutional values in the erstwhile feudal society of quasi-urban India. To expedite this democratization process of Indian administration, the terms 'merit selection' and 'merit promotion' need aptitudinal definitions, so that right kind of civil servants may be screened for recruitment and further subjected to meaningful training. Personality behaviour of civil servants is not a matter of law or brilliance only. The perception and attitudes have to change and this requires an aptitudinal exploration in their personality structures.

Chapter 4

Rational Maturity and Emotional Intelligence

The Dilemmas of Ethical Conduct

The Union Minister Veerappa Moily, in the fourth report of Administrative Reforms Commission (ARC) on 'Ethics in Governance' writes: 'Good governance must be founded on moral virtues ensuring stability and harmony. The art of good governance simply lies in making things right and putting them in their right place'.

In public administration, what is right, about rights and which place is the right place are determined by the values enshrined in the constitution. The legal codes, rules and regulations exist so that the civil bureaucracy may conform to and follow them as a procedure. When Max Weber described the one best way of getting things done, he termed it 'legal-rational'. Law has to have a rational basis as was construed by Hegel. The Hegelian idealism was that 'real is rational and rational is real'. The concept of rationality in Weber's judgement was something that makes human beings responsible and accountable. Rational individuals or civil servants can depersonalize themselves and ensure maximum justice, objectivity and excellence. The present-day meritocracies, swear by Weber and believe that legal-rational approach can maximize responsiveness, transparency and compassion in administrative decisions and actions. With rationality, ruling his or her behaviour, a civil servant can conceptualize public good and perform his or her tasks with integrity, probity and discipline. A number of reports on code of ethics, including the one prepared by American Society for Public Administration, stress upon the rational-moral aspects of administrative action. Ethical activities in administration are followed only when civil servants:

- Exercise discretionary authority to promote public interest.
- Recognize and support the public's right to know the public business.
- Exercise compassion, benevolence, fairness and optimism.
- Prevent all forms of mismanagement of public funds by establishing and maintaining strong fiscal and management controls, by supporting audits and investigative activities.
- Protect constitutional principles of equality, fairness, representativeness, responsiveness and due process in protecting citizen's rights.
- Maintain truthfulness and honesty and do not compromise them for advancement, honour, or personal gain.
- Zealously guard against conflict of interest or its appearance, e.g. nepotism, improper outside employment, misuse of public resources or the acceptance of gifts.
- Establish procedures that promote ethical behaviour and hold individuals and organizations accountable for their conduct.

For long, it was argued that rationality is a distinctive human quality of the brain and possessing rationality will imply its use also. The ideal-type mental construct of bureaucracy, propounded by Max Weber, highlighted the ethical imperative of bureaucratic behaviour in a far-fetched manner. Weber observed: 'In the rational type, it is a matter of principle that the members of the administrative staff should be completely separated from ownership of the means of production and administration. Officials, employees and workers attached to the administrative staff do not themselves own the non-human means of production and administration .... There exists, furthermore, in principle, complete separation of property belonging to the organization, which is controlled within the sphere of office, and the personal property of the official, which is available for his own private uses'.

By 1770, a centralized recruiting system for bureaucracy and a superior examination commission for that purpose began to operate in Prussia. By the end of the 18th century a merit system of recruitment applied to all posts there. However, the 'Prussian organization gradually degenerated into a sort of caste system ... which was characterized by exclusiveness, contempt for outsiders and ... social discriminations of paternalism'.

This analysis of Weber underscores the need to check the misuse of an official position for the sake of personal gains. Although his ideal-type construct on bureaucracy is not 'empirical' in a methodological sense, yet it has an empirical flavour, for it appears to have taken into account the existential reality of bureaucratic behaviour in cross-national and cross-temporal contexts. Although Weber was certainly not normative while constructing his ideal types, yet the message is clear: 'Do not misuse official property for personal benefit'.

In his *Economy and Society,* Max Weber observes that bureaucracy gives birth to a new species of human beings. Man's social relations have been converted into control relations. Skills affirming the ascendancy of technical means, whether of administration or production, have replaced norms and beliefs of man concerning human ends. Psychologically, the new personality type is that of rationalistic expert, incapable of emotion and devoid of will. Bureaucracy has created a person who is nothing but a little cog in a big machine. Language, as a means for bringing people into communication, has become the secretive tool of command. Administration everywhere has replaced politics, particularly democratic politics, and the methods of determining social goals are being based on human needs. This has necessitated the utility of rational application of law in administration. The modern, western society experienced this growth of rationalism in many spheres. For instance, it was evident in the development of protestant ethic which encouraged hard work and self-discipline. This ethic was the basis of the spirit of capitalism which called for the rational investment of time and efforts so as to maximize profits and development of rational capitalism. The general trend towards rationality was also evident in other spheres like development of science and governance. Thus, protestantism, capitalism, science and bureaucracy are all parts of one cluster of human development – the process of rationalization. The legal-rational authority depends on the availability of a legal code which could be established to claim obedience from the members of the bureaucratic organization.

Rationality as Right Brain Management

Administration looks after the interests of the organization within the limits of law which as a system of abstract rules is applied to particular cases. The man exercising authority obeys this impersonal order and obedience is not to the person who has the authority but to the impersonal order which has appointed him or her to that position. The rationalist studies focus mainly on the over-valued skills of critical analysis. They sadly neglect the powerful right brain modes. Dr. Harry Alder found that most of the top British CEOs he studied, had actually learnt to access their right brain capacities, and they trust the resultant outputs. This trend towards the 'right brain management' has been called 'creative management' by Gareth Morgan.

Weber's conception of bureaucracy can be found in his ideas on power, domination and authority. Weber defined power as 'the probability that one actor, within a social relationship, will be in a position to carry out his own will despite resistance'. Imperative control or domination is power in a hierarchy; it is the probability that with a given specific content it will be obeyed by a given group of persons. The exercise of authority requires that a person successfully issues orders to a group of subordinates who respond because of their belief in the legitimacy of the order. Thus, legitimacy turns into power and domination into authority.

Bounded Rationality

The later researches of post-Weber era conclusively prove that rationality is neither organic, nor permanent, nor static. For instance, Simon, Bernard and a host of other writers talk about the 'flexibility of rationality'. Objectivity of rational action was questioned when Simon advanced his concept of 'bounded rationality' of values which can neither be fixed nor called final in Weberian sense. The six-fold classification of this rational behaviour, as attempted by Simon, is given below:

1. Subjectively rational
2. Objectively rational
3. Individually rational
4. Organizationally rational
5. Deliberately rational
6. Consciously rational

This pluralist view of rationality brings interest groups into the orbit of political analysis and focuses on the power of such groups as countervailing factors in policy making in the modern state. It emphasizes that not only governments and political elites but bureaucracies and bureaucratic elites too are boxed in between divergent and intricately related interests and pressures, which they must placate in order to survive. It clarifies the internal complexity and interplay of contending forces within the modern government and its bureaucracy. It convincingly makes out the case that the modern state, including bureaucracy, is not as systematic and rational as it might have widely been thought out to be. It thus includes an implicit, and perhaps inadvertent, but largely well-taken criticism of Weber's model, together with a shift to a more down-to-earth image and a more realistic emotional appraisal of the limits of bureaucratic effectiveness. It proves that Weberian civil servants cannot be 'objectively rational' all the time and in all sorts of varied situations. Once rational, does not mean rational always and everywhere. Weber has been subjected to a scathing criticism and the irrational behaviours of his rational public servants are quoted day in and day out in instances of corruption and ethical malpractices.

IQ as Right Brain Mapping

Starting from philosophy, the research in brain behaviour has crossed the frontiers of psychiatry and now the neurological deficiencies and disorders are establishing the fact that 'rationality' is neither exclusive nor infallible. Gone are the days when research about cortex, vertebra and thalamus could give some hazy measurements of IQ or brain mapping. The rational behaviour has its limitations, obstructions and distortions. So Weber's availability of rationality is no guarantee of its neutrality or maturity. People with rationality or high IQ can be criminals and may indulge in unethical practices without any qualms of conscience. A holistic view of probity is being advocated in 'value-centric civil service'. Weber is not only to be revisited but needs to be improved upon in the light of new neurological researches in the areas of reason and emotion to discover administrators of ability, compassion and empathy. Rationalism has to be combined with intuition and common sense. A man with reason and vision can foresee, comprehend and even decide with his mental faculty of right reason but mere reason, cannot fight with the ethical dilemmas of allurements in administrative compulsions. The presence of a rational faculty and high IQ, which is a part of brain management, is a prerequisite, but it should be mature enough to subjugate itself to other emotional pressures present inside the lobes of the brain and their consequent fights with right reason.

According to experts, an individual's creativity depends essentially on the ability to make conceptual associations, whereby he or she is able to generate innovative ideas. This is a mental process that is eminently facilitated by techniques of right brain tapping. It enables one to bypass the routine functioning style of the left brain mode, and enter into the visual mode of the right brain. This latter holistic mode permits one to make the imaginative leaps that constitute what Edward de Bono calls 'lateral thinking'. The creative ideas thus generated can subsequently be evaluated for their practicality and feasibility, by using the logical activity of the left brain. The net result is that one has to learn to operate the whole brain in the most effective manner. The CEOs and other top organizational leaders, like Harry Alder, have demonstrated it. According to management writers, such as Edward de Bono and Harry Mintzberg, even the most well-known management schools are unable to produce the appropriate kind of managers that modern society needs. In Alder's diagnosis, the main reason for this is the management training programmes which woefully neglect the left lobe of the brain.

Psychiatry and neurosciences find 'reason' as a quality of behaviour, which may diminish or even get polluted, if the person does not possess the requisite emotional intelligence in the other lobe. Rationality can distinguish between a moral and immoral action or practice, but it cannot prevent unethical doings if the civil servant finds himself or herself poor or devoid of emotional intelligence of the brain.

IQ tests of rationality measure the brain power of comprehension, its twitching, speed of mental activization and interpretation of the results. They are extremely important as an administrative equipment, but mere reason or faculty of logic can reduce an intelligent man to the position of a human robot with the mechanical mind of a computer. Though useful, the extra-developed rational faculty of the administrators causes the following situations:

1. Relativity of interpretations in human situations which is natural. The hierarchy may attempt to resolve conflicts at rationality levels, but it breeds senior-subordinate conflicts because of relativity and hierarchy of rationality itself.
2. Rationality makes people rigid, authoritarian and even arrogant.
3. Being hostile to human rights of liberty and equality, a hierarchy of rationality renders bureaucracy somewhat incompatible with democratic values of liberty and equality.
4. Equating law with right reason may be a need but discovering moral action and justice through mere rational manipulations can be equally disastrous.

Weber never thought of bureaucracy as an independent social unit. He tended to view it as a machine. Hence, the question of control over bureaucracy becomes easy. It subordinates itself to anyone who is able to master the economic and legal techniques necessary for its proper functioning. Since Weber regarded bureaucracy as an apparatus, it can work for anyone who knows how to gain control over it. He considered it essential that non-bureaucratic leaders be selected who might control the controllers. The other checks which Weber considers necessary for reducing the influence of bureaucracy to its rightful proportions are openness, elimination of official secrets and the introduction of effective parliamentary control. It covers all those non-rational and extra-situational factors which emotional intelligence suggests.

The Lateral Thinking

Rationality, law and morality are not only interrelated but they make a trio, each becoming the baseline of the triangle at different occasions and in different situations. Law wants to cover the moral ground in a selective manner and just as legality cannot be the morality of a society, similarly, rationality of the few cannot define law or morality either. Weber was trying to be rational by propounding authority as legal-rational. But, Bentham will call it legal-moral, which Kant will not accept. So, the problem boils down to a distinction between morality and rationality. The latter has to be extra-developed and disciplined to encompass law and morality. Weber offers a sound pillar to legal-rational conduct, but this has to be supported by the second pillar of emotional intelligence and rational maturity to keep the administrative edifice human, social and moral. Emotions are generally seen as a sphere of heart rather than that of the head. An emotional brain, which a neuro-psychologist Daniel Goleman examines in his celebrated study, separates the rational from the emotional. He refuses to call human reason or rational temperament as his or her destiny. 'Very often emotions hijack reason and the smart people become dumb', says Goleman. 'Most people allow their emotions to overwhelm their weak reason and they need emotional relearning. Human beings, if they do not know the anatomy of head and heart, are liable to be the slaves of their passions. The lack of emotional intelligence may conspire with their intimate enemies and they may fall a prey into a neurological trap without any 'master aptitude'. Emotions represent a powerful source of human energy and if human beings are weak in channelizing their emotional resurgence, they may lose the roots of empathy or pleasant memories of happy unions and incidents.'

The Oxford English Dictionary defines emotion as 'an agitation or disturbance of mind, feeling, passion, or a vehement or excited mental state'. Goleman refers to emotion 'as a feeling with its distinctive thoughts, psychological and biological states, and a large range of propensities to act'. There are hundreds of emotions, along with their blends, variations, mutations and nuances. Indeed, there are many more subtleties of emotions than we have the words for them in any language. Each emotion offers a distinctive readiness to act; each points us in a direction that has worked well to handle the recurring challenges of human life. As these eternal situations are repeated and have been repeated over evolutionary history, the survival value of the emotional repertoire is attested by its becoming imprinted in our nerves as innate, and automatic tendencies of the human heart.

To quote Goleman again, 'A view of human nature which ignores the power of emotions is sadly shortsighted. The very name *homo sapiens,* the thinking species, is misleading in the light of the new appreciation and vision of the place of emotions in our lives that science now offers. As we know from experience, when it comes to shaping our decisions and our actions, the feeling counts every bit as much – and often more – than our thought. We have gone too far in emphasizing the value and significance of the purely rational or of what IQ measures as worth while in human life. For better or worse, intelligence can come to nothing when the emotions hold sway'.

The Bono Research of Two Lobes

Emotions are as basic and decisive in human action as is reason because all pleasures and pains are not physical. There shall always be a difference between a 'pin push' and a piece of poetry. The emotions in essence are impulses to act, the instant plans for handling life that evolution has instilled in human beings. The very root of the word 'emotion' is 'motere'. The latin verb 'to move', plus the prefix 'e-' connote 'move away'. It suggests a tendency to act which is implicit in every emotion. How do emotions lead to actions is obvious if we watch animals or children. It is only in the so called 'civilized' adults that we find the anomaly. In the animal kingdom, emotions or root impulses act to divorce them from obvious reactions.

The Emotional Repertoire

In emotional repertoire each emotion plays a unique role, as revealed by their distinctive biological signatures. With new methods to peep into the body and brain, researchers are discovering more physiological details of how each emotion prepares the body for a very different kind of response. To quote Goleman, 'With anger blood flows to the hands, making it easier to grasp a weapon, the heart rate increases, and a rush of hormones like adrenaline generates a pulse of energy strong enough for vigorous action. With fear, blood goes to the large skeletal muscles, such as in the legs, making it easier to flee, at the circuits in the brain's emotional centres trigger a flood of hormones that put the body on general alert, making it edgy and ready for action, and attention'.

Goleman further says, 'Among the main biological changes in *happiness* there is an increased activity in the brain centre which inhibits negative feelings and fosters an increase in available energy. The configuration offers the body a general rest and enthusiasm striving toward a great variety of goals. Love, tender feelings, and sexual satisfaction entail parasympathetic arousal, the physiological opposite of the 'flight-or-fight' mobilization shared by fear and anger'. For example, when a marriage breaks, a wife may say, 'I really do not care now' but then her eyes momentarily well up with tears and that moment of teary eyes could easily pass unnoted. But, the empathetic understanding that someone's watering eyes means she is sad despite her words to the contrary, is an act of comprehending just as surely as is distilling meaning from words on a printed page. One is an act of the emotional mind, the other of the rational mind. In a very real sense, we have two minds, one that thinks and one that feels.

The Right-Left Brain Interactions

The two fundamentally different ways of knowing the phenomenon, interact to construct a mental life. The rational mind is the mode of comprehension which makes persons typically conscious and more prominent in awareness, thoughtful, and able to ponder and reflect. But, alongside this, there is another system of knowing which is impulsive and powerful. It is the illogical, and can be called the *emotional mind*.

Apparently emotional intelligence seems like a contradiction in terms. The philosophers may see a dichotomy between the emotional and the intellectual sides of mental life of human beings. The skill sets include intellectual abilities and moral qualities which converge into emotional intelligence. IQ tests measure general ability to solve problems and understand concepts. They in turn include

1. reasoning ability,
2. problem-solving ability,
3. ability to perceive relationships between things and ability and
4. to store and retrieve information. Rationality is considered as an innate, unalterable and natural endowment.

Gardner questions this conventional method of measuring intelligence as a single, one-dimensional skill or a golden key to success in life. He identified six varieties of intelligences namely

1. logical,
2. linguistic,
3. spatial visualization,
4. kinaesthetic genius,
5. musical, and
6. personal intelligence.

Emotional intelligence refers mainly to 'personal intelligence' that helps in getting along well with people and in prudently ordering one's own life. It is essentially an ability to understand the physical, mental and social impact that negative emotions have on human bodies, minds, relationships and ability to pursue and achieve goals. It creates ability to moderate one's own emotions and overcome strong negative emotions to achieve goals. It facilitates the understanding of emotions of others where by one can adapt to situations and extract the best out of their teams. The ability to overcome the emotional obstacles help to recover from setbacks and resolve crises and conflicts. The emotions represent a way in which the body conveys about an unmet desire or need. It may create serious consequences on mental and social well-being. The state of awareness about emotions of self and that of others can rightly be called emotional intelligence (EI). The psycho-rational analysis of the two lobes of the brain inform about the level of EI. The medical professionals have worked out three specific models of EI. They are

1. The Ability Model of Peter Salovey and John Mayers
2. The Trait Model of Konstantin Petridis
3. The Mixed Model of Daniel Goleman

The Ability Model, of Peter Salovey and John Mayers, defines emotional intelligence as, 'the subset of social intelligence that involves the ability to monitor one's own and others' feelings and emotions, to discriminate among them and to use this information to guide one's thinking and actions'. It comprises four abilities:

1. perceiving emotions,
2. using emotions,
3. understanding emotions, and
4. managing emotions.

The Ability Model strives to measure the EQ level through the Mayer-Salovey-Caruso Emotional Intelligence Test (MSCEIT) which is based on a series of emotion-based problems that seek solutions.

The Trait Model of Konstantin Petridis locates the constellation of emotional self-perceptions at the lower levels of personality. 'People have a number of emotional self-perceptions and traits which can be measured through the respondent's self-assessment. The assumption is that the person can accurately describe his or her own traits. It explores emotional intelligence through personality framework. Here the emphasis is on environmental aspect of personality rather than on the assumption of emotional intelligence as a brain-based activity. The Swinburne University Emotional Intelligence Test (SUEIT), and the Scheutte Emotional Intelligence Model along with Trait Emotional Intelligence Questionnaire (TEIQue) test Emotional Intelligence on 15 subscales which are organized under four factors. These factors are:

1. well-being,
2. self-control,
3. emotionality, and
4. sociability.

The Goleman Model is more elaborate, mixed and exhaustive. It gives a list of four kinds of competencies. In fact self awareness is the mother emotion, which gives birth to (1) self assessment, (2) self confidence and (3) self management. Goleman says that these competencies are not necessarily inherent or natural, but must be developed over time. Unlike IQ which is stagnant beyond a stage in life, the emotional intelligence continues to develop throughout life. Self awareness increases with patience, which requires a check in practice. Emotions need to be identified and acknowledged, when they occur. Going to the roots of emotions helps in understanding their cause. Otherwise they get mixed up with symptoms. With increasing self-awareness, one can be able to forecast the feelings and the triggers which might lead to such feelings. This will help in preparing for such situations. Initially it is not easy or comfortable when one starts acknowledging or recognizing the emotions. It requires lot of self-confidence to accept the strengths and weaknesses, and start working on improvement.

The competency skills like self control, reflection, reframing and rehearsal help to enhance trustworthiness, conscientiousness, adaptability, initiation and achievement orientation. Social awareness involves an understanding of how others are feeling. According to Goleman, it requires three specific skills:

1. empathy,
2. acknowledgement, and
3. sensitivity.

Organizational awareness and service orientations can contribute to the growth of social skills which in turn help in strengthening:

1. influence patterns,
2. leadership styles,
3. team management,
4. communication patterns, and
5. change catalytic abilities.

All this builds bonds to improve collaborative teamwork and makes conflict management effective and workable.

Emotionally intelligent behaviour is a necessity to build bridges of mutual understanding and trust. To promote effective, efficient and empathetic governance, the social capital has to be built across the government structures. The administration works in a complex environment involving constant interaction with the public, elected representatives and the media etc. The administrators are always under pressure to perform and deliver the results, irrespective of the constraints. Goleman puts interpersonal skills in the centre of his concept of emotional intelligence which pertains to all about the ability to connect one self with people and understand their emotions for a harmonious co-existence. Emotional intelligence positively influences individual performance. It can improve the quality of work leading to better success in careers.

Howard Gardner's study 'The Frames of Mind', is a path breaking research about interpersonal ability to understand our own feelings and interpersonal intelligence as ability to understand the feelings of others.

The Wayne Payne's study (1985), entitled 'E.I.: A Study of Emotions', presents the psychiatric implications and prescriptions of mental-emotional disorders. A decade later Daniel

Goleman explained why emotional intelligence matters more than intelligence quotient. He found that the emotions have a biological purpose. They are indication that something has gone wrong or that some desire or need has not been fulfilled. They can be heightened or down played. The teams which have positive interpersonal relations have happy members who work for their goals and possess a balance and self control. They enjoy peace of mind and high motivation and concentration. Contentment and happy social life are always the end-results of appreciation. These people have good social relations and generally keep good physical health as well. They are generally successful in their careers also. On the contrary people with low EI develop negative feelings that cause frustration, depression, disappointment, anger and anxiety.

The emotional-rational dichotomy approximates to the folk distinction between 'heart' and 'head'. Knowing something as right 'in one's heart' is a different order of conviction. Somehow a deeper kind of certainty than thinking always exists in the rational mind also. There is a steady gradient in the ratio of rational-to-emotional control over the mind. More intense the feeling, more dominant becomes the emotional mind and the rational gets more and more ineffectual. This is an arrangement that seems to stem from eons of evolutionary advantage to having emotions and intuitions which guide our instantaneous response in situations.

These two minds, the emotional and the rational, operate in close harmony for the most part, intertwining their very different ways of knowing to guide us through the world. Ordinarily, there is a balance between emotional and rational minds, with emotion feeding into and informing the operations of the rational mind, and the rational mind refining and sometimes vetoing the inputs of the emotions. According to Goleman, 'the emotional and rational minds are semi-independent faculties, each reflecting the operation of distinct, but interconnected, circuitry in the brain. In many or most moments, these minds are exquisitely coordinated; feelings are essential to thoughts and thoughts to feelings. But when passions surge and the balance tips, it is the emotional mind that captures the upper hand, swamping the rational mind'.

The Emotional Brain in Neural Architecture

The neocortex of *homo sapiens* is much larger than that of other living beings. It makes them rational as well as emotional. The neocortex is the seat of thought; it contains the centres that put together and comprehend what the senses perceive. It adds a feeling to what we think about it and allows us to have feelings about ideas, symbols, imaginations, etc. Then, there are several other higher centres through which behaviours and relations are processed.

Goleman's study on emotional intelligence asserts: 'These higher centres do not govern emotional life; in crucial matters of the heart and most especially in emotional emergencies, they can be said to defer to the limbic system. Because so many of the brain's higher centres sprouted from or extended the scope of the limbic area, the emotional brain plays a crucial role in neural architecture. As the root from which the newer brain grew, the emotional areas are intertwined via myriad connecting circuits to all parts of the neocortex. This gives the emotional centres immense power to influence the functioning of the rest of the brain – including its centres for thought'.

Talking about the challenge of emotional life, Aristotle writes: 'Anyone can become angry that is easy. But to be angry with the right person, to the right degree, at the right time, for the right purpose, and in the right way is not easy'. In *The Nicomachean Ethics,* Aristotle's philosophical enquiry into virtue, character and good life, his challenge is to manage our emotional life with intelligence. Our passions, when well exercised, have wisdom; they guide our thinking, our values and our survival.

But they can easily go away, and do so all too often. As Aristotle found, the problem is not with emotionality, but with the *appropriateness* of emotion and its expression. The question is, how can we bring intelligence to our emotions.

The Alarm System of the Amygdala

Goleman compares amygdala with an alarm system. He writes about the brain's architecture: 'The amygdala is poised something like an alarm company where operators stand ready to send out emergency calls to the fire department, police and a neighbour whenever a home security system signals trouble. This amygdala orchestrates as it commandeers areas throughout the brain. The amygdala's extensive web of neural connections allows it, during an emotional emergency, to capture and drive much of the rest of the brain – including the rational mind. Our emotions have a mind of their own, one which can hold views quite independently of our rational mind. This amygdala arousal seems to imprint in memory most moments of emotional arousal with an added degree of strength. One reason we can be so battled berried by our emotional outbursts, is that they often date from a time early in our lives when things were bewildering and we did not have words for comprehending events. We may have the chaotic feelings, but not the words for the memories that formed them. The connections between the amygdala (and related limbic structures) and the neocortex are the hub of the battles or cooperative treaties struck between head and heart, thought and feeling. This circuitry explains, why emotion is so crucial to effective thought, both in making wise decisions and in simply allowing us to think clearly'.

The Complementarity of Limbic System and Neocortex

The emotions matter for rationality. In the dance of feeling and thought, the emotional faculty guides our moment to moment decisions, working hand in hand with the rational mind, enabling or disabling thought itself. Likewise, the thinking brain plays an executive role in our emotions – except in those moments when emotions surge out of control and the emotional brain runs rampant. In a sense we have two brains, two minds and two different kinds of intelligence: rational and emotional. How we do in life is determined by both, it is not just IQ, but *emotional intelligence* that matters. Indeed, intellect cannot work at its best without emotional intelligence. Goleman writes, 'Ordinarily, the complementarity of limbic system and neocortex, amygdala and prefrontal lobes, means each is a full partner in mental life. When these partners interact well, emotional intelligence rises, as does intellectual ability. This turns the old understanding of the tension between reason and feeling on its head. It is not that we want to do away with emotion and put reason in its place, but instead find the intelligent balance of the two'. The Goleman study concludes that 'the old paradigm held an ideal of reason freed of the pulls of emotion. *The new paradigm urges us to harmonize head and heart*. To do that well in our lives means we must first understand more exactly what it means to use emotion intelligently'.

Thus, the meaning of emotional intelligence, within its neurological claptrap, simply means:

1. Intelligence is neither rational nor emotional, but a composite of the two with a shifting balance in human operations.
2. Emotional starvation causes deviant behaviours and unethical practices.
3. Uncontrolled and exuberant emotions may overpower reason and the people with high IQ may commit crimes, offences and deficient behaviours.

In public administration, in India, there is an overemphasis on the quest for merit which is regarded as synonymous with rational faculty. Mental ability is tested at every point of recruitment and training includes all those exercises that challenge left brain to be more and more reason and result-oriented. The result is obvious. The plain emotional prejudices of extra love for family, kinship, caste, community and religion, region, etc. make the Indian official behaviours parochial, selfish and even anti-national. In fact, 'corruption' has been and can be defined as 'loving one's family more than the society'. People prefer to harm and loot the society and the country for the affluence and an ostentatious living of their children and the close kins. Government officials are accused of their irrational and unethical decisions because they are too emotional to widen their loyalty circle to society and the country. Emotional attachment to family, to jobs and to the wide world is healthy emotional intelligence. But it is the right ordering and systematic disciplining of emotions which makes rationality or ability purposive. All government rules, regulations, laws and institutions expect public servants to be merely rational, impartial, compassionate and tolerant but this kind of objectivity, dedication and aptitudes of impartiality can come only when they are emotionally mature and know how to discipline their excessive and exuberant parochial emotions. The aptitudinal values are essentially a field of emotions and the rational irrigation cannot make them fertile or productive. The rational fears of punishment do not deter the corrupt because the emotional compensation which they derive from 'feeding the family' is much more satisfying than the sacrifice which the legal-ethics entails.

The Unschooled Emotions of Public Servants

Public service anywhere has to be a mission but in fact it is a profession. In India, those who come to join government service are rationally alright but their emotional intelligence is either too low or too much family-oriented that they indulge in unethical practices for greed and kinship obligations. Here, the emotional intelligence either does not exist or has never been schooled or disciplined in rationality. Helping a brother is an emotional duty, no matter the rational laws call it 'nepotism' (भाई-भतीजावाद). In

Indian society, 'rationality' is generally a casualty when it confronts emotions of a wild variety without maturity training. Public servants have difficulty in being impartial or non-partisan for the simple reason that their intellectual brain cannot coexist or conquer the emotional part of the brain. They tend to relapse into subjectivity or intolerance, partly because the emotive mix in their rationality is too strong to be extricated. Examples are not rare, where their ability or merit forces them to be sympathetic rather than to be empathetic at all. Dedication to public service requires a strong emotion of compassion towards the weaker sections of society, but the rationality of public service does not stir the emotional being of a civilian. His or her emotional self has either been brutalized by the system of status or he or she can always rationalize his or her behaviours, which were not trained in emotional intelligence. The application of emotional intelligence of government employees in India normally follows three patterns:

1. They pride in being extra-rational and isolate themselves emotionally from the society without understanding the meaning of the term 'emotion'.
2. They are either too emotional or extra-secretive about their emotions assuming that only illiterate people obey emotions.
3. They do not distinguish between the healthy and unhealthy contents of reason and emotion and consequently cancel them out rather than blending them into a purposeful decision of good governance.

The Emotional Illiteracy of Weberian Rationals

This situation is responsible for irresponsible and indifferent behaviours of government employees. More recently, transparency and participations are being tried but the emotional involvement of officials in governance is either too low or extra-rational. There is emotional illiteracy and people do not know how to manage with a heart. The cost of this illiteracy is that some of them suffer from dilemmas and depressions. They encounter trauma and become intolerant in the process. Without a basic aptitude of empathy they shed crocodile tears on the plight of the governed and keep striving for their power positions and job extensions. Emotional intelligence is not even a criterion of their self-assessments or annual confidential reports. What matters is legal performance for which an overemphasis on Weberian rationality is an unfortunate legacy of the British Raj.

The psychologists and neuroscientists are warning and constantly suggesting a happy blend of Weberian rationality with Simonian objective emotionalism in the application of 'satisficing decisions' or heuristic decisions of intuition. This can be accomplished by:

1. Understanding reason and emotion and their proper mix in human affairs. It requires a high level of self-awareness.
2. Schooling emotions since early childhood, so that the later behaviours may sprout on a fertile aptitudinal soil of 'otherliness'.
3. Disciplining the emotional mind with a high-level of intelligence, so that mere intellectual excellence may not result in a robot-like mechanical efficiency with disastrous conclusions.

The Goleman Paradigms

Here are some excerpts from the Goleman's study of emotional intelligence (why it can matter more than IQ). The readers may reflect upon them and use them whenever they find them gainful in their administrative experience.

1. Emotional entertainment is the heart of *influence*.
2. Emotions that simmer beneath the *threshold of awareness* can have a powerful impact on how we perceive and react, even though we have no idea that they are at work.
3. Let that reaction be brought into awareness – after being registered in the cortex – he or she can evaluate things anew, decide to shrug-off the feelings left earlier in the day, and change his or her *outlook and mood*.

4. Interpersonal intelligence is the *ability to understand* other people: what motivates them, how they work, and how to work cooperatively with them. It is a capacity to form an accurate, *vertical model of oneself* and to be able to use that model to operate effectively in life.
5. IQ offers little to explain the *different destinies of people* with roughly equal promises, schooling and opportunity. Ninety-five Harvard students with a wider spread of IQ when followed into middle age, the men with the highest test scores in college were not successful compared to their lower-scoring peers. Nor did they have the greatest life satisfaction, nor the most happiness with friendships, family and romantic relationships.
6. The feelings of *enthusiasm and pleasure* in what we do – or even by an optimal degree of anxiety – the emotions propel us to accomplishment. The emotional intelligence is *a master aptitude*, a capacity that profoundly affects all other abilities, either facilitating or interfering with them.
7. When emotions overwhelm concentration, what is being swamped is the mental capacity which cognitive scientists call 'working memory', the ability to hold in mind all information relevant to the task at hand. The prefrontal cortex executes working memory – remembering, where feelings and emotions meet. When the limbic circuitry that converges on the prefrontal cortex is in the thrall of emotional distress, it costs the effectiveness of working memory.
8. The goal-directed, self-imposed delay of gratification is the essence of *emotional self-regulation.* Walter Mischel's finding underscores the role of emotional intelligence as a *meta-ability*, determining how well or how poorly people are able to use their other mental capacities.
9. When the emotional brain is driving the body with a strong reaction – in the heat of anger – there can be little or no empathy. *Empathy requires enough calm and receptivity* so that

the subtle signals of feeling from another person can be received and mimicked by one's own emotional brain.

10. *Empathy* underlies many facets of moral judgement and action. One is 'empathic anger', which John Stuart Mill described as '*the natural feeling of retaliation* ... rendered by intellect and sympathy applicable to ... those hurt. It wounds us through wounding others'. Mill dubbed this the '*guardian on justice*'. There is some evidence that the level of empathy shades people's moral judgements.
11. Just as the mode of the rational mind is 'word', the mode of the emotions is non-verbal. When a person's words disagree with the tone of voice the non verbal gestures tell the 'Emotional Truth'.
12. *Compassion:* A mere hand-holding is a good medicine. EI is the crucial capacity to learn.

Continuous training programmes for the employees to develop the desired emotional competencies help in creating the right ecology for the organization to perform. This is based on the belief that all individuals have a profile of strengths and development areas in the emotional intelligence competencies. The leaders in administration and governance are expected to possess a wide range of emotional competencies. These areas include; people orientation with sensitivity to diversity, behavioural and cultural norms, interpersonal skills, team work, social skills and networking etc. Integrity, honesty, trustworthiness, support the value system with importance to public interest over self interest. Commitment and empathy towards the underprivileged sections strengthen credibility and reliability in terms of a role model performance. Focus on employees and their feelings set clear goals. The administrative leaders have a responsibility to increase the employees' performance, morale and motivation. To succeed in promoting an emotionally intelligent culture, the leaders must promote openness, transparency and diversity. They must tolerate constructive disagreements and values of flexibility.

Communication patterns among various wings of the organizations is a necessity to achieve the varied goals of organization.

The basic belief that leads to optimism is that setbacks or failures are due to circumstances. We can do something to change them for the better. The art of the critique is intricately entwined with the art of praise. So, in administration, one has to be solution giving, sensitive and a patient listener. A public servant can develop this curriculum of emotional disciplining in his or her own way. Goleman has prescribed the following one dozen guidelines for this self-science curriculum of emotional intelligence. Accordingly, a public servant should:

1. Develop self-awareness, which implies observing oneself and recognizing one's feelings. He or she can build a vocabulary for feelings; and know the relationship between thoughts, feelings and reactions;
2. Examine his or her actions and know their consequences, particularly, when thought or feeling rule a decision;
3. Manage feelings, monitor 'self-talk' to catch negative messages such as internal put-downs; realize what is behind a feeling; find ways to handle fears, anxieties, anger and sadness;
4. Practise to handle stress, i.e. learn the value of exercise, guide imagery and relax his or her methods;
5. Develop empathy by understanding others' feelings and concerns and consider their perspective; appreciate the differences in how people feel about things;
6. Review his or her communication skills, talking about feelings effectively, becoming a good listener and question-asker; distinguishing between what someone does or says and his or her own reactions or judgements about it; sending 'I' messages instead of blame;
7. Try self-disclosure, value openness and build trust in a relationship; which means to know when it is safe to risk talking about one's private feelings;

8. Deepen his or her insight by identifying patterns in emotional life and reactions; recognizing similar patterns in others;
9. Try to be humble enough to develop self-acceptance, feel pride and see oneself in a positive light; recognize strengths and weaknesses, and be able to laugh at oneself;
10. Strive to take responsibility, which requires recognizing the consequences of one's decisions and actions, accepting one's feelings and moods, following through commitments;
11. Strive to be assertive, which is also a character of mature emotion. It means stating concerns and feelings without anger or passivity; and
12. Should understand group dynamics which implies cooperation; knowing when and how to lead, when to follow.

Conflict resolution becomes easy if an administrator knows how to fight fair with colleagues, subordinates and seniors with a win-win model for negotiating compromise. The aptitudinal values of civil service are essentially ethical, which means no law, rule or code can force civil servants to be honest, objective, tolerant or compassionate. The rules provide the guidelines, remind about their desirability and at worst threaten public servants to suffer punishment, if they were found guilty of violating the basic minimum moral order. It is almost impossible to define the terms like integrity, empathy, tolerance or dedication in legal terms. They are subjective and interpretative. An endless discussion may follow about their degrees, quantum, applicative methods and demonstrability in public affairs. Yet, a working definition has to be agreed upon so that this kind of morality can be legislated or implemented by the bureaucracy and the law courts. The lexicon meanings may be putting words for certain phrases used in administration. The meanings may overlap and translations may create cultural nuances, giving contradictory meanings. Still, as in jurisprudence, law is interpreted at different levels of the courts and their benches, the moral codes can be debated in the contemporary contexts of society and an operational consensus can be arrived at. Unanimity in any moral justice is not a matter of evidence or intentions alone, yet they play a decisive role in any notion of justice, duty or moral obligation also. Society and government, when prescribe the aptitudinal ethical values for the civil servants, they normally define these terms as under:

1. *Integrity:* The dictionary synonyms for integrity are wholeness, unimpaired state, righteous purity and honesty. The Hindi translations of Father Bulke use the terms as सत्यनिष्ठा, न्यायनिष्ठा, अक्षत्ता and सुस्वास्थ्यता. The Latin word integer means whole or complete or perfect condition. The dictionary meaning is – adherence to moral and ethical principles; honesty; moral character, i.e. being sincere without being deceitful or untruthful, guided by one's own judgment. It implies that a person of integrity of character is one who is engaged in the search of truth and is making experiments with truth like Mahatma Gandhi. As an ethical being, Gandhi started with the proposition that God is truth but he ended by finding that truth is God. Any human being who has an unflinching faith and devotional belief in this kind of searchable truth is a person of integrity. The truth does not dawn upon human beings. It has to be discovered, for which a regimen of moral virtues is a precondition. Gandhi prescribed अहिंसा, आस्तेय, बह्मचर्य, अपरिग्रह, etc. for his *satyagrahis*. Hence, an average civil servant must guard himself or herself against falsehood, prejudices or conventional beliefs, deeply seated in his or her psyche.

   They should make recommendations and decisions only to serve public interests. They should carry out their functions to the best of their abilities and strive to meet the highest professional standards at all times. They should be mindful of their position of public trust and set a good example to others. Civil servants should be guided by a sense of propriety and conduct themselves in a manner that would bear the closest public scrutiny. This obligation is not fully discharged merely by acting within the law. They should not place themselves under any financial or other obligation that might influence them in the performance of their functions, including the receipt of gifts. They should promptly declare private interests relating to their functions. Civil servants should take steps to avoid conflicts of interest and the appearance of such conflicts. They should take swift action to resolve conflicts that arise. This obligation continues even after leaving the office. The civil servants should be impartial, open-minded, guided by evidence, and willing to hear different viewpoints. They should be ready to acknowledge and correct mistakes. In procedures involving comparative evaluations, civil servants should base recommendations and decisions only on merit and factors expressly prescribed by law.

A faith in truth is possible, but the person has to have a liberal orientation of his or her soul. A brilliant civil servant has a right to interpret the law and rules, provided he or she takes the law as something vibrant, dynamic and live in its administrative context. Integrity of character is human truthfulness, something total, which is pure, because it is unimpaired by subjective experiences of the self. It may look like an unworkable ideal, but सत्यमेव जयते is a human effort to approximate to this abstract. As Gandhi will say, 'One step is enough for me'. A civil servant may heave a sigh of relief and close his or her note by saying to oneself, 'I did, what I should' as per demand of the rules or law.

The UK civil service code reduces integrity to some dos and don'ts. They are:

1. Fulfil your duties and obligations responsibly;
2. Act in a way that is professional and that deserves and retains the confidence of all those with whom you have dealings;

3. Carry out fiduciary obligations responsibly, that is make sure public money and other resources are used properly and efficiently;
4. Deal with the public and their affairs fairly, efficiently, promptly, effectively and sensitively, to the best of your ability;
5. Keep accurate official records and handle information as openly as possible within the legal framework; and
6. Comply with the law and uphold the administration of justice.

Similarly the don'ts are:

1. Never misuse your official position, by using official information to further private interests or those of others;
2. Do not accept gifts or hospitality or receive benefits from anyone which might reasonably be seen to compromise your personal judgement or integrity.
3. Do not disclose official information without authority even after retirement.
4. Do not deceive or knowingly mislead ministers, parliament or others.
5. Never get influenced by improper pressures from others for the prospect of personal gain.

2. *Impartiality:* As an ethical quality of human conduct, impartiality literally means 'not favouring one person more than other'. Its Hindi version निष्पक्षता can be called समदर्शिता, which is the crudest definition of the term 'justice'. Impartiality, as an ethical virtue, implies refusing to align or getting inclined to or side against the other. Judges must be impartial and so should be the administrators. Those who execute the law have to interpret it also at every step of its implementation. Civil servant, in fact, is an administrative judge who operationalizes the administrative law. Impartiality or 'इमानदारी' has to be his or her cherished credo. Like a judge, he or she should not only be

impartial, but should appear to be impartial also, to gain credibility and import legitimacy to his or her action. If the civil servant is cautious and alive to the fact that समदर्शिता can be inculcated as an ethical value, he or she has to know the two sides of the coin or the various shades of the event to avoid his or her prejudices which might inhere in his or her attitudes or perceptions. Taking sides cannot be avoided in administration, but the situation should come only after knowing and weighing the sides without biases.

The British Civil Service Code ensures impartiality by prescribing the following dos and don'ts. The dos are:

1. Carry out your responsibilities in a way that is fair, just and equitable and reflects the civil service commitment to equality and diversity;
2. Serve the government, whatever its political persuasion, to the best of your ability in a way which maintains political impartiality, no natter what your own political beliefs are;
3. Act in a way which deserves and retains the confidence of political masters ensuring that you will establish the same relationship with future government; and
4. Comply with restrictions on your political activities.

The don'ts are:

1. Do not act in a way that is determined by party political considerations.
2. Do not allow your personal political views to determine any advice you give or your actions.
3. Do not use resources for any other purpose but only for the authorized public purposes for which they are provided.
4. Do not violate discipline to do actions unbecoming of a public servant.

3. *Non-partisanship:* Partisanship is generally associated with blind faith or अन्धभक्ति. Non-partisanship of a civil servant

requires a neutrality of character. Loyalty to government is regarded as a healthy trait but it should not be stretched too far in a democracy. People are the masters and political rulers keep coming and going. Hence, loyalty (भक्ति) to the office and not to the officer has to be the criterion. Political neutrality permits a civil servant to vote freely and boldly during elections but his or her administrative conduct has to avoid personal involvement in political affairs of the government. He or she has to sit on the fence (तट) and offer his or her professional expertise to political masters like a professional lawyer (*vakil*) or an expert doctor. The UK Civil Service Code defines non-persuasions and impartiality as acting solely according to the merits of the case and serving equally well governments of different political persuasions. The constitutional protection provided for the civil service under Article 310, 311 in India has assured bureaucracy to work non-politically in spite of the changing governments. The conduct rules ban a civil servant from taking part in politics and elections. They are expected to maintain absolute political neutrality which alone ensures work impartiality irrespective of their political persuasions and attitudes.

4. *Objectivity*: It is often glorified as a great ethical virtue in civil service. In common parlance, it means कर्मवाची, वस्तुनिष्ठ or वास्तविक. Again, as an antonym of subjectivity, in ethics, it will mean a principle which does not aim at a particular object. So, by implication, it will be called 'honesty' or seeing all objects as things without any value-loaded interpretations. A public servant may have strong values but he or she should also possess a stronger capacity to accept things as mere things or objects without putting his or her personal self into them. As defined in UK CS code, objectivity implies that advice and decisions be based on rigorous analysis of the evidence. The civil servants are expected to

take decisions based on rationale and not on emotion. In a country like India, where a complex societal context exists, the civil servants should be guided solely by public interest in their official decision making and not by any financial or other consideration either in respect of themselves, their families or their friends. In carrying out their official work, including functions like procurement, recruitment, delivery of services etc. they should take decisions based on merit alone. This value neutrality helps in imparting a fair deal. The civil service objectivity is the strength of the administrator because the lay citizens are quite subjective in their perceptions and value judgements.

5. *Dedication:* Dedication to duty can be called a professional virtue, which maximizes performance. Those who think that civil service is not mere employment, but it has to be a mission, they want that public servants should give more to society as compared to what the government gives to them. It fosters the spirit of sacrifice and abnegation. Those who serve genuinely do not put conditions. Public service is a notion of surrender, where the job-joy compensates. The pinpricks and the material returns are nominal. If some people want to rule the masses, they have to be humble. In fact, they are superior beings, with higher moral caliber. They should command respect and exhibit the spirit of dedication and sacrifice in times of crisis and turbulence. Some people have these self-effacing qualities in their personalities and they should be preferred in recruitment and promotions for their sincere zeal and extra enthusiasm for public service.
6. *Empathy*: As an ethical aptitude, it is quite different from sympathy. It is easy to experience or exhibit pity or sorrow if someone is in distress. The civil service value has to be that of empathy which means a capacity to enter into another person's personality and experience his or her miseries. It is to feel (परानुभूति), as the other person is feeling. It is a state of

realization which goes much beyond or much further to the expansion of sympathy. It comes only when one can transplant himself or herself into another person's place or situation. "काश मैं यह होता", think this way and the situation will get sized up without arguments. Mahatma Gandhi called it a 'Tilsman' and asked his people to close their eyes and feel that 'He is Me'. The answers and solutions will spontaneously follow. Empathy is not only an ethical virtue, but it is receptivity, objectivity and an honest involvement in other's affairs.

7. *Tolerance*: As an ethical virtue, it is what the animals lack. The life of sensory reactions and reflections can make people hostile, stale and even vindictive. Those who can cultivate rationality and empathy, alone can love the people with whom they violently disagree. Tolerance is an ability to endure, a disposition to permit the rage of variation. It is patience (धैर्य, सहनशक्ति) which permits differences, mistakes and even wrong assertions and decisions to coexist. It is a mega virtue, for all those who are saddled with higher responsibilities in administration. All public servants are not equal. The senior ones should show tolerance because they are superior. Even, the lower categories of public servants have to learn tolerance, because they owe a responsibility to people, who might occasionally become intolerant because of being aggrieved.
8. *Compassion*: It is another name of sympathy. It is a fellow feeling (सम्वेदना) that generates pity, mercy and sorrow for the sufferings of others. Buddha preached 'करुणा' because it is a virtue of virtues. It puts all human virtues in their proper place. It ennobles all human beings and yields a very special kind of human joy in providing human bond with one's own species. It is universal and architectonic in nature. Civil servants have ample opportunities to exhibit compassion in

their official duties, especially when the poor, the weak, the women and the disadvantaged fellow beings are involved.

Thus, the above mentioned aptitudes provide special equipment in the armoury of a public servant. He or she can be a real servant in his or her own eyes and also in the estimation of the government and the people at large. His or her assignments and responsibilities might be quite, tough and challenging, but all these tasks become easier, if the aptitudinal values of any ethical being are sagaciously practised by him in his long career as a public servant. All these characteristics of personality stress upon self awareness; self regulation; motivation; empathy; and social skills. The forces of globalization and information technology have transformed the operations of government and business. It has also altered the emotional environment within the organizations. Harry Levinson believes that the work done by subordinates should be criticized constructively based on the factors of specificity, providing solutions, face to face contact and empathy. With knowledge work, team replaces the individual as the work unit. As a result, emotional intelligence which comprises skills that promote harmonious group working has become important. The government servants need to show personal commitment in implementing welfare programmes for the deprived groups. Empathy is the quality which enables government servants to address the problems of the poor, deprived and the vulnerable sections of the population. The ability to read the emotions of others is critical for all tasks. It is the basis of other-regarding behaviour, which can be called the first step in cultivating social skills needed in government. The ability to defer gratification and control and channel one's urges to act is a basic emotional skill, or will. Being able to put away one's self-centered focus, the impulses can be diverted to social benefits. It opens the way to empathy, to real listening, to take another person's perspective into account. EI leads to caring, altruism, and compassion.

The Goleman's study on 'emotional intelligence' present the research situation about this neurological area which was unknown to Weber and other classical writers on rationality and bureaucracy. He convincingly and conclusively proves that rationality cannot become mature without emotional intelligence. The recruitment of Indian civil servants was never conceived this way. Even training courses are devised to sharpen the intellect and now when a modernizing society of democratic India has to be administered by middle-class graduates, the entire merit has to be redefined in terms of emotional maturity of the two brains. It is over-emotionalism that explains public servants' loyalty behaviours very much like that of caste, class and community. Reservation policies damage intellectual maturity and heighten emotional sentimentalism. The untrained and uncontrolled emotions generate casteist and communal behaviours. More so, these emotional riots inside the brain blind brilliant people to surrender to over-emotionalism. Power and money cannot be the pursuit of right reason. But, if emotional intelligence is under-weighed in any merit selection or promotion, it filters a very risky kind of merit which is condemned to subjectivity, corruption and inefficiency. The definitions of social justice in independent India require a solid commitment of administration to the weak, the welfare of deprived, the women and the disadvantaged groups all over the country. Reservation has helped them to improve their own lot. But, the beneficiaries and opponents of social justice policies are emotionally upset and their merit-based behaviour is far from desirable. Both are ethically wrong in their subjective interpretations of laws, rules and policies, objectively prescribed by the governments.

Emotional intelligence is the quality which enables government servants to address themselves to the problems of the poor, the deprived and the vulnerable sections of the population. It lies at the root of human altruism and concern for others. Its total absence leads to criminal phychopathic behaviours as in that of murders and molesters. Self awareness opens the gates to empathy. If one cannot gauge one's emotions, he or she will hardly know how others feel. The inability to note the feelings of others is a notable failing of emotional intelligence. It means that one misses out on what it is to be a human. Concern for fellow human beings arises from attuning oneself to the emotions of others or from capacity for empathy. The ability to read the emotions of others is critical for public tasks. Deep interest in fellow human beings is a mark of otherliness. This does not mean unwholesome curiosity about the personal life of others or maliciously gossiping about them. One should not be indifferent to others or ignore their existence and well-being. It means that one should observe them and guess their moods and feelings. Emotional states of people are usually revealed through their bodily clues, facial expressions and general movements, gestures and postures. The purpose is not to take advantage of their emotional vulnerability but to understand and to help them better.

Government servants implement the programmes according to the prescribed rules and procedures. But mere mechanical efficiency is inadequate for successful implementation of these programmes. They have to put their heart and soul into the effort. Programmes for scheduled castes, scheduled tribes, women and children fall into this category. These programmes are hard to design and execute. Unlike other sectoral programmes, they lack adequate infrastructure, committed and knowledgeable staff and suffer from low visibility. They lack glamour. Government servants find it much harder to implement these programmes than those in infrastructure or in core industry. This is true for all social and poverty alleviation programmes. The client groups are poor, illiterate and unorganized. They confer no benefits of any sort on government servants. Government servants often view them as a troublesome and avoidable burden, and seek transfers to other departments. This is where young officers have to display idealism and compassion even at the cost of undergoing some personal inconveniences.

Ethical behaviours of honesty and probity emanate from reason and emotion both. Rational comprehension and emotional compassion are the two major pillars on which stand the edifice of administrative structure and behaviour. A new definition of merit should explore the value systems and aptitudinal rational-emotional fields to ensure 'ethics' in areas of public concern. This will ensure 'ethics' in public administration. Mere recognition of the dichotomy and exhortations of moral values cannot render bureaucracy ethical. The public service commissions have taken a welcome initiative in this regard. Reason has to be nurtured and emotions have to be disciplined. Hopefully after sometime the two together will build the 'temple of an ethical pyramid' which will have its pillars cemented by rational maturity and emotional intelligence of public servants right from a *chaprasi* to the chief secretary in the hierarchy.

CHAPTER 5

The Sources of Ethical Inspiration

Lessons from the Lives of Leaders, Reformers and Administrators

Human experience originates in the practice of ideas which, in turn, ignites a thought process of newer ideas for change and growth. The theory-praxis dichotomy is puerile, because the persons and ideas which inspire future generations represent the end products of those ideas and experiences of individuals who themselves were inspired by their worthy predecessors. Gandhi inspired millions and millions to stay in non-violence, but he himself inherited a valuable legacy of truth and non-violence from a host of Indian and western thinkers and reformers. From whom should an administrator borrow his or her ethical values and conduct is just impossible to discern and discover. Consciously speaking, even administrators do not know, who is their 'role model' and to what extent this model inspires them when their situations and circumstances are different. The heroes in history are like characters of a fiction to whom its readers do not know in their entirety. Even these so-called great men have their own weaknesses. Similarly, achievements in one field do not *ipso facto* render a person great and acceptable in other walks of life. Then, there can be an unending discourse on the term 'eminent'. Mahatma Gandhi's candidature for Nobel Peace Prize was summarily dismissed by the Nobel Committee, while this so-called 'eminence' was deservingly accepted for a Mother Teresa and a Henry Kissinger.

Who renders service to mankind and who should be regarded as a great leader, a reformer and a benefactor of oppressed humanity, is difficult to identify and still more difficult is to reach to a consensus about his work and worth. There are great men, who prefer to stay unsung in history and there are tombs of unknown soldiers, who made a supreme sacrifice without asking for a return. The history is full of examples of fake leaders and the genuine reformers who were given a cross by their own people. The criteria and degrees of successes may vary from time and context, but human history according to historian Will Durant, has a tendency to honour those who show exemplary courage and make willing sacrifices so that the pain and misery of others may get mitigated.

The Role Models of Inspiration: Read, Watch and Think

All kinds of societies and governments make conscious and unconscious efforts to identify their great people of outstanding merit. A variety of awards, prizes, honours, etc. are conferred by the governments, the media and the philanthropic or volunteer organizations to express their gratitude towards those great men and women, who do not crave for these honours and recognitions. The jury which selects and elects these eminent persons, from amongst the people, have its own problems of evolving a criterion or preferential weightage system. The eminent people, like a beautiful woman not participating in a Miss World Contest, seldom participate in these competitions and one may reject the total list of participants because the members of the jury themselves may lack the basic credentials. But then, this eminence is quite different from the ethical wealth, which an ordinary invisible human mortal can possess. People rarely think of great moral leaders, reformers and thinkers, when it comes to performing individual ethical deeds. The value system of the unconscious is generally prepared by these role models with whom one may compare his or her current situations and dilemmas. Very often the individuals personify virtues and their lives of tension, torture and sacrifices earn admiration which sustains a person in the moments of ethical crisis. Nelson Mandela's situation may be somewhat different from that of Mahatma Gandhi. They were also different in many ways but what inspired them were the common indomitable courage and the human spirit of incessant struggle against the brutalities of their contemporaries. It is a universal truth and their experiments with this kind of eternal truth inspire people to fight and promote the notion of human dignity.

Although success or prizes have little meaning and relevance in making an ethical human being adorable and admirable, but when these eminent awardees are selected the usual criteria applied by the jury consist some of the following considerations:

(a) *Contribution* to society in general.
(b) Personal *achievements* of high order against odds.
(c) *Distinctiveness* of personality and the extraordinary qualities or virtues.
(d) Efforts made for the *amelioration of human sufferings* and misery.
(e) *Successes* achieved by noble means in the *pursuit of noble ends.*
(f) *Recognition* of quality service or *innovative accomplishments* by the peer groups.

There can be a big debate about the meanings and interpretations of terms such as contribution, success, recognition and achievements, etc. and the differences may be quite honest. Hence, success or no success, the ethical qualities of eminent leaders are a great reward unto themselves. Their admirers may not need arguments. The deeds speak louder than their words and even the words which they leave behind are interpreted and evaluated, when they are no more. This appraisal gives to their ethical messages a longevity and a social selectivity, which effectively shape the lives of people at large. An average administrator may search and look for these fountain heads of inspiration, who teach him or her virtues like (1) objectivity, (2) empathy, (3) tolerance, (4) compassion, (5) impartiality and (6) objective analysis of events. The lives of moral thinkers and philosophers can teach brilliant young administrators to understand ideas in their abstraction and isolation and then pursue them in their respective social situations. In fact, moral ideas of the world do not recognize national frontiers. What Kant, Whitehead and Russell think and advice can gainfully be applied everywhere and anywhere in human circumstances in all times and all climes.

Biographical Accounts for Identification

Candidates for viva voce examinations of civil services are generally evaluated on the basis of their hobbies and the value dispositions which they enjoy to pursue. The reading of biographies and autobiographies is one popular hobby from where the candidates select their inspirational role models. Apparently, these brilliant people think that their eminent heroes have some unique qualities, which enabled them to attain such great heights. Reading books is a very creative hobby, provided one has a searching mind to scan his or her hero and his or her doings. Vivekanand offers an exciting reading but can these preachings of a Sanyasi help the administrator, who is overburdened with the responsibilities of his or her office and family? Yes, a Sanyasi's preachings can be interpreted by a public servant and a citizen although the comparison is invidious and untenable. Religious scriptures and books of history provide a vast canvas on which the ocean of ethical values can be explored and charted out for individual navigation. A civil servant has to equip himself or herself with insights for which he or she should collect his or her own storehouse of knowledge. One should read autobiographies of Hitler and Churchill to explore the truth and conclude how history books have falsified facts or coloured them with their own brush. A reading habit as a hobby, is administrator's strength and this lame excuse is untenable that he or she is too busy to find time for reading. The great people, whether they are entrepreneurs or scientists or men of arts and letters, always have a refreshing perspective to add to one's thought process. For instance, reading Amartya Sen's *Argumentative Indian* and then reading *A Train to Pakistan* by Khushwant Singh, one gets those rare glimpses of Indian psychology and Indian history which no textbook can even attempt. A civil servant is not an ordinary executive to obey the dictates of elected political leaders. He or she is a leader of society in his or her own right. The so-called status system of power and pelf has disfigured his or her image as a person of ignorance and affluence. In fact, he or she should be a person in the image of Colonel Tod, Woodruff and Metcalf. He or she should reflect and learn continuously for which a reading habit is a prerequisite.

Reading Maketh a Full Man

The lives of great men everywhere, in all cultures and in all times, have been a saga of courage and creativity. The contemporary people do not do justice to these extraordinary people. Their works and accomplishments represent sincere hard work, dedication to some mission and a non-conformism against the established order. Newton, Copernicus, Einstein and for that matter Rousseau, Sir C.V. Raman, Abdul Kalam, Sam Pitroda and hundreds of others, carry an eternal message which may be revised to shape the notions of human civilization and culture. A public servant should read and know what the NASA scientists are up to. He or she can implement development plans with far-sight and insight if he or she knows what kind of food will constitute a balanced diet of future. By reading the life account and the message of Mother Teresa, one begs the question: Why build cities glorious, if man unbuilded goes, in vain we do the work, unless the builder grows?

The Light House of Self Regulatory Discipline

Literature, philosophy and psychology may not look very useful instantly when an executive sits in his office and asks his junior to carry out his legal orders. But they enrich his mind and stir the reason and emotions to ask more meaningful questions, which a public servant can ignore only at the peril of his career enjoyment. Bhartari Hari's three Shataks about romance, morality and detachment offer a world-view of life which maketh a full-man of Francis Beacon. Even film personalities have their leaders and one can read Harivansh Rai Bachchan with profit to appreciate the outstanding contribution of Amitabh Bachchan in the film *Sholay* or *Coolie*. The civil servants have to be versatile in tastes and dispositions. Their career requires an interactive approach to human relations and behaviours which men of art, literature and music keep enriching all the time.

A daily newspaper, if read with care, presents enough food for thought. One has to read the scriptures to comprehend the truth of religious terrorism. Naxalite violence looks senseless to all those who do not appreciate the problems of human frustrations, aspirations and failures. Even a judge and a police officer should read poems of Jai Shankar Prasad and Ramdhari Singh Dinkar to develop the requisite emotional intelligence, which is more basic to their jobs and professional fulfilments. The messages and the lessons from the lives of the leaders, reformers and tall administrators are so many and so diverse that an intelligent administrator can use them as his lighthouse for self-regulatory discipline. Public servants should know how to use their personal libraries in the mid-life careers of their public service. The messages are clear.

Believe in Positive Thinking

It is not even worth an attempt to make a list of these great men from all walks of life. Some of the stereotype areas are politics, science, literature, art, social service and business. But then, there are hundreds of fields and millions of unknown leaders, who can be perennial sources of inspiration. It depends on one's value system and aptitudinal response to the deeds of people in history, religion, politics and society. Anything can be inspiring and/or depressing. But, the analysis based on reading and observation can convert the pessimistic outlook into an incredible power of positive thinking. People have natural instincts of greed and domination but when you read Abdul Kalam's *Wings of Fire* and see his pictures, while vacating the Rashtrapati Bhawan after an illustrious presidency of five years, in two hired taxies only, as compared to 50 truck loads of his successor, one understands and gets transformed into a new ethical mould of public service. Such stories can be multiplied. What is important is the habit of reading and separating the 'ethical' from the 'unethical'. A tentative list of these eminent leaders, reformers, scientists and litterateurs can be prepared to which the future administrators may make their individual additions and deletions. It includes persons, living and active in public life of India and also deceased persons, whose life itself is a message for those who have not seen them in flesh and blood. The political leaders and their legacies may be controversial, but what the scientists have achieved is before everybody to see. The men of letters are inspiring for the words they have left behind in print. Modern India owes its progress and development to some of these outstanding men and women who have successfully made impressions of their footprints on the sand of time. Hopefully, the posterity will scan their achievements with pride.

Political leaders in democratic India do not inspire young people. But then, those who made their contributions to freedom struggle are gratefully remembered. Mahatma Gandhi is a unique case in point and by and large the younger generations feel that he was a great man in his own right. They may not accept his political and economic philosophy in the present-day world context, but they accept the fact that India lost the opportunity of building a new model of development in the illusive pursuit of the western model. Even in its impractical overtone, the model has relevance and young administrators may keep searching and experimenting with Gandhian truth, which ultimately triumphs (*Satyamev Jayate*). They may blend the Gandhi and Ambedkar models of social justice for the weak, women and the deprived. Leaders like B.G. Tilak gave the message of 'Real Swarajya' which is yet to be achieved with the help of science and technology. The political leaders of pre-independence era urge upon the new generation to continue with the 'Second War of Indian Independence'. The words of Netaji Subhash Chandra Bose or Maulana Abul Kalam Azad can stir the younger people into national awareness and ask them to guard themselves against complacency and stagnation.

Simplicity and Scarifies Sublimate

After 1947 also, we have a galaxy of leaders who have left a glorious legacy of patriotism, simplicity and commitment to the Constitution. Rajendra Prasad and Zakir Hussain symbolize what presidency should be like. Jayaprakash Narayan and Vinoba Bhave explain the messages of Mahatma Gandhi which can never be ignored by those who wish to see India developing with a difference. In fact, political leaders of varied shades and ideologies may not be that popular as were the freedom fighters, but young civilians can learn a lot from the political careers of Aruna Asaf Ali, or Ram Manohar Lohia and even P.V. Narasimha Rao. The polemics apart, the post-freedom generation of political leaders should be honestly evaluated and their styles and value systems may be inculcated. Leaders like Morarji Desai, A.B. Vajpayee, George Fernandes, V.K. Krishna Menon, Sardar Patel, Namboodripad or even Manmohan Singh have stood to the test of times. The patience, perseverance and the far-sightedness which these great leaders have exhibited in talking about the most sensitive issues like integration of native states, Babri demolition, or nuclear explosion and social justice battles in the country need commendation and the children of modern Indian history can take very valuable lessons from their insights and far-sights. Even very many great leaders like Charan Singh, Jagjeevan Ram or Mamta Banerjee should be studied for their handling of the caste, class, poverty and regional situations in the country.

Adversaries also Inspire

Any list of political leaders will be illustrative and suggestive. The young administrator will have to read history from varied sources. He may get impressed by the indomitable courage of a Bal Gangadhar Tilak and the amiable and assertive creativity of Gopal Krishan Gokhale, whom Gandhi compared with the Himalayas and the Ganges. Gandhi himself was an open, simple and humble man and he learnt a great deal from his seniors like Dadabhai Nauroji, Annie Besant and Aurobindo Ghosh. His contemporaries, though an anathema to his thought and political style, inspired him in very many ways to struggle for freedom of the motherland. In this sense Gandhi owed his ethical inspiration to his adversaries like Mohammad Ali Jinnah, Subhash Chandra Bose and Bhim Rao Ambedkar. One can learn from the lives and deeds of Pt. Jawahar Lal Nehru, Jai Prakash Narain, Ram Manohar Lohia, Purshottam Das Tandon and Madan Mohan Malviya, who very happily worked with Gandhi, but had their basic and violent differences with him in public life on public issues. A galaxy of political leaders from National Movement and after independence, like Sarojini Naidu, Maulana Abul Kalam Azad, Rajgopalachari, Rajendra Prasad, Sardar Patel grew under Gandhi's shadow, but were leaders, thinkers and activists in their own right. Their lives and careers should not be compared nor evaluated on the basis of their failures or successes in history. A discerning administrator may evaluate their contributions in terms of (1) honesty of purpose (2) will to serve and sacrifice (3) envisioning a free India, and (4) making their respective contributions. These known and unknown heroes of freedom struggle cannot be compared with each other and never with a Gandhi or with a Jawahar Lal Nehru. Everybody has an option to pick and choose and to combine a variety of virtues and commitments which maybe contradictory. Getting inspiration from some body is not mere imitation. Similarly making somebody a role model does not work, especially when that person is no longer alive or involved in the actual operations of history. Leaders likes Radha Krishnan, P.V. Narsimha Rao, George Fernandis, Krishna Menon and Rama Swami Nicker were not freedom fighters in the historical sense but the modern generation can take inspiration from their commitments to principles, simplicity and unadulterated patriotism.

Every brilliant administrator can draw his or her own lessons from the lives of leaders and reformers, provided he/she studies these lives and actions dispassionately. Reading the experience of 'Insiders' from biographies or autobiographies stirs an open mind and the more and more one discovers, he or she may be fascinated or disillusioned by the message, which his or her life has left behind. The young administrator is a recipient of this variegated legacy of history which his hero has furthered and preserved in his own way with caution.

Naturally, therefore, no one leader or his life should be or can be selected for inspiration. The young brilliant mind should equip himself with what he could not read as a formal student. Heroes should be discovered by making and using personal libraries, otherwise there exists a risk of dogmatizing the virtue, subjectively selected in younger years.

Business or corporate leaders also play a decisive role in Indian economy. They are increasing in number and their roles and contributions are changing very fast. A look on their profiles can inspire the young entrants to civil service about their changed role vis-à-vis these corporate houses or leaders. For instance, a young entrant may take some captains of industry and study their success stories: Dhirubhai Ambani, Adi Godrej, Azim Premji and Ratan Tata are the accredited stalwarts. M.S. Oberoi, Mukesh Ambani, Narayan Murthy and Rahul Bajaj are not great because of their parentage. Laxmi Mittal, Indra Nooyi and Nandan Nielkeni have burnt midnight oils to touch the pinnacle.

Innovation is Merit

Birla, Tata and Bajaj are the Indian entrepreneurs, who were monopolizing family capitalism before independence. Their contribution in funding the national movement and supporting Mahatma Gandhi's efforts have not been properly researched. An objective assessment may be controversial and may denigrate Gandhi as a protogonist of capitalism. The ideological controversy apart, the old and new capitalism can be evaluated as an instrument in nation-building. After 1993, the new economic policy has been a challenge and Tata could come out with a Nano car for the common man. The NRIs opened up world market for Indian goods and capital. What should inspire a young Indian is the flexibility, resilience and innovative character of Indian initiatives taken up by corporate magnates like Narayan Murthy, Ambani brothers, Oberoi and dozens of others, whom *Forbes* magazine keeps calling the 'High and the Mighty' of India. Most of these corporates of Indian origin are competing in the open market of the world and the civil servant should appreciate how have they changed the course of events and the flow of foreign funds from Gulf countries and other retail trade pockets of Indian economy.

The civil service career today cannot be a romantic dream of ruling bureaucratic fiefs of rural India. The private-public partnership (PPP) presents a challenge and a civil servant in government should do wonders and miracles like Oberois and Ambanis. There is no point in harping upon the differences between public and private administrations. The new concepts like good governance, digital governance, citizen orientation of transparent public administration offers newer opportunities to seek inspiration from a Narayan Murthy or a Bill Gates for new Public Management (NPM). A new wave of liberalization and globalization has been sweeping all over the world and the young aspirants in bureaucracy must get inspired, *'To Be the Change'*, which they want to see in the Indian administration. Notwithstanding their limitations, the urge to compete and excel is the secret of success in corporate world. Public administration must compete, innovate and deliver goods and services, qualitatively better than what private entrepreneurs are delivering. There is little wrong in having profit or money incentives of corporate administration in place of power and status orientation of traditional bureaucracy. If civil servants feel inspired by the success stories of corporate entrepreneurs, the development administration will acquire a new meaning and a higher height of ambitional success in their mission.

Pursue Excellence

Leadership of Creative Artists and Scientists has immensely contributed to society by launching a revolution of connectivity, mobility and popular awareness. Some of the outstanding names in media and literature like: Dileep Kumar, Madhuri Dixit, Hema Malini, Shahrukh Khan and Amitabh Bachchan are household names in India. V. Shanta Ram, Premchand, Rabindranath Tagore, Mulk Raj Anand, Salman Rushdie or Jaishankar Prasad leave an indelible mark of their originality and creativity. Those who have read Amrita Pritam, Mahadevi Verma, Khushwant Singh and Mahasweta Devi feel rewarded and Hasrat Jaipuri and Majrooh Sultanpuri if listened to, will knock at the closed gates of young personality.

The eminent personalities have their own 'influence zones'. They have succeeded and made a headway as the brilliant sons and daughters of the soil. Some of them had no family background. Rather, they are people who have fought against odds and made a niche. Amitabh went to Bollywood without any godfather. He was allured to contest elections and join politics, which he boldly turned down to stay in a career of his choice. With the kind of talent that he has he could successfully anchor the game show 'Kaun Banega Crorepati'. As an uncrowned king of Bollywood, he does not mind doing even petty advertisements. The lesson that most of these film stars give, is that honest and hard work pays. Lata Mangeshkar or Shabana Azmi may sit in the Rajya Sabha but they are not, what they are in the studios. Actors or artists just work, and the social status follows. Pran and Rajesh Khanna could become what they were capable of becoming. This is the message for those who aspire for succeeding in any career of their choice.

The field of literature may not offer money, but this gives an opportunity for the expansion of one's personality. Away from money and power, it is an area of knowledge, where people leave indelible mark on the social and cultural fabric of society. A young civil servant should read the latest, the best and all sort of literature, available in varied languages of the world. This company of the best brains permits the sharing of ideas with people, who are no longer alive to share the most exciting experiences of their intellectual life. The men of letters like Tagore, Prasad, Dinkar and Mahadevi have something very substantial to offer and inculcate in life. A public servant without a sound literary disposition cannot enjoy his or her administrative assignments, which is another name of literary life in social action.

Similarly, there are very many fields of art like music, dance, painting, singing, etc. where the finer instincts of life contribute to the quality of aesthetic sense and high tastes. A civil servant is not a mere file pusher. He or she should use his or her talent in the secretariat, but must keep polishing it by pursuing some hobby, which can keep his or her tastes refined and alive. The middle-class influx in civil service is a challenge for which the artistic tastes are a prerequisite. The performances of Ustad Amjad Ali Khan,

Hariprasad Chaurasia, Beghum Akhtar and Bismillah Khan may thrill a civil servant but to learn from a Lata, Asha and Mohammed Rafi requires more than an inspiration. The talent of a Sonal Mansingh, Yamini Krishnamurthy, Bhimsen Joshi and M.F. Hussain cannot be duplicated by mere appreciation but one becomes a better Civil Servant if inspired by excellence.

Love Thy People

The judges, sports persons, medical doctors and a host of others also lead productive lives. Dr Naresh Trehan earned a fortune, touched the pinnacle of success and then decided to perform open-heart surgery in Gurgaon. Madhuri Dixit married a doctor, raised her family and returned to her film career as a mother. Justice P.N. Bhagwati showed a way and judges after judges are trailing on to intensify this judicial revolution, which seeks to cleanse the electoral dirt of Indian politics.

We owe the quality of our national life to the dedication of professional people who have burnt midnight oils to win their laurels. India would have been poorer with out a C.V. Raman, a Homi Bhabha, a Jagdish Chandra Bose and a Meghnad Saha. Scientists like M. Visvesvaraya, A.P.J. Abdul Kalam, Sam Pitroda, and M.S. Swaminathan inspire every body with their astounding creativity. The lives of G.B. Kurian, Shridharan and Raja Ramanna evoke respect. Justice P.N. Bhagwati, Justice J.C. Verma, Anna Hazare, Medha Patkar, Baba Amte and Dr Naresh Trehan leave messages of selfless social service. Sachin Tendulkar, M.S. Dhoni and Virat Kohli are not mere cricketers but are inspirers to success.

A good civil servant should make his or her own contribution to develop the quality of our national life. The administrators should promote a Sam Pitroda to head a knowledge commission. The vision of these men of ideas transforms a society. We have remained in backwaters because our administrators could not look beyond the contours of money and power. Our country is extremely rich in talent but the political and administrative rulers somehow could not discover it. Naturally, they cannot promote it with blinkers of rules or procedures. No wonder we stand sunk in a mess of our policies in the areas of games and sports.

Fortunately, our civil service still attracts the best. But we have failed to preserve this best. Mere training programmes cannot improve the situation. The probationers should be encouraged to take inspiration from the success stories of our scientists, judges, men of letters, artists and players. These stories are live and a debate about these national records, unique triumphs and global recognitions should guide the path of those who have come to administration to make a career of national service.

When Justice J.C. Verma vacated his official residence as the Chief Justice of India after retirement, he moved into a rented house in Delhi. He was an upright judge with extraordinary virtues of personality. Owning a private house was well within his means but his aptitudinal simplicity without an exhibitional disposition made his ethical excellence worth emulating for the VIPs. Ram Manohar Lohia, a veteran socialist leader, never sat in a rickshaw pulled by a human being and asked for a quiet cremation at Pach Kui Road electric crematorium in 500 rupees without any noise of condolences. The West Bengal Chief Minister, Mamta Banerjee, notwithstanding her acrobatics, lives like a mother-didi model with three simple sarees without any jewellery or ostentatious luxurious living of an upper class. Abdul Gaffar Khan and Maulana Abul Kalam Azad lived and fought as valiant secularists. They have left models for Indian Muslims, who should work for a reunion of partitioned Indians like Germans, Koreans and Vietnamese.

Shun Attitudes of Class Character

Foundational values for civil services are usually talked about or taught in public service training programmes. Normally, it does not work because good or desirable values cannot be inflicted or forced upon people. The young entrants, who have made their way through a very tough competition, find certain values justified in the name of merit and heavy public responsibilities. The English system of bureaucracy taught them alienation from people and dedication to duty, when they were fascinated by these values of social status and privileged living. In later years they found them justified and well-earned. In the post-entry period of their careers, even when some of them think of simple living and high thinking, the class attitudes come in conflict with human aptitudes of simplicity, compassion and objectivity. They think that they are neutral and have love and sympathy for the weak and the underprivileged. But, the alienation and the class character of the colleagues hardens the undesirable attitudes of a closed group, bordering on the behaviour of a 'professional caste'. Whenever challenged, they blame the other group and find fault with the system. In a democracy it ends up by passing the buck to the elected representatives, who are less cohesive, but who keep imitating the elitist value system of bureaucracy. For instance, most of the high-ranking civil servants in India accuse politicians for politicizing public services by their meddlesomeness and unethical interventions. But, the truth is that the public bureaucracy has bureaucratized the elected political leaders to collectively enjoy a life of privileges within the framework of the so-called law. This game of mutual mud slinging goes on and the poor masses are being exploited by both the elitist groups, operating as caste groups, in the mass culture of a feudal society.

All Works are Noble and Work Alone is Noble

Lives of great leaders, reformers and administrators all point out to the fact that they could outshine only because they loved their people. Living in a *Bhangi* colony by Gandhiji was symbolic and those who joined his ashramas at Sevagram and Sabarmati were subjected to a rigorous discipline of simplicity and sacrifice. This quasi-military kind of discipline could throw up satyagrahis, and a Meeraben was assigned the task of preparing manure from the night soil of public toilets. Today, the governments sanction crores of rupees for '*sulabh shauchalaya*' projects and the civil service values of legality and subjectivity blame the people and their political leaders who are relatively more corrupt and more manipulative. A public debate between elites and the masses is not possible. Rather it deepens the chasm with the conclusion that people do not have desirable values. A student of ethics will say that no political leader has read Gandhi and they keep inaugurating Gandhi Vidyalayas as a ritual. Political leaders can perhaps be forgiven because they are the lesser developed species, but a public servant who claims to be intellectual and well-acquainted with the preaching of great men cannot and should not excuse himself or herself, if he or she is genuinely an educated person of virtues and of ethical human values. Lessons from the lives of great men are generally dismissed by the educated people on the ground that the times have changed. Even Gandhi is irrelevant for development, then how can his life and messages inspire those who do not want to learn. The argument has a partial truth and must be examined in depth. V.P. Menon was the secretary of Sardar Patel. Both of them had a mission and that was to integrate princely India. A civil servant must read Menon's book to discover to his surprise that the two did not agree on several vital issues like privy purse. Yet, Patel will ask Menon to negotiate on his behalf. It may be true even today but a Menon will not ask for a transfer and a Sardar admits that it was Menon who accomplished the integration of princely states. Differences are a part of political game but bitterness, hostility and abuse was pettiness which both the actors abhorred. By reading biographies, history books or psychological researches, one does not change his or her basic views, but they evoke interest in human conflicts and their peaceful resolution.

Respect Dissent

There is a Chinese saying that great people discuss ideas, not individuals. All human beings have their frailties and if individuals start personifying ideas then ideas lose their appeal. A civil servant cannot get inspiration from his God fathers, but the idea which thrilled his mentor may thrill him or her much more. So great men always leave a legacy of dissent. 'Yes men' are found only in religious congregations. Administrators should learn to 'agree to disagree'. This culture of dissent strengthens democracy. Unfortunately, disagreements in Indian society are over-stretched to the extent of hostility, which in its ultimate form destroys creativity. Hierarchy should be respected but the seniors should not develop an administrative culture of conformism or slavery in the name of discipline. Senior civil servants can be a perennial source of inspiration for their juniors, it they allow dissent and practice dissent from their respectable seniors.

Let Your Life be the Message

Ethics is neither law nor conscience nor social customs and practices. A public servant is a human being with a conscience. He is a social being who should share and respect social customs and mores. But more than this, he is a man of law. The rules and regulations govern his conduct and behaviour but all this cannot render him into a 'Super Being' or an ideal paper pusher in the secretariats.

A civil servant does not represent people in the political sense of electoral politics. Yet, he votes and contests for political office after retirement. His neutrality may cause non-conformism or disagreements which again does not mean hostility and alienation. Naturally, an average human being with mere commonsense cannot be a civil servant of British variety. Free India retains this British legacy of civil service neutrality but the generalist kind of professionals who are entering into civil service positions lack that catholicity of mind which comes from a life long pursuit of noble ideas or goodness. This requires a commitment to truth and professional ideals of public service. With out sensitivity and sincerity, no body can inspire or get inspired by any body. It is neither accident nor achievement. In fact, it is a receptive faculty, endowed with three potentialities:

1. A conscious and continuous search and research of the 'Noble' which cannot be a dead letter of law.
2. A capacity to identify and welcome new ideas and separating the grain from the chaff.
3. A response to accept the unacceptable and integrate the change values in human personality .

Work Anonymously

Naturally, not anybody can be a total role model for any civil servant. The predecessors who did wonders in the past will cut a sorry figures today. If Metcalf and Woodruff come to life and are posted as collectors in Indian districts today, they will either resign or create chaos with the value they upheld or practiced. An inspirer has to demonstrate and deliver goods as public servant. Those who do not know or know pretty little, do not inspire or get inspired. Knowledge, commitment and revision are the composite elements of inspiration. Even a mediocre can learn and improve but those who take civil service as mere employment or a status game of power and pelf; for such incumbents there are no lessons and messages in the lives of great leaders or administrators. 'My life is my message' said Gandhi. This eternal truth needs reiteration to check-mate hypocrisy of sublime colonial value in a decadent mass society of India. The civil servant has to create, revise and transmit new resurgent values for which he should learn to work anonymously. This can be inspiring for the future generations.

The Woodruff Model Still Inspires

The tall administrators of British period hailed from London. They had their differences with the Governors and Governor-Generals.

But, one could read how they used to play golf in the evening. They did not observe any protocol and called each other by first name. The ethical norms of Christian living was the meeting point and excellence in jobs is what all of them cared for under the alien stars. Philip Woodruff, in his monumental book, *The Men Who Ruled India*, narrates innumerable episodes, anecdotes and stories from the lives of Charles Metcalf, MaCenze Brown, Charles Anderson and a host of others who shared their differences without any rancour, backbiting and silent conspiracies. It is not possible today, because civil servants at Mussoorie or Hyderabad do not share common professional ethos and ethics. They come from different strata of society and caste, class, religion and region divide them much more than it was conceivable in British or Mughal days. But, the great administrators, as ever, remained a pillar of searchlight. Their prejudices can be identified but their love for the job, its excellence, and professional dedication even at the cost of patriotism can be appreciated by their successors, who are performing similar functions under different circumstances in the system. Police officers, judges, civil servants and doctors were public servants then and now. The differences may be enjoyed but the baseline of aptitudinal values of tolerance, empathy, compassion and objectivity should serve the source of inspiration.

Inspiration is Not Imitation

Taking inspiration does not mean imitation or a revision of one's ideas. Every epoch of history has its own constraints and provocations. Those who understand and comprehend events and leaders properly, get inspired and keep them as role models. Administration is qualitatively different from politics and business. But what inspires an administrator is the zeal, the perseverance, the honesty of purpose and above all the qualities of character. At young age, these characteristics of one's personality fascinate youngsters who cherish dreams and ambitions for a successful life which is productive and enterprising. Every field offers opportunities and there are odds also that frustrate the plans, the dreams and the honest endeavours. The reading of biographies can equip administrators to see through the chaos and make their own path. For instance, the late Prime Minister Narasimha Rao had an unprecedented dilemma of his lifetime, when the Babri structure was demolished and the socialist economy got stuck in a bind. His autobiography *The Insider* is a mine of administrative ideas and techniques which can inspire all those who want to learn secularism from history and practise liberalization, privatization and globalization with or without mental reservations.

The learning theories tell us that people learn only when they partake in the ideas and experiences. Mere sermonizing does not inspire. The lessons from the lives of great men are more enduring because the survival of the ideas represents their strength and triumph. Great administrators are generally anonymous and social reformers confront opposition. Even political leaders become out of date, but the test of greatness is in the life of ideas. The aptitudes of service, sacrifice and commitment inspire while selfishness, violence and parochialism evoke derisive feelings. A public servant should have the capability to separate the grain from the chaff. Discovering role models, rather than accepting heroes as role inspirers, is a challenge. A civil servant has to be mentally alive and vigilant. He or she should have no illusion that success is a matter of chance because even chances are not a matter of accident. Civil servants work anonymously and what their predecessors or seniors have accomplished falls as a gain or an obstacle to their lot. They have to take life in the stride. The inspirational aspect should keep them working tirelessly, irrespective of the fact that the result will depend upon the perseverance of their successors. He or she should realize that incomparable achievements of their predecessors have gone unsung and unrecognized. It is a lesson which a conscientious administrator should learn from history.

Work is noble and work alone is noble. Mistakes and failures are a part of the game but the lives and messages of great leaders, reformers and administrators constantly remind that what matters is the spirit of service to the people. An honest commitment to this cause of public service is a reward unto itself, no matter the contemporaries recognize it or not. Excellence sublimates all professions into missions and this is what makes the contributions meaningful.

Chapter 6

Moral Philosophies and Moral Philosophers

As a seminal branch of the discipline of philosophy, moral philosophy can be distinguished from ethics, religion and socio-political philosophies. It has no geographical frontiers and is not supposed to fall in the framework of historical experiences. The universal and eternal man is the focus of its study. The existence, security and survival needs of rational human being is what the moral philosophers seek to enquire about. The developmental needs of a human being, which emanate from his or her historical and cultural contexts, are relevant, but they are neither primary nor basic, because of the relativistic perspectives of society and culture. What Aristotle, Buddha, Emmanuel Kant and Jean Paul Sartre discuss is the concept of a 'moral man' and logically their moral philosophies are the subjects of polemical discussions in deontological ethics, which has come up to the philosophies of alienation, ethics of care and the deep ecology ethics of our times.

Moral thinkers have a unique place in the inculcation of moral values. No moral value can be called final or closed.

Relativism and revisions are a need to understand moral philosophies. The contribution of moral philosophers has very little to do with geography, history or law. People everywhere should pursue moral ideas for their ideational joy, validity and excellence. After all, the core social morality is survival or perpetuation of rational quality in human society. Human beings are not food. Hence, extermination of human society for any philosophical reason of morality will be untenable.

Ethics focuses on human actions, which include its morality also. Once it is decided that an action is human, then that action becomes a subject matter for ethics. It is an important function of ethics to figure out whether particular human actions are moral or otherwise. Morality involves an examination of human action to decide if it is good, bad or indifferent – to figure out if it is right or wrong, good or bad. Psychology has established that humans have a free will. People have the capacity to choose one action and reject another. They also have the capacity to choose what is right and reject what is wrong or vice versa. Free will plays a vital role in human action and in its morality. Ontology involves the nature of causality, the difference between cause and effect and the principle of sufficient reason. Epistemology further elaborated on judgements arrived at by generalizations. By combining these two studies, it can be said that if one knows the nature or purpose of something or some being, it can fairly and accurately be decided what kinds of activities are good or bad for that particular person or thing. For example, if one knows what the nature or purpose of a knife is, he can fairly and accurately figure out what activities are good or bad for a knife so that it can achieve its purpose. If one knows what activities a 'being' does, it can fairly and accurately decide the purpose of that being.

Humans can perfect their knowledge if they so like. The ultimate purpose of every human action is to cultivate the human mind or acquire knowledge. Materialism maintains that people's happiness consists in acquiring material goods. The acquisition of wealth is or should be the ultimate purpose of human action. Humanism holds that the ultimate end of human action is in achieving prosperity and progress for the human race. This is equivalent to the theory of economic plenty. Other forms of humanism are narrower in that they see the ultimate end of human action as achieving prosperity and progress for a nation. This can lead to extreme nationalism. Humanitarianism sees the ultimate end of human action as service, whether it be service to humankind in general, to a nation, to an organization or to a group. The highest good people can achieve is to serve. The scholastics base the ultimate end of human action on philosophy. From theodicy, they claim that a supreme being exists and that humans ultimately depend on and can be completely satisfied only by association with the supreme being. The goals of life cannot be decided unanimously. Rousseau went to the extent of saying that the 'logical goal of life is suicide'. Nisbet calls life and its philosophies as 'absurdism'. Nietzsche argues that superman has a special moral right to enforce his morality. Scholars conclude that universal judgements are neither possible nor feasible.

Some actions are morally right and others are morally wrong or both. While these philosophers cannot agree on the morality of all actions, or perhaps on much of anything else, they have agreed that some actions such as murder, robbery, rape or treachery are morally wrong by their very nature. They may not agree on the number and kind of human actions that fit into the intrinsic evil category. For instance, Patrick Buchanan said: 'Cardinal O'Connor has done nothing but has asserted Catholic doctrine on homosexuality and abortion; both are intrinsically wrong'. Although Buchanan cited the Bible and not ethics as the source of his claim, he illustrates the point made here that sometimes at least there is an intrinsic difference between a good action and an evil action. But how does a person decide the difference between the two? What constitutes the essence of morality? Morality concerns the fundamental reason why some actions are good and others are evil. There has to be a test to find out what actions are good and what actions are evil. It is a search for criteria to assess the goodness or badness of human action. There are several schools of thought on this issue, such as utilitarianism, institutionalism, rationalism, scholasticism, etc. It is reasonable to consider all elements in determining what is right and what is wrong. Both the deontological and teleological schools of thought probably concur on this point. Yet, the teleological school might consider departing from this theory if it limits the application of criteria to an action before commission, as opposed to concomitant or subsequent applications.

Criteria of Human Action

What part of a human action should one examine to decide if the action occurs within the ambit of human nature. There are three parts to every action that one should examine: (1) the object of the action, (2) the circumstances in which the action was performed, and (3) the end or purpose of the act. Sometimes these three components are the only practical criteria based on which a public administrator will have to decide the morality of a public action. Essentially, this is the basis of the teleological approach. The same physical action may at different times be morally good or morally bad. For example, driving through a red light may be morally bad. But if authorities remove the light, the same physical act of driving through the intersection may be morally good. What makes the difference between a morally good action and a morally bad one? Does the difference rest in some extrinsic circumstance, such as a law or a red light, or in some intrinsic circumstance or nature of the action itself? The fundamental question is: Are all human actions right or wrong because of some extrinsic circumstances, such as rules of law, or are at least some human actions intrinsically evil? There are different schools of thought on this point.

The Divine Positivism

Divine positivists claim that actions are good or evil only because God has freely commanded them to be so. They say, God, who has forbidden lying, could just as easily have forbidden telling the truth. Positive laws of God determine the morality of human actions, therefore, these theorists are called 'divine positivists'. The problem with this theory is that it is difficult to comprehend how God could command a murder to be right and moral at one time and at another time to be immoral or evil. This is contrary to the common experience of people of all times and of all places, who have determined that murder is evil. If the divine positivist position is correct, ethics serves no useful purpose because human reason is incapable of distinguishing between right and wrong – only God can do that.

The Human Positivism

Human positivists, on the other hand, hold that the difference between right and wrong arose from tribal custom or because of education or social influences. Rousseau held that actions are good when the state or general commends them and evil when the state forbids them. Circumstances are those qualities that make an abstract act concrete and individual. Circumstances include such things as being done at a particular time, in a particular place, by a particular agent, and in a particular manner. Moral circumstances, not physical, are the criteria for assessing the goodness or badness of a human action. Moral circumstances may also increase the goodness or badness of a human action. To strike another person in self-defence is one thing; to strike another without any provocation or justification is another matter. Some moral circumstances are aggravating when they increase the goodness or badness of an action. Thus, stealing from a homeless person is an *aggravating* circumstance that increases the badness of an already bad act. Circumstances are *extenuating* when they decrease the amount of badness of an action.

When the great moral philosopher Jean Paul Sartre was awarded the coveted Nobel Prize, he assertively returned it by saying that human beings are petty mosquitoes, sitting on a potato in a sack of potatoes and the award winning event by mutual commendation is an act of immorality. One may disagree with Sartre but Sartres are needed to keep the moral dialogue alive. A discussion on the issues of moral philosophy contributes to human understanding of the 'being'. A civil servant is no exception. If the public service is an act of moral intercourse, the participants must be aware of its causes and consequences. To a practical administrator, the debate may be trivial, mundane and confusing. But then public service is neither power nor a 'dominance value' of sheer coercion. Civil servants in India, who know too much of history and law, find the moral philosophy debates too abstract and even boring. But then, one cannot prove one's credentials of merit if a free and open debate on moral scruples is regarded as taboo in a given society.

Morality Assessment

The object of an action is the first part of any action in a morality assessment. In other words, the object of any action is its essence. It is that which makes an action what it is and not something else. Every action has an object. The object distinguishes the act from every other act. That object can be something good, bad or indifferent, that is, neither good nor bad. Lying and telling the truth are examples of two actions that are distinguished from each other according to moral criteria. The following principles apply to the object of every action:

1. An action whose object is bad by its very nature will remain bad and nothing can improve it – neither circumstances, nor purpose, nor intention. A lie, defined as speaking contrary to what is in the speaker's mind, remains a lie despite the purpose or circumstances involved. Purpose and circumstances do not make it anything (another object) except a lie.

2. An action that is good may become bad because of circumstances or purpose. For example, telling the truth is a good act. By telling the truth, when silence would suffice, to destroy another person's good name or character makes the good act of telling the truth a morally bad act because of the speaker's purpose or intention.
3. An action that is indifferent (neither good nor bad) may become good or bad because of circumstances or purpose. Walking may be an indifferent act. But walking into a store to steal becomes a morally evil action because of the purpose.

The Purpose Principle

Similarly, the end of a human action is the purpose the person had in mind while doing the act. It is the intention. People can have only one purpose or have a variety of purposes in doing a particular act. One can deduce certain principles based on the purpose in mind when performing the act:

1. An action that is indifferent because of its object may become good or bad because of the purpose. For example, jogging in itself is an indifferent act. But, when it is done to maintain good health, it becomes a good act, and when it is done to arrive at a place where the person commits theft or murder, it becomes an immoral action.
2. An action that is good because of its object may become more good or less good or even bad because of the purpose. For example, to give a donation to a homeless person is a good action. If you give the donation just to get rid of the person, it is still a good action, but not as good as in the first case. If you give the donation to lure the homeless person into doing something evil or immoral for you, the donation becomes an immoral act.
3. An action that is evil by its object may become more wrong or perhaps less wrong, but never good by its purpose. For instance, telling a lie is morally wrong. But telling a lie to

defame another person is more wrong. Telling a lie to get out of trouble or to protect the interests of another person is still lying and still wrong, but less wrong because of the purpose. A good end does not justify bad means.

The Situational Morality

Interpretivists do not limit their consideration of morality to mere circumstances; they also consider the nature of the action and its purpose. The most difficult problem in situation ethics is that it often makes morality subjective and relative. There is nothing to prevent two persons in same circumstances from giving two diametrically opposite meanings to the same action. This implies that an action that is morally good for one person can be morally evil for another. Although interpretivists do subscribe to human reason as an interpreter of human actions, the person who focuses on the situation alone cannot be sure of the morality of at least some actions. Human beings have a rational nature, and psychology has established that once we know the nature of something, we can also come to know its purpose and what will help it to attain it. For humans, it is proximately a rational nature that determines what is good and what is bad. The scholastics go one step further and argue that the decision on the morality of human action rests with the supreme being, on whom humans ultimately depend.

The criterion for assessing the morality of human action is a fundamental issue that has intrigued philosophers. Philosophers have overfocused on one part and have put forward different criteria for assessing morality. But, a single criterion of pleasure or the existence of a categorical imperative is an insufficient explanation of the state of morality.

When are the individuals responsible for the effect of their actions? To be responsible for an evil effect one must advert at least vaguely to the fact that the action is bad. If we so advert, we are presumed to have willed the effect. For instance, a hunter sees an object but is unsure whether it is a man or a deer. The hunter adverts, at least vaguely, to what the consequences of firing a shot may be. The hunter shoots anyhow, and therefore the presumption is that the hunter willed the effect of his or her action. On the other hand, for a good effect to be imputed, the actor must advert to the good effect and intend it. For example, after a presentation by an official on government travel regulations, a junior in the audience decides to reimburse the government for over-reimbursement. If the senior official never considered – much less intended – the good effect, the official is not responsible for it. Similarly, there are certain actions that have two effects – good and bad. How does someone decide the morality of such actions? Ethicists provide a few general principles to help decide the morality of acts of double effect. They are: (1) When the actor physically does the act, the action is physically imputed to that person – the person is responsible for his or her action. (2) If the actor does not perform the act but causes another to do it, the first person is still morally responsible for the consequences of the act to the degree that he or she foresaw those consequences. (3) Whatever increases, lessens or destroys the liberty and knowledge that are essential for a moral act also increases, lessens or destroys the responsibility of the actor. (4) On the other hand, the actions of other people may be imputed to others if they have helped, encouraged or persuaded them to do something or if they have remained silent when these people clearly needed advice. It is a real problem in the management of bureaucracy at various levels.

The Biblical Morality

There is an unending discourse whether legality or morality are supplementary or contradictory. Some maintain that they partially overlap, while others argue that they can be coeval or coextensive. This boils down to an intimate relationship between sin and crime. Bible said that 'man was born of sin' and he is incapable to police and adjudicate his sinful actions. Several moral philosophers believe that if a man cannot control his sinful activities on his own, it is another sin to put him under the overall control of sinning individuals, who may be dishonest, selfish and corrupt. Similarly, all guardians of law will uphold the theory of moral man and ask the witnesses to take a moral oath in the court room that 'they are speaking the truth and nothing but the truth only'. The moral scruples fight against criminality and even the worst criminal may confess before a church father and own his or her guilt. Naturally, the ethics of law and ethics of moral man may meet at some point to produce the workable delivery of fair justice.

Nozick's Version of Moral Rights

Nozick's version of moral rights creates a debate about willing inheritance of property. Nozick maintains that an individual is capable of taking care of himself or herself, if allowed by others in general and the state in particular to do so. The theory allows that a minimal state be established, which helps people to protect their rights and regain their property, if someone steals from them. It is possible, according to Nozick, for rational individuals to agree to an arrangement where the police protect the individuals' right to physical integrity, where courts of law ensure that contracts are upheld, and so forth. However, there is no room, according to the theory, for a system where the state uses taxation to oblige individuals to give up their property, only because a system of education or health care needs to be funded in society. The modern welfare state, at least to the extent that it is motivated by a desire to meet urgent needs (and not to correct injustices in the past), is considered to be a sophisticated system of slavery by Nozick.

Natural Right of Property and Inheritance

The property and its inheritance has been an area of moral debate. What makes ownership moral? John Locke, the celebrated English philosopher in his theory of social contract, takes a position that a moral order of human beings existed much before they created a legal order by contracting for the state. His natural rights theory of life, liberty and estate has today evolved into a theory of natural rights, which makes human rights as sacrosanct, moral and inviolable. Another moral philosopher from Harvard, Robert Nozick, does not accept Locke's proviso about acquisition and inheritance of property on the basis of labour which the owner had spent upon it. Locke has observed: 'God has given us all things richly .... But how far has he given it to us to enjoy? Whatever is beyond this, is more than his share, and belongs to others. Nothing was made by God for man to spoil or destroy'. Locke also states explicitly that there exists a right to charity. Charity gives every man a title to spend so much out of another's plenty, as will keep him from extreme want, where he has no means to subsist otherwise.

Existentialism and Philosophies of Alienation

The 20th century closed with a critical debate on the young Marx and the mature Marx. The economist and revolutionary Marx has been supplemented by a philosopher-anthropologist Marx, who propounds the 'dialectics of alienation'. The complete return of Marx to his human self is his 'return from religion, family and state to his real existence'. This existentialism in the humanistic ethical philosophies gave birth to Frankfurt School of Critical Sociology. The social rebels, like Eric Fromm, find modernization as the sole cause of maladies making 'security' more important than freedom, Nisbet feels disenchanted and lonely and ruefully asks, 'who am I and what am I?' and Herbert Marcuse, Rosa Laxumberg, T.W. Adorno and Hanna Arendt ask the meanings of *human happiness* and advance *performance principles, pleasure doctrines* and *surplus repression* theories of morality. Marcuse's plea for a new kind of man and a new kind of society elaborates the existing situations, goals to be achieved and methods to be adopted. Actually these questions of moral philosophy should be debated in the realm of public administration also. Mere Weber's rationalism does not produce the moral philosophy of man and his universe. Locke, Marx, Nisbet, Fromm and Marcuse offer the backdrop and provide an ethical insight into the problems of liberty, property, inheritance, gender justice and ecological ethics which is needed to execute the administrative policies for ensuring of moral rights of man.

Moral philosophies and philosophers have initiated debates and have offered polemical conclusions, which create intellectual chaos rather than social clarity. The administrator should not get confused or overawed with this but should feel challenged in studying the various schools of moral theorists and the moral problems which they have raised.

1. *Kantian Categorical Imperatives of Conscience*: Kant refers to his supreme moral principle as the 'categorical imperative' – categorical because it does not depend on anyone's particular desires, and imperative because it is a command of reason. Kant also claims that the categorical imperative can be reformulated as 'an act that you use humanity, whether in your own person or in the person of any other, always at the same time as an end but never merely as a means'. Using this version, Kant argues that a deceitful promise is immoral, because a person making such a promise is using another person only as a means. He is not treating that individual as an end or a rational being, worthy of his or her respect.
2. *John Stuart Mill's Individualist Utilitarianism:* It provides a means of dealing with the quandary of conflicting obligations. To illustrate this, he gives an example. An individual promised to meet someone for lunch, but on the way he encountered a woman in need of immediate aid. What should he do? Utilitarianism solves the problem by telling to give priority to help the woman, because that course of action will produce more happiness. But then should one not keep

his own promises? Mill's answer is that usually one should, because the practice of keeping one's promises generates productive social benefits. An exception should be made, however, on those occasions when more happiness can be produced by not keeping a promise.

3. *Aristotle's Virtue Ethics:* Aristotle grounds morality in human nature. He views 'good' as the fulfilment of the human potential to live well. According to him, to live well is to live in accordance with virtue. But how does one acquire virtue. Aristotle's answer is that we acquire it by habit. One becomes good by doing good. Repeated acts of justice and self-control result in making a just and self-controlled person. Such a person not only performs just and self-controlled actions but does so from a fixed character. The virtuous act in practice is a mean between the two extremes, which are vices; for example, courage is the mean between rashness and cowardice.
4. *Nietzsche's Master and Slave Morality*: A controversial figure in the history of moral philosophy, Friedrich Nietzsche, a German philosopher, claimed that traditional notions of 'good' and 'evil' embody a 'slave morality'. According to him, this slave morality needs to be transcended by a higher form of human morality. It would lead towards the enhancement of life in a world which should be conceived without God. He offers his unconventional views in aphoristic style and transforms the theological version of the biblical moral man.
5. *Susan Wolf's Philosophy of Moral Saints:* Bernard Mayo urges that we all try to be a little like saints. But, Susan Wolf argues that a saintly life is not a model towards which human beings should strive. She defends the view that human beings should not sacrifice their values to protect the so-called moral values. Saintliness may talk of morality but

the latter covers a much wider spectrum than mere renunciation or even sacrifice in ignorance.

6. *John Rawls' Theory of Justice:* Redrawing the framework of social contract, John Rawls, the Professor of Philosophy at Harvard University, views justice as a social arrangement that ensures that the interests of some should not be sacrificed to the arbitrary advantages enjoyed by others. Like Hobbesian rational self-preservation, Rawls defends his views by appealing to an implied agreement among individuals to engage themselves in social cooperation in accord with certain principles. But, then Hobbes and Rawls derive their principles from different chains of reasoning and reach at widely different conclusions also. Rawls' veil of ignorance enables the unequal individuals to participate in a system of distributive justice of a given society with their implicit consent. So, they continue to be 'moral' even in their unmoral pursuits.
7. *Female Ethics of Carol Gilligen:* It is called ethics of care, which Dr Susan Jaggar takes to the point of Feminist Practical Discourse (FPD). Gilligen stretches the equality principle to care principle of the female sex, by virtue of its maternal anatomy. It requires a practical discourse and mere equality of two sexes does not ensure moral justice to women. Gender is not an abstraction and gender justice is a vital issue of human morality.
8. *Environment Ethics:* Now going much beyond the problems of the planet earth, it encompasses cosmos and space research with all sorts of future implications. Denuding the planet earth does not yield sustainable development. Morally, we owe our planet to our children rather than to our ancestors. Depleting the resources is immoral. Science can do it, it is an achievement of human ingenuity, but 'should science do it?' – is a big question of human ethics and morality.

Ethical guidance to civil service behaviour can be sought from (1) moral standards (2) or from an analysis of action or (3) from the laws (4) or conscience. A law is an enactment of legislature which historically arises from religion, philosophy or social norms. The legal branches include criminal law, civil law and laws covering specific sectors. The laws can be substantive and procedural. The former defines offences or crimes, while the latter specifics the modalities, which the courts have to follow in dispensing justice. The constitution of a nation is regarded as its fundamental law, which embodies the basic values and ethos of the society. The concept of ethical law is the outcome of centuries of philosophical and moral speculations. St. Thomas Aquinas believed that law imposes an obligation on people and makes people act or desist from acting. It prescribes some actions and prohibits other actions.

Rules or regulations can be laid down by private persons or corporate houses. The law can only be made in exercise of sovereign power by legislature. Aquinas mentions the primary, secondary and tertiary principles of natural law. Primary principles of natural law are universal rules of conduct and can be easily perceived by human reason. The natural law tells what is good and what casts a moral duty to follow. It has to meet certain conditions to qualify for people's obedience. In modern democratic parlance, no citizen is above the law. The public servants must follow constitutional values while performing their official duties. The theory of a special moral sense is called 'dogmatic intuitionism'. It believes that conscience does not give us infallible knowledge of the right or wrong of particular acts. It only indicates general principles which apply to classes of acts.

Conscience has three aspects (1) knowledge, (2) authority and (3) associated emotions. The conscience or value commitments can be explained as results from moral development, education and social environment. People generally remain loyal to social morality, imbibed in their formative years. Moral reformers seek changes even in social ideals and institutions regarded as sacred. Moral relativism questions the validity of universal, objective and moral values. They can be seen as individual or cultural. The path of reflective conscience has to find a mean between capricious self-conceit and dead conformity of law. Public servants cannot act mechanically in applying these rules. They have to identify situations with moral implications and think through the possible alternatives.

Moral debates in the fields of capital punishment, war, abortion, euthanasia, obscenity, female care, etc. are highly provocative and raise penetrating issues of values. For instance, the administrators can peruse Carol Gilligan's ethical study, *In a Different Voice* (1982), and then compare her views on 'ethics of care' with the sexual prejudices in moral philosophies of Immanuel Kant and Herbert Marcuse. They will be amused to see Nel Nodding's objection to abstraction of women in moral philosophy. Herbert Marcuse's philosophy of 'Male Repressive Tolerance' can be contrasted with Susan Jaggar's FPD. These insights in feminine moral philosophies of female philosophers will lead to the conclusions that there is no way to solve the moral dilemmas of legal crimes like rape, infanticide, surrogacy, lesbian marriages, etc. unless one is prepared to go through a hard normative thinking of the ethical philosophers.

The deep ecological problems of environmental ethics are knocking at the threshold of space and the cosmos. The technological social order hurts the liberals with the situations which can be harsh or liberal with the situations in other planets. The officers in civil services cannot evade or ridicule these moral issues of philosophy, because they will gradually be pressurized to make laws for gender ethics and ecological degradation of our planet. The 'right' reason of Kant is not the only answer. The ethical issues, being somewhat narrower and more practical in scope, stop earlier than moral problems of human existence. Social concerns become more vital in ethical appraisals but the moral philosophy and moral philosophers take a worldview of human problems as Bertrand Russell rightly puts it that 'the sin cannot be geographical'. Similarly, poverty, violence, human health, human rights and human backwardness cannot be viewed from national or geographical perspectives. If gay and lesbian marriages are legalized in USA, the people all over the world should be concerned about human birth, surrogacy and animal farming of human beings that shall follow. Abortion is not a matter of maternal health only; it is a downright murder which has been called a crime in all civilized societies of the world. Conscripting able-bodied males for 'war' is the denial of human rights, because a war, whatever may be the reasons, remains a 'multitudinous murder' and a ghastly crime against humanity in its consequences. Issues of medical ethics, female care, human life and deep ecology need to be sorted out first, before the administration launches its administrative agenda for legal action. The moral issues and moral problems that border on human ethics are varied and innumerable. They defy rational classifications, but can broadly be grouped as under:

1. Moral Rights Area
   (a) World Hunger
   (b) Affirmative Action
   (c) Satyagraha
   (d) Famine
   (e) Weaker Sections and Backward Classes
   (f) Property and Inheritance

2. Medical Area
   (a) Euthanasia
   (b) Prohibition
   (c) Drug Abuse
   (d) Sterilization
   (e) Human Husbandry
   (f) Organ Transplant and Organ Sale

3. Violence and Protest Movements
    (a) Terrorism
    (b) Conscription
    (c) Capital Punishment
    (d) Animal Rights and Cruelty
    (e) Collective Punishments
4. Women's World
    (a) Pornography
    (b) Abortion
    (c) Child Abuse
    (d) Prostitution
    (e) Trafficking
    (f) Surrogacy
    (g) Lesbian Marriages
    (h) Rape
    (i) Infanticide
5. Ecology
    (a) Biodiversity
    (b) Wildlife Protection
    (c) Pollution
    (d) Deforestation
    (e) Eco-degradation
    (f) Animals in Bio-research

To this, the specific problems of culture and countrywise practices may be added. For instance, India has special moral problems in the areas of tribal population, caste stratifications, religious conversions and a verity of backwardnesses for which laws and theories are needed. Social justice is a broad rubric and public administrator should theorize morality rather than merely legalizing it for implementation of laws without comprehending the meanings of reservation for backwards or development of the so-called underdeveloped.

Morality as Liberty

The moral issues in philosophy are debated because of their unique human character. Human beings are not food. They are not even tools to be employed as a means to achieve some ultimate end. The so called Supreme End, even if Divine, cannot be justified at the cost of human freedom or collective good represented through institutions of state, society or government. Naturally, all the moral philosophies accept that *Life is Sacred* and its decoration or termination by anybody for any reason has to be regarded as an unpardonable sin against humanity. This raises perennial and irresoluble questions on issues like conscription, abortion, terrorism, capital punishment, armament and nuclear wars. Pacifists may argue against violence but the very institutions of laws and government are social-violence institutionalized. Even functional anarchy will require some sort of mild violence paraded as non-violent or non-killing punishment. This endless debate in the area of moral responsibility of moral man in moral society, ends with minimization of violence and practice of more sustained and sophisticated ways of punishment and military systems in the world.

Morality as Gender Justice

The other sensitive area where the moral law of conscience matters, is gender justice. Male female gender discriminations divide the philosopher. Even women philosophers do not accept the abstraction of women. The gender justice is neither mercy nor any special kind of a call of conscience. Family, society and state have to protect this human species against violence, torture and gender victimization. The procreation function even with advancements of reproduction biology puts the female gender in crisis and pain situations for the benefit of male human-kind. Hence crimes like pornography, prostitution, abortion, marital cruelty, infanticide, child trafficking and abuse are not mere ordinary crimes, but instances of moral turpitude, because women's right alone can be called 'Human Rights'. The social consciousness of the moral society has to be aroused so that gender justice may be conceptualized and practised with more stringent laws to meet the ends of justice.

The Medical Intervention

The medical morality is more than medical ethics. The knowledge of science and technology with its new interventionist approaches and equipments can make life 'more and less' human. Euthanasia or mercy killing today, will be called the 'Shame of Science'. Man should conquer disease because there by he conquers life and death. Organ transplants, blood transfusions, coma convulsive surgery and regeneration of cells have created situations for the dawn of a new scientific morality. The science of eugenics, in-vitro fertility and surrogacy have opened new vista of birth morality through sperm banks and egg donation centres. This sort of human husbandry divides moral philosophers into naturalist and interventionist camps. Homo-marriages have separated sexuality from fertility and if lesbian marriages are accepted by law and society, the socio-cultural contents of moral philosophy will wane and may be replaced by a uni-sex society of human colleagues. But all this will have to pass through a hard test of non-human systems of mixed breeds, hybrid human species and their longevity and utility. The moral issues will dominate the transition till the immoral society gets settled as 'moral'.

Eco and Bio Degradations as Human Perversions

Climate pollution, eco degradation and decline in bio-diversity is another area of soft morality, where in fierce debates have surfaced in the 21st century. The other planets have become reachable and inter planetary travels and exchange will encourage a new facility and terror to human civilization bordering on human morals. Today it is everybody's guess, but if the earth is denuded and air and water resources get pollute, will the human morals violate the sanctity of other planets in the name of creativity and development? The philosophers must brood, '*Where stands the limit',* because the sky has already ceased to be the limit. The space research also has innumerable moral issues like the planetary climate and ocean resources. The human beings on the planet earth will have to provide a moral leadership to life on other planets in terms of enduring values of social living.

Man, in all systems and cultures, has to be accepted as a moral being and if he dies just because of hunger or famine around, it must stir the conscience of humanity. Civil disobedience and affirmative action are moral rights because no government can have a right to rule a moral society in an immoral manner. People must assert to remove backwardness, irrespective of their right to property and legal inheritance. Like liberty and equality, property and its inheritance should be morally acceptable in terms of limitations only, which the law should keep revising as per consensus of the community. Medical ethics, in the western societies, go much beyond the Christian morality of the Bible. Mercy cannot be extended to mercy killing. God or no God, human judgement cannot be trusted to terminate a life that is sacred. Should a woman has a right to abort the foetus or a man should be sterilized as a measure of social punishment? Should the sale of human organs or even selling of blood for donation purposes be called moral or a mere unethical practice of a given society? The medical doctors cannot be allowed to take decisions about the patient, no matter the latter does not understand the complications of his or her disease. Even cloning is viewed as 'immoral' because it disturbs the natural procedure of birth. There are innumerable women's areas wherein the immoral laws of surrogacy, rental wombs, motherless motherhood and lesbian wedlocks will be called immoral, because of their consequences and unnatural human processes of artificial action.

The big debates on pornography, obscenity, prostitution and child abuse ultimately end up with the problems of consent and awareness. Terrorism cannot be justified at any cost because crude violence to terminate life violates what is inviolable in human existence. The ecology ethics again puts forward a moral argument, 'Can people damage and destroy a planet which they have inherited for a transfer to their children?' This is grossly immoral to damage the future for the crash advantages of the present. The limit to growth and development does not mean that 'sky is the limit'.

In fact, the law-morality debate is an introspectional ethical realm of public administration. Morality cannot be legislated and the law will always be observed in breach if it does not have a moral grounding. Naturally, therefore, it is in the interest of administration to understand and appreciate why laws are systematically violated in social systems. A perfect congruence between law and morality is an unworkable proposition, but a police officer, a magistrate and a judge must struggle with the morality of law which is much more than a mere right or 'jus naturale' of Roman variety.

Ever since the dawn of human civilization, the primitive man has been struggling to become a 'social animal' of Aristotle. Sociability sublimated him as an ethical being but the Hobbesian animalism compelled him to accept the Lockian law of preserving a moral order through law. The two are not contradictory but supplementary. Ethical practices are imposed as legal codes, where human frailties or greed tend to perpetrate an immoral or unnatural order in human society. Negative codes or laws against corruption, terrorism, prostitution, human husbandry and organ transplant may fall in this category of ethical living. But there are eternal and universal questions of human nature. Should female body be abused against her will? Should air and water be allowed to get polluted? Should homo-sexuality be promoted into a lesbian marriage? Do people be given a moral right to indulge in affirmative action against conscription or capital punishment? These are big big questions, which transcend the limits of time and space. Non-vegetarian food may have nothing to do with ethics or morality, but if an egg eating society procreates human infants for 'flesh food', it will be down right immoral and violative of human conscience. In these areas, several issues pertain to gender justice and professional ethics of medical profession. A vast ocean of immorality extends to the areas of human rights application of science, technology and preservation of ecology against human degradation. The moral philosophy dimension of female ethics raises its voice against cruelty, abortion, cloning techniques and capital punishment to rid the society from crimes against humanity. Here, the ethical laws may not exist or may be in the offing. At one point, the ethical protest may join hands with morality protagonists. But there are morality areas which can be called unethical at the level of social customs and practices. Prohibition, surrogacy, pornography, wildlife protection are areas on the border line. As human societies advance with science and technologies, the ethical problems enter into a wider and more complex problem zone of moral ethics or ethical morality. The scope, nature and consequences have to be spelt out to extricate human issues from a mess of natural interactions and societal value crises of a given society.

In India, where public administration is viewed as a narrow application of law or conformity to legal rules and procedures, an administrator has to be a petty moral philosopher of his or her own variety. Disasters can follow if he or she thinks that moral clap traps are a philosophical nuisance and 'law is what he or she thinks it is, or it should be'. Even judiciary, which has the sole prerogative to interpret and defend the law, takes the judicial pronouncements and juristic precedents literally and mechanically. Naturally, the incidence and quantum of injustice do not decline. It is tragic that administrators imitate their seniors only and very few of them have genuine interests in questions of moral philosophy. The moral philosophers of the world have a self-willed responsibility to make this world a better place for human habitation and enjoyment. The administrators should continuously learn from their moral theories and their utilitarian nuances in their day-to-day practice of law.

Ethics in family, society, business, medical world, environment or administrative affairs is nobody's monopolistic preserve. Law or no law, the moral order exists for the human beings. It enjoins upon the human communities to define norms, prepare codes and implement those policies which sublimate human existence from the animal value of mere survival. The ethical issues may be stretched to God or scriptures, but the human ethics has to be simplified even for an atheist or an agnostic. The civil servants in India are highly educated persons and they can proudly boast of their high moral standards. But this elitist bragging of a tiny minority does not make much sense, where the lower echelons of bureaucracy are deeply sunk in corruption and unethical practices of exploitation and domination over the poor. To be ethical, *ipso facto,* implies – to make others ethical. Ethical values do not get inspired by writing Annual Confidential Reports (ACRs) of juniors or by being extra-legal or rational in a Weberian sense. The civil servants will have to generate a climate of ethical harmony and moral justice around them to enhance their own faith and confidence in a life of virtue and social service. 'Virtue is knowledge', said the Greeks and social service needs a moral commitment, which philosophy alone can inspire. The fountain heads of ethical inspiration are spread all over and all around. The administrator can and should screen and choose the lifestyles, noble missions and exemplary sacrifices of great leaders, tall reformers and their worthy predecessors. It is a part of civil service duty and this will equip them with the right kind of aptitudes necessary to launch conscious attempts to lead a life of reason and compassion. The Aristotelian 'golden mean ethics' is one such path, which can be traversed with rational and emotional intelligence. The Weberian decisions may be recorded on the files but a satisfying emotional decisioning may be strived in the field.

A little musing in the area of moral philosophy can enable an administrator to have an interface with great human minds, which will push his or her laws and rules into the realm of an idea or a theory. The right law will get strengthened, but if there is a dichotomy between law, morality and politics, the conscience of a civil servant should revolt. The study of moral philosophy is a healthy restraint on legal jurisprudence. The law everywhere has to be humanized. Similarly, there exists a need to legalize morality. The area of administrative ethics represents the golden mean. A civil servant can be civil, only when he or she has his or her orientation in moral philosophies, propounded by all-time moral philosophers. May it be Gautam, the Buddha or a Karl Marx, the Messiah of the Proletariat.

Chapter 7

The Ethics of Accountability

Status and Civil Service Values in India

The term 'civil service', if contrasted from 'public service', gives a civilizational connotation to the former. No Hindi translation of the term comes even close to it. A civilian dress, a residential area called civil lines and even Mahatma's 'Satyagraha' which he named as civil disobedience movement give different meanings of the term 'civil'. It is widely used in English-speaking world as something opposed to military. A military dress is called uniform, while a civilian dress code will stress upon the freedom to choose. Similarly, a civil lines or a Bengali 'Bhadralok' is where the aristocrats of society reside. Here, it denotes an elitist cluster which does not include the masses or the commoners in general. Gandhiji used it in the British sense of civility, politeness and his civil disobedience (सविनय अवज्ञा) was a protest movement to disobey with all respect to authority of the state and society.

The term 'civilian', when used for administrators in government, often excludes the political masters. The latter are public servants but are not members of the civil service of the state. Here, the term is reserved for permanent government servants, who constitute the career bureaucracy as an executive wing of the government.

A civil servant in UK is an epitome of civility, liberty and elitism. Though a ruler, he or she behaves like a 'ruling servant', which seems like a contradiction in terms. He or she is required to be politically neutral, and allows the political game of power to be played by the elected leaders according to the rule of procedure. He or she has his or her umpire's liberty and neutralist elitism of a professional, who does not play foul but only blows the whistle, when others violate the rules and play foul in the game.

As a generalist civilian, the civil servant possesses the culture of mind and intellect and behaves in the most polite manner with the people and with their elected political leaders in the government. He or she advises the political masters to handle sensitive public issues with care and utmost public concern in a civil manner in accordance with the civilizational norms of a Christian society. The British government, which evolved its constitutional structure for centuries, never set down to frame administrative rules and regulations of civility or civilianism in obedience to any theory of ethical civility or civilian responsibility. The conventions, which gradually laid the foundations of rule of law in England, crystallized the role of civil servants, which included the inculcation of a value system of a civilized society. The Christian ethics was the primary and eternal source of strength to these British civilians. What the military commanded with the use of a gun or coercion, these civilian public servants were asked to accomplish with a smile and the moral power of their character which comprised virtues of honesty, neutrality and objectivity. In fact, whatever they heard from the pulpit in the church by way of sermons of the church father, they were urged upon to follow in administration as children of God. These civil service values in England, like that of the British Constitution, were unwritten, conventional and were a proud possession of the nobility, from which the civil service was recruited. This blue blood royalty laid down the traditions of British Civil Service. The moral-legal distinctions were not neatly demarcated in White Hall or in India, till the Hanoverian royal dynasty switched over to the rudiments of a parliamentary form of government in UK.

Later on, when these Christian civilians from London had to establish the administration in the non-Christian colonies, particularly India, they had to revise their civil service values of Christianity in codified forms. The natives were heathens or pegans, and their value system was so different, that a Viceroy Lord Cornwallis had to respond with a prescribed code of conduct for the Indian civil servants. The company government devised training programmes for British civilians who had to work in India. The English Victorian ethics or the Christian virtues of civil service were outlined in rules and codes and the native officials who were not civil in their judgements were legally made to obey their seniors in their respective areas of ethical behaviours.

The East India Company had two different sets of values for the English officers and the native Indian employees. The discriminations were echoed in protests like Ilbert Bill controversy. The military code for the British rulers was also different from this civil code and seldom did the British officers mix with the native officials, who were totally a discriminated and an inferior lot in terms of Hindu-Muslim values.

The native civil servants in India, during the Crown's rule, were encouraged to stay away from the people and imitate the alien values of their English seniors. They ridiculed all those who looked patriotic and nationalistic in their ideas, dress codes and language. Over a period of time these civil service values of honesty, integrity, tolerance, impartiality or objectivity, which have nothing to do with European geography, ultimately got symbolized with a 'sahib culture' of Western dress and English language. The hybrid value system of the native Indian officials attempted to legalize and operationalize some of the universal ethical values through rules and procedures. But, the Indian secretariats followed the iron law of oligarchy with the result that public service ethics became a handmaid of bureaucratic rules and their colonial manipulators.

The Non-Moral Values of Non-Gazetted Employees

As compared to the Mughal system of administrative values, the Christian value system of English rule was much superior, but it could not make a dent in the Indian social system. The petty officials were the worst affected and they lost the best of both the oriental and occidental worlds. They pretended to conform to laws to please their British seniors, but in practice they remained corrupt, parochial and dishonest without any healthy traditions of a Hindu civil service. After the Mutiny or the First War of Indian Independence in 1857, Her Majesty's government pursued a policy which Dadabhai Naoroji very aptly called the 'UnBritish Rule in India'. This unBritish rule bisected the Indian society into urban and rural segments. The English-knowing Macaulay elite of India was to rule and administer the rural masses in the districts and the contradictions of cultural values become sharper and deeper with the passage of time.

The divide was so deep and so fundamental that the administrators of the British Raj had to be given values of loyalty, impartiality and objectivity to rule a vast colony of native Indians, with the cooperation of brilliant Indian youngsters. Lord Cornwallis made no secret of his opinion, when he openly said that most of the civil servants under the Company rule were cheats, dishonest and corrupt. His regime made the most degrading arrangement of 'gazetted' and 'non-gazetted' public servants. The latter were and are not trusted even today. These third- and fourth-class public servants were employed in the British administration to demonstrate the association of the natives in public service. Functions, powers and security of job were ensured without much moral responsibility or legal accountability of these non-gazetted free booters who have been enjoying spoils since the Mughal times. These ranks are seeped into corruption even today and a 'Babu Raj' is ridiculed for its valuelessness in public services. These 'Babus' and peons, who acquired a ruler status, imitated the 'Sahibs' and misbehaved, harassed and tortured their own people to demonstrate their personal loyalty to the 'Raj'. This anti-people attitude which the British government symbolized during freedom struggle made these 'Babus' as 'Babu Sahibs'. Even a *chaprasi* thinks that he is superior to a *rikshawala*, although their moral statures may be poles apart. These cadres of civil servants, numbering into millions are notorious for their harassment, extortion, antipathy and exploitation of the masses. The rural people in India believe that getting a government job is a licence to misbehave and indulge in immoral deeds in lieu of their loyalty to the Christian rulers. All efforts to induct or inculcate probity in governance or evolve an ethical code of conduct founders on this rock of irresponsibility. They want to rule the people and refuse to accept the fact that public service implies an ethical value of higher responsibility. The Englishmen never cared to arrest these ethical malpractices of their petty officials, partly because they were aliens and partly because they enjoyed the vicarious pleasure in boasting that English officers were far far superior to the best of the natives. The civil service values of these non-gazetted employees are a living legacy of the British Raj. A petty *patwari*, a semi-literate *thanedar*, a manipulative accountant and a money minter PWD overseer, have been rolling in superfluous wealth without paying any income tax. These people somehow manage their entry into lower ranks of services without any rigorous system of competitive merit and these are the officials who have brought a 'notoriety' to public services in India. All efforts to downsize this corrupt and manipulative army of 'Babus' is resisted by seniors in the name of their indispensibility, poverty and increasing workload. Security of job and seniority based promotions permit them to reach to higher echelons without much moral fibre. These junior functionaries have family values of nepotism and are known for obliging the members of their own caste, class and kinship with the result that certain departments in governments like PWD or a municipality have become the exclusive preserves of these perverse groups who do not work and some of them are living much beyond their means. The challenge of 'ethicizing' these so called educated and anti-social employees in lower government positions is insurmountable. They are loyal and respectful to their seniors but they fleece the citizens and the poor Indian masses like the Mughal officials or the British masters of the past.

'India, that is, Bharat' Dichotomy

The term 'public' in India has a different meaning as compared to people in other parts of the world. Even the Constitution says 'India, that is, Bharat' which implies an English-knowing ruling India and a Bharat, which consists of the teeming millions, i.e. the masses. The urban public servants were called 'civil' and they still continue to 'rule' rural India in the 21st century under the garb of public service. A civil servant everywhere is supposed to have the values of civility, humility and compassion, which are missing even at the lowest level of a Babu or a *chaprasi* in India. On the contrary, they are arrogant, greedy, dominating and irresponsible to the people. The right to information, citizen charter and accountability rules are now being enacted to change the value behaviours of these semi-literate employees. Yet, it is a Herculean task to transmit ethical values of objectivity, empathy, dedication and tolerance in their public relations. The answer does not lie in punishing them or training them in higher values. Like other developed countries, the government must get rid of this low paid non-gazetted bureaucracy by replacing it with part-time non-career workers. Women, weaker sections and neo-educated youngsters with scientific temper have to be inducted as new professionals. For genuine civil service values the clerical (third class) and *chaprasi* (fourth class) services have to be abolished selectively and gradually as career jobs. This unscrupulous and unethical bunch cannot be weeded out, but can conveniently be downsized and phased out of government employment in instalments.

Status as an Elitist Ethics

The situation is relatively better in case of gazetted employees in class I and II public services. But here too, there are invidious distinctions and discriminations between all-India services and central services, technical services and administrative services, the state services and the corporate services, etc. The pay commissions are constantly reducing these anomalies but the general problem of status system in government jobs creates ethical concerns and dilemmas. The British rule strengthened an anti-people and alienated bureaucracy. It has moral virtues of honesty, sincerity, integrity and objectivity, but simultaneously it had no compassion for the weak and the poor. Tolerance to human situations or loving the natives was frowned upon during the British Raj. The conformity to rules was called discipline and keeping distance from the natives was stressed over and over again to maintain the level of efficiency. This philosophy of public service made the British and the Indian officials in senior positions absolutely unsocial and unequal.

The public officials isolated themselves in the name of status, dignity and decorum. Knowingly or inadvertently, they did not mix with the people and had their secluded offices with peons at the gates. They were accorded special privileges and protocol facilities to overawe the common man. These 'Sahibs' did not do any manual work and peons were made available to serve them even water, what to talk of tea or coffee. The manual jobs were regarded as 'degrading' and the 'Sahibs' degenerated into new official Brahmins and the juniors are still playing the neo-Harijans. The concepts of isolation, authority and privileges were stretched too far and the senior officials never used public transport or sat in petty town eateries or restaurants. They were elites and the Mussoorie academy has taught them to look like

VIPs even after independence. This VIP status system, which spoiled the Gandhian political leaders, is also a 'bureaucratic infection' and together the two find it convenient and comfortable to perpetrate their authority over the people who accept them like British masters of the past. Today, the status conscious politicians only inaugurate the functions or make pronouncements, while the public servants keep fighting for their transfers and privileges and blame the people and the politicians for the 'moral terpitude' for Indian society. The race of privileged status and VIP red-light cars attracts the most brilliant youngsters to civil service, and the status system fixes them into a caste frame which erodes their moral character. Like the scholarly Brahmin class of antiquity, the senior public servants deride manual work and live in a false paradise of domination, without compassion. Like the proverbial Nero or scholarly Pandit Brahmins, they love the people but from a distance. They do not suffer from any moral guilt, so long as the law permits unsolicited comforts and privileges. They have an inflated super ego, which gives them a sense of superiority and they firmly believe that moral scruples should be subordinated to rational instincts, which they honestly command in abundance.

A-moral Bureaucracy of Rules

Democracy all over the world has this problem of non-moral or an a-moral bureaucracy, which legally claims that it is not immoral. The bureaucrats will concede that all discriminations are condemnable and reprehensible but the discriminations based on merit or intellect are healthy and should be duly rewarded. This compensation has to be in the form of money, power and honour, which ultimately boils down to the status system in a social hierarchy. This argument can be taken as valid but then the status system, howsoever rational, weakens merit and creates conditions of immorality. Virtue ethics does not justify it, because exhibition of superiority over ignorant and innocent people is not a life of virtue. 'Status' in social situations cannot be a Kantian categorical imperative of conscience either. Benthamite utilitarianism, in its utter hedonistic sense, will call bureaucratic status as 'the greatest good of the select few' at the cost of 'a huge pain of a large number'. The moral theorists cannot accept Weber because his 'one best way' has proved to be a 'continental nuisance' in Carlyle's experience. Status system is immoral because it rests on a theory of permanent and fixed lifetime rationality, which is not tenable in any ontological and epistemological sense. The critics who believe that status hierarchy in administration is hostile to liberty and equality will argue that it is *ipso facto* immoral and no objective rational law will uphold it in a rule of law democracy with equalitarian cravings.

The personal qualities of a civil servant comprise intellect and character. Aristotle pioneered the study of virtue ethics in his *Nicomachean Ethics* which emphasizes that moral agents should transcend their self interests. This idea found expression in later thinking of Roman stoics, Christianity, Renaissance, and Enlightenment. Traditional moral thinkers consider prudence, justice, fortitude and temperance as the cardinal virtues. Civil servants have to correct their moral frailties. Their virtues can be classified as: (1) family virtues, (2) aesthetic virtues, (3) intellectual virtues, (4) religious virtues, (5) administrative virtues, and (6) professional virtues, with charity. Honour, benevolence and justice are the foundations of public administration. The civil servant should follow appropriate processes and procedures and show respect to colleagues and people. David Hart has propounded the ideas of a 'benevolent bureaucrat' and lists moral qualities that breed benevolence. It needs superior prudence, moral heroism, love of humanity, and a continuing effort towards moral improvement of society.

Goodness of character involves, moving one's mental focus from self interest and pulling it towards others. All public servants need good character. In difficult administrative situations the government servants have to follow the existing codes of conduct and other virtues which apply to a variety of jobs. In the traditional Weberian model, the government servants were politically neutral. Their ethical conduct consists in obeying rules or orders of superiors. The acts of omission and commission which flout rules, are called unethical. The principles of public administration prescribe that public servants should actively pursue policies of economic and social equity. The public choice theory, New Public Management (NPM) advocates that governments should follow private sector norms and focus on customers. Government agencies need to be 'customer-driven and service-oriented'. They have to be 'responsive, user-friendly, dynamic, and competitive providers of public services to customers'. They recommend that public servants should cultivate entrepreneurial spirit and creativity to optimize productivity and give results. Communitarianism, unlike public choice theory, disagrees with free market economics, but it emphasizes on a healthy community, and minimization of individual choices, as a desirable public goal. It proposes values based on community participation in government.

The English society, which boasted of its Victorian morals, is no longer what it has been in the 19th century. The post-war scenario and mass migration from former colonies of the empire have rendered the so-called Christian ethics polluted. The White Man's Burden, which was an ethical cover to pursue colonial interests, stands exposed. Now, the ethical codes are being prepared and their rigorous implementation is stressed upon. The Nolon Committee on Standards in Public Life is one such attempt which confesses that British civil servants are losing their high ethical standards of character. The civilians should be equipped with a checklist to measure their intellectual calibre and the moral fibre in a more rigorous manner.

The Nolon's Software for Ethical Odyssey

The rules provide the road map but the conscience directs the behaviour. A plethora of recommendations exist to comprehend the nuances and structural implications of reforms that have been undertaken to revise the rules. Still, there is no litmus test of human morals. The checklists, suggested by Peak and Blanchard, seems like a blueprint for ethical odyssey. The Nolon Committee's report, on standards in public life in UK, is an excellent document to develop the software aspect of ethics in government. The report identifies six characteristics in the midst of present-day ground realities of black money, abundant corruption, hedonistic culture and debasement of virtue ethics. The principles for public service standards, as enumerated in the Nolon Committee's report, are:

1. Integrity
2. Selflessness
3. Objectivity
4. Honesty
5. Accountability
6. Demonstrative Leadership

These ethical values in public life engender and strengthen a host of allied values or virtues known by different names. Some of them emanate from the core values which cris-cross the main highways of the road map.

An average public servant may get confused in selecting, pursuing and then moderating these core and secondary values. His or her judgement may be different from that of the society. Yet, an extrication is possible if the person makes a sincere attempt to opt for the right kind of core values. The ancillary values can be:

1. Commitment
2. Sensitivity
3. Righteousness
4. Justice
5. Fairness
6. Altruism
7. Accountability
8. Empathy
9. Compassion

The list can be longer. The real dilemma is that every code of ethics has to have intrinsic (self) regulation and extrinsic control of institutions. The former needs appeals and reiterations and the latter stresses upon core and quasi-judicial mechanisms. Both are being tried in India and both have proved equally ineffective. The cultural pollution blackens the clean laws of conscience, and the dirty men in administration require 'policing the police' or 'judging the judges'. Sin and crime can be viewed as two kinds of pervasive or ethical behaviours. Sinners should feel ashamed of their deeds and criminals need to be handled by the iron arm of the law. This plain truth everybody knows and perorates. The crux of the problem is how to make civil servants accountable for their sins and crimes of omission and commission in their public service career.

Every individual roughly knows that the civil service values in their ultimate analysis are ethical. Law can only make public servants aware of their duties and punishments, which generally hinder this self-awareness. Still, some people in every public service will be black sheep. They should not have been recruited, because the disciplinary codes cannot correct the 'congenitally unethicals'. Yet, as a practical measure, all governments indulge in this exercise of pinpointing lapses, assigning responsibility and accepting non-accountability as a last resort. Civil service values of higher order need to be inculcated, propagated and promoted at every level, but associating terror with their violation goes unnoticed by those who are habitual criminals and conscience evaders. Accountability, as a civil service value, is precious but the perennial issues are to whom, what for and how much.

Accountability: To Whom, What For and How Much?

Accountability, in a democratic political system, is the outcome of delegation of authority and responsibility which is made to public functionaries. It simply means that the official should render an account of one's action. It reflects the measurement of one's performance in terms of predetermined, well-understood and accepted standards. The implication is that the authority entrusted should be used effectively, impartially and honestly in consonance with the purpose stipulated. It is specifically legal, but the overreaching 'ethical question' is 'to whom are the public servants accountable, for what purpose and to what extent'. It requires identification of standards and evaluation mechanism at various levels of hierarchy. The macro and micro applications entail imagination, efforts and moral values to pinpoint accountability in each case.

Here, accountability gets confused with responsibility. Responsibility may be accepted as a moral precept, but accountability will imply punishment for default or misconduct. The code of public service prescribes characteristics: like sensitivity, responsiveness and transparency. These supporting pillars of legal accountability are basically ethical. Sensitivity is a psychological aptitude of empathy. It gives a sense of fairness and appreciation. Responsiveness is not succumbing to undue pressures. It implies a modicum of courtesy, which leads to attentiveness to other's problem. Transparency is regarded as a stimulus to good governance. Negatively, it can be viewed as an antidote to corrupt practices. In the absence of transparency, people attribute graft, venality, nepotism, cronyism and wrong doings in high places. It ultimately undermines the legitimacy of administrative authority. The administrative adage is that 'there is no authority without corresponding responsibility'. Even the judges owe it to society whether their authority to send people to gallows should be circumscribed by layers and levels of accountability. Delayed justice is a lesser evil than executing innocents in the name of procedural accuracies. Responsibility is the other side of authority and no public servant howsoever tall or wise can be allowed to use authority or power which has an inherent tendency to get corrupted when practised.

Accountability is a legalized version of this ethical obligation and all public servants, including judges, must accept this cognitional value of their conscience.

Responsibility: A Cognitional Obligation of Conscience

Different writers have conceptualized responsibility as:

1. specific accountability,
2. a causal phenomenon, and
3. an obligation as an ethical being.

The causal and consequential factors are relevant and decisive and render it different from answerability and accountability.

H.L.A. Hart, in his celebrated treatise *Punishment and Responsibility* (2008), classifies administrative responsibility into four categories:

1. Role responsibility
2. Liability responsibility
3. Culpability responsibility
4. Caused responsibility

Apparently, the cause, the culpability, the liability and role factors will fix accountability differently and even assign different kinds of punishments to those found guilty of dereliction of duty. The assigned responsibility has to be viewed differently from an assumed responsibility.

Donald W. Smithburg distinguishes between (a) obligation, (b) responsibleness, (c) accountability and (d) legitimacy. The first two may be called ethical but accountability is a juristic concept of punishments. One of the considerations in legitimacy may be accountability and the official may accept his or her moral responsibility. Similarly, mere legitimacy may not invoke any legal obligation.

In practice, all these meanings and shades or nuances overlap. They reinforce each other. In deeper connotation it means something, what one feels from within. In fact, responsibility, in behaviour, ultimately boils down to one's perception of right or wrong. It is a psychological perspective, a kind of cognitional value, or a reflection from within. Naturally, it gets linked up with the administrator's conscience, what Gandhiji called 'inner voice'. This ethical dimension of responsibility transforms legal duty into a Kantian imperative of conscience. Accountability may be to oneself or to society or to the organization, and in each case it becomes a quest for excellence or a search of eternal values of *dharma* or a reconciling value of conflicting interests in social situations. The men of law make a juristic difference between answerability, responsibility and accountability. But, a civilian without a right kind of value system may get away by evading individual answerability to collective responsibility. Then collective responsibility will be confused with moral responsibility and moral responsibility will have to be spelled out as legal accountability of damages or liabilities. The Hindi translation makes it *uttar* plus *dayitva* (उत्तरदायित्त्व). *Dayitva* is obligational and again the legal accountability gets merged into moral or ethical responsibility. The judges may have the satisfaction of deciding the 'onus' and quantum, but the 'intention' and 'will' parts of duty cannot be underscored in any accountability-responsibility syndrome of moral nature.

The public servants in India, may not like to indulge in academic debates or discussions, but even from a practical or field point of view, the concept of accountability in an organization gives a ladder of accountability. It can be arranged as under:

1. Policy accountability
2. Programme accountability
3. Process accountability
4. Probity and legal accountability

Whatever may be the model of government, public or corporate, the responsibility in governance will be explored with the fundamental question of 'legitimization of power' under a particular constitutional government. A government is a 'structure of responsibility' and the problem of citizen's responsibility for government is as important as is the justification of his or her obedience to government.

The legal-moral debate of accountability is an egg and hen conundrum. The public servant must face administrative enquiries, Public Interest Litigation (PIL), judicial action or judicial review and public audit including that of the CAG, so that his or her legal and moral role may be spelled out in terms of social change, which he or she seeks to catalyse.

Laws and rules guide the conscience of a public servant, which needs to be, so that he or she is strengthened in the enforcement of public law. The government must create conditions conducive for the attainment of this ultimate goal. If a public servant has the right kind of ethical values and aptitudes, the laws are only a guidance, but if he or she refuses to listen to his or her conscience, the laws must frighten him or her in terms of monetary loss, social ignominy and physical pain. Corruption, subjectivity, harassment, delays and evasion of laws are violations of Civil Conduct and Append (CCA) rules. Hence, the special institutions like Anti Corruption Bureau (ACB), Central Bureau of Investigation (CBI), Central Vigilance Commission (CVC), Lokpal, Lokayukta, etc. are needed. The public awareness and institutional traps keep the misguided people on track. But, the real answer is to strengthen the ethical values by education, exposure and putting inspiring examples before the juniors. The administrative climate promotes moral values and that is what stands wanting in the Indian milieu. This positive ethicization of public servants is called *communitarian ethics*. Jurgen Habermas, in his *Moral Consciousness and Communicative Action* (1990), argues that moral consciousness is not a mere appendix of social conventions, but is grounded in self-chosen ethical principles. The ethical demand does not always square with social demand, nor the ethical standards always coincide with the social standards. Man obeys an inner ideal, not to a social claim or a collective necessity. The ethical imperative comes not from around, but from within and above.

The Ethical Concerns in Public Service

The social status notion pertains to ethical concerns both in government departments and in private institutions, but the dilemmas are more serious in the former because the government seeks to serve and the citizen is not a tool or a mere labourer. The private organizations, even when they tend to promote production or enhance profit, cannot be oblivious to moral concerns. The dilemma in corporate governance can be somewhat eased by the fact that customer is free to choose or reject. But, in government service, the citizen has a little choice and may have to surrender his or her freedom, if the government servant opts to be unethical. If civil servants keep a respectable distance from people and overawe the citizens with their privileged positions, they are indulging in immoral malpractices for which no law can or should protect them. The modern theories of corporate governance extend their net in the name of social responsibility of business. Charity and philanthropy apart, the corporate world cannot be allowed to run a mad race on unethical tracks of business. The dilemmas in government may be more serious, yet the ethical concerns and issues are the same in both the enterprises. Some of them are:

(a) Should people suffer coercive structures of government and monopolistic freedoms of business which tend to violate the parameters of ethical norms?

(b) Should bureaucratic merit and corporate adventurism be permitted to manipulate situations detrimental to moral good of the people?

(c) Should power in government or money in business determine the nature of distributive justice, which constitutes the core of moral living?

These ethical concerns and considerations overweigh notions of law and innovation. Power and money shape social values and if bureaucracy and business are to provide contents to public service values in private and public sectors, then, the ethical values will confront a critical crisis in both. The present-day Indian scenario confirms and validates these hypotheses. The Indian society, and for that matter all societies, are increasingly degenerating into corruption, violence, disintegration and anomie, because the unethical values of crude power and monetary greed are threatening the higher values of social harmony and family affection.

The Administrative Rules and Discretionary Ethics

The civil service ethics codifies the norms of work and workers into laws, rules and procedures. The rationale was to introduce uniformity, permanence and similarity in behaviours and relationships. The code of public servants, called as CCA rules, prescribe the 'dos and don'ts' and thereby clarify the duty ethics, which an employee should keep in mind before acting. He/she should be loyal, honest and objective in his/her decisions. The rules objectify the dictates of his conscience, what Kant will call the 'categorical imperatives'. The laws and rules may seemingly be violative of the moral order but at a deeper and higher level they express the 'real will of the public servant' and 'general will of the society' as a whole. Naturally, therefore, the law offers an ethical guidance and the civil servant may interpret the rules and procedures according to his/her conscience. At higher levels of public service it is called 'discretionary ethics'. There is no specific or well-defined law to which the conscience of the public servant should respond. He/she is a rational being. His/her administrative laws must conform to the higher law of the land, i.e. the constitution. The rule of law conventions of UK, as Dicey defines, is 'the customary law' which represents the collective wisdom or conscience of the community. Green calls it 'the common consciousness of the common good'.

Law, Morality and Conscience

Thus, the laws and morality in an idealist political philosophy represent two sides of the same coin. Laws, rules and procedures make the working conscience practical for purposes of accountability. Notwithstanding the minor contradictions, it is safer and more correct for a public servant to follow the laws and rules. Conformity to laws and procedures makes the civil servants politically neutral and professionally competent. It also helps in maintaining the high standards of personal integrity and probity. It reminds about the value system for nation-building. The laws and rules emanate from the higher constitutional law of the land. The civil servants have a special responsibility to promote a culture of excellence, probity in public conduct and concern for social equity. The cardinal maxim of ethics is 'be good and do good'. This applies to all realms whether personal, governmental or professional. In a governance system, ethics becomes a multi-dimensional phenomenon. It encompasses (a) legality of public action, (b) rationality in policy decisions and (c) ensuring responsibility and accountability of public action. Ethical rightness of rules strengthens the end work commitment, spurs excellence and promotes fusion of individuals' pursuit of personal and public goals. Ethical action nurtures resilience, exhibits compassion and safeguards the spirit of justice. The ideal of dedication makes a civil servant transparent and his integrity of character feels rewarded. The senior civil servants underline this integrity in a wide connotation, wherein it includes:

(a) Intellectual honesty.
(b) Free and frank expression of views.
(c) A scientific temper of mind.
(d) A high degree of objectivity.
(e) A powerful sense of justice.

More laws or less rules and the conscience of man in human affairs shall always play a role in ethical decisiveness. Even corporate world believes that strong political will, radical legislation, greater transparency, civic awareness, alert media, a vigorous civil society and idealistic businessmen can do wonders to create a moral climate in the social order.

Conscience is the Brush, that Paints the Laws

All discussions of law focus on principles of morality outside human conscience. It is something that determines the morality of human actions. Conscience is a special act of the mind that comes into being when the intellect passes judgement on the goodness or badness of a particular act. It is a practical judgement on particular and concrete human actions. From an ethical perspective, a conscience is judgemental – an act of the intellect. It is not a feeling or an emotion, but an intellectual decision. It is also a decision with a view to a particular action. Conscience can make a practical judgement on the morality of a past or future action.

The conscience is different from law. Law states a *general* rule concerning actions whereas conscience lays down a *practical* rule for specific action. Conscience applies the law or rule to specific actions, therefore, it is wider than law. Some say that conscience is to law, what a brush is to paint. Conscience is quite similar to completion of the ego identity, whereby 'every ego is, in some sense a code of ethics'. If ego and conscience are similar or identical, people have the capacity of determining the meaning of a particular action, past or present, and at the same time assess the morality of that action. Both approaches involve reflection, assessing meaning as well as morality. The individuals use conscience to apply the law to a particular action. The teleologist may not admit application of a particular law to give meaning or morality to an action, but this process involves application of 'a set of value commitments' developed by human beings from childhood. In practice, both schools use the same process but with different tools. The moral decisions may be different, but since both approaches involve the same human reason, moral judgements will often be the same.

Conscience Classified

It is argued that human beings can have different kinds of conscience, such as:

1. *A true conscience* means that judgement is in accordance with fact. The judgement is a correct or accurate application of law to the action.
2. *An erroneous conscience* when the judgement is false – the practical judgement incorrectly applies law to the action. The erroneous judgement can be vincibly or invincibly false, and is identical with ignorance.
3. *A certain, doubtful or probable conscience:* A conscience is certain when the judgement on the morality of an action is without prudent fear of error. Prudent fear of error does not involve metaphysical certainty, but generally a normal person has no doubts about the judgement. That certainty can apply to both a correct and an erroneous conscience. A conscience is doubtful when the judgement does not exclude prudent fear of error. The person is aware of some doubts about the practical judgement to be made. A conscience can be both doubtful and erroneous at the same time. A judgemental conscience is a probable conscience when the judgement 'almost' excludes the prudent fear of error. A normal person is almost certain that the judgement is correct, even though it may be erroneous.

The principles that govern the conscience are that a person must take reasonable care to ensure a correct conscience. He or she is bound to follow a certain conscience even if that conscience is false. For example, if somebody is certain that it is morally right to lie to save another's life, he or she is bound to lie. It is ethically not correct to act on a doubtful conscience. Vincible ignorance is no excuse – the person must make some effort to resolve the doubt. If such efforts fail, the principle *lex dubia non obligat* ('a doubtful law does not bind'), comes into play.

If the law is doubtful, then, the administrator can apply any of the principles that appeal him or her the most. A law is doubtful and does not bind when there is more probable evidence in favour of liberty than against it. This is probabilism. A second version of probabilism states that the person may follow an option in favour of liberty, provided the evidence in favour of liberty is solidly probable, even though the evidence against liberty is more probable. Another version of probabilism, known as *equiprobabilism*, states that the person may follow an opinion in favour of liberty if the evidence on both sides is equally balanced. The principle implicit in compensationalism to pinpoint accountability has to be based on the facts that the person has as considered the evidence not only favouring and opposing liberty but also (1) the gravity of the law, (2) the reason for acting against the law, (3) the inconvenience arising from the strict interpretation of the law and (4) the justness of the cause for selecting the option offering most liberty.

Accountability Obligation to Educate Conscience

Some laws may be doubtful and provide options for people. They serve as additional guidelines to the principles of conscience. But the final question on conscience is: whether there is an additional obligation for people according to their state in life or educational status to have correct consciences. Are public administrators bound to educate their consciences according to the responsibilities they have? It is a moot question because conscience cannot have a hierarchy of values. Management means getting things done right. Here, the argument is that getting things done right is only one side of the coin. Management also involves getting the right thing done in a right manner. But what is the right or ethical thing to do? If public servants must not only do things right but also do what is right, they have an obligation to educate their consciences according to their state in life. This includes not only management theory and practice but also ethical theory and practice. If managers do not do both, they run the risk of not only being outdated but also of neglecting true managerial responsibility. If administrators are educators and teachers, they must learn both aspects of the job. In educating and updating the conscience, the two extremes need to be avoided. One is not caring about conscience at all – making no effort to learn what is right or what is wrong, or perhaps showing no interest in right and wrong. Some public managers exhibit this characteristic. There are some public servants who fit this description. Both the extremes may be in accordance with the concept of conscience, which involves a practical judgement on the morality of human action.

Besides reliance on the nature of an action, its consequences and purpose, laws, rules and conscience provide guidance in determining what is right and what is wrong. However, in spite of the help that laws, rules and conscience may provide to a public administrator, they do not guarantee infallible judgement. While laws and rules would seem to be a deontologically sound frame of reference in making ethical decisions, there may be many flaws. The teleological approach acknowledges that there are too many civil laws, rules, regulations, court decisions and opinions governing almost everything, including ethical decision. It is virtually impossible for a public administrator to know all the laws or rules. However, a framework for understanding civil laws, rules and regulations is needed by linking them with natural law and human reason. The conscience framework can provide a basis for ethical decision-making. The end result is far from perfect, but at least it offers a starting point.

From virtue perspective, if conscience and ego represent the same, there are flaws resulting from the interpretations or decisions of what is right and what is wrong. There is no doubt that reflection on the meaning of an action is an important factor in determining its morality. Rather than the public administrator attempting to understand all the laws, rules, regulations, court decisions and opinions, the virtue approach may be the one to apply in discretionary decision-making. This may not always satisfy top management, but it is not without a solid philosophical support and practical merit. But, regardless of whether public administrators follow a deontological or a teleological approach, thinking, reasoning and reflection must occur. Otherwise, there is no way to enforce accountability ethics on administrators for their actions. In considering what is right and what is wrong, public administrators have at their disposal information (1) on the nature of the action performed or about to be performed, (2) the circumstances surrounding the action, and (3) the purpose of the action.

A review of these three factors can make the administrator conscious about his obligation or his ethics of accountability. The fear of punishment by law protects this obligation. In government offices legal ethics is stressed, so that accountability ethics may *ipso facto* be protected. The law, morality and conscience trio, which a civil servant personifies, guards public funds. Every penny that comes and goes out of the treasury has to be accounted for. Utilization of public money has to be certified and frauds, embezzlement and corrupt practices need to be punished. This converts conscience into law and many good intentioned public servants do not utilise assigned and sanctioned public funds to avoid or escape the procedures of accountability. It has created a new problem of 'Accountability of Non-utilization of Public Funds' in several development departments of the government.

The Corporate Accountability

The business leaders in corporate sector all over the world are surrounded with questionable policies and moral practices. The instances are many. The setting up of the Treadway Committee in USA (1987) and the Cadbury Committee in UK (1991) prove the point. There were rampant cases of exploiting of minority shareholders, siphoning of funds, blatant violations of laws, non-compliance of rules/laws, surreptitious dealings and inadequate non-disclosures. On the initiative of Confederation of Indian Industries (CII) in 1996, the Desirable Code of Good Governance was framed in 1998, followed by the Kumaramangalam Birla Committee (1999) recommendations.

Scandals in number of countries, especially the United States, triggered reforms in corporate governance, accounting practices and disclosures, the world over. The provisions of some of the reform acts include: (i) creation of the 'Public Company Accounting Oversight Board' to monitor auditors, (ii) independence of auditors, and (iii) corporate governance.

One dominant driver of this changing business-society relationship is globalization. It offers a point where international relations and corporate governance meet. Here, the international relations determine the ethical parameters of national economy. Ever since India joined the global markets and the economy got opened to retail foreign trade, a floodgate of scams and scandles has taken over the operations of corporate funding. Money laundering and international investments have polluted the administrative ethos of probity and integrity.

It has given rise to what is called 'corporate social responsibility' (CSR) in India also. The CSR concept is developing its ethical norms and codes through a variety of institutions. Its four specific models have been championed by eminent ethicists like (1) Mahatma Gandhi, (2) Pandit Nehru, (3) Milton Friedman, and (4) Edward Freeman, respectively:

1. The first model is totally ethical, which talks of voluntary commitment by private companies likes of Birlas and Bajajs, to public welfare.
2. The second model can be called statist, wherein the state ownership and legal requirements determine corporate responsibilities.
3. The third model advocates that corporate responsibilities should remain limited to private owners, i.e. the shareholders of the companies.

4. The fourth model requires the market to respond to the needs of stakeholders, customers, employees and communities.

The post-globalization model of Freeman replaces the shareholders' interest model by corporate philanthropy of stakeholders. India has a long and commendable heritage of corporate philanthropy. Community service, as a part of the business culture, is also being welcomed by modern multi-national corporations (MNCs), who want to take community service as a non-profit business collaboration. Commenting upon CSR, James Campell of North West Minnesota Bank writes: 'There is something magical here, a feeling of giving back to the community and making everyone's life better. It is an ingrained expectation.'

The PPP Accountability

Various Indian companies, trusts or NGOs or developmental agencies, are working to make villages self-sufficient, provide livelihoods to the villagers and develop sustainable partnerships with communities. The Corporate Social Responsibility in India is a multi-stakeholder approach. This is partly because NGOs are not well-organized and partly because the corporate understanding of CSR policy does not include the participation of civil society. The new concept of Private Public Partnership (PPP) accountability as a joint or shared notion of accountability ethics, is yet to develop in post-Liberalized, Privatized and Globalized (LPG) India. As the trends are irreversible, the PPP models should work out ethics compatibility in the two.

Democracy, whether in government or in corporate world is another name for public accountability. Electoral system makes the political rulers responsible and accountable to people for their laws and policies. The corporate world enjoys Darwinism but in public administration the responsibility and accountability are legal and judicial. The rules and regulations are adhered to, so that responsibility may not get evaded. Nonetheless, no government servant can be acquitted just because he does not know his moral responsibility. To make it more specific, coercive and punishable, the juristic procedures are resorted to and civil servants are punished for violation of rules and laws. This is accountability which is moral as well as legal.

The accountability ethics in government is underlined in varied ways of procedures and hierarchical accountability to seniors and ministers. ACR is one way to ensure this accountability for which both the senior and junior are made morally responsible. Transparency promotes ethical accountability and participation and social audits are the mechanisms to ensure responsibility in terms of legal accountability. Developmental budgets make this responsibility grave and enormous. The methods to avoid accountability, including the non-utilization of public funds are regarded as immoral as embezzling public funds.

The level of monitoring of CSR being low, most of the companies do not even publish their annual CSR report. The Gandhian notion of 'ethical trusteeship' continues to be on the CSR agenda. Liberalization, privatization and globalization as keynotes of new international economic order have now come to stay. The world market has its healthy and unhealthy impacts on Indian economy and politics. The civil servants in India have an opportunity to exploit these developments for national good but the selfish and unethical use of these opportunities has added to corruption. The exploitation of these opportunities by corporate sector is being welcomed as growth and development.

The nation-states in the world comity of nations are not equally developed materially as well as ethically. The superpowers are and will exploit the middle-range powers in open competition as is the situation today. But, the ethical situation in scientifically advanced countries is forcing business to be more ethical. Former CEO of Microsoft, Bill Gates and Bono, an Irish singer and businessman, are donating their wealth for the welfare of African society. This is capitalism in reverse. Actually, it is the result of the disintegration of family system in the West. The citizen's welfare is replacing family welfare and succession of property and wealth needs a change in inheritance laws there. The affluent businessmen want to do justice to their stakeholders rather than leaving a fortune for their biological progeny. This development, coupled with advances of technology and connectivity revolution, widens the frontiers of family loyalty. The parochialism is yielding place to universalism of the international era which is creating a 'world without borders'. It can be termed as an 'ethical revolution' of business values, transforming the profit motto into a service mission of business. As this globalization gets stabilized and the family loyalty becomes weaker in the urban industrial economy of India, the feminist revolution will have its impact on corrupt familial practices of Indian society. As the sanctity of the institution of marriage declines in India, the family values will change the perspectives on property and inheritance of wealth. The corporate capitalism and the nucleus family will contribute to the dawn of new values of possession, greed and inheritance. Hopefully, it will revise the 'over-familial values' of an agricultural society into societal values of equitability, equity and gender justice.

Thus, from the distrust of non-gazetted public servants to the socio-ethical responsibility of business managements, there is a wide area of ethical debates and disputes in a plural society of India's size and diversities. The historical legacies, howsoever obnoxious, cannot be wished away. The ethical behaviours of ruling servants are to be regulated by the laws but their conscience also needs to be aroused in matters that pertain to the masses. A democratic government will have to be accountable and hence a public servant has to be alive to his or her ethical concerns, inherent in the operations of good governance. The funding of development by national and global corporations is a necessity of the future. A brilliant civil servant should visualize this distant future, stay away from the status feudalism of the past, meticulously follow the laws of governance and also that of his or her conscience. It shall keep him or her accountable in the PPP global economy of the country.

Accountability of Non-Utilization of Public Funds

Development administration in India in the earlier years used to starve for funds. Now a days, surprisingly it has a spate of unutilized resources sanctioned under various schemes, projects and plans. It can be called highly unethical to get these funds sanctioned by competent authorities and then permitting them to lapse unused. The concept of audit being too legal and too narrow, either there is a colossal waste of public funds or there are several departments which leave the public funds unspent. The civil servant has a moral responsibility to spend these public funds as desired by Planning Commission or the Parliament. There are several undefined pockets of discretion in the rules and the discretionary unaccountability represents an unethical practice in the non utilization of public funds, particularly when it is resorted to avoid audit.

Government departments have the practice to pass on money in the form of grants to non-government organizations (NGOs). Revenue expenditure is only for current or ongoing expenditure. The capital expenditure generally results in the creation or acquisition of assets. In budget, the expenditure is separately shown for individual items like pay, daily allowance (DA), travel allowance (TA), office consumables, conveyance, office rent, telephone bill and a host of other contingencies. The full utilization of sanctioned funds or achieving the financial targets of a scheme is important. Actually the utilization of funds is the first indicator of a scheme's performance. Unutilized funds mean that financial targets of the scheme have not been met. This emphasis is being shifted to project outcomes from physical targets. The implementing agencies have to utilize the funds fully within the prescribed time limit, (usually 31st March) for the purposes for which they are intended.

The state ratio of expenditure is usually around 20 per cent to 30 per cent in Centrally Sponsored Schemes (CSS), the states cannot afford it. Central Ministries tend to formulate schemes with the same all-India pattern without allowing for regional or state variations. The financial approvals of schemes get delayed. In many schemes like mid day meals and hostels, costs are estimated on per unit per head basis. In an inflationary situation, such unit costs escalate, and it becomes difficult to operate the programme. A major difficulty in social sector schemes, arises from inadequate staff and lack of project planning and management skills.

The Rangarajan Committee examined this mode of transfer of funds from the Centre to implementing agencies for various programmes. The funds are transferred in two ways (1) the treasury mode and (2) the society mode. In the treasury mode, these funds are sent to states through the Reserve Bank of India (RBI). The state governments transfer funds to District Rural Development Agencies (DRDAs), Panchayati Raj Institutions (PRIs), Non Government Organizations (NGOs) and other Implementing Agencies (IAs). In the society mode the central ministries transfer funds directly to IAs – DRDAs, PRIs and NGOs and others.

The unutilized funds according to rules have to be surrendered to the finance department every year and they are not made available to the concerned agencies or programmes in the ensuing year. Naturally, the unfinished plan budgets, whether at the centre or in states, are seldom fully utilized. This is particularly the case in social sector programmes which have a vital bearing on human development index. Generally, the large, capital intensive sectors are able to utilize their plan budgets fully. These expenditures consist mostly of a small number of relatively lumpy items. In contrast to such sectors, social programmes are unable to utilize funds speedily. The social sectors include education, health and family welfare, water supply and sanitation, social security and welfare, and nutrition. The inability of the state governments, to utilize the available funds fully in the central schemes, is due to systemic weaknesses in the government apparatus in social sectors across many states. Moreover the rigidity in the norms, guidelines and unit costs that govern the Central schemes, lack fiscal decentralization from Centre to states.

The Central Plan Monitoring Committee (CPMC) has recently set up its portal which integrates tens of thousands of implementing agencies through a common system and tracks fund movement at successive stages, starting with the initial till the money actually reaches to the ultimate beneficiaries. The Comptroller and Auditor General (CAG) reports and other studies have revealed many problems of fund utilization. The purpose of fund utilization is to realize value for money, and achieve the programme objectives. Achievement of these objectives depends on provision of facilities, inputs and services. Physical targets of programmes are necessary but not sufficient for achieving their ultimate goals. As a result, there is considerable emphasis in recent times on the final outcome of the programmes. Expenditures on all public funds have to be properly accounted for and have to go through the audit of the Comptroller and Auditor General. Major irregularities which emerge are also examined by parliamentary committees. The Comptroller and Auditor General of India is the head of the Supreme Audit Institution of India (SAI). The CAG is the sole auditor of the accounts of the Central Government and the State Governments.

The CAG examines various aspects of government expenditure. The conduct of audit is done on the basis of accounts, vouchers and records. This audit may be a regularity audit (compliance) or performance audit. Performance audit assesses: (a) economy (b) efficiency, and (c) effectiveness. The CAG examines and certifies the Finance Accounts and the Appropriation Accounts of the Centre and the states. The Parliament and State Legislatures have constituted specialized committees like the Public Accounts Committee and the Committee on Public

Undertakings (COPU), to whom CAG's audit reports and annual accounts automatically stand referred. The government servants have to follow the canons of this financial propriety.

It restrains the misuse of public funds. But keeping the funds unutilized and then allowing them to lapse is also an unethical practice of avoiding accountability. Public funds are a fiduciary trust for public good. The civil servants who avoid this accountability may not get legally punished but they commit a moral lapse of accountability by being non-functional. Not to act as civil servant can be called as immoral as violating the law codes of departments.

CHAPTER 8

Probity in Governance

Instrumentalities to Curb Unethical Action

The Chamber's Dictionary defines 'probity' as 'an act of deep investigation undertaken in search of truth'. Father Bulke has translated it into Hindi as 'इमानदारी' or 'सत्यनिष्ठा'. *Iman* in Urdu language will imply a religious conviction to one's own conscience. So, when Mahatma Gandhi wrote his *My Experiments with Truth*, he started from the premise that 'God is Truth' but towards the end of his exploration, he concluded that 'Truth is God'. One may interpret this experience or experiment as an objective approach, and a rationalist secular way of exploring the mystical phenomenon, called God. Gandhi was a great theist but his God was the truth. This 'truth' (सत्य) for which he had a devotional commitment made him a religious person whose conscience was coiled by all sorts of politically poisonous snakes involved in the mundane struggles for power. *'Imandari'* or *'satyanistha'* costed him his life, but the moral of his life story is that the 'truth' does not dawn, it has to be discovered. People will always violently disagree with you or with one another, but resisting them non-violently makes the truth triumph. 'सत्यमेव जयते' is not a moral euphemism. It is an ethical precept and one must assert and fight for it (सत्याग्रह) religiously with the courage of conviction, i.e. निष्ठा, which he calls an article of faith.

The students and practitioners of public administration instantly jump at the definitions of morality and catalogue a long list of virtues or codes to manufacture the moral man. From Weber to McGregor, every blind man has defined his proverbial elephant in perceptional segments. They all are correct, yet, all of them can be called wrong, because ethics defies definitions. Cooper will say, 'Morality involves the ultimate ends, while ethics may be confused with right rules of conduct or professional standards'. Others may maintain that 'probity requires inquiry and contemplation about truth, which may question the adequacy and meaning of proposed action suggested by the senior officials'. Gibson Winter raises a controversy, when he writes, 'Ethics must look to the future, because it concerns with the goodness and rightness of civil servants, doing and deciding.' A public official may judge the past but the future may revise it for new possibilities. Administrators have to draw a line, what ought to be allowed and what should be prohibited. Hence, in order to be moral, an administrator must engage himself or herself in the process of:

1. examining and questioning the standards in the light of which administrative decisions are made;
2. relating with the social concerns and organizational goals and reflecting a commitment to these goals;
3. adapting to the changes in the environment; and
4. preparing to be held responsible and accountable for the decisions made in the individual and professional capacities.

The Code of Conduct and Hierarchy of Controls

This will require detailed rules and procedures to legislate the moral action. The codes of conduct exist in all governments but they are given meaning while in operation by those seniors who preside over their small kingdom of morality as chieftains. They are wise people and more rational than their juniors but this does not imply that they are more moral than their juniors in hierarchy. Hence, the consensus in bureaucracy is that these codes are only the guidelines. The moral code, according to Kathrin Denhardt, is one which must serve as a norm of behaviour and according to which fresh entrants in the service can be counselled. It must serve as a comprehensible guide for everyday behaviour at the workplace, a standard on which sanctions could be based and by which behaviours could be evaluated; and ultimately it must also serve as a tool of administrative control.

The juniors will never accept this kind of a moral code which the seniors would like to use as a tool of administrative control. Their argument will be that certain moral norms like honesty, truthfulness, discipline, fairness, tolerance, justice, etc. are a part of the moral order of administrative society and the administrative code of ethics has to be based on them. To say that it is impossible to agree on a basic moral foundation, leaves public servants without any ethical guidance for solving their decisional problems and they become free to operate in a state of confusion, ambiguity and amorality. Here, the intention is not to evolve some static and never-changing moral standards for all times. The broad moral order may remain the same but the understanding and interpretations of these standards must change with time. The junior may opt for a more local ethics. These ethical relativists detest rigid codification of morals since they believe in 'situationism' and are not in favour of universality of ethical standards. The anti-foundationalists and post-modernists are also in the same league, but for different reasons. They do not recommend any long-term ethical codes. They believe that such meta-narratives marginalize concepts of difference and otherness. The crucial issue is: Can probity in governance be practised by separating morality from the hierarchical discipline. An Annual Confidential Report (ACR) is an instrument of evaluation of work and the worker both.

But should it be viewed as a tool of control of the juniors in organizational hierarchy? This latter view hierarchies the very notion of morality as being more moral and less moral. The senior has a right to control, but he or she may be morally much inferior to his or her junior, whom he or she finds immoral because of his or her indisciplined behaviour.

ACR for Work Performance or Worker Excellence

It will be argued that all indiscipline in administration is not immoral. The right to protest and organize unions is a moral right against the coercive authority of the seniors. Hence, the philosophical basis of governance is legal and mere submissive and obedient juniors cannot be called moral. The seniors and juniors both have to ponder over and probe into what should be the acceptable contents of this code. Probity will demand acceptance of the code of conduct but a mere imposition of rules in the name of conformity or discipline will make probity debatable.

The administrative concepts like efficiency, neutrality, integrity, objectivity, commitment and compassion are nebulous and inclusive terms, which even a church father cannot define or still less, prescribe. A judge also sees their meanings only in a legal framework and his or her judgments are subject to be challenged or revised in appeals. The administrator being an executive controller is on a more shaky ground. In a military situation this may be justified in the all-absorbing morality of national security but a civil government cannot enforce a moral code of conduct as a tool of discipline. The civil servants have to be persuaded to accept a moral code but forcing them to be morally free will be regarded as a contradiction in terms.

The British rule used morality, probity and integrity almost interchangeably. The senior British civil servants then had a very special responsibility to promote a 'culture of excellence' in the colony. Today, the employees at the junior ladders of bureaucracy expect it the other way round. The seniors do not know how to motivate their teams and take recourse to legal actions without any passion for excellence and compassion for the weak, the poor and the disadvantaged. Naturally, therefore, accountability, commitment to social justice and responsiveness to people's problems are at a very low ebb. Moral exhortations and fear of damaging ACRs cannot foster effective work culture and result orientations as required. The bureaucratic apparatus, which is extremely conscious of its status position, keeps the juniors and citizens disempowered and even insulated from social audit. The concept of public service in a democratic government and society needs a metamorphosis in the very notion of probity, which is more a matter of sharing rather than imposing. The very idea of senior-junior dichotomy and the former controlling the moral character of the latter, is highly degrading and is inconsistent with the philosophical basis of governance and probity. The junior is a colleague and, as in the West, the senior cannot be a custodian of his or her moral conduct. The way the senior public servant in our country perpetrates this superiority notion through code of conduct is violative of the moral culture of administration. In India, character certificates are asked as a ritual before one enters into a government job and everybody for sure knows that a notary public sells them for a petty pittance. Moral guardianship of public servants through control mechanisms has rendered them irresponsible. No wonder corruption increases and more and more controlling instrumentalities are resorted to. The result has been that public servants enjoy 'politician-bashing' and 'senior-ridiculing' in the secretariats as their pleasant pastime. As imposing probity in the conduct of millions and millions of junior functionaries is simply unpractical or a problem unsurmountable, it will be worthwhile to think about their replacement by non-career part-time workers, who will be more controllable and much more ethical to justify the rationale of public service without organized trade unions. Providing more jobs to more educated people, particularly housewives in all age groups, will serve the moral purpose. It will protect the integrity of senior public servants and that of the junior staff also, without any legal code of conduct, or an ACR because of which the seniors are presently accused of abusing their junior ones as menials or mere domestic servants.

Probity in administration, is generally confused with a fight against corruption. But from an ethical angle it needs a strategy to transform the system. A three pronged attack upon the malignant system of administration can make the dent to make people realise that things are changing. The strategic planning must include:

1. An informed and empowered citizenry widely participating in transparent administration.
2. A strong instrumentality of law to curb corruption and malpractices with an iron hand.
3. A new kind of work culture, assuring quality of work life and efficient service delivery to the people at the cutting edge.

This kind of positive, negative and long range strategies can cumulatively cleanse the system and enhance probity.

Transparency as Probity in Administration

This raises a natural demand and a need to democratize Indian bureaucracy at lower levels of hierarchy. The government is also realizing, though somewhat reluctantly, that secrecy in public administration should be minimized and transparency should be encouraged to induct participation of people in administration. It will empower the citizens and will also prove to be the surest road to probity.

Transparency is a key characteristic in any democratic working. The political rulers must fight elections on the basis of transparent facts and the civil servants should be punished, if they abuse their discretion under the garb of secrecy. The Official Secrets Act of 1923, made information and knowledge of government policies, rules, regulations, decisions, accounts and discretionary acts inaccessible to people. Naturally, the citizens were unable to obtain justice at the hands of manipulative and 'intelligent' bureaucrats. This Act was a replica of the British Act as amended in 1920. The provisions of the section 5 of the Act were so comprehensive that almost all information about the government could qualify to be categorized as an official secret. The worst was that the words 'secret' or 'official secret' were not even defined in the Act, thus giving a lot of leeway to civil servants to interpret the provisions of the law to their defence. This Act was thus a convenient smokescreen to deny the public a legitimate access to government information.

During the late 1990s and early part of the 21st century, legislative measures were adopted by several states, such as Rajasthan, Tamil Nadu, Maharashtra and Goa, as Right to Information Acts at the state level, which paved the way for enforcing transparency in the administrative system. Consequently, the Freedom to Information Act, 2002, was enacted which enabled a common man to have access to the records of the central and state governments and other authorities established by or under the Constitution and by any law made by the appropriate government and include any other body owned, controlled or substantially financed by funds, provided directly or indirectly, by the appropriate government.

Later on, the 'freedom' to information was converted into 'right' to information. To distinguish this, the legislation had to be upgraded into the Right to Information (RTI) Act of 2005. Presently, there are several pockets of resistance in the administrative system against this legal measure, but as time passes, this new component will become an integral part of administrative culture of the country. Perhaps no other innovation in administration has such a phenomenal potentiality of positivism as does this Right to Information. There is an inverse correlation between transparency and corruption and the hope is that with an increasing stress on transparency, people's control over the governance will be augmented and, in this process, corruption will be mitigated.

The acceptance of this idea in the non-government sector will cover all sections of society, such as private companies, corporations and firms, trade unions, non-government organizations (NGOs) and voluntary agencies like trusts, associations and organizations, including the bodies of professionals, and so on, whether owned or controlled by the government or by private individuals and institutions. By this piece of legislation, India has entered into an age of authenticity in public affairs, which will help the sustenance of respectable levels of integrity in public life.

A large number of fresh entrants to public services in India implicitly accept that they want to gain power, wealth and status. Values and morality do not count much for a large number of aspirants. Resultantly, even the component of values in the training does not have any impact on their mindset. Devoid of ethics, the public service to them is an instrument of unbridled lust for money and power. Transparency will not only frighten them but will also force them to introspect about the probity component in their lives and careers.

Probity through RTI

Transparency means minimum secrecy or making the maximum information public. Mere legislation is not enough. Its genuine enforcement requires a will on the part of the state, a willingness on the part of administrators and an initiative, coupled with courage, on the part of citizens themselves. The state machinery should be ready to punish those civil servants who obstruct the implementation of RTI Act. Their age-old orientation to treat every information as 'secret' must give way to greater openness and transparency in public affairs. This would require a transformation of the mindset of administrators at all levels, more particularly at the cutting-edge level, of the administration.

Citizens, once awakened, must share information and create a network of information systems in a knowledge society, which may, in turn, bring a moral pressure on administration to respect people's desires and aspirations. Thus, transparency through RTI in administration means

1. information gathering,
2. information sharing,
3. information networking,
4. information exposing scams and scandals, and
5. information participation and social audit.

In simple words, it is the beginning of a democratic administration. Informed people are aware and aroused. In place of being afraid of officials, they frighten them and make them public-oriented. The age-old alibi that people do not deserve and the misuse of the RTI might spell disaster is a deliberate and mischievous lie. The democratic governance of last 65 years has exposed the conspiratorial nature of this elitist argument.

The undeserving people of India have become more deserving with this right to information sharing, because a demand for popular participation and social audit has alerted the bureaucracy to be responsive. The media, the NGOs, the political parties and a host of other pressure groups have come forward and the erring bureaucrats are being brought to the book every day.

The Culture of Accountability

Transparency in administration makes public service 'civil' and accountable. The accountability ethics makes democratic administration responsive and sensitive. People may continue to have their grievances but the administrator has to be civil, accessible and smiling. Transparency generates information and information sharing creates an ethos of citizen participation in the day-to-day functioning of the administrative agencies. Gradually, it becomes a popular force and the demands of social audit become irresistible. All administrative activities and transactions need legal screening. If administration confronts social audit, it may strengthen the hands of senior administrators, who are honest and hardworking.

The information transformation, coupled with computer and cyber networking, is popularly called as the 'revolution of connectivity'. It has linked government with millions and millions of people in an unprecedented manner. It has inadvertently given birth to an allied revolution, known as 'revolution of rising expectations'. These expectations may be false or phony, but they have to be there, if people are to be aroused and activated in the field. There are two ways to activise people or making them partners in the running of administration:

1. *The Right to Information:* It implies an active citizenry which should knock at the gates of the Information Commission or the government office, where an information officer will have to provide him or her an authentic piece of information, on the basis of which he or she may move to the court and make the government pay compensation for the damages or the liabilities caused by public officials.
2. *The Citizen Charter:* It lets the citizen know his or her rights vis-à-vis the administration at the cutting edge or in the field. Here, the government supplies the information even which it is not asked for or desired by the citizen. The administration at its own should come forward and educate people what their rights are and what they can demand from a civil administrator as a part of their rights – civil or human. The government organizations are being asked to prepare and put these citizen charters for public display and anybody who visits these offices or officers for any reason, may know what are the duties of administration as a corollary of his or her right of citizenship. For instance, a suspect person in police custody has a right to ask for a seat, a glass of water or a daily newspaper to read, if he or she had to wait for his or her turn in a police station. This is mere civility or courtesy

which must not be viewed as a violation of police authority. These citizen charters in banks, post offices and railway/bus stations, etc. should inform the citizen at the cutting edge that he or she has a right to be helped rather than harâssed by power and status-hungry babus of bureaucracy. The office procedures and delivery systems of service should be explained in writing so that citizens may know where to go and what is to be asked for. The unwanted harassment, the callousness of attitude, extortions and corruption in the delivery of service should be minimized by time-bound schedules or calendars. This information service by a democratic government is a facilitation and it can go a long way to protect citizens from the horrifying tyranny of 'babudom', so notoriously practised in the district administration and below.

Public administration during the British days ruled over Indians as subjects. The civil servant was the representative of the British royalty and people of the colony were not citizens. They were supposed to obey and follow rather than to participate or suggest. Naturally, administration had its own elitist or ruling ethics, governed by the senior officials or rules and regulations framed by the alien government. Today, when the Republican Constitution of India assures liberty, equality and justice to every citizen without distinctions of colour, caste, sex or creed, the citizen has a right to know that who is violating the spirit of the Constitution and where should he or she go for an appeal or redressal of grievances.

Moreover, the Constitution guarantees the dignity of the individual to every citizen in its preamble. The citizen has a right to protect his or her dignity and the administration has a corresponding duty to let the citizen know why has his or her dignity in question been outraged. The contempt of the citizen is a more critical question than the contempt of the government or the law courts.

This shift in constitutional paradigm has to be understood by the administration of the country. The RTI and the citizen charters are not just paper assurances. The law is making concrete institutional arrangements so that the people of India may know, understand and act for the achievement of the constitutional goals through their active and effective participation. Again, this participation, like an electoral mandate, has to be meaningful. The cry for social audit, howsoever elusive and abusive it may be, is a democratic imperative of the Constitution, which can be called legal as well as ethical.

Dignity through Participation and Empowerment

Popular participation and social audit are nowadays called as pillars of democratic bureaucracy. Adult suffrage has introduced wholesale democracy in Indian politics and people are effectively participating in elective bodies at national, state and village levels. Notwithstanding the minor aberrations and malfunctionings, our political democracy has singular and spectacular achievements to its credit. But then, we have relatively achieved much less in democratizing our bureaucracy. Perhaps, it was necessary in early years to balance the social system from political subversion. But, now, when the socio-economic foundations have become strengthened, it is high time to associate people with public service administration and empower them to perform social audit of these institutions at every level. This democratization of public bureaucracy implies the following:

1. The bureaucratic pyramid must be pluralized at the apex with the association of committees, consisting of representatives from all walks of public life.
2. The civil servants misbehaving, neglecting and harassing people by showing their superiority or authority must be legally punished.
3. The polite culture of reception offices and female officers welcoming the aggrieved must be encouraged and promoted to make people participate in governance at all levels.

4. Decision-making in administration should be time-bound and public decisions be made open through media, websites or notice boards with facilities to protest and correct the lapses.
5. Informed people should be invited to administrative offices frequently and should be welcomed with open arms and encouraged to offer their innovative suggestions. Their acceptance can be reported in the media and the government must express its thankfulness to the people for their cooperation.

Campaigns like 'प्रशासन जनता के संग' are a beginning in this direction. Such camps should be organized once in every six months to clear the arrears. The MPs/MLAs/Pradhans should compulsorily attend such popular camps and administrators should educate them about possible misuse and incidents of corruption. Conflicts are a natural phenomenon in a democracy and to resolve them, rather than to suppress them, is a democratic exercise, howsoever illiterate or ignorant the people may be. Administrators in India will have to stop boasting and bragging of their educational superiority, which does not necessarily lead to popular welfare. It is all the more relevant, where women and weaker sections are involved. Giving them equal status and equity ethics may rob the administrative status of the official to begin with, but a democratic transformation from a colonial approach is the real freedom for which the national struggle was fought against an alien power. The foreign rulers could not respect a common man of India, even when he or she was honest and sincere. Our fellow civilians cannot be allowed to behave with contempt with the mass citizenry, although it may be true that the former has genuine love for the people of India. This is the way the Indian society has been operating since antiquity. The high-caste Hindus had both love and contempt, for the untouchables.

Social Audit and Informed Citizenry

The citizen participation in administration being too new or radical is bound to cause some chaos and discomfort. The panchayat politics is accused of interfering in district administration. This can be rectified by the awareness of legal audit supplemented by social audit. Social audit is an instrumentality of identifying the loopholes which the executive should plug to the best of its capacity.

A systematic audit of the accounts of government ministries, departments, enterprises and agencies is instrumental in pointing out irregularities in financial dealings, mal-administration and corruption. The Comptroller and Auditor General (CAG) of India, assisted by the Accountant Generals in various states, has considerable opportunity to go into those cases where corrupt practices are suspected to have influenced government actions. However, because of delays in audits and the slow process involved in the consideration of audit reports by the Public Accounts Committees (both central and state), the immediate impact of an audit is substantially diluted. A penetrating report of the CAG can highlight a case like the Bofors scandal, 2G spectrum scam, CWG scam, etc. but the time lag between the occurrence of financial crime and its detection and reporting is so long that corrupt practices are rarely prevented or punished on time. Besides, the CAG is only a recommendatory authority and hence, much depends on the executive agencies in taking effective action on its recommendations. True and healthy traditions give the CAG sufficient clout, but to predict that such respect for the CAG will continue undiminished would be presumptuous. Nevertheless, it cannot be denied that the CAG has been instrumental in causing several corrective actions on the part of the central as well as state governments. These include modifications in system and procedures which help in reducing the number of cases that are likely to promote corruption. There has been a widespread feeling that the existing legal provisions and the conventional instruments of combating corruption have not proved sufficiently effective. There are a series of loopholes in the functioning of Vigilance Commissions at the central and state levels. Also, the investigating agencies like the CBI have been overburdened with cases. The cases filed in judicial courts linger on endlessly and constitutional protection to civil servants comes in the way of taking appropriate punitive action against them. In 1951, the A.D. Gorwala Committee recommended the setting up of an independent tribunal to investigate cases of corruption against public servants, but this suggestion was not accepted by the then government.

Social audit is needed to keep public servants politically neutral. They should comprehend their role vis-à-vis people rather than vis-à-vis political rulers in power. The informed public opinion and free media should protect civil servants. Investigative journalism, which is developing quite fast in India, must expose the political leaders and defend the civil servants in their heroic struggle against corrupt rulers. Strict accountability can be improved by an independent and powerful machinery of audit. The CAG has started playing this role. The auditors are the main gatekeepers of financial probity. Framers of the constitution, in practically all democracies of the world, have created a role for public audit as being the cornerstone on which the credibility of government is built up in the eyes of the people. Public audit provides independent assurance to all stakeholders that audited institutions have complied with the intent of the legislature as well as the orders of the executive. An effective audit strengthens governance by providing for accountability and protecting the core values of government. Public audit helps in bringing transparency in operations of the government and bringing to light improprieties committed by persons holding high positions. Various reports of the CAG have highlighted improprieties in the award of high-value contracts and cases of fraud and misappropriation.

One of the imperatives of social audit is to blow the whistle. Ethical working does not necessarily mean working strictly according to rules, which in any case should be a norm generally, but also working with a view to make life smooth and easier for the common man. The litmus test would be, whether the rules and procedures are circumvented for self-interest or for the good of society at large. From social audit point of view civil servants should be classified into several categories: (i) those who are dishonest and do work without wasting time if a consideration is received; (ii) those who are dishonest and do not work leading to the harassment of citizens; (iii) those who are honest but do not do any work, apprehending action against them; and (iv) those who are honest and still take decisions to get the work done without fear of attracting action against them. The need of the society at present is to increase the number of officers belonging to the last category so that the citizenry can be assured of the desired performance in time, without paying bribe.

One of the preconditions of social audit is informed citizenry. The 2005 RTI Act, coupled with the Right to Education (RTE), fulfils the basic legal requirement, i.e. right to know, as a fundamental human right. The UN General Assembly, in its first session, resolved that 'freedom of information is a fundamental human right and touchstone of all the freedoms to which the United Nations is consecrated'. It changes public accountability of public administration. The UN Economic and Social Council elucidated it as one of the prerequisites of democratic or good governance. It entails holding elected or appointed officials charged with a public mandate responsible and answerable for their actions, activities and decisions. It is the role of civil society to hold those in public office, accountable. Accountability seeks to know who is liable for what and what kind of conduct is illegal. In fact, it is 'giving an account of government policies and/or decisions, whether proactively (of one's own volition) or reactively (in response to a request for information)'. Giving account and being held to account includes:

(a) making mistakes public and rectification, and
(b) explaining why decisions have been taken, by whom and how outcomes are arrived at.

Taking responsibility may entail rectification of maladministration.

Information, participation and audit should go hand in hand with democratic awareness. The public interest litigation (PIL), which this triple process will generate, gives birth to a new kind of human rights jurisprudence. The administration will have to compensate citizens for their acts of commission and omission. It is a great democratizing power in emerging societies like India. Kofi Annan, the former Secretary General of the United Nations, has put it as under: 'The power of information has given us all the chance to effect change and alleviate poverty in ways we cannot even imagine today. Our task is to make that change real for those in need, whatever they may be. With information on our side, with knowledge of a potential for all, the path of poverty can be reversed'. An open, transparent and corruption-free governance is a democratic tool of citizen empowerment. As it gets sharpened, the administration in developing societies is frightened about its de-powerization. A healthy balance is workable and the pinpricks of transition can be sorted out by mutually accommodating the conflicting interests.

An ethical code of conduct for public servants is recognized as a universal need. Such code has been codified and enacted also. But the dilemma persists because of the lack of consensus and worse still, the use of immoral methods. To enforce morality, an administrator has to handle decisional dilemmas. His or her discretionary powers call for a fair utilization of the influence of private corporate sector in the areas that were hitherto in the domain of public administration. It forces him or her to lay more emphasis on flexible procedures, qualities of decisiveness, self-regulation, answerability and achievement-orientedness. An administrator's behaviour entails personal choice, biases, values, likes, dislikes and capacity for reasoning. All play a distinct role in tackling decisional dilemmas. For instance, some of these ethical dilemmas are; what kind of favours are acceptable without being considered discourteous and rude? Should any and all kinds of gifts and hospitality be avoided? Or, should it be limited to a specified minimum? If so, what should be that minimum? Is public servant only a public servant during office hours? Or ethical norms should be practised outside office hours also? Should all public servants interpret policies and programmes according to their individual perceptions of right and wrong or should they only adhere to the values of the institutions they are serving? Finally, what should the public servants do if their personal honesty and integrity appear to be out of place in their work environment? Situations cannot be generalized and it will be unfortunate if the administrator is reduced to a mere robot and final mandates are delivered to him or her about the people and the problems that he or she is expected to handle. His or her personal and public ethics require inquiry and contemplation into truth, that is, seeking the right answer to one's question with the help of ethical deliberations. The administrator should question the 'adequacy' and 'meaning' of proposed action in the light of his or her obligations to the organization as well as to the public at large.

Corruption: A Bogey and the Reality

In recent years so much has been written, discussed and debated around corruption that perhaps an encyclopaedic study in volumes will be inadequate to define, combat and evolve ground strategies to curb and kill the monster. The truth is, that the new policies of liberalization, privatization and globalization have taken the lid off the bottle and the Imp is out. Now lo and behold! here he is in his monstrous colours. Veerappa Moily, Chairman of Second Administrative Reforms Commission, before issuing the fourth report on 'Ethics in Government', had the age-old dilemma, when he writes: 'We have alibi for our lapses by quoting trespass from other democratic institutions, by resorting to a blame game. The executive/civil services blame interference by the political executive or legislatures and vice versa. If any of the democratic institutions leaves space, the mafia or extra-constitutional authority occupies that space. Realization of its own authority and discharging its sphere of responsibility, developing accountability and responsiveness are the real solutions to the conflicting situations of eroding democratic polity'.

Moily consults and quotes from Confucius, Plato, Napoleon, Tony Blair and Mahatma Gandhi and ultimately comes to the conclusion: 'So, in the ultimate analysis, it is a question of ethics. Ethics is a set of standards that helps guide conduct. One of the problems is that the present codes of conduct are not direct and to the point. They are full of vague sermons that rarely indicate prohibitions directly.' Then, he further bemoans that the absence of rules is not the problem: 'One cannot mandate honesty. The rule of law can only defeat the perverse mind. However, it cannot defeat the perversity of the heart. The line separating good and evil passes not between states nor between classes ... but through the middle of every human heart. We have no destinies other than those we forge ourselves'.

Quoting Gandhi, Moily says, 'You must change, if you wish to see the change in this world'. But then his 300-page report enumerates the institutions, which will reverse the slide by prescribing stringent standards of probity in public life. Like a poet, he comments, 'These standards should be not only the conduct of Ceasar's wife, but of Ceasar himself'. The standard for probity in public life should be not only conviction in a criminal but propriety, as determined by suitable independent institutions specifically constituted for the purpose. Deregulation, liberalization and privatization are not necessarily the solution to addressing the problem. Prevalent institutional arrangements have to be reviewed and changes be made where those vested with power are made accountable, their functioning be made more transparent and subjected to social audit with a view to minimize discretionary decisions. All procedures, laws and regulations that breed corruption and come in the way of efficient delivery system will have to be eliminated. The perverse system of incentives in public life, which makes corruption a high-return low-risk activity, need to be addressed.

The Santhanam Report - 1964

Corruption in public life is not a legal malaise, and it has to be minimized by an iron hand of law, which is not easy to be hammered out in Indian milieu. Yet, a workable definition of unethical practices can be worked out if there is consensus about (1) public good, (2) law and rules about personal gains in official positions and (3) pecuniary advantages in action and non-action. India's legal bureaucracy frowns at misuse of official positions and deviations from rules and calls corruption a universal phenomenon. The Indian history and society learnt little from the British but continues to languish in medieval Mughal time corruption for which the *patwaris* and the *thanedars* are the most notorious. Independence adds a developmental dimension which brings millions and billions of rupees for these petty 'booty grabers' to have their family development. The Santhanam Committee identified some 71 cases in 1964, to which dozens more may be added to update the list. The Prevention of Corruption Act, 1988 remains the key document for the police and the judiciary to detect and punish. With its innumerable amendments or revisions, every public servant knows that these 'toothless laws' are only for the *Vakils*. Consequently, justice is sold in India and it is not even costly for the corrupt.

The debates on and about corruption started during the Nehru era of Indian Politics. The Santhanam Report represents the beginning of Indira Gandhi era after a short interregnum of Lal Bahadur Shastri. It is a detailed and systematic probe into the phenomenon, listing its causes and consequences this Committee on Prevention of Corruption (1964) has remarked about the phenomenon as under:

'For a country like India, development of her material resources and raising the standards of life of all classes are, indeed imperative. At the same time, the deterioration in the standards of public life has to be arrested. Ways and means have to be found to ensure that idealism and patriotism have the proper place in the ambition of our youth. The lack of moral earnestness, which has been a conspicuous feature of recent years, is perhaps the greatest single factor which hampers the growth of strong traditions of integrity and efficiency.' Values like altruism and empathy for poor, are hard to imbibe after joining the civil services. They need to be instilled in childhood, in family and in school. The Indian public services have many established traditions. Many of these are in the form of conventions of propriety and acceptable behaviour without formal sanctions. However, there is also a need for higher code of ethics. For the codes of conduct, while containing some general norms like 'maintaining integrity and absolute devotion to duty' and not indulging in 'conduct unbecoming of a government servant', are generally directed towards cataloguing specific activities deemed undesirable for government servants. There is no Code of Ethics prescribed for civil servants in India although such codes exist in other countries. What we have in India are several conduct rules, which prohibit a set of common activities. There is, of late, a concern that more 'generic norms' need to be added to the list of accepted conduct. A number of generic expectations from civil servants, are referred as 'values'. These salient 'values' are:

1. Allegiance to the various ideals enshrined in the preamble to the Constitution.
2. Apolitical functioning of administration.
3. Good governance for betterment of the people to be the primary goal of civil service.
4. Duty to act objectively and impartially.
5. Accountability and transparency in decision-making.
6. Maintenance of highest ethical standards.
7. Merit to be the criteria in selection of civil servants.

8. Ensuring economy and avoidance of wastage in expenditure for a healthy and congenial work environment.
9. Communication, consultation and cooperation in performance of functions to facilitate participation.
10. Acceptance of codes of conduct to cover an individual's official or professional conduct.

The violations of code of conduct should constitute breach of official rules. Some violations of these codes may be grave. The professional ethics should cover the personal and job-related standards of behaviour expected of professionals. Because of their specialized knowledge and training, the professionals have to bear higher responsibility in their work areas. The integrity based codes merely outline the desired values. The civil servants are expected to imbibe these values and convert them into suitable behavioural principles of conduct.

A public service code outlining commitment to ideals of the Preamble of the constitution; good governance; transparency in decision-making; economy in expenditure; can create a healthy and congenial work environment and conducive atmosphere for participatory management. It seems like a prudent attempt to legalise ethical desirability.

Santhanam made it clear that controlling corruption only through administrative vigilance is impossible. It requires a multi pronged approach – with public participation and systemic economy and administrative reforms. Government departments' independent professional agencies have to be used to contact persons and get their responses. He suggests that provisions for social audit should be introduced in all schemes which have many scattered beneficiaries. Social audit, unlike CAG audit, can be based on information which beneficiaries provide. It is not possible to consign economic problems to oblivion through legislation. Corruption arises not so much from human moral weakness as from inherent systemic weaknesses which create opportunities for corruption. Minimization of discretionary decision making can reduce discretionary benefits which public officials control. One way of simplifying procedures can be the system of a single window clearance or one-stop service centre.

The Post-Indira Politics

The Indira Gandhi phase of Indian politics was marked by the tragic events of Bangladesh (1971), declaration of National Emergency (1975) and the Operation Blue Star (1984). These events shattered the economy and the efforts to combat corruption were placed on the back burner. Even a Mr Clean, Rajeev Gandhi could not stay that clean and his assassination inaugurated an era of instability. The two regimes of Narsimha Rao and Atal Bihari Bajpai could hardly do any damage-control, when the new economic policy of liberalization, privatization and globalization of 1993 was announced. It has opened the flood gates of corruption in public life. Inflation, price rise and developmental tensions have been too heavy to protect the democratic institutions.

There is a widely held view that self disciplinary mechanisms even within judiciary are no longer effective. Moreover, the role of executive in judicial appointments has reached a vanishing point. The collegium system of appointing judges is seen by many as opaque. The selection committee has recommended: 'The appointment process cannot be allowed and should not be allowed to continue in the hands of a self-appointed common law mechanism created by judicial order operating since the early 1990s. Now a National Judicial Commission has been set up to create a broad-based and comprehensive model for judicial appointments, by amending of Articles 124 and 217 of the Indian Constitution.'

The UPA Government of Manmohan Singh and Sonia Gandhi had the most trying decade from 2004 to 2014. It witnessed the corruption phenomenon at its worst. Its manifestations in scams, scandals, black money politics like

Commonwealth Games, 2G Spectrum, Adarsh Housing Society, Coal Block Allocations etc. made the people desperate and a civil society movement rose under the leadership of a veteran Gandhian Anna Hazare. It was joined by social activists like Prashant Bhushan, Swami Ramdev, Kiran Bedi, Arvind Kejriwal and a host of Aam Admi Party (AAP) leaders of later era. The civil society pressure expedited the strong Jan Lokpal demand, to which the government response was slow and halting. The UPA government willy-nilly conceded to the demand of a Lokpal Lokayukt Agency (2011) and 116th Amendment could also got processed.

The Preventive Instrumentalities

The causes responsible and the cures to be attempted to arrest the infectious epidemic of corruption can be lifted up from any computer inventory. The discussions have been ad infinitum. The conclusions will be that the above-mentioned institutions of union and state governments should be strengthened until people in India decide and opt to have a better society. Hopefully, some day they will. Till then, we have to hold on the system and make the laws more and more ethical and stringent. A brief review of these preventive instrumentalities will be relevant here.

Curbing Corruption by Vigilance

Evolving and enforcing codes ultimately ends up with the prevention of corruption and vigilance machinery to punish the delinquent. The Government of India has an elaborate framework for the conduct of public servants in a variety of public service categories. First of all, there are five mega documents detailing these rules. These are:

1. All India Services (Conduct) Rules, 1968
2. All India Services (Discipline and Appeal) Rules, 1969
3. Central Civil Services (Conduct) Rules, 1964

4. Central Civil Services (Classification, Control and Appeal) Rules, 1965
5. Railway Servants (Conduct) Rules, 1966

Then, there is a general requirement in all the service rules that government servants at all times will maintain absolute integrity. Besides, it has been laid down that no civil servant shall use his or her office to secure employment for any member of his or her family in any private undertaking. He or she will not accept, or permit any member of his or her family to accept any gift (a term which covers any pecuniary advantage). He or she will not engage directly or indirectly in any trade or business or undertake any other employment. He or she cannot speculate in any investment, or make an investment which is likely to embarrass or influence the discharge of his or her duties.

The conduct rules require that every government servant, holding a supervisory post, shall take all possible steps to ensure the integrity and devotion to duty of all government servants for the time being under his or her control and authority. A large number of conduct rules contain the provisions of a series of orders issued by the British government before independence. Some of them pertain to (1) receiving and giving of loans by gazetted officers (1860) and by non-gazetted officers (1869); (2) receiving of gifts (1876); (3) selling of houses and valuable property (1881); (4) management of companies and private trade and employment (1885); (5) collection and subscription by government servant (1885); (6) creditors and solvency (1885); and (7) employment in commercial organizations after retirement (1920).

There are procedural and fundamental definitions because of the constitutional safeguards guaranteed to civil servants. There are twelve stages involved in the departmental proceedings undertaken to inquire into the misconduct or misbehaviour of government servants under the Central Civil Services (Classification, Control and Appeal) Rules. These stages start with the preparation of a definite charge-sheet ending with the imposition of a penalty. Major penalties include downgrading, compulsory retirement, removal from service and dismissal (which involves a ban on future government employment), while the minor ones range from censure to the withholding of increments.

The first Administrative Reforms Commission (ARC) study team found both the conduct rules and the classification, control and appeal rules too brief and perfunctory to be really useful. It also found many loopholes in the procedures. The courts have taken too narrow a view in this regard to protect the security character of civil service. Article 311 of the Indian Constitution, along with Article 311(2), as amended after the Constitution (42nd Amendment) Act, 1976, lays down that no person who is a member of a civil service of the union or an all-India service or a civil service of a state or holds a civil post under the union or a state shall be dismissed or removed or diminish in rank (1) except after an inquiry in which he/she has been informed of the charge against him or her, and (2) given a reasonable opportunity of being heard in respect of those charges.

Prior to the 42nd Amendment, the whole procedure followed under Article 311 was so cumbersome that it generally went in favour of the accused. The Santhanam Committee remarked that Article 311 of the Constitution, as interpreted by our courts, had made it very difficult to deal effectively with corrupt public servants. It was during the emergency that an amendment to Article 311 was introduced, which, after permitting a 'reasonable' opportunity to the accused, now lays down: 'Provided that where it is proposed after such an inquiry, to impose upon him any such penalty, such penalty may be imposed on the basis of the evidence adduced during such inquiry and it shall not be necessary to give such person any opportunity of making representation on the penalty proposed'. This provision can cause an indefinite protraction of the disciplinary procedure. Experience shows that over-security in service to a civil servant is a spur to misconduct. The impact of constitutional provisions on the state of discipline, integrity and work ethos is highly demoralizing. It requires political will and sagacity on the part of public servants.

Moreover, evidence problems are obstructed by various quarters in the performance of their duties. Notwithstanding anti corruption bodies, there is massive corruption at lower levels which is hardly investigated. There is collegial unity among officers which comes in the way of proper inquiry against the accused. Officers generally save their brother-officers from inquiries and possible punitive measures. Corrupt politicians lose moral authority to correct their delinquent subordinates and protracted inquiries dampen the enthusiasm of senior officers to initiate proceedings against their juniors suspected of indulging in corruption. Similarly, the permission to investigate corruption cases involving government servants and to prosecute them is granted to the investigating and prosecuting agencies by the administrative departments and ministries concerned after a great deal of reluctance and delay. Various remedies are suggested to reduce corruption through deregulation and privatization, placing greater reliance on competition to ensure low prices and good quality. Incentives for good performance and disincentives for corrupt practices in government need to be increased. Moreover, administrative procedures may also reduce corruption by increasing accountability, transparency and the role of citizen's voice. Specific measures have been listed by various committees and commissions. The governments should simplify laws and procedures, enforce immediate and compulsory retrenchment of officials whose record and reputation is tainted, and against whom there is an evidence of corruption. Strengthening of power of the state vigilance departments, Lokayuktas and the anti-corruption branch of the state police, to enable them to effectively initiate and pursue investigations independently of government direction, is usually talked about as an alibi. Guaranteed protection of civil servants who expose corrupt practices is advocated. Annual awards in recognition of the contribution made by such persons in exposing wrong-doings in the government is also suggested as a positive measure. In addition, states are being asked to pass the Corrupt Public Servants (Forfeiture of Property) Act, already drafted by the Law Commission. The Benami Transaction Prohibition Act, 1988, exists on the statute book. The states have been asked to frame rules and procedure for this law also.

The Instrumentalities to Combat Corruption

Central Vigilance Commission

Central Vigilance Commission (CVC) was set up in 1964 to advise the central government on matters pertaining to the protection of integrity in administration. It has been conceived to be an apex vigilance institution, free of control from executive authority, monitoring vigilance activity under the union government and advising various authorities in the central government organizations in planning, executing, reviewing and reforming their vigilance activities. The government has authorized the CVC to receive written complaints for disclosure on allegations of corruption or misuse of office and recommend appropriate action.

The CVC exercises superintendence over the functioning of the Delhi Special Police Establishment (DSPE) with respect to investigations under the Prevention of Corruption Act, 1988 or offences under Criminal Procedure Code (CrPC) for certain categories of public servants. It reviews the progress of investigations conducted by the DSPE into offences alleged to have been committed under the Prevention of Corruption Act. It undertakes an inquiry or causes an inquiry or investigation to be made into any transaction, to which the executive control of the Government of India extends, or is suspected or alleged to have acted for an improper purpose or in a corrupt manner. It tenders independent and impartial advice to the disciplinary authorities in cases involving a vigilance angle at different stages, i.e. investigation, inquiry, appeal, review, etc. It also exercises a general check and supervision over vigilance and anti-corruption work in ministries or departments of the Government of India. The CVC also undertakes or causes an inquiry into the complaints received under the Public Interest Disclosure and Protection of Informer Programme and recommend appropriate action. Though the jurisdiction of the Commission extends to all employees of the central government and its organizations, it advises on individual vigilance cases only with regard to senior high level personnel. The role of the CVC is advisory, almost in the same sense as that of the UPSC.

The primary responsibility for the maintenance of integrity and efficiency of each department/organization rests with the respective chief executives who are assisted by a Chief Vigilance Officer. The overall supervision of the work of this Chief Vigilance Officer is done by the CVC. The Commission has its own secretariat, Chief Technical Examiners' Wing (CTE) and a wing of Commissioners for Departmental Inquiries (CDI). The CTE constitutes the technical wing of the Commission and is manned by two engineers of the rank of Chief Engineers. The main functions assigned to this organization are: technical audit of construction works of governmental organizations from a vigilance angle, investigation of specific cases of complaints related to construction works and extension of assistance to Central Bureau Investigations (CBI) in their investigations involving technical matters.

The Commission receives complaints against central government employees allegedly involved in corrupt practices and misconduct either directly from the complainants or through the various departments/enterprises concerned. Wherever prima facie allegations exist, complaints are forwarded to the administrative authorities concerned, including the Central Bureau of Investigation (CBI) or the CVOs, for detailed investigation and reporting.

During the year 2010, the Commission tendered first stage advice in 3,424 cases, of which 256 cases were based on the investigation reports forwarded by the CVOs concerned. It appears that the number of complaints received by the CVC is not even the tip of the iceberg. Perhaps the office of the CVC is not being utilized by the aggrieved as much as it should be.

The Commission operates a project called 'VIGEYE'. It consists of Vigilance Complaint Management System (VCMS), which enables the use of mobile phones and web-based technologies. Citizens can lodge complaints through telephones or mails. They can provide better information and evidence along with their complaints by using mobile phones with a software application especially designed for this purpose. Thus, the VIGEYE is characterized by simplified process of filing complaints, providing authentic identity of the complainant, digitalization of the complaint procedure, better classification and indexing of complaints and complete availability of complaint trial.

Central Bureau of Investigation

In 1941, the Government of India created a Special Police Establishment to investigate cases of bribery and corruption. In 1963, it became part of the newly created Central Bureau of Investigation (CBI), which was established as an attached office of the Ministry of Home Affairs. Presently, it is attached to the Ministry of Personnel, Public Grievances and Pensions. It is responsible for

1. preparing and implementing a comprehensive programme of vigilance and anti-corruption;
2. collecting information on such cases with the help of governmental as well as non-governmental agencies;
3. preparing lists of persons and organizations engaged in malpractices;

4. checking and searching definite information about the prevalence of malpractices; and
5. taking the subsequent necessary action to bring forth the culprits.

The CBI has eleven functional divisions as under:

(i) Anti-Corruption Division
(ii) Special Crimes Division
(iii) Economic Offences Division
(iv) Technical Advisory Units
(v) Directorate of Prosecution
(vi) Policy Division
(vii) Administration Division
(viii) System Division
(ix) Coordination Division
(x) Central Forensic Laboratory
(xi) Training Division

During 2010, the number of cases registered by the CBI was 1,009 which included 867 regular cases and 142 preliminary enquires. While 212 cases were registered for demand of bribe by public servants for showing official favours, 66 cases were registered for possession of assets disproportionate to known sources of income. Out of total 1,009 cases, 731 cases related to the Anti-Corruption Division, 129 pertained to Special Crimes Division and 149 to Economic Offences Division.

Not all the states have vigilance commissions. Some of them have well-organized anti-corruption departments which, though preserving their autonomy, are an extension of the police administration. In a few states, the anti-corruption departments have been turned into regular bureaus. In Rajasthan, for instance, the Anti-Corruption Department has been reorganized as the Rajasthan State Anti-Corruption Bureau. It is headed by a Director General of Police, who is assisted by several Inspector Generals of Police, Deputy Inspector Generals of Police,

Superintendents of Police, Additional Superintendents of Police and Deputy Superintendents of Police. The Bureau enjoys considerable functional autonomy. The state anti-corruption machinery, comprising police officials, does not show grit and gumption to catch with required skills and alacrity, suspected police and administrative officials of senior ranks. An administrative will to act with firmness is conspicuous by its gross absence. Apart from the Indian Penal Code, the Prevention of Corruption Act and the vigilance machinery at central and state levels, there are several conduct rules and other government orders which act as checks on administrative corruption.

Civil Society and Lokpal

It is generally agreed that legal institutions against corruption need support from civil society, which is yet to be organized in India. The stray movements got an extraordinary fillip when a veteran Gandhian Anna Hazare took up the command and his fast techniques revived the Gandhian 'satyagraha' for the 'Second War of India's Independence'. The movement was to liberate the country from the clutches of the corrupt elites and unscrupulous nationals, who are more atrocious and rapacious than the former British colonialists. It was necessitated because several Prime Ministers, in spite of their solemn assurances, could not get the Lokpal Bill passed in the parliament of India in last 20 years or so. The earlier efforts were so frustrating that a huge crowd gave a standing ovation to a Hazare and the Lokpal Bill could get a shape. The debate on a strong Lokpal versus weak Lokpal continues even today but the bill has reached to the Statute Book.

The Lokpal and Lokayukta Bill 2011, was passed by the Lok Sabha on 27 December 2011 but it could not be conclusively debated and voted upon in Rajya Sabha. The bill is a result of intensive parleys in the Joint Parliamentary Committee and extensive discussion in the Lok Sabha in which all political parties presented their views. Many of the recommendations of the Anna Hazare team could not be fully included in the proposed bill. Yet, notwithstanding the weak or strong Lokpal debate, the UPA government of Manmohan Singh has cleared the Bill and the final position is as under.

The Government of India at the centre will have a body named Lokpal. This Lokpal will have a Chairperson and up to eight members. Four of these will be judicial members. The President of India will appoint the Chairperson and Members of Lokpal based on the recommendations of a Selection Committee under the chairmanship of the Prime Minister. The Selection Committee will have at least seven persons of standing.

Lokpal will have a wide jurisdiction covering the Prime Minister, Ministers, MPs, all categories of government and public sector employees and employees of NGOs receiving sizeable funding from government. Lokpal will have an in-house Inquiry Wing headed by the Director of Inquiry for conducting preliminary inquiry into any allegations of corruption. Lokpal will also have a Prosecution Wing headed by the Director of Prosecution. The bill lays down the procedure for handling the complaints.

No sanction or approval of any authority is required when the Lokpal orders a preliminary inquiry or an investigation or prosecution. This will not apply to those who hold constitutional offices and are removable by procedures separately laid down in the constitution.

- The Lokpal shall consist of a chairperson, who is or has been a Chief Justice of India or is/has been a judge of the Supreme Court or an eminent person who fulfils the eligibility specified in the Act and such number of members not exceeding eight, out of whom 50 per cent shall be judicial members. Out of the total members, not less than 50 per cent shall be from amongst the persons belonging to the SCs, STs, OBCs, minorities and women.

- A person is eligible to be appointed as a judicial member if he or she is or has been a judge of the Supreme Court or is or has been a Chief Justice of a High Court. Besides, a person is eligible to be appointed as a member other than a judicial member if he or she is a person of impeccable integrity and outstanding ability having special knowledge and expertise of not less than 25 years in the matters relating to anti-corruption policy, administration, vigilance, finance, law and management. The chairperson and members shall be appointed by the President of India after obtaining the recommendations of a selection committee which will consist of:
  (a) the Prime Minister as chairperson,
  (b) the Speaker of Lok Sabha as member,
  (c) the Leader of Opposition in the Lok Sabha as member, and
  (d) the Chief Justice of India or a judge of the Supreme Court nominated by him or her as member.

This selection committee shall prepare a panel of persons to be considered for appointment, constitute a search committee consisting of at least seven persons of standing and having special knowledge and expertise in varied areas. However, the selection committee may also consider any person other than the persons recommended by the search committee.

- The chairperson and members shall be appointed on the recommendations of the selection committee by the President of India for a period of five years from the date on which the chairperson or a member enters his or her office or until he or she attains the age of 70 years, whichever is earlier. The salary, allowances and other conditions of service of the chairperson shall be the same as those of the Chief Justice of India, while for other members, they shall be the same as those of a judge of the Supreme Court.
- There will be an Inquiry Wing in the office of Lokpal that will be headed by the Director of Inquiry to conduct

preliminary inquiry of any offence alleged to have been committed by a public servant punishable under the Prevention of Corruption Act, 1988. The administrative expenses of the Lokpal shall be charged on the Consolidated Fund of India. The jurisdiction of Lokpal will include Prime Minister, ministers, Members of Parliament, Groups A, B, C and D officers and officials of the central government. Matters pending before any court or committee or authority for enquiry prior to the commencement of this Act will continue to be under the jurisdiction of such authorities.

- On receipt of a complaint, the Lokpal will first decide whether prima facie a preliminary inquiry is needed. If so, he or she can order a preliminary inquiry that will be conducted by the Inquiry Wing or an agency (including the Delhi Special Police Establishment). A bench consisting of not less than three members of the Lokpal will consider a preliminary inquiry and order further investigation, departmental proceedings or closure of proceedings. Further, a bench consisting of not less than three members of the Lokpal shall consider every report based on such investigation or enquiry.
- The Lokpal or the investigating agency may require any public servant or any other person who is able to furnish information or produce documents relevant to preliminary enquiry or investigation. After the conclusion of investigation, where the findings of the Lokpal disclose commission of an offence under the Prevention of Corruption Act, 1988, by a public servant, the Lokpal may file a case in the Special Court and shall also sent a copy of the report together with its findings to the competent authority. The Lokpal shall have the power of superintendence and direction over the Delhi Special Police Establishment in respect of matters referred by it. The Central Vigilance Commission (CVC) shall send a statement to the Lokpal in respect of action taken on complaint referred to it, by the Lokpal. The Inquiry Wing of the Lokpal shall have all the

powers of the civil court under the Code of Civil Procedure, 1908, in the fulfilment of its responsibilities. The Lokpal may also utilize the service of any officer or organization or investigating agency of the central government or any state government as the case may be.

The Lokpal, on the basis of evidence presented before it, can recommend to the central government for transfer or suspension of a public servant involved in corruption, from the post held by him or her till such period as may be specified in the order. The chairperson or any member of the Lokpal shall be removed from his or her office by the President on grounds of misbehaviour after the Supreme Court, on reference being made to it, recommends for such removal. Every public servant shall make a declaration of his or her assets and liabilities as per the provisions made in this legislation. The Lokpal will present to the President an annual report on its work done during a specified year. The President shall cause a copy thereof to be laid before both houses of parliament. The Lokpal shall function as the final appellate authority in respect of appeals arising out of any other law related to providing public service and redressed of public grievance by any public authority. It shall not inquire or investigate into any complaint that is made after the expiry of a period of seven years from the date on which the offence mentioned in such complaint is alleged to have been committed. It shall provide legal assistance to every person against whom a complaint has been filed, to defend his or her case before the Lokpal, if such assistance is requested for.

The Lokpal and Lokayuktas Bill, 2011, prescribes that the Lokayukta in the state shall consist of:

(a) a chairperson, who is or has been a Chief Justice of a High Court or a judge of the High Court or an eminent person who fulfils the eligibility specified in this legislation; and
(b) such number of members, not exceeding eight, out of whom 50 per cent shall be judicial members, and of these eight

members, not less than 50 per cent will be from SCs, STs, OBCs, minorities and women.

The chairperson and members shall be appointed by the governor after obtaining the recommendations of a selection committee consisting of the Chief Minister as chairperson, and the Speaker of the Legislative Assembly, the Leader of Opposition in the Legislative Assembly, the Chief Justice of the High Court of the state or a judge of the High Court nominated by him or her and an eminent jurist nominated by the Governor, as members. The person and every member shall be appointed for a term of five years or till he or she attains the age of 70 years, whichever is earlier.

All other provisions concerning the structure, powers and functioning of the Lokayukta will be on the pattern of the Lokpal as given in the proposed legislation.

The Whistleblowers Protection Bill was also approved by the Union Cabinet on 9 August 2010. This is officially known as the Public Interest Disclosure and Protection to Persons Making the Disclosure Bill, 2010. The bill was passed by the Lok Sabha in December 2011.

Right to Information (RTI) 2005

Institutional arrangement cannot be effective, unless people are well informed and transparency shakes and shocks the administration to do its duties. In 2005, The Union and State governments took a historic decision to end secrecy in government. The RTI Act 2005, gives a wide meaning to the term information. For purpose of sharing it with the citizens the main strategy is based on disclosure of information. For supply of information, the Act creates an elaborate machinery. It consists of Public Information Officers, Assistant Public Information Officers, Departmental Appellate Authorities, independent Central Information Commission (CIC) and independent State Information Commissions. RTI Act entrusts the Central

Information Commission (CIC) with the responsibility of monitoring the implementation of the Act. CIC prepares a yearly report on the implementation of the RTI Act. State Information Commissions (SICs) perform similar functions at state level.

The Act contains provision for imposing penalties on those who fail to provide information within the prescribed time limits. All government departments, agencies and undertakings including banks have designated PIOs to handle RTI requests. CIC has significantly increased the openness and transparency of the government.

Practices of investigative journalism, internet and international initiatives encouraged transparency. There was a growing recognition that secrecy in government breeds misuse of power and corruption. The laws for freedom of information seek to ensure that government activities are transparent, fair and open. Except in matters of defence, atomic energy and national security, no secrecy is normally necessary in government affairs.

The Citizen Charter

People now have a right to seek information from the government. It creates a corresponding duty of the government to equip the citizen with information about his rights even with out asking for the same. Former UK Prime Minister, John Major, took the lead in 1991 and the Citizen Charter (CC) movement followed. The modern states are democratic and welfare states and they must provide a range of public services to their citizens. The services cover areas such as education, health, housing and transport. Services also include such requirements as a driving license, telephone connection, gas connection, tax refund, Adhaar Card, passport, and copies of public records of one's property, educational qualification and date of birth etc. The Citizen Charters are a means of solving the day-to-day problems which citizens experience while dealing with the organizations, providing public services. The Conservative Party government under John Major was the first to introduce the Citizen's Charter in 1991. Tony Blair's Labour government relaunched it in 1998 under the new name 'Services First'. The six principles of the Citizen's Charter movement as originally framed were to facilitate.

1. quality
2. choice
3. standards
4. value
5. accountability
6. transparency

The Commissioners for citizen charter services will be appointed by the President (or by Governors in States) on the recommendation of a selection committee. The bill contains a mechanism for dealing with complaints. There is a provision for three appeals. There are provisions for penalties also.

A Citizen's Charter includes: (1) vision and mission statements; (2) identification of services; (3) identification of levels; (4) identification of client groups/stakeholders/users; (5) specification of time-frames for each service; specification of time-frames at each level; specification of service quality standards; (6) specification of service delivery standards; and providing information about the grievance redressal procedures. Citizen's charters represent application of the concept of reinventing government on the managerial model of successful private enterprises. The citizens are treated as the customers of the department for that service. The service becomes the product which the department provides. The service delivery model casts government servants in a different role as providers of services to people. They have to render service with sympathy and ensure public satisfaction. Government also introduced the 'Right of Citizens' for time bound delivery of goods and services and redressal of their grievances. The main provisions of the Bill are: Public authorities should publish a citizen's charter. They have to specify the services and the quality of services to be provided. The heads of department are responsible for disseminating and updating the citizen's charter. 'Public authorities' have been defined widely covering all kinds of publics.

Article 311 and Security of Civil Servants

One dilemmatic problem that confronted public administration in India was to protect the honest civil servants against the abuse of anti-graft law. The guilty must be punished but the honest has to be protected against the unscrupulous. Some administrators quote the old colonial procedures and want that corrupt officials, even when caught red handed in the act, must be given a chance by their seniors and the government to be heard and protected. This gave them protection under Article 311, under which a government sanction was needed to prosecute a senior civil servant of the rank of joint secretary and above. It delayed matters and brother administrators showed undue favours to save the guilty.

Apparently, the Article 311 was unduly overprotective to senior civil servants. The idea was that simple and honest civil servants way not get trapped and the CBI or police officials may not harass the so called guilty. But this very approach in a democracy is pernicious and all sorts of criminals caught red handed, evaded departmental enquiries and avoided prosecution by getting the government sanctions stalked under legal technicalities. It took years to seek the necessary permission. The bureaucracy made efforts to protect the image of brother civilians. The legal battles cannot be allowed to delay the procedures that cause the miscarriage of justice. Delay in the denial of justice and with the passage of time the corrupt officials honourably retire with retirement benefits.

The Second ARC exhibited courage and recommended the dropping of the Article 311, which was unwanted and was a legacy of the British rule. The Supreme Court has openly come against this kind of over protection of senior civil servants. The honourable Apex Court has maintained that Article 309 offers a sufficient guarantee of job security and the corrupt officials should not be given extra time to distort the evidence. The CBI and the senior justice officers have to be trusted as in cases of other accused. The government permission for prosecution does not help in meeting the ends of justice. It has been viewed as a historic reform, where by the guilty will be brought to book and the anti graft agencies of the government will not feel demoralized in trying the high and the mighty.

Corruption in India after 1993, has touched a new high of uncountable zeros. The senior officials above the rank of a Joint Secretary cannot be unduly protected in the name of delatory government sanctions. The law must take its due course and the judiciary has preserved the constitution which is its responsibility.

Informed and empowered citizenry, along with a strong and civil police force, are a condition necessary but they are not sufficient to make administration civil, polite and people oriented. The centuries of foreign rule has created an anti-people administration culture in our offices because of which, even very honest and well meaning people neither greet nor smile at the visitors. They rarely come forward of their own to help the citizens in trouble. Mere laws, rules and sermons by senior officers do not help the common man here. Unlike the West, where every receptionist smiles with a question 'Are you being helped?', the junior employees in India are rude, discourteous and even avoiding and evading the harassed victim. The work culture of holidays, status system, power fulminations and political manoeuvring dominates. The seniors will have to take the lead and place a new model of work-life and service-delivery by new leadership. The problems are there. It is not easy also but the senior officials must appreciate that the junior employees will change only when they will see the change rather than they merely hear about it from others.

Work Culture, Quality of Work Life and Service Delivery

If a young person from the school visits a bank, police station and a hospital, he or she will get a contrast of the three kinds of work cultures of education, police and health administrations. The teacher, the sub-inspector and the nurse all the three are government servants, but their functions and the climate which the performance of these functions creates, are so different that their work cultures determine the quality of work-life and service delivery in each one of these organizations. In school, there will be noise and boys and girls will be loitering around during interval. The police sub-inspector will have tensions on his or her face and will be hanging on the phone and the nurse will have a queue of waiting patients asking for instant relief. The functional difference will shape the behaviours of the employees and when they get used to these experiences over a long period of time, they become 'prisoners of these work cultures' and do not even know what they are doing and what is right or wrong in their behaviours.

The work culture of a typical Indian government office follows a pattern. It will open late and the babus will take an hour or so to settle down. The environs will be dirty and the sweeper will make it dirtier, complaining about detergent. People will bring enquiries and without an enquiry officer they will be made to disperse or asked to wait in a long queue. The seniors will come leisurely and become busy in meetings. The babus will start their sessions of gossiping and tea taking. Then, they will walk out of their seats leaving the chairs empty. Everybody will ask the people to come later or the other day and the office will be practically closed by the lunch hour. Some employees will be buried in the files, others will be moving around manipulating their selfish or political errands. The seniors keep on calling juniors into their rooms and the people are asked to wait without any rule of 'first come first served'. All this can be summed up in the following characteristics of a 'Babu-Sahib Culture' of Indian administration:

1. It is relaxed, anarchic and disorderly, without any concern of service delivery to the citizen.
2. It is too formal, where nobody smiles or shakes hands with the citizen who is supposed to wait without any welcome or information.

3. It is quasi-political. Employees are always busy with their demand charters and Trade Union activities of *hartals* and *bandhs* to be organized in near future.
4. It is manipulative. The rich, the powerful and the VIPs straight away go to the head without looking at the babus or *chaprasis* (peons). The common man keeps struggling with pushing his or her papers and documents and the babus conspire to manipulate and strike the deals for the Sahib.
5. The Sahib attends to political bosses only and the lay citizen has to reach to the decisional centres through some tout or a middleman charging for the deal.

This kind of work culture cares little about the quality of work. Employees always feel that they are low paid and petty graft is a part of their work ethics. The beneficiaries willingly and happily pay for it. Why should one work in a system where nobody works and is punished or rewarded for doing nothing? People suffer and manage or manipulate their own affairs. This kind of work ethos creates jobs of non-work and non-involvement. People discuss only transfers and promotions and in the absence of job-joy, job-satisfaction or job-enrichment they are reduced to do the routine work and avoid any innovation or adventure. The quest for excellence does not motivate employees because there is nobody to appreciate their good work. The Sahib likes to be in the good books of his or her own Sahib. The female workers are denied fair treatment and the union leaders keep giving the message, how to civilize their seniors by burning their effigies. The undignified scenes in offices and the stories of corruption may be exaggerated, but the work culture as a whole is uncomfortable to the employee of conscience. He or she works lonely and sincerely for some time and then finally decides to opt for gang or the crowd behaviour of their colleagues.

The Absence of Quality of Work Life

The quality of work life is not only poor, but in fact it does not exist. People feel very happy if some VIP dies and a holiday is declared. The work life from 9 am to 6 pm is extremely boring. There is no teamwork and still less, if any, concern for the citizen or the customer. Corrupt practices keep searching victims and job standards. Nobody teaches to anybody, nor anybody cares to know. In USA or Europe, these junior employees are part-time and the job does not exhaust them. The quality of work life in India is poor because:

1. The career jobs for nine hours a day for 35 years in life are absolutely dull and boring, particularly at non-gazetted levels of hierarchy.
2. Drudgery has to be suffered because the jobs very rarely change or get renewed.
3. Transfers are resented because of the non-mobility of the family and employees keep manipulating for the cancellation of transfers or getting placements of their choice.
4. The status system isolates the juniors and seniors and they do not enjoy any teamwork.

All this makes the job a 'salary quest' and a pay packet justification. Employees do not like their jobs, but they cannot quit them either just because they have no other options or they cannot give up mid-career promotional benefits. The non-workers, when promoted on account of mere seniority, develop a relaxed outlook towards indiscipline. They enjoy being surrounded by flatterers and sycophants. Dissent causes hostility and perverse groups keep sabotaging the harmony of the system.

The Delivery of Service

This adversely affects the delivery of service. Whether it is a post office or a railway station or a hospital, the citizen at the receiving end is harassed or victimized. Corruption is the offshoot of this work culture and the poor quality of work-life in every office. No pay packet satisfies such employees. They need extra money to show off and exhibit their inflated egos.

Procedures, delays and corruption damage the quality of public service and its delivery system. People settle for inferior or poor quality of service rather than to pay a heavy price in terms of grafts, delays, commissions or booty sharing. No one department can be singled out and no one Lokpal or Lokayukta can clean these Augean stables. Poor quality of service delivery can be identified and verified in any government department, if one cares to make a check on the following:

1. The period of delay and violation of rules and procedures involved in obtaining the public services from the agency.
2. Inordinate delays in the delivery system of service, including a fire brigade service or an ambulance for medical emergency.
3. Low professional standards of public service for which the employees or officers have neither any regret nor repentance.
4. Reluctant and unwilling public service by the corrupt officials and malpractices prevalent in their offices.
5. Irritating and humiliating reactions of government servants, who do not know the art of serving people with a smile.

This kind of work culture, quality of work life and service delivery pollutes the probity efforts in government. The bogey of corruption and the institution of Lokpal as a panacea are the popular reactions against this frustration. A student of ethics will ask many more searching questions about these propositions.

Professionalism: The Answer

Corruption is regarded as an antonym of probity in government. The coercive structure of power should perform the 'hold on operation' and punish the guilty, but the positive efforts of building a middle-class polity and a middle-class morality should simultaneously be strengthened through rights to education and information. Popular participation in administration and social audit of civil service performance, ensures probity and integrity in democratic governance. Professionalism in civil service is the answer of ethical malpractices, but more decisive is the social ethos, which can empower people to assert and show the officials their place. Honest efforts are being made and with the entry of weaker sections and women in administration, a middle-class morality will sooner than later replace the rural values of the feudal structures, and exhibitional values of exploitation by semi-literate elites in the Indian society.

People all over the world are entering into an era of post-modernism. Science has disillusioned them from the so-called joys of family life and communitarian ethics. The aversion is so serious that marriage as an institution has given way to 'live-in' and property is losing its charm without a successor. Women's liberation is adding to the life of isolation and social insecurity. Naturally, 'work' alone is becoming the primary source of happiness and pain. In place of loving children or cherishing family values of agricultural society, human beings are falling upon their professional lives for their sustenance. This professionalism or job-joy is the hope of the future. Professionalism implies professional code of conduct, professional ethics, professional discipline and professional excellence. As it develops, the loyalties to family, caste, class and region will decline, which can be seen as the root cause of malpractices and corruption in public life. In India, the civil servants under the Mughals and the Britishers never cared about the excellence of their professions in comparison to the honour of their birth, family relations and caste connections. These values of agricultural society account for massive corruption in civil service ranks of both, junior and senior categories. The future job patterns will be profession-oriented. In high professional profiles and image of excellence, lies the hope for a more ethical society which is currently plagued by over-affection to children and family members, caste fellows and co-religionists. The reforms of liberalization, privatization and globalization will necessitate 'contract professionalism' and second and third career public services will gradually replace the overprotected and lifetime career civil service in India.

Chapter 9

Corporate Social Responsibility and Global Transparency

The Ethical Issues

When Mikhail Gorbachev announced Perestroika and Glasnost in the Soviet Union, the World Bank celebrated it as a new wave of liberalization. This openness and relaxed state of economy gave impetus to privatization, popularly known as corporate governance. The decolonized world of the cold war era, which was waiting in the wings to welcome it as 'New Rightism', started practicing it as a global phenomenon of new markets and technology exchange in their developmental endeavours. The dawn of the 21st century witnessed a mixed model where in notwithstanding the continuation of Marxist economies, the so called democratic world of the third world countries started experimenting with Private Public Partnership (PPP) and Technology Transfers (TT) with the risk of Neo Capitalism staging a come back. The bipolar world of yester-decades bloomed into a multi polar world with new business centres at Beijing, Mumbai, Brazil and Johannesburg. The World Trade Organization (WTO), which was ill prepared to struggle with world trade problems of intellectual property rights and patents, succumbed to the pressures of big economies, monopolized by multinationals. The oil producing nations created the energy crunch and the threats of growing nuclear proliferation clouded over the international horizons with secrecy, aid underpinnings and human rights violations in the Afro-Asian world. The African resurgence and the Latin American participation in world economy, to which China and India add a new dimension, have resulted into a number of new regional security pacts, international monetary funds and development banks for Africa, Latin America, Asia and Islamic countries. Pacts like G-8 and G-20 represent a new kind of pluralism for economic cooperation. Consequently, the world trade in spite and despite of desperate problems of labour, infrastructure, taxation, loans and technology growth have marked a phenomenal growth for the benefit of the participants. But then, it continues to be a game without a referee and worse still without rules of the game. The foul play and unethical practices are galore in the absence of global transparency and universal acceptance of unfair trade practices. The governments being weak and instable, work hands-in-gloves with the corporate sector. Sudan, Iran and Afghanistan are the weak spots, but the conditions in Brazil and South Africa are no better, where as China and India are viewed as rivals. The non-European, non-Soviet and non-American worlds are developing new patterns of global partnership, corporate social responsibility and business transparency, which are far far away from being ethical or non-colonial.

The subject can be broadly approached from two distinct perspectives. One, the corporate governance in the wake of Liberalization, Privatization and Globalization (LPG) reforms and its social responsibility popularly known as Corporate Social Responsibility (CSR). Secondly, the live issues of partnership frameworks, global ethical leadership and international regulatory mechanisms for funding and aid effectiveness which the CSR and global transparency needs have evoked.

The Principles of Corporate Governance

The term 'corporate governance' can be defined as 'a system of law and sound approaches by which corporations are directed and controlled, focussing on the internal and external corporate structures with the intention of monitoring the actions of management and directors and thereby mitigating agency risks which may stem from the misdeeds of corporate officers.' In contemporary business corporations, the main external stakeholder groups are shareholders, debt holders, trade creators, suppliers, customers and communities affected by the corporation's activities. The internal stakeholders are the board of directors, executives, and other employees. Much of the contemporary interest in corporate governance is concerned with mitigation of the conflicts of interests that exist between the stakeholders. The ways of mitigating or preventing these conflicts of interests include the processes, customs, policies, law, and institutions which have an impact on the way a company is controlled. An important theme of governance is the nature and extent of corporate accountability. A related but separate thread of discussion focuses on the impact of a corporate governance system on economic efficiency, with a strong emphasis on the welfare of shareholders. In large firms, where there is a separation of ownership and management and no controlling shareholders, the principal-agent issues arise between upper-management (the 'agent') – which may have very different interests and by definition considerably more information – and shareholders (the 'principals'). The corporate governance as a set of conditions, shapes the ex-post-bargaining over the quasi-rents generated by a firm. The firm itself is modelled as a governance structure acting through the mechanisms of contract. Here, corporate governance may include its relation to corporate finance. The principles of corporate governance stand some what settled in three documents released since 1990: (1) The Cadbury Report (UK, 1992), (2) the Principles of Corporate Governance (OECD, 1998 and 2004) and (3) the Sarbanes-Oxley Act of 2002

(US, 2002). The Cadbury and OECD reports present general principles around which businesses are expected to operate to assure proper governance. The Sarbanes-Oxley Act, informally referred to as Sarbox or Sox, is an attempt by the federal government in the United States to legislate some of the principles recommended in the Cadbury and OECD reports. These principles champion the rights and equitable treatment of shareholders, the interests of stakeholders and the role and responsibilities of the board. The integrity and ethical behaviour of the corporate officials have to develop a code of conduct for executives that promotes ethical and responsible decision making. The disclosure and transparency procedures have to be timely and balanced to give access to factual information.

The other set of guidelines has been the OECD Principles of Corporate Governance which were published in 1999 and revised in 2004. The OECD guidelines are often referenced by countries developing local codes or guidelines of their own. Building on the work of the OECD, the other international organizations and private sector associations have formed about 20 National Corporate Codes under the United Nations inter-governmental Working Group of Experts called International Standards of Accounting and Reporting (ISAR). They have produced their guidance on good practices in Corporate Governance Disclosure. This internationally agreed benchmark consists of more that fifty disclosure items across five broad categories:

1. Auditing
2. Board and management structure and process
3. Corporate responsibility and compliance
4. Financial transparency and information disclosure
5. Ownership structure and exercise of control rights

As a result of separation between the investors and managers, the corporate governance mechanisms include a system of controls intended to help and align managers' incentives with those of shareholders. It makes the agency concerns necessarily lower for a controlling shareholder.

The board of the directors is responsible for the successful perpetuation of the corporation. This responsibility cannot be relegated to the management. A board of directors has a key role in corporate governance. It has the responsibility for: (1) CEO selection and succession; (2) providing feedback to management on the organizations; (3) strategy; (4) compensating senior executives; (5) monitoring financial health, performance and risk; and (6) ensuring accountability of the organization to its investors and authorities. Boards have various committees (e.g. Compensation, Nominating and Audit) to perform their work.

All parties of corporate governance have an interest, whether direct or indirect, in the financial performance of the corporation. Directors, workers and management receive salaries, benefits and reputation, while investors expect to receive financial returns. For lenders, it is specified interest payments, while returns to equity investors arise from dividend distributions or capital gains on their stock. Customers are concerned with the certainty of the provision of goods and services of an appropriate quality; suppliers are concerned with compensation for their goods or services, and possible continued trading relationships.

In some countries of Continental Europe, ownership is not necessarily equivalent to control due to the existence of dual-class shares, ownership pyramids, voting coalitions, proxy votes and clauses in the articles of association that confer additional voting rights to long-term shareholders. Ownership is defined as the ownership of cash flow rights whereas control refers to ownership of control or voting rights. The control and ownership structures are measured by using observable measures of control and ownership concentrations.

In some corporations thc family interests dominate ownership and control structures. It is argued that the oversight of family controlled corporations is superior to that of corporations 'controlled' by institutional investors with diverse share ownership. The companies in which 'founding families retain a stake of more than 10 per cent of the company's capital generally enjoy a superior performance over their sectorial peers. One of the biggest strategic advantages a company can have is blood ties,' concludes a *Business Week* study.

The significance of institutional investors varies substantially in different countries. In developed Anglo-American countries, like Australia, Canada, New Zealand, U.K., U.S. the institutional investors dominate. The Japanese investors are not institutional. Their holdings are largely with one group. The large pools of invested money are designed to maximize the benefits of diversified investment.

There are both internal monitoring systems and external monitoring systems. Internal monitoring can be done, by one (or a few) large shareholder(s) in the case of privately held companies or a firm belonging to a business group. Furthermore, the various board mechanisms provide for internal monitoring. External monitoring of managers' behaviour, occurs when an independent third party (e.g. the external auditor) attests the accuracy of information provided by management to investors. Stock analysts and debt holders may also conduct such external monitoring. An ideal monitoring and control system should regulate both motivation and ability, while providing incentive alignment towards corporate goals and objectives. Care should be taken that incentives are not so strong that some individuals are tempted to cross lines of ethical behaviour, by manipulating revenue and profit figures to drive the share price of the company up.

The Internal Corporate Controls

Internal corporate governance controls monitor activities and then take corrective action to accomplish organizational goals. Examples include: the board of directors, with its legal authority to hire, fire and compensate top management, safeguards invested capital. Regular board meetings allow potential problems to be identified, discussed and avoided.

Corporate Governance: The World Models

There are many different models of corporate governance around the world. These differ according to the variety of capitalism in which they are embedded. The Anglo-American model tends to emphasize the interests of shareholders. The coordinated or multi-stakeholder model associated with Continental Europe and Japan also recognizes the interests of workers, managers, suppliers, customers, and the community. A related distinction is found between market-orientated and network-orientated models of corporate governance.

The Continental European Models

Some continental European countries, including Germany and the Netherlands, require a two-tiered Board of Directors as a means of improving corporate governance. In the two-tiered board, the Executive Board, made up of company executives, generally runs day-today operations while the supervisory board, made up entirely of non-executive directors who represent shareholders and employees, hires and fires the members of the executive board, determines their compensation, and reviews the corporations major business decisions.

The Indian Model

India's SEBI Committee on Corporate Governance defines corporate governance as the 'acceptance management of the corporation and of their own role as trustees on behalf of the shareholders. It is about commitment to values, about ethical business conduct and about making a distinction between personal and corporate funds in the management of a company.' The so-called 'Anglo-American Model' of corporate governance emphasizes the interests of shareholders. It relies on a single tiered Board of Directors which is normally dominated by non-executive directors, elected by shareholders. Because of this, it is also known as 'a unitary system'. Within this system, many boards include several executives from the company (who are ex officio members of the board). Non-executive directors are expected to outnumber executive directors and hold key posts, including audit and compensation committees.

The US and UK Models

The United States and the United Kingdom differ in one critical respect with regard to corporate governance: In the United Kingdom, the CEO generally does not serve as Chairman of the Board, whereas in the US the dual role is the norm, despite major misgivings regarding the impact on corporate governance. In the United States, corporations are directly governed by state laws, while the exchange (offering and trading) of securities in corporations (including shares) is governed by federal legislation. Many US states have adopted the Model Business Corporation Act, but the dominant state law for public trade corporations is Delaware, which continues to be the place of incorporation for the majority of publicly traded corporations. Individual rules for corporations are based upon the corporate charter which is less authoritative than the corporate bylaws. Shareholders cannot initiate changes in the corporate charter although they can initiate changes in the corporation by-laws.

The practice of having the CEO as the Chair of the Board is known as 'Duality'. This practice is common in the US. It is relatively rare elsewhere. In the UK, successive codes have recommended against duality. External corporate governance encompass the controls of external stakeholders over the organization. These controls are exercised by competition, debt covenants, demand for and assessment of performance information, government regulations, managerial labour market, media pressures and takeovers.

The Problems

Today the Corporate Governance has emerged as a system and some of its systemic problems like the monitoring costs and the supply of accounting information demand immediate solutions. Internal control procedures are policies implemented by a'board of directors, audit committee, management, and other personnel. It provides reasonable assurance of achieving objectives related to reliable financial reporting, operating efficiency, and compliance with laws and regulations. It generates the problem of balance of power. The simplest balance of power requires that the President be a different person from the Treasurer. This application of separation of power is further developed in companies where separate divisions check and balance each other's actions.

Performance-based remuneration is another measure which is designed to relate proportion of salary to individual performance. It may be in the form of cash or non-cash payments such as shares and share options, superannuation or other benefits etc. The large shareholders, monitoring banks and large creditors, pose problems. Given their large investments in the firm, these stakeholders have the incentives, combined with the right degree of control and power, to monitor the management.

The corporate governance is generally equated with private administration which works for a profit motto and has little place for rules and regulations. The cut-throat competition makes it unethical and big business houses are condemned for their unprincipled methods, resulting in scams and scandals. India had a train of these unethical practices of the corporate world since 1990. This threatens to taint or pollute the merit bureaucracy of rules. After the collapse of the Soviet system in the nineties, the LPG wave had made the corporate world more conscious about its social responsibilities. Today, it is not enough to build Birla Temples or charity institutions. Even to pay tax obligations have also nothing to do with philanthropy. The break down of the family system due to women's emancipation, unleashes a wave of private property regulations. Naturally, these is a growing demand that Corporate Governance should manage itself better in social interest. Social responsibility of business in 21st century is viewed as corporate responsibility of the private sector which has to work for the social good of the social sector. It raises a host of moral issues including corporate transparency.

Corporate Transparency

Corporate transparency means the extent to which a corporation's activities are observable by outsiders. This is a consequence of regulation, local norms, and the set of information and privacy. The business policies, concerning corporate decision-making and operations, openness to employees, stakeholders, shareholders and the general public determine its extent. Standard and Poor's Governance Services publishes the corporate transparency guidelines which describes the extent to which a corporations actions are observable by outsiders. This is a consequence of regulation, local norms, set of information, privacy, and business polices. Transparency, as used in science, engineering, business, the humanities and in a social context generally implies openness, communication, and accountability. Transparency is operating in such a way that it is easy for others to see what actions are being performed. For example, a cashier making change at a point of sale by segregating a customer's large bills, counting up from the sale amount, and placing the change on the counter in such a way as to invite the customer to verify the amount of change, demonstrates transparency.

The stakeholder attention and scrutiny has given rise to a powerful shareholder movement. Shareholder activists, composed of large multi-billion-dollar pension funds, religious and socially responsible investment groups, and other institutional investors, are now using a variety of vehicles to influence board behaviour, including corporate governance standards of excellence and filling shareholder resolutions. These investors are concerned with areas such as board diversity, independence, compensation, and accountability, as well as social issues like employment ethics, environmental policies, and community involvement. The corporate responsibility implies a discharge of responsibilities or obligations that a company has toward its stakeholders. When examining a particular corporate practice, like profit versus environmental protection, corporate responsibility can help to distinguish between a stakeholder expectation and a corporate obligation, i.e. is the company obligated to provide absolute environmental protection at all costs or is it obligated to maximize profits for its investors at the cost of damaging the environment. The CSR can be understood in terms of corporate responsibility, but with greater awareness upon the obligations which a company has to the community, with respect to charitable activities and environmental stewardship. Corporate and social responsibility is described as a tacit contract between business and a community. The community permits the business to operate within its jurisdiction to obtain jobs for residents and revenue through taxation. Additionally, the community expects the business to preserve the environment and to make the community a better place to live and to work through charitable activities. Business for Social Responsibility (2001) defines CSR as 'Socially responsible business practices strengthen corporate accountability, respecting ethical values in the interests of stakeholders. Responsible business practices respect and preserve the natural environment. Helping to improve the quality and opportunities of life, they empower people and invest in communities where a business operates.' It should be noted that some business ethics organizations believe that corporate responsibility encompasses all responsibilities that a company has, to all of its stakeholders, which includes ethical, social and environmental responsibilities. The corporate sustainability means aligning an organization's products and services with stakeholder expectations, and thereby adding economic, environmental and social value to it. The Global Reporting Initiative, that grew out of environmental work by the Coalition for Environmentally Responsible Economies (CERES) and the United Nations Environment Programme (UNEP), produced the GRI Sustainability Reporting Guidelines in 2000, which cover economic and social performance as well as the more 'traditional environmental' ones.

Social Accountability

The end of the cold war; spreading democratization has brought a shift in balance among the state, the market and civil society. Globalization; and changing social mores – are the factors which are altering the environment in which governments are operating. The explosion of new information and communication technologies is also causing global diffusion of ideas and practices, enabling the public to demand higher standards of ethics, transparency and accountability in the public sector. These prerequisite values of good governance and sustainable development not only buttress responsive public policy and high levels of public sector performance but also play a crucial role in preventing the onset of systemic corruption. There is increasing international recognition to the fact that corruption impedes economic development, undermines stability and erodes trust in public institutions. The pernicious effects of corruption – the poor quality of essential public infrastructure and services – are borne by those who are least able to afford.

If a company is truly committed to CSR, it regards it as an integral part of the business decision making process and prominently places it in the company's core mission, vision, and values documents. These simple but important statements state company goals and aspirations. They also provide insight into a company's values, culture, and strategies for achieving their aims. The mission or vision of a socially responsible business frequently references a purpose beyond 'making a profit' or being the best. It specifies that it will engage in ethical business practices and seek to create value for a variety of stakeholders, including shareholders/owners, employees, customers, vendors, communities, and the natural environment. Sample companies satisfy this indicator if they stated CSR as an intricate part of their corporate objectives and conducted their business in a manner that was consistent with their statements. After measuring the sample companies' performance on the indicators, performance was compared to whether or not they are rated on the Dow Jones Sustainability Indexes (DJSI). Many social investors consider the DJSI the most competitive index to be listed on because of its high social, ethical, and environmental standards. Dow Jones Sustainability Indexes track the financial performance of the leading sustainability companies worldwide, providing asset managers with reliable and objective benchmarks to manage sustainability-driven portfolios. The DJSI world covers the largest 2,500 companies by market capitalization in the Dow Jones Global Index.

GlobeScan's 22 nation survey on CSR explores the attitudes, and behaviour of consumers, shareholders, and corporate employees relating to current CSR issues. The survey has been conducted annually since 1999, using face-to-face or telephone interviews with representative samples of 1,000 citizens in each of the selected countries (GlobeScan, 2003). Topics in the survey include: trust in companies, corporate governance, communications, company ratings, ethical consumerism, and socially responsible investing. The 2003 Management Barometer surveys top executives in large multinational corporations spanning technology, financial services, and consumer and industrial products and services (Ascolese, 2003). The polling is developed and compiled with assistance from the opinion and economic research firm of BSI Global Research Inc. The survey looks at the stronger emphasis European headquartered multinational companies place on reporting their environmental and social performance.

The Image and Distrust

The corporate scandals of last few years have helped to drive a surge in regulation and decline in public trust. Citizens on both sides of the Atlantic, have a hard time believing multinational company executives and have lost some faith in the governments that are supposed to be regulating them. More and more citizens are putting their trust in NGOs to hold global companies accountable for their actions. Trust is the single largest driver of public attitudes on a whole range of issues from globalization to terrorism to the role of governments. Trust is also the primary driver of corporate and country brands. Companies realize that they now face new conditions in their efforts to build corporate reputation and public trust.

At the global level, the problems become complex because there is a historic distrust and the former colonies have a very poor image of their business leaders. The big multinationals are still a monopoly of rich nations. These multinational companies are powerful drivers of international trade and investment, and have a critical role to play in upholding and advancing business ethics, corporate governance and social and environmental standards, especially in countries which are less developed. Companies in Europe and America offer shareholders the power to unseat board members through voting proxy. The chief executives fill their boards with allies leading to conflicts of interest and low levels of governance. In UK, only around one in three listed companies fully comply with the country's combined code on corporate governance. What is needed is that all multinational companies fully disclose their executives pay to primary shareholders since the corporate frauds are directly tied to greed. The executives are not allowed to boost their own pay at the expense of others. UK recently failed to pass legislation that would curb executive pay and the US has yet to even make an attempt. The corporate world should clearly outline whistle-blowing framework with code of conduct to all employees, who need a base level of support and counsel when an individual's ethics is challenged. A strong whistle blowing process can be a company's best means of reducing the impact of fraud.

The Corporate Social Responsibility

The CSR, now broadly accepted by business and companies, must move to the next stage by embedding CSR into core activities and not treating it as an add-on. At the start of the decade, CSR was often seen as an optional extra by business leaders and as an adjunct of public relations. But with a spate of corporate scandals rocking faith in business ethics, that position appears to have changed for good. Acknowledging CSR and publishing reports to the next stage by embedding CSR into core business activities has to be accepted. More and more NGOs feel that CSR is an adjunct of company public relations. Those that do not embed social and environmental performance throughout the corporate culture, risk losing credibility with stakeholders.

As stakeholders take a growing interest in corporate social responsibility, many companies are finding that they are responsible not only for their own CSR performance but for that of the companies 'upstream' and 'downstream' – that is, their suppliers as well as their customers and even their customers' customers. Leadership companies are imposing codes of conduct on their suppliers and customers to ensure that other companies' policies or practices do not reflect unfavourably on them.

Applying these standards to other businesses has a cascading effect and allows the company to make a larger impact towards improving the social and environmental performance of the private sector. The CSR communications efforts need focus on staff and suppliers, by sending them tailored social reports. Internal stakeholders are widely unaware of their company's social and environmental performance making them an underutilized resource. All employees and suppliers have enormous reach and influence with external stakeholders. People are more likely to believe things they hear about a CSR programme from a source they know than they get from a glossy report. A 2004 GlobeScan survey of 1,000 employees in European large companies found that 84 per cent of the respondents agreed with the phrase, 'CSR increases my motivation and loyalty.' Only 64 per cent felt that their company had done a good job informing them about its social responsibility commitments.

The ethics of corporate business is increasingly under the scan of public accountability. The media and the parliamentary institutions document and publish reports. Special commissions are appointed to unearth true facts and culprits are brought to book. In India, 2 G Spectrum can be called a case in point which lowered the ethical image of government and corporate world in collusion. Corporate transparency is a look of accountability. The stockholders and stakeholders need to be protected against frauds which secrecy generates. The private public partnership projects add a new dimension to this unethical relationship which democratic accountability threatens to expose in public interest. The effective provisions of social accountability improve the ethical quality of CSR and can save the healthy competitive system of free trade from governments intervention and control in changing economies of third world countries.

Ethics in International Relations

International ethics is an area of international relations theory which concerns the extent and scope of ethical obligations between states, in the era of globalization. Schools of thought include cosmopolitanism and anti-cosmopolitanism. Realism, Liberalism, and Marxism are ethical traditions that conceptually address moral issues in international relations. The Realists start with the premise that ethics is secondary, or inapplicable to the affairs of international politics. They believe in the primacy of self-interest over moral principle. The pursuit of self-interest by states is viewed as a *right*, or *duty*, making it a principle for

Realists to uphold. From their standpoint, the international environment is perpetually anarchic and competitive over resources. There is no overarching authority over states. Without a superior power to enforce order, ethics cannot be sustained in international affairs. Out of necessity, international conditions compel states to defend their interests by immoral means, and this compulsion of self-defense dissolves moral duties. It would be considered unethical by the principle of pursing self-interest, for a state to compromise its goal for power and security.

International relations is the study of relationship among countries, the roles of sovereign states and inter-governmental organizations which effect the political and economic relations of varied nations across the globe. The nation states freely permit foreign or international organization to function and shape relationships and behaviours. These international institutions form a vital part of contemporary international relations. Much interaction at the system level is governed by them, and they outlaw some traditional institutions and practices of international relations, such as the use of war.

United Nations Organization

The United Nations (UN) is an international organization that describes itself as a 'global association of governments facilitating co-operations in international law, international security, economic development, and social equity'. It is the most prominent international institution. Many of the legal institutions follow the same organizational structure as the UN.

The Organization of Islamic Cooperation (OIC) is an international organization, consisting of 57 member states. The organization attempts to be the collective voice of the Muslim world (Ummah) and attempts to safeguard the interests and ensure the progress and well-being of Muslims. Some of the other generalist inter-state organizations can be identified as:

1. African Union
2. Association of Southeast Asian Nations
3. Arab League
4. Commonwealth of Independent States
5. European Union
6. G8
7. G20
8. League of Nations
9. Organization of American States

Economic Institutions

1. Asian Development Bank
2. African Development Bank
3. Bank of International Settlements
4. Inter-American Development Bank
5. International Monetary Fund
6. Islamic Development Bank
7. World Bank
8. World Trade Organization

International Legal Bodies

Human rights

1. European Court of Human Rights
2. Human Rights Committee
3. Inter-American Court of Human Rights
4. International Criminal Court
5. International Criminal Tribunal for Rwanda
6. International Criminal Tribunal for the Former Yugoslavia
7. United Nations Human Rights Council

Legal

1. African Court of Justice
2. European Court of Justice

3. International Court of Justice
4. International Tribunal for the Law of the Sea

Additionally there are several Regional Security Pacts. They include:

(a) Council for Security Cooperation in the Asia Pacific
(b) GUAM Organization for Democracy and Economic Development
(c) Maritime Security Regime
(d) NATO
(e) Shanghai Cooperation Organization
(f) South Asian Association for Regional Cooperation
(g) Union of South American Nations

In international relations, overseas aid or foreign aid is a voluntary transfer of resources from one country to another. Humanitarianism and altruism are the objectives for giving this aid. It may have other functions as well: For instance, it can be given as a signal of diplomatic approval (1) to strengthen a military ally, (2) to reward a government for behaviour desired by the donor, (3) to extend the donor's cultural influence, (4) to provide infrastructure needed by the donor for resource extraction form the recipient country or (5) to gain other kinds of commercial access. Aid may be given by individuals, private organizations, or governments. Standards delimiting exactly the kinds of transfers that count as aid, vary. The aid figures may or may not include transfers for military use.

The foreign aid agenda today, covers a wide ground and all sorts of programmes and pacts exist to float foreign currency in weaker countries. This double edged weapon is used to offer philanthropic assistance and also to over-power the economies to subserve the interests of donor countries. With the thaw in the Cold War the middle range powers like India, China, Germany and Japan have taken to a new role in international economic relations in the multipolar world. They have signed mutual assistance facts and are entering into the global arena to promote their national, political and economic interests along with the growth of the region. The EU model, though not feasible in non-European world, is being imitated by African, Asian and Latin American countries. A number of these Aid-Agendas are criticized for their ulterior motives. Others believe that they have supported developing economies and poverty stricken societies. Some analysts of the Overseas Development Institute, argue that current support for the developing world suffers from a policy incoherence and that while some policies are designed to support the third world, other domestic policies undermine its impact. For instance, encouraging developing economies to develop their agriculture with a focus on exports is not effective on a global scale. The collection of code lists for representing information is manipulated. The donors publish data and use the standards to encourage submission of meta-data to the IATI registry.

Aid effectiveness is the effectiveness of development aid in achieving economic or human development. Aid agencies are always looking for new ways to improve effectiveness, including conditionality, capacity building and support for improved governance. As recognized by the OECD's Working Party or Aid Effectiveness at the beginning of the 21st century, it became apparent that promoting widespread and sustainable development was not only about amounts of aid given, but also how aid was given. Aid flows have significantly increased over the last decade, but at the same time aid has become increasingly fragmented.

The Accra Agenda and Paris Declaration, 2005

In a research by the Overseas Development Institute in Ethiopia, Sierra Leone and Zambia suggests that the Accra Agenda for Action (AAA) and Paris Declaration on Aid Effectiveness's indicators are too narrowly defined and lack depth. The principles of 'predictability' and 'transparency' are highlighted as lacking depth and important sub-dimensions not given enough emphasis, on adaptation to local contexts. The recipient governments felt 'predictability' meant donors should provide funding within the quarters scheduled. The Paris Declaration embodied a new, broad consensus on what needs to be done to produce better development results. Its principles lay open the possible ways to undertake, which can be interpreted also as the major objectives of good aid: fostering recipient countries' ownership of development policies and strategies, maximizing donors' coordination and harmonization, improving aid transparency and mutual accountability of donors and recipients. The Accra Agenda for Action states that transparency and accountability are essential elements for development results, as well as drivers of progress. Mutual accountability and transparency is one of the five partnership commitments of the Paris Declaration. Through 'transparency', donors and recipients can be held accountable for what they spend and aid can be made more effective by knowing: Who gives money to which recipient? What project is being funded and for what purpose and where?

Transparency offers a valuable answer to insecurity, making aid 'predictable' and 'reliable'. Transparency has been shown to improve service delivery and to reduce opportunities for diversion and therefore corruption. Transparency can be defined as a basic expression of mutual accountability. Mutual accountability can only work if there is a global culture of transparency that demands provision of information through a set of rules. These rules should provide data and the donor country should agree on adopting a standardized format for providing information on volume, allocation and results, such as the International Aid Transparency Initiative (IATI), or other similar standards, and commit to improve recipient countries' data bases with technical, financial and informational support. The format should be easily downloadable and with sufficient disaggregation to enable comparison with other data. Making aid data public and comparable among donors, would be likely to encourage a process of positive emulation towards a better usage of public funds. After all, official development assistance (ODA) is a voluntary transfer that depends on the support of donor country tax payers.

To improve accountability, while building evaluation capabilities in aid recipient countries and systematically collecting beneficiaries' feedback, different mechanisms to evaluate and monitor transparency should be considered, such as independent third-party reviews, peer reviews or mutual reviews.

Paris Declaration, 2005

The international community came together at the Paris High Level Forum on Aid Effectiveness, hosted by the French government and organized by the OECD. In February 2005, the role of aid in promoting development was attracting increasing public scrutiny in the run-up to the G8 Summit in Gleneagles, Scotland, and the global campaigns such as 'Make Poverty History'. The aid process was still too strongly led by donor priorities and administered through donor channels, making it hard for developing countries to take the lead. Aid is still too uncoordinated, unpredictable and non-transparent. At the Paris meeting, more than 100 signatories – donor and developing-country governments, multilateral donor agencies, regional developments banks and international agencies – endorsed the Paris Declaration on Aid Effectiveness. The Paris Declaration represented a consensus among the international community about how to make aid more effective. At its heart, was the commitment to help developing-country governments formulate and implement their own national development plans, according to their own national priorities, using, wherever possible, their own planning and implementations systems. The Paris Declaration contains 56 partnership commitments aimed at improving the effectiveness of aid. It lays out 12 indicators to provide a measurable and evidence-based way to track progress, and sets targets for 11 of the indicators to be met by 2010. The Declaration is focused on five mutually reinforcing principles:

1. *Ownership:* Developing countries must lead their own development policies and strategies, and manage their own development work on the ground.
2. *Alignment:* Donors must line up their aid firmly behind the priorities outlined in developing countries' national development strategies.
3. *Harmonization :* Donors must coordinate their development work better amongst themselves to avoid duplication and high transaction costs for poor countries.
4. *Managing for results:* All parties in the aid relationship must place more focus on the result of aid, the tangible difference it makes in poor people's lives.
5. *Mutual accountability:* Donors and developing countries must account more transparently to each other for their use of aid funds, and to their citizens and parliaments for the impact of their aid.

A first round of monitoring of the 12 Paris Declaration indicators was conducted in 2006, based on activities undertaken in 2005 in 34 countries. A second survey was organized in early 2008, in which 54 developing countries examined progress against the targets at country level. The evidence so far suggests that progress has been made. For example, more than one third of developing countries surveyed had improved their systems for managing public funds. The predictability of aid flows also remains low making it hard for governments to plan ahead. In some quarters, the Paris Declaration is almost synonymous with aid effectiveness; it is expected that aid will be effective and achieve development outcomes when the principles are observed for government sector aid. Independent NGOs, such as Eurodad, also release their own evaluations, showing that the Declaration is not being implemented as envisaged.

Third High Level Forum Accra, 2008

The Third High Level Forum on Aid Effectiveness (HLF-3) was held in Accra, Ghana from 2–4 September 2008. Its aim was to build on the work of the two previous meetings, in Rome and Paris, to take stock of progress so far, and to accelerate the momentum of change. The forum was attended by senior ministers from more than 100 countries, as well as representative of multilateral aid institutions such as the European Commission (EuropeAid), the World Bank, the United Nations (UN), private foundations and civil society organizations. It was the first of three major international aid conferences in 2008, all aimed at speeding up progress toward the Millennium Development Goals. The Accra Forum took place against a rapidly changing international aid landscape. Donor countries such as China and India are becoming increasingly important and there are more global programmes and funds that channel aid to tackle specific problems, such as the Global Fund to Fight Aids, Tuberculosis and Malaria. Private funding sources such as the Bill and Melinda Gates Foundation are becoming major players, and civil society groups are increasingly active. The Accra meeting was different from its predecessors in that developing countries played a more active role in the preparations of the agenda. Some 80 developing countries took part in the regional preparatory events. Fifty-four developing countries participated in the OECD's 2008 survey of progress against the Paris Declaration targets. There is broad acknowledgement that new global challengers, such as rising food and fuel prices and climate change, bring added urgency to efforts to make aid as effective as possible.

Attention is being focused on stepping up progress towards the commitments outlined in the Paris Declaration by committing signatories to accelerating the pace of change by focusing on key areas that should enable them to meet the 2010 targets agreed at Paris. Drawing on evidence, the Accra Agenda for Action (AAA) identifies three main areas where progress towards reform is still too slow. (1) The Accra Agenda for Action says, developing-country governments still need to take stronger leadership of their own development policies and engage further with their parliaments and citizens in shaping them. (2) The Accra Agenda for Action aims to incorporate the contributions of all development players – middle-income countries, global funds, the private sector, civil society organizations – into more inclusive partnerships. (3) The Accra Agenda for Action says, the demonstration of impact must be placed more squarely at the heart of efforts to make aid more effective. There is a strong focus on helping developing countries to produce stronger national statistical and information systems to help them better monitor and evaluate impact.

The Accra Agenda for Action sets out a list of commitments for its signatories, building on those already agreed in the Paris Declaration. It asks the OECD's Working Party on Aid Effectiveness to continue monitoring progress on implementing the Paris Declaration and the Accra Agenda for Action. All these international conventions and declarations represent an effort to create consensus in the area of business ethics. The old notion of 'Private Profit' is to be replaced by the newer slogan on 'Corporate Social Responsibility'. Aid or/and Trade are the traditional patterns and both can be abused for exploitative ends. So long the nation states dominate, the weaker nations stand in a danger of being exploited under one pretext or the other. Aid is a humanitarian devise, while trade is a self respecting contractual system of national and international intercourse.

The World Trade in Decolonized World

The study of colonialism indicates that European powers entered the Afro-Asian continents as traders with the help of missionaries. The so-called white man's burden was practiced at the cost of black nations interests which became weak, poor and backward in the process. After second World War, the national resurgence has liberated these former colonies and with decolonization, a new era of world trade and commerce has opened new vistas of economic relationships. The WTO, as an international organization, is vainly struggling to ensure fair conditions of economic justice and business equity. The unethical practices of super and bigger powers dominate the world market. Efforts are needed to ensure economic justice and fair play to all the strong and weak nations of the world.

Globalization, as a world trade phenomenon, has several new and inbuilt challenges, which are unprecedented. The global markets are different from colonies and the so called developed countries and their business leaders cannot be accepted as superior partners. The demands of world economy are compulsive and mere customs and conventions do not allow the desired scenario to emerge. The global trade and commerce of the corporate world has international dimensions of foreign funding, and involvements in whole sale and retail trades. The marketing practices, rates of interest, labour laws, technology transfer and contracts arrangements in alien lands, flood the entire area with unethical practices with an impossibility to punish the miscreants. The political nature of the governments does not permit transparency or a business democracy with ethical standards. The international law does not have teeth and the neocolonial game continues in the name of so called sound business practices and WTO conventions.

In India, the multinationals have arrived with a bang. The fragile structures of politics and corrupt bureaucracy are vainly struggling to regulate the flow of foreign capital and protection of the ecology. The super powers play their nasty game of foreign aid, the NGO politics and the free trade areas with soft conditions. The corporate governance, like world governance of UN, has not become global. The glaring inequities paralyse the UN intervention and WTO has failed to ensure commercial justice between developed and developing worlds of post-war era.

Foreign aid and foreign trade apart, the international community has to go a long way to develop international law and international ethics to build an honest world with out economic barriers.

The reason for this was that the United Nations Global Compact Principles of CSR are still not integrated into the business processes of the companies. The level of monitoring of CSR in India is still regarded as very low as many of the companies do not even publish their annual CSR report. Thus, the notion of 'ethical trusteeship' remains a notional feature of the Indian CSR agenda.

Liberalization, privatization and globalization as keynotes of new international economic order have come to stay. The world market has its healthy and unhealthy impacts on Indian economy and politics. The civil servants in India have an opportunity to exploit these developments for personal ends or for national interests. Selfish and unethical use of these opportunities is called corruption, while the exploitation of opportunities in national interest is welcomed as development.

The nation-states in the world comity of nations are not equally developed, materially as well as ethically. The superpowers are and will exploit the middle-range powers in open competition, as is the situation today. But, the ethical situation in scientifically advanced countries is forcing business to be more ethical. Former CEO of Microsoft, Bill Gates and Bono, an Irish singer and businessman, are donating their wealth for the welfare of African society.

Capitalism in Reverse

This is capitalism in reverse. Actually, it is the result of the disintegration of family system in the West. The citizen's welfare is replacing family welfare and succession of property and wealth needs a change in inheritance laws there. The affluent businessmen want to do justice to their stakeholders rather than leaving a fortune for their biological progeny. This development, coupled with advances of technology and connectivity revolution, widens the frontiers of family loyalty. The parochialism is yielding place to universalism of the international era which is creating a 'world without borders'. It can be termed as an 'ethical revolution' of business values, transforming the profit motto into a service mission of business.

As this globalization gets stabilized and the family loyalty becomes weaker in the urban industrial economy of India, the feminist revolution will have its impact on corrupt familial practices of Indian society. As the sanctity of the institution of marriage declines in India, the family values will change the perspectives on property and inheritance of wealth. The corporate capitalism and the nucleus family will contribute to the dawn of new values of possession, greed and inheritance. Hopefully, it will revise the 'over-familial values' of an agricultural society into societal values of equitability, equity and gender justice.

Thus, from the distrust of non-gazetted public servants to the socio-ethical responsibility of business managements, there is a wide area of ethical debates and disputes in a plural society of India's size and diversities. The historical legacies, howsoever obnoxious, cannot be wished away. The ethical behaviours of ruling servants are to be regulated by the laws but their conscience also needs to be aroused in matters that pertain to the masses. A democratic government will have to be accountable and hence a public servant has to be alive to his or her ethical concerns, inherent in the operations of good governance. The funding of development by national and global corporations is a necessity of the future. A brilliant civil servant should visualize this distant future, stay away from the status feudalism of the past, meticulously follow the laws of governance and also that of his or her conscience. It shall keep him or her accountable in the Private Public Partnership (PPP) global economy of the country and the world.

Case Studies

Case Study 1

You are working as an Executive Engineer in the construction cell of a Municipal Corporation and are presently in-charge of the construction of a flyover. There are two Junior Engineers under you who have the responsibility of day-to-day inspection of the site and are reporting to you, while you are finally reporting to the Chief Engineer who heads the cell. While the construction is heading towards completion, the Junior Engineers have been regularly reporting that all construction is taking place as per design specifications. However, in one of your surprise inspections, you have noticed some serious deviations and lacunae which, in your opinion, are likely to affect the safety of the flyover. Rectification of these lacunae at this stage would require a substantial amount of demolition and rework which will cause a tangible loss to the contractor and will also delay completion. There is a lot of public pressure on the Corporation to get this construction completed because of heavy traffic congestion in the area. When you brought this matter to the notice of the Chief Engineer, he advised for further expediting the project for completion in time. However, you are convinced that this was a serious matter which might affect public safety and should not be left unaddressed.

What will you do in such a situation? Some of the options are given below. Evaluate the merits and demerits of each of these options and finally suggest what course of action you would like to take, giving reasons. (250 words)

(i) Follow the advice of the Chief Engineer and go ahead.
(ii) Make an exhaustive report of the situation bringing out all facts and analysis along with your own viewpoints stated clearly and seek for written orders from the Chief Engineer.
(iii) Call for explanation from the Junior Engineers and issue orders to the contractor for necessary correction within targeted time.
(iv) Highlight the issue so that it reaches superiors above the Chief Engineer.
(v) Considering the rigid attitude of the Chief Engineer, seek transfer from the project or report sick.

Case Study 2

Sivakasi in Tamil Nadu is known for its manufacturing clusters on firecrackers and matches. The local economy of the area is largely dependent on firecrackers industry. It has led to tangible economic development and improved standard of living in the area.

So far as child labour norms for hazardous industries like firecrackers industry are concerned, International Labour Organization (ILO) has set the minimum age as 18 years. In India, however, this age is 14 years.

The units in industrial clusters of firecrackers can be classified into registered and non-registered entities. One typical unit is household-based work. Though the law is clear on child labour employment norms in registered/non-registered units, it does not include household-based works. Household-based work means children working under the supervision of their parents/relative. To evade child labour norms, several units project themselves as household-based works but employ children from outside. Needless to say that employing children saves the cots for these units leading to higher profits to the owners.

On your visit to one of the units at Sivakasi, the owner takes you around the unit which has about 10-15 children below 14 years of age. The owner tells you that in his household-based unit, the children are all his relatives. You notice that several children smirk, when the owner tells you this. On deeper enquiry, you figure out that neither the owner nor the children are able to satisfactorily establish their relationship with each other.

(a) Bring out and discuss the ethical issues involved in the above case.
(b) What would be your reaction after your above visit? (300 words)

Case Study 3

You are heading a leading technical institute of the country. The institute is planning to convene an interview panel shortly under your chairmanship for selection of the post of professors. A few days before the interview, you get a call from the Personal Secretary (PS) of a senior government functionary seeking your intervention in favour of the selection of a close relative of the functionary for this post. The PS also informs you that he is aware of the long pending and urgent proposals of your institute for grant of funds for modernization, which are awaiting the functionary's approval. He assures you that he would get these proposals cleared.

(a) What are the options available to you?
(b) Evaluate each of these options and choose the option which you would adopt, giving reasons. (250 words)

Case Study 4

As a senior officer in the Finance Ministry, you have access to some confidential and crucial information about policy decisions that the Government is about to announce. These decisions are likely to have far-reaching impact on the housing and construction industry. If the builders have access to this information beforehand, they can make huge profits. One of builders has done a lot of quality work for the Government and is known to be close to your immediate superior, who asks you to disclose this information to the said builder.

(a) What are the options available to you?
(b) Evaluate each of these options and choose the option which you would adopt, giving reasons. (250 words)

Case Study 5

You are the Executive Director of an upcoming Infotech Company which is making a name for itself in the market.

Mr. Anirudh who is a star performer is heading the marketing team. In short period of one year, he has helped in doubling the revenues as well as creating a high brand equity for the company so much so that you are thinking of promoting him. However, you have been receiving information from many corners about his attitude towards the female colleagues; particularly his habit of making loose comments on women. In addition, he regularly sends indecent SMSs to all the team members including his female colleagues.

One day, late in the evening, Mrs. Anuradha, who is one of Mr. Anirudha's team members, comes to you visibly disturbed. She complains against the continued misconduct of Mr. Anirudh who has been making undesirable advances towards her and has even tried to touch her inappropriately in his cabin.

She tenders her resignation and leaves your office.

(a) What are the options available to you?

(b) Evaluate each of these options and choose the option you would adopt, giving reasons. (250 words)

Case Study 6

You are posted as the Medical Superintendent of a district level government hospital in Rajasthan that caters to the need of poor patients from surrounding rural areas along with the local people from the district town. As such, the hospital has very good infrastructure and adequate equipment to cater to this need. It also receives sufficient funds to meet the recurring expenditure. In spite of this, there have been repeated complaints, particularly from the patients, which include the following:

1. Very poor maintenance and unhygienic conditions in hospital premises.
2. The hospital staff frequently demanding bribes from the patients for the services rendered.
3. The negligent attitude of the doctors resulting at times in casualties.

4. Siphoning of a substantial stock of medicine by the staff and selling it out.
5. Strong nexus between the senior doctors of the hospital and the owners of local private nursing homes and testing labs as a result of which the patients are strongly misled and dissuaded from availing the hospital facilities and rather compelled to purchase costly medicines from market and get medical tests and even operations done from private medical houses.
6. There also exists a notorious employee union which puts undue pressure and resents any reformative step by the administration.

Ponder over the situation and suggest effective ways to tackle each of the above-mentioned problem.

Case Study 7

A Public Information Officer has received an application under RTI Act. Having gathered the information, the PIO discovers that the information pertains to some of the decisions taken by him, which were found to be not altogether right. There were other employees also who were part to these decisions. Disclosure of the information is likely to lead to disciplinary action with possibility of punishment against him as well as some of his colleagues. Non-disclosure or part disclosure or camouflaged disclosure of information will result into lesser punishment or no punishment.

The PIO is otherwise an honest and conscientious person but this particular decision, on which the RTI application has been filed, turned out to be wrong. He comes to you for advice.

The following are some suggested options. Please evaluate the merits and demerits of each of the options:

(i) The PIO could refer the matter to his superior officer and seek his advice and act strictly in accordance with the advice, even though he is not completely in agreement with the advice of the superior.
(ii) The PIO could proceed on leave and leave the matter to be dealt by his successor in office or request for transfer of the application to another PIO.
(iii) The PIO could weigh the consequences of disclosing the information truthfully, including the effect on his career, and reply

in a manner that would not place him or his career in jeopardy, but at the same time a little compromise can be made on the contents of the information.

(iv) The PIO could consult his other colleagues who are party to the decision and take action as per their advice.

Also please indicate (without necessarily restricting to the above options) what you would like to advise, giving proper reasons (250 words)

Case Study 8

You have been asked to give an explanation for not attending an important official meeting. Your immediate boss who has not informed you about the meeting is now putting pressure on you not to place an allegation against him/her. You would:

(a) Send a written reply explaining the fact.
(b) Seek an appointment with the top boss to explain the situation.
(c) Admit your fault to save the situation.
(d) Put the responsibility on the coordinator of the meeting for not informing.

Case Study 9

A local politician (bad element) has started illegal construction on your vacant plot. He has refused your request to vacate and threatened you of dire consequences in case you do not sell the property at a cheap price to him. You would:

(a) Sell the property at a cheap price to him.
(b) Go to the police for necessary action.
(c) Ask for help from your neighbours.
(d) Negotiate with the goon to get a higher price.

Case Study 10

You are an officer-in-charge for providing basic medical facilities to the survivors of an earthquake affected area. Despite your best possible effort, people put allegations against your for making money out of the funds given for relief. You would:

(a) Let an enquiry be set up to look into the matter.

(b) Ask your senior to appoint some other person in your place.
(c) Not pay attention to allegations.
(d) Stop undertaking any initiative till the matter is resolved.

Case Study 11

You have been made responsible to hire boats at a short notice to be used for an area under flood. On seeing the price mentioned by the boat owners you found that the lowest price was approximately three times more than the approved rate of the Government. You would:

(a) Reject the proposal and call for a fresh price.
(b) Accept the lowest price.
(c) Refer the matter to the Government and wait.
(d) Threaten the boat owners about a possible cancellation of the licence.

Case Study 12

You have taken up a project to create night-shelters for homeless people during the winter season. Within a week of establish ing the shelters, you have received complaints from the residents of the area about the increase in theft cases with a demand to remove the shelters. You would:

(a) Ask them to lodge a written complaint in the police station.
(b) Assure residents of an enquiry into the matter.
(c) Ask residents to consider the humanitarian effort made.
(d) Continue with the project and ignore their complaint.

Case Study 13

You, as an administrative authority, have been approached, by the daughter-in-law of an influential person regarding harassment by her in-laws on account of insufficient dowry. Her parents are not able to approach you because of social pressures. You would:

(a) Call the in-laws for an explanation.
(b) Counsel the lady to adjust, given such a circumstance.
(c) Take action after her parents approach you.
(d) Ask her to lodge complaint with the police.

Case Study 14

You have differences of opinion regarding the final report prepared by your subordinate that is to be submitted urgently. The subordinate is justifying the information given in the report. You would:

(a) Convince the subordinate that he is wrong.
(b) Tell him to reconsider the results.
(c) Revise the report on your own.
(d) Tell him not to justify the mistake.

Case Study 15

You are handling a time bound project. During the project review meeting, you find that project is likely to get delayed due to lack of cooperation of the team members. You would:

(a) Warn the team members for their non-cooperation.
(b) Look into the reasons for non-cooperation.
(c) Ask for the replacement of the team members.
(d) Ask for the extension of time citing reasons.

Case Study 16

You are a chairperson of a state sports committee. You have received a complaint and later it was found that an athlete in junior age category who has won a medal has crossed the age criteria by five days. You would:

(a) Ask the screening committee for a clarification.
(b) Ask the athlete to return the medal.
(c) Ask the athlete to get an affidavit from the court declaring his/her age.
(d) Ask the members of the committee for their views.

Case Study 17

You are involved in setting up a water supply project in remote area. full recovery of cost is impossible in any case. The income levels in the area are low and 25 per cent of the population is below poverty line (BPL). When a decision has to be taken on pricing, you would:

(a) Recommend that the supply of water be free of charge in all respects.
(b) Recommend that the users pay a onetime fixed sum for installation of taps and the usage of water be free.
(c) Recommend that a fixed monthly charges be levied on the non-BPL families and for BPL families water should be free.
(d) Recommend that the users pay a charge based on the consumption of water with differentiated charges for Non-BPL and BPL families.

Case Study 18

As a citizen you have some work with a government department. The official calls you again and again; and without directly asking you, sends out feelers for a bribe. You want to get your work done. You would:
(a) Give a bribe.
(b) Behave as if you have not understood the feelers and persist with your application.
(c) Go to the higher officer for help, verbally complaining about feelers.
(d) Send in a formal complaint.

Case Study 19

You are the head of your office. There are certain houses reserved for the allotment to the office and you have been given the discretion to do so. A set of rules for the allotment of the houses has been laid down by you and has been made public. Your personal secretary, who is very close to you, comes to you and pleads that as his father is seriously ill, he should be given priority in allotment of a house. The office secretariat that examined the request as per the rules turns down the request and recommends the procedure to be followed according to the rules. You do not want to annoy your personal secretary. In such circumstances, what would you do?
(a) Call him over to your room and personally explain why the allotment cannot be done.
(b) Allot the house to him to win his loyalty.

(c) Agree with the office note to show that you are not biased and that you do not indulge in favouritism.
(d) Keep the file with you and not pass any orders.

Case Study 20

While travelling in a Delhi-registered commercial taxi from Delhi to an adjacent city (another State), your taxi driver informs you that as he has no permit for running the taxi in that city, he will stop at its Transport Office and pay the prescribed fee of Rs. forty for a day. While paying the fee at the counter you find that the transport clerk is taking an extra fifty rupees for which no receipt is being given. You are in a hurry for your meeting. In such circumstances, what would you do?

(a) Go up to the counter and ask the clerk to give back the money which he has illegally taken.
(b) Do not interfere at all as this is a matter between the taxi driver and the tax authorities.
(c) Take note of the incident and subsequently report the matter to the concerned authorities.
(d) Treat it as a normal affair and simply forget about it.

Case Study 21

A person lives in a far off village which is almost two hours by bus. The villager's neighbour is a very powerful landlord who is trying to occupy the poor villager's land by force. You are the District Magistrate and busy in a meeting called by a local Minister. The villager has come all the way, by bus and on foot, to see you and give an application seeking protection from the powerful landlord. The villager keeps on waiting outside the meeting hall for an hour. You come out of the meeting and are rushing to another meeting. The villager follows you to submit his application. What would you do?

(a) Tell him to wait for another two hours till you come back from your next meeting.
(b) Tell him that the matter is actually to be dealt by a junior officer and that he should give the application to him.
(c) Call one of your senior subordinate officers and ask him to solve the villager's problem.

(d) Quickly take the application from him, ask him a few relevant questions regarding his problem and then proceed to this meeting.

Case Study 22

There is shortage of sugar in your District where you are the District Magistrate. The government has ordered that only a maximum amount of 30 kg sugar is to be released for wedding celebrations. A son of your close friend is getting married and your friend requests you to release at least 50kg sugar for his son's wedding. He expresses annoyance when you tell him about the government's restrictions on this matter. He feels that since you are the District Magistrate you can release any amount. You do not want to spoil your friendship with him. In such circumstance, how would you deal with the situation?

(a) Release the extra amount of sugar which your friend has requested for.
(b) Refuse your friend the extra amount and strictly follow the rules.
(c) Show your friend the copy of the Government instructions and then persuade him to accept the lower amount as prescribed in the rules.
(d) Advise him to directly apply to the allotting authority and inform him that you do not interfere in this matter.

Case Study 23

You are in-charge of implementing the Family Planning Programme in an area where there is a strong opposition to the present policy. You want to convince the residents of the need for keeping small families. What would be the best way of communicating this message?

(a) By logically explaining to the residents the need for family planning to improve the health and living standards.
(b) By encouraging late marriages and proper spacing of children.
(c) By offering incentives for adopting family planning devices.
(d) By asking people who have been sterilized or are using contraceptives to directly talk to the residents.

Case Study 24

You are a teacher in a university and are setting a question paper on a particular subject. One of your colleagues, whose son is preparing for the examination on that subject, comes to you and informs you that it is his son's last chance to pass that examination and whether you could help him by indication what questions are going to be in the examination. In the past, your colleague had helped you in another matter. Your colleague informs you that his son will suffer from depression if he fails in this examination. In such circumstances, what would you do?

(a) In view of the help he had given you, extend your help to him.
(b) Regret that you cannot be of any help to him.
(c) Explain to your colleague that this would be violating the trust of the University authorities and you are not in a position to help him.
(d) Report the conduct of your colleague to the higher authorities.

CASE STUDIES 2014 (IAS MAINS)

Case Study 25

Now-a-days, there is an increasing thrust on economic development all around the globe. At the same time, there is also an increasing concern about environmental degradation caused by development. Many a time, we face a direct conflict between developmental activity and environmental quality. It is neither feasible to stop or curtail the developmental process, nor it is advisable to keep degrading the environment, as it threatens our very survival.

Discuss some feasible strategies which could be adopted to eliminate this conflict and which could lead to sustainable development. (250 words)

Case Study 26

Suppose one of your close friends, who is also aspiring for civil services, comes to your for discussing some of the issues related to ethical conduct in public service. He raises the following points:

(i) In the present times, when unethical environment is quite prevalent, individual attempts to stick to ethical principles may cause a lot of problems in one's career. In may also cause hardship to the family members as well as risk to one's life. Why should we not be pragmatic and follow the path of least resistance, and be happy with doing whatever good we can?
(ii) When so many people are adopting wrong means and are grossly harming the system, what difference would it make if only a small minority tries to be ethical? They are going to be rather ineffective and are bound to get frustrated.
(iii) If we become fussy about ethical considerations, will it not hamper the economic progress of our country? After all, in the present age of high competition, we cannot afford to be left behind in the race of development.
(iv) It is understandable that we should not get involved in grossly unethical practices, but giving and accepting small gratifications and doing small favours increases everybody's motivation. It also makes the system more efficient. What is wrong in adopting such practices?

Critically analyze the above viewpoints. On the basis of this analysis, what will be your advice to your friend? (250 words)

Case Study 27

You are a no-nonsense, honest officer. You have been transferred to a remote district to head a department that is notorious for its inefficiency and callousness. You find that the main cause of the poor state of affairs is the indiscipline of a section of employees. They do not work themselves and also disrupt the working of others. You first warned the troublemakers to mend their ways or else face disciplinary action. When the warning had little effect, you issued a show cause notice to the ringleaders. As a retaliatory measure, these troublemakers instigated a woman employee amongst them to file a complaint of sexual harassment against you with the Women's Commission. The Commission promptly seeks your explanation. The matter is also publicized in the media to embarrass you further. Some of the options to handle this situation could be as follows:

(i) Give your explanation to the Commission and go soft on the disciplinary action.

(ii) Ignore the Commission and proceed firmly with the disciplinary action.

(iii) Brief your higher-ups, seek directions from them and act accordingly.

Suggest any other possible option(s). Evaluate all of them and suggest the best course of action, giving your reason for it. (250 words)

Case Study 28

Suppose you are the CEO of a company that manufactures specialized electronic equipment used by a government department. You have submitted your bid for the supply of this equipment to the department. Both the quality and cost of your offer are better than those of the competitors. Yet the concerned officer is demanding a hefty bribe for approving the tender. Getting the order is important both for you and for your company. Not getting the order would mean closing a production line. It may also affect your own career. However, as a value-conscious person, you do not want to give bribe.

Valid arguments can be advanced both for giving the bribe and getting the order, and for refusing to pay the bribe and risking the loss of the order. What those arguments could be? Could there be any better way to get out of this dilemma? If so, outline the main elements of this third way, pointing out its merits. (250 words)

Case Study 29

Rameshwar successfully cleared the prestigious civil services examination and was excited about the opportunity that he would get through the civil services to serve the country. However, soon after joining the services, he realized that things are not as rosy as he had imagined.

He found a number of malpractices prevailing in the department assigned to him. For example, funds under various schemes and grants were being misappropriated. The official facilities were frequently being used for personal needs by the officers and staff. After some time, he noticed that the process of recruiting the staff was also not up to the mark. Prospective candidates were required to write an examination in which a lot of cheating was going on. Some candidates were provided external help in the examination. Rameshwar brought these incidents to the notice of his seniors. However, he was advised to keep his eyes, ears and mouth shut and ignore all these things which were taking place with the connivance of the higher-ups. Rameshwar felt highly disillusioned and uncomfortable. He comes to you seeking your advice.

Indicate various options that you think are available in this situation. How would you help him to evaluate these options and choose the most appropriate path to be adopted? (250 words)

Case Study 30

In our country, the migration of rural people to towns and cities is increasing drastically. This is causing serious problems both in the rural as well as in the urban areas. In fact, things are becoming really unmanageable. Can you analyze this problem in detail and indicate not only the socio-economic but also the emotional and attitudinal factors responsible for this problem? Also, distinctly bring out why—

(a) educated rural youth are trying to shift to urban areas;
(b) landless poor people are migrating to urban slums;
(c) even some farmers are selling off their land and trying to settle in urban areas taking up petty jobs.

What feasible steps can you suggest which will be effective in controlling this serious problem of our country? (250 words)

Annexure A

Central Civil Services (Conduct Rules), 1964

1. Short title, commencement and application.

(1) These rules may be called the Central Civil Service (Conduct) Rules, 1964

(2) They shall come into force at once.

(3) Save as otherwise provided in these rules and subject to the provisions of the Indian Foreign Service (Conduct and Discipline) Rules, 1961, these rules shall apply to a civil service or post(including a civilian in Defence Service) in connection with the affairs of the Union:

Provided that nothing in these rules shall apply to any Government servant who is :-

(a) (i) a Railway servant as defined in Section 3 of the Indian Railways Act,1890(9 of 1890);

(ii) a person holding a post in the Railway Board and is subject to the Railway Service(Conduct) Rules;

(iii) holding any post under the administrative control of the Railway Board or of the Financial Commissioner of Railways;

(b) a member of an All India Services;

(c) a holder of any post in respect of which the President has, by a general or special order, directed that these rules shall not apply:

Provided further that Rules 4,6,7,12 and 14, sub-rule(3) of Rule 15, Rule 16, sub-rule(1),(2) and (3) of Rule 18, Rule 19,20 and 21 shall not apply to any Government servant who draws a pay which does not exceed Rs.500/-per mensem and hold a non-Gazetted post in any of the following establishments, owned or managed by the Government, namely:-

(i) Ports, docks, wharves or jetties;
(ii) defence installations except training establishments;
(iii) public works establishment, in so far as they relate to work charged staff;
(iv) irrigation and electric power establishments;
(v) mines as defined in clause (j) of Section 2 of the Mines Act, 1952 (35 of 1952);
(vi) factories as defined in clause (m) of Section 2 of the Factories Act, 1948(63 of 1948); and
(vii) field units of the Central Tractor Organisation employing workmen governed by labour laws:

Provided further that these rules shall apply to any person temporarily transferred to a service or post specified in clause (a) of the first proviso to whom but for such transfer these rules would have otherwise applied.

3. General

(1) Every Government servant shall at all times-
   (i) Maintain absolute integrity;
   (ii) Maintain devotion to duty ; and
   (iii) do nothing which is unbecoming of a Government servant.

(2) (i) Every Government servant holding a supervisory post shall take all possible steps to ensure the integrity and devotion to duty of all Government servants for the time being under his control and authority;
   (ii) No Government servant shall, in the performance of his official duties, or in the exercise of powers conferred on him, act otherwise than in his best judgment except when he is acting under the direction of his official superior;
   (iii) The direction of the official superior shall ordinarily be in writing. Oral direction to subordinates shall be avoided, as far as possible. Where the issue of oral direction becomes unavoidable, the official superior shall confirm it in writing immediately thereafter.
   (iv) A Government servant who has received oral direction from his official superior shall seek confirmation of the same in

writing as early as possible, whereupon it shall be the duty of the official superior to confirm the direction in writing.

EXPLANATION I-A Government servant who habitually fails to perform the task assigned to him within the time set for the purpose and with the quality of performance expected of him shall be deemed to be lacking in devotion to duty within the meaning of Clause (ii) of sub-rule (I).

EXPLANATION II-Nothing in Clause (ii) of sub-rule (2) shall be construed as empowering a Government servant to evade his responsibilities by seeking instructions from, or approval of, a superior officer or authority when such instructions are not necessary under the scheme of distribution of powers and responsibilities.

3-A. Promptness and courtesy

No Government servant shall-

(a) In the performance of his official duties, act in a discourteous manner;

(b) In his official dealings with the public or otherwise adopt dilatory tactics or willfully cause delays in disposal of the work assigned to him.

3-B. Observance of Government's policies

Every Government servant shall, at all times-

(i) act in accordance with the Government's policies regarding age of marriage, preservation of environment, protecting of wildlife and cultural heritage;

(ii) Observe the Government's policies regarding prevention of crime against women.

3-C. Prohibition of sexual harassment of working women

(1) No Government servant shall indulge in any act of sexual harassment of any woman at her work place

(2) Every Government servant who is in-charge of a work place shall take appropriate steps to prevent sexual harassment to any woman at such work place.

EXPLANATION-For the purpose of this rule, "sexual harassment" includes such unwelcome sexually determined behaviour, whether directly or otherwise, as-

(a) Physical contact and advances;

(b) Demand or request for sexual favours;

(c) Sexually coloured remarks;

(d) Showing any pornography; or

(e) Any other unwelcome physical, verbal or non-verbal conduct of a sexual nature.

GOVERNMENT OF INDIA'S DECISION

(23) Acts and conducts which amount to misconduct. The act or conduct of a servant may amount to misconduct:

(1) if the act or conduct is prejudicial or likely to be prejudicial to the interests of the master or to the reputation of the master;
(2) if the act or conduct is inconsistent or incompatible with the due or peaceful discharge of his duty to his master;
(3) if the act or conduct of a servant makes it unsafe for the employer to retain him in service;
(4) if the act or conduct of the servant is so grossly immoral that all reasonable men will say that the employee cannot be trusted;
(5) if the act or conduct of the employee is such that the master cannot rely on the faithfulness of his employee;
(6) if the act or conduct of the employee is such as to open before him temptations for not discharging his duties properly;
(7) if the servant is abusive or if he disturbs the peace at the place of his employment;
(8) if he is insulting and insubordinate to such a degree as to be incompatible with the continuance of the relation of master and servant;
(9) if the servant is habitually negligent in respect of the duties for which he is engaged;
(10) if the neglect of the servant through isolated, tends to cause serious consequences

The following acts and omissions amount to misconduct:

(1) Willful insubordination or disobedience, whether alone or in combination with others, to any lawful and reasonable order of a superior.
(2) Infidelity, unfaithfulness, dishonesty, untrustworthiness, theft and fraud, or dishonesty in connection with the employer's business or property.
(3) Strike, picketing, gherao-striking work or inciting others to strike work in contravention of the provisions of any law, or rule having the force of law.
(4) Gross moral misconduct-Acts subversive of discipline-Riotous or disorderly behaviour during working hours at the establishment or any act subversive of discipline.
(5) Riotous and disorderly behaviour during and after the factory hours or in business premises.

(6) Habitual late attendance.
(7) Negligence or neglect of work or duty amounting to misconduct-Habitual negligence or neglect of work.
(8) Habitual absence without permission and over-staying leave.
(9) Conviction by a Criminal court.

4. Employment of near relatives of Government servants in companies or firms

(1) No Government servant shall use his position or influence directly or indirectly to secure employment for any member of his family in any (company or firm)

(2) (i) No Class I Officer shall, except with the previous sanction of the Government, permit his son, daughter or other dependant, to accept employment in any (company or firm) with which he has official dealings or in any other (company or firm) having official dealings with the Government:
Provided that where the acceptance of the employment cannot await prior permission of the Government or is otherwise considered urgent, the matter shall be reported to the Government; and the employment may be accepted provisionally subject to the permission of the Government.
(ii) A Government servant shall, as soon as he becomes aware of the acceptance by a member of his family of an employment in any (company or firm) intimate such acceptance to the prescribed authority and shall also intimate whether he has or had any official dealings with that (company or firm):
Provided that no such intimation shall be necessary in the case of a Class I Officer if he has already obtained the sanction of, or sent a report to the Government under Clause (i).

(3) No Government servant shall in the discharge of his official duties deal with any matter or give or sanction any contract to any (company or firm) or any other person in any member of his family is employed in that (company or firm) or under that person or if he or any member of his family is interested in such matter or contract in any other manner and the Government servant shall refer every such matter or contract to his official superior and the matter or contract shall thereafter be disposed of according to the instructions of the authority to whom the reference is made.

5. Taking part in politics and elections

(1) No Government servant shall be a member of, or be otherwise associated with, any political party or any organization which

takes part in politics nor shall he take part in, subscribe in aid of or assist in any other manner, any political movement or activity.

(2) It shall be the duty of every Government servant to endeavour to prevent any member of his family from taking part in, subscribing in aid of, or assisting in any other manner any movement or activity which is, or tends directly or indirectly to be, subversive of the Government as by law established and where a Government servant in unable to prevent a member of his family from taking part in, or subscribing in aid of, or assisting in any other manner, any such movement or activity, he shall make a report to that effect to the Government.

(3) If any question arises whether a party is a political party or whether any organization takes part in politics or whether any movement or activity falls within the scope of sub-rule (2), the decision of the Government thereon shall be final.

(4) No Government servant shall canvass or otherwise interfere with, or use his influence in connection with or take part in an election to any Legislature or Local Authority:

Provided that –

(i) a Government servant qualified to vote at such election may exercise his right to vote, but where he does so, he shall give no indication of the manner in which he proposes to vote or has voted;

(ii) a Government servant shall not be deemed to have contravened the provisions of this sub-rule by reason only that he assists in the conduct of an election in the due performance of a duty imposed on him by or under any law for the time being in force.

EXPLANATION-The display by a Government servant on his person, vehicle or residence of any electoral symbol shall amount to using his influence in connection with an election within the meaning of this sub-rule.

6. Joining of associations by Government servants

No Government servant shall join, or continue to be a member of, an association the objects or activities of which are prejudicial to the interests of the sovereignty and integrity of India, or public order or morality.

7. Demonstration and strikes

No Government servant shall-

(i) engage himself or participate in any demonstration which is prejudicial to the interests of the sovereignty and integrity of India, the security of the State, friendly relations with foreign States, public order, decency or morality, or which involves contempt of Court, defamation or incitement to an offence, or

(ii) resort to or in any way abet any form of strike or coercion or physical in connection with any matter pertaining to his service of any other Government servant.

8. Connection with press or other media

(1) No Government servant shall, except with the previous sanction of the Government, own wholly or in part, or conduct or participate in the editing or management of any newspaper or other periodical publication or electronic media.

(2) Nothing in sub-rule (1) shall apply in case a Government servant in the bona fide discharge of his official duties publishes a book or participates in a public media.

(3) A Government servant publishing a book or participating in a public media shall at all times make it clear that the views expressed by him are his own and not that of Government.

9. Criticism of Government

No Government servant shall, in [any radio broadcast, telecast through any electronic media] or in any document published in his own name or anonymously, pseudonymously or in the name of any other person or in any communication to the press or in any public utterance, make any statement of fact or opinion:

(i) Which has the effect of an adverse criticism of any current or recent policy or action or action of the Central Government or a state Government:

[Provided that in the case of any Government servant included in any category of Government servants specified in the second proviso to sub-rule (3) of Rule 1, nothing contained in this clause shall apply to bona fide expression of views by him as an office-bearer of a trade union or association of Government servants for the purpose of safeguarding the conditions of service of such Government servants or for securing an improvement thereof.];or

(ii) Which is capable of embarrassing the relations between the Central Government and the Government of any State; or

(iii) Which is capable of embarrassing the relations between the Central Government and the Government of any foreign State:

Provided that nothing in this rule shall apply to any statements made or views expressed by a Government servant in his official capacity or in the due performance of the duties assigned to him.

10. Evidence before committee or any other authority

(1) Save as provided in sub-rule (3), no Government servant shall, except with the previous sanction of the Government, give evidence in connection with any enquiry conducted by any person, committee or authority.

(2) Where any sanction has been accorded under sub-rule (1), no Government servant giving such evidence shall criticize the policy or any action of the central Government or of a State Government.

(3) Nothing in this rule shall apply to-
   (a) evidence given at an enquiry before an authority appointed by the Government, Parliament or a State Legislature; or
   (b) evidence given in any judicial enquiry; or
   (c) evidence given at any departmental enquiry ordered by authorities subordinate to the Government.

11. Communication of official information

Every Government servant shall, in performance of his duties in good faith, communicate information to a person in accordance with the Right to information Act, 2005 (22 of 2005) and the rules made there under:

Provided that no Government servant shall, except in accordance with any general or special order of the Government or in performance in good faith of the duties assigned to him, communicate, directly or indirectly, any official document or any part thereof or classified information to any Government servant or any other person to whom he is not authorized to communicate such document or classified information.

12. Subscriptions

No Government servant shall, except with the previous sanction of the Government or of the prescribed authority, ask for or accept contributions to, or otherwise associate himself with the raising of, any funds or other collections in cash or in kind in pursuance of any object whatsoever.

13. Gifts

(1) Save as otherwise provided in these rules, no Government servant shall accepts, or permit any member of his family or any other person acting on his behalf to accept any gift.

EXPLANATION – The expression "Gift shall include free transport, boarding, lodging or other service or any other pecuniary advantage provided by any person other than a near relative or personal friend having no official dealings with the government servant.

Note 1 – A casual meal, lift or other social hospitality shall not be deemed to be a gift.

Note 2 – A Government servant shall avoid accepting lavish hospitality or frequent hospitality from any individual, industrial or commercial firm, organization, etc having official dealings with him.

(2) On occasions such as wedding, weddings anniversaries, funerals or religious functions, when the making of gift is in conformity with the prevailing religious and social practice, a Government servant may accept gift from his near relatives or from his personal friends having no official dealings with him, but shall make a report to the Government, if the value of such gift exceeds -
   (i) rupees (seven thousand) in the case of a Government servant holding any Group 'A' post;
   (ii) rupees (four thousand) in the case of a Government servant holding any Group 'B' post;
   (iii) rupees (two thousand) in the case of a Government servant holding any Group 'C' post; and
   (iv) rupees (one thousand) in the case of a Government servant holding any Group 'D' post; and

(3) In any other case a Government servant shall not accept any gift without the sanction of the Government, if the value exceeds –
   (i) rupees (one thousand five hundred) in the case of Government servants holding any Group 'A' or Group 'B' post; and
   (ii) rupees (five hundred) in the case of Government servants holding any Group 'C' or Group 'D' post.

(4) Notwithstanding anything contained in sub rules (2) and (3), a Government servant, being a member of the Indian delegation or otherwise may receive and retain gifts from foreign dignitaries, if the market value of gifts received on one occasion does not exceed rupees one thousand. In all other cases, the acceptance and retention of such gift shall be regulated by the instruction issued by the Government in this regards from time to time.

(5) A Government servant shall not accept any gifts from any foreign firm which is either contracting with the Government of India or is one with which the Government servant had, has or is likely to have official dealings. Acceptance of gifts by a Government servant from any other firm shall be subject to the provisions of sub-rule (3).

13. A. Dowry

No Government servant shall:

(i) give or take or abet the giving or taking of dowry; or

(ii) demand directly or indirectly, from the parent or guardian of a bride or bridegroom, as the case may be, any dowry.

EXPLANATION-For the purpose of this rule, "dowry" has the same meaning as in the Dowry Prohibition Act, 1961 (28 of 1961).

14. Public demonstrations in honour of Government servants

No Government servant shall, except with the previous sanction of the Government, receive any complimentary or valedictory address or accept any testimonial or attend any meeting or entertainment held in his honour; or in the honour of any other Government servant:

Provided that nothing in this rule shall apply to-

(i) a farewell entertainment of a substantially private and informal character held in honour of a Government servant or any other Government servant on the occasion of his retirement or transfer or any person who has recently quitted the service of any Government; or

(ii) the acceptance of simple and inexpensive entertainments arranged by public bodies or institutions.

15. Private trade or employment

(1) Subject to the provisions of sub-rule (2), no Government servant shall, except with the previous sanction of the Government-

(a) Engage directly or indirectly in any trade or business; or

(b) negotiate for, or undertake, any other employment, or

(c) hold an elective office, or canvass for a candidate or candidates for an elective office, in any body, whether incorporated or not, or

(d) canvass in support of any business of insurance agency, commission agency, etc., owned or managed by any member of his family, or

(e) take part except in the discharge of his official duties, in the registration, promotion or management of any Bank or other company registered or required to be registered, under the Companies Act, 1956 (1 of 1956), or any other law for the time being in force, or of any co-operative society for commercial purposes.

(f) Participate in or associate himself in any manner in the making of-

(i) a sponsored media (radio or television) programme; or
(ii) a media programme commissioned by Government media but produced by a private agency; or
(iii) a privately produced media programme including video magazines;

Provided that no previous permission shall be necessary in case where the government servants participates in a programme produced or commissioned by Government media in his official capacity.

(2) A Government servant may, without the previous sanction of the Government:
(a) undertake honorary work of a social or charitable nature, or
(b) undertake occasional work of a literary, artistic or scientific character, or
(c) participate in sport activities as an amateur, or
(d) take part in the registration, promotion or management (not involving the holding of an elective office) of a literary, scientific or charitable society or of a club or similar organization, the aims or objects of which relate to promotion of sports, cultural or recreational activities, registered under the Societies Registration Act, 1860 (21 of 1860), or any other law for the time being force, or
(e) take part in the registration, promotion or management (not involving the holding of elective office) of a co-operative society substantially for the benefit of Government servants, registered under the Co-operative Societies Act, 1912 (2 of 1912), or any other law for the time being in force:

Provided that:
(i) he shall discontinue taking part in such activities, if so directly by the Government; and
(ii) in a case falling under Clause (d) or Clause (e) of this sub-rule, his official duties shall not suffer thereby and he shall, within a period of one month of his taking part in such activity, report to the Government giving details of the nature of his participation.

(3) Every Government shall report to the Government if any member of his family is engaged in a trade or business or owns or manages an insurance agency or commission agency.

(4) Unless otherwise provided by general or special orders of the Government, no Government servant may accept any fee for any work done by him for any private or public body or any private person without the sanction of the prescribe authority.

EXPLANATION-The term 'fee' used here shall have the meaning assigned to it in fundamental Rule 9 (6-A).

15-A. Subletting and vacation of Government accommodation

(1) Save as otherwise provided in any other law for the time being in force, no Government servant shall sublet, lease or otherwise allow occupation by any other person of Government accommodation which has been allotted to him.

(2) A Government servant shall, after the cancellation of his allotment of Government accommodation vacate the same within the time-limit prescribed by the allotting authority.

16. Investments, lending and borrowing

(1) No Government servant shall speculate in any stock, share or other investment:

Provided that nothing in this sub-rule shall apply to occasional investments made through stock brokers or other persons duly authorized and licensed or who have obtained a certificate of registration under the relevant law.

EXPLANATION-Frequent purchase or sale or both, of shares, securities or other investments shall be deemed to be speculation within the meaning of this sub-rule.

(2) (i) No Government servant shall make, or permit any member of his family or any person acting on his behalf to make, any investment which is likely to embarrass or influence him in the discharge of his official duties. For this purpose, any purchase of shares out of the quotas reserved for Directors of Companies or their friends and associates shall be deemed to be an investment which is likely to embarrass the Government servant.

(ii) No Government servant who is involved in the decision-making process of fixation of price of an Initial Public Offering or follow-up Public Offering of shares of a central Public Sector Enterprise shall apply, either himself or through any member of his family or through any other person acting on his behalf, for allotment of shares in the Initial Public Offerings or Follow-up Public Offerings of such Central Public Sector Enterprise.

(3) If any question arises whether any transaction is of the nature referred to in sub-rule (1) or sub-rule (2), the decision of the Government thereon shall be final.

(4) (i) No Government servant shall, save in the ordinary course of business with a Bank or a public limited company, either himself

or through any member of his family or any other person acting on his behalf,-

(a) lend or borrow or deposit money, as a principal or an agent to, or from or with, any person or firm or private limited company within the local limits of his authority or with whom he is likely to have official dealings or otherwise place himself under any pecuniary obligation to such person or firm or private limited company ; or

(b) lend money to any person at interest or in a manner whereby return in money or in kind is charge or paid

Provided that a Government servant may give to, or accept from a relative or a personal friend a purely temporary loan of a small amount free of interest, or operate credit account with a bona fide tradesman or make an advance of pay to his private employee:

Provided further that nothing in this sub-rule shall apply in respect of any transaction entered into by a Government servant with the previous sanction of the Government.

(ii) When a Government servant is appointed or transferred to a post of such nature as would involve him in the breach of any of the provisions of sub-rule (2) or sub-rule(4), he shall forthwith report the circumstances to the prescribed authority and shall thereafter act in accordance with such order as may be made by such authority.

17. Insolvency and habitual indebtedness

A Government servant shall so manage his private affairs as to avoid habitual indebtedness or insolvency. A Government servant, against whom any legal proceeding is instituted for the recovery of any debt due from him or for adjudging him as an insolvent, shall forthwith report the full facts of the legal proceedings to the Government.

18. Movable, immovable and valuable property

(1) (i) Every Government servant shall on his first appointment to any service or post submit a return office assets and liabilities, in such form as maybe prescribed by the Government, giving the full particulars regarding-

(a) the immovable property inherited by him, or owned or acquired by him or held by him on least or mortgage, either in his own name or in the name of any member of his family or in the name of any other person;

(b) shares, debentures and cash including bank deposits inherited by him or similarly owned, acquired, or held by him;

(c) other movable property inherited by him or similarly owned, acquired or held by him; and

(d) debts and other liabilities incurred by him directly or indirectly.

NOTE. 1.-Sub-rule (1) shall not ordinarily apply to Class IV servants but the Government may direct that it shall apply to any such Government servant or class of such Government servants.

NOTE. 2.-In all returns, the values of items of movable property worth less than [2][Rs. 10,000] may be added and shown as a lumpsum. The value of articles of daily use such as clothes, utensils, crockery, books, etc., need mot be included in such return.

[3]NOTE 3.-Where a Government servant already belonging to a service or holding a post is appointed to any other civil service or post, he shall not be required to submit a fresh return under this clause.

[4](ii) Every Government servant belonging to any service or holding any post included in Group 'A' and Group 'B' shall submit an annual return in such form as may be prescribed by the Government in this regard giving full particulars regarding the immovable property inherited by him or owned or acquired by him or held by him on lease or mortgage either in his own name or in the name of any member of his family or in the name of any other person.

(2) No Government servant shall, except with the previous knowledge of the prescribed authority, acquired or dispose of any immovable property by lease, mortgage, purchase, sale, gift or otherwise either in his own name or in the name of any member of his family:

[1]Provided that the previous sanction of the prescribed authority shall be obtained by the Government servant if any such transaction is with a person having official dealings with him.

[2](3) Where a Government servant enters into a transaction in respect of movable property either in his own name or in the name of the member of his family, he shall within one month from the date of such transaction, report the same to the prescribed authority, if the value of such property exceeds 3twenty thousand rupees in the case of a Government servant holding any Class I or Class II post or 3fifteen thousand rupees in the case of Government servant holding any Class III or Class IV post:

[1]Provided that the previous sanctions of the prescribed authority shall be obtained by the Government servant if any such transaction is with a person having official dealings with him.

(4) The Government or the prescribed authority may, at any time, by general or special order, require a Government servant to furnish, within a period specified in the order, a full and complete statement of such movable or immovable property held or acquired by him or on his behalf or by any member of his family as may be specify in the order. Such statement shall, if so required by the Government or by the prescribed authority, include the details of the means by which, or the source from which, property was acquired.

(5) The Government may exempt any category of Government servants belonging to Class III or Class IV from any of the provisions of this rule except sub-rule (4). No such exemption shall, however, be made without the concurrence of the Cabinet Secretariat (Department of personnel).

EXPLANATION I. - For the purposes of this rule:

(1) the expression "movable property" includes:

(a) jewellery, insurance policies, the annual premium of which exceeds 1[Rs. 10,000] or one-sixth of the total annual emoluments received from Government, whichever is less, shares, securities and debentures;

[2][(b) all loans, whether secured or not, advanced or taken by the Government servant;]

(c) motor cars, motor cycles, horses or any other means of conveyance; and

(d) refrigerators, radios 1[radiograms and television sets].

(2) "prescribed authority" means:

(a) (i) the Government, in the case of Government servant holding any class I post, except where any lower authority is specifically specified by the Government for any purpose;

(ii) Head of Department, in the case of a Government servant holding any class II post;

(iii) Heads of Office, in the case of a Government servant holding any class III or class IV post;

(b) in respect of a Government servant on a foreign service or on deputation to any other ministry or any other Government, the parent department on the cadre of which such Government servant is borne or the ministry to which he is administratively subordinate as member of that cadre.

EXPLANATION II.-For the purpose of this rule 'lease' means, except where it is obtained from, or granted to, a person having official dealings with the Government servant, a lease of immovable property from year to year or for any term exceeding one year or reserving a yearly rent.

GOVERNMENT OF INDIAN'S ORDERS

S.O. 114. In pursuance of sub-rule (1) of rule 18 of the Central Civil Service (Conduct) Rules, 1964, read with Note 3 (since substituted) thereto, the Central Government hereby:

(a) prescribes the forms specified in the schedule to this Order, as the forms in which the return referred to in the side rule shall be submitted by-

(i) every Government servant on his first appointment after the date of issue of this Order to any service or post, and

(ii) every Government servant who is in service on the date of issue of this Order;

(b) directs that-

(i) the first return in respect of a Government servant on his first appointment to any service or post shall be as on the date of such appointment and shall be submitted within three months from that date and every such return, after the first, shall be submitted as on, and by, the dates specified in Clause (c) in respect of returns after the first return, provided that if the interval between the date of submission of the first return and the date on which a subsequent return is due is less than six months, the latter return need not be submitted;

(ii) the first return in respect of every Government servant who is in service on the date of issue of this order, shall be as on the 31st December,1972 and specifies the 31st day of March, 1973, as the date on or before which such return shall be submitted;

(c) further directs that every Government servant shall submit such returns after the first, at an interval of five years, on or before the 31st day of March of the year immediately following the year to which the return relates an every such return shall be as on the 31st day of December of the year immediately preceding the said 31st day of March; and

(d) also directs that every such return shall be handled as secret document and the provisions of Rule 11 of the Central Civil Service (Conduct) Rules, 1964, shall, as far as may be, applied thereto.

GOVERNMENT OF INDIA'S DECISIONS

(11) Authorities from whom valuation report may be accepted. In accordance with the instructions contained in Decision (4) a government servant is required to submit, after the completion of the construction of a hose or additions and alterations to an existing house, a valuation report in Form 4 prescribed therein, signed by a firm of Civil Engineers or a Civil engineer of a repute. Doubts were expressed whether the valuation certificate could be accepted from engineers working in the same or other department or as public servants elsewhere. The matter has been considered in consultation with Ministry of Home Affairs and the advice given by them in individual case is summarized below –

(1) For building constructed at a cost not exceeding Rs. 10,000/-in villages and town area, a certificate from a Tashildar could be accepted. Certificate from Overseers should not be accepted.

(2) Even if the Government servant who has constructed a house is himself a qualified Engineer, a certificate of valuation given by him cannot be accepted as he is a party to the transaction. He should be asked to produced a certificate from an independent Civil Engineer.

(3) Certificate issued by Engineer employed in the same department where the Government servant concern is employed, cannot be accepted.

(4) Certificates issued by Engineers who are public servants and are employed in a department other than the Department of the Government servant concern, with whom the Government servant has no direct official dealings, can be accepted.

(5) Valuation certificates from retired Engineers of the Government with whom the Government servant might have worked, can be accepted provided the retired Engineers are engaged in regular private practice.

(12) Charge of Corruption reasonably arises where a Government servant is unable to satisfactorily account for his assets in moveable and immoveable property. A presumption of corruption fairly and reasonably arises against an officer who cannot account for large accretion of wealth which he could not possibly have saved from his own source of income. This principle has received statutory recognition in Section 5 (3) of The Prevention of Corruption Act, 1947 and its application in a departmental enquiry against an officer charge with corruption could not, therefore, be unjust or inequitable. In fact this principle has recently been upheld by the Supreme Court in the case of Shri G.R. Mankar v. Union of India (Civil Appeal No. 160 of 1963). Ministry of Finance, etc are requested to ensure that in Departmental enquiry against an officer charge with corruption and found to be in possession of assets disproportionate to his known sources of income, the presenting officer concern brings the legal positions, as set out in Paragraph 1 above, to the notice of the enquiry officer.

(23) Punitive action for failure to submit Annual Immovable Property Returns in time. In accordance with the provisions of Clause (ii) of Rule18 (1) of the CCS (Conduct) Rules, 1964, every Government servant holding a Group 'A' or 'B' post is required to submit an annual return giving full particulars regarding the immovable property inherited by him or owned or acquired by him or held by him on lease or mortgage either in his own name or in the name of any member of his family or in the name of any other person. It has been prescribed in M.H.A.,O.M.No.25/10/55-Estt.(A),date 12-1-1956, that such reports shall be submitted in the month of January, every year The form used for this purpose has also been prescribed under the said OM. The need for obtaining these returns regularly and making careful scrutiny of the same was reiterated from time to time.

2. It has, however, been noticed that these returns are not submitted in time in many cases. Ministries/Departments are, therefore, requested to ensure that these returns are submitted by all Groups 'A' and 'B' Officers under their control in respect of every calendar year by 31st January of the next year. It may be impressed upon them that failure on the part of a Government servant to comply with the requirement of the aforesaid can form good and sufficient reason for instituting disciplinary proceeding against him. **Strict action may be taken against employees who failed to submit the returns in time or furnishing wrong information.**

18 A. - Restriction in relation to acquisition and disposal of immoveable property outside India and transactions with foreigners, etc.

Notwithstanding anything contained in sub-rule (2) of Rule 18, no Government servant shall, except with the previous sanction of the prescribed authority –

(a) acquire, by purchase, mortgage, lease, gift or otherwise, either in his own name or in the name of any member of his family, any immoveable property situated outside India;

(b) dispose of, by shall, mortgage gift or otherwise or grant any lease in respect of any immovable property situated outside India which was acquired or is held by him either in his own name or in the name of any member of his family;

(c) enter into any transaction with any foreigner, foreign Government, foreign organizations or concerns, -

  (i) for the acquisition, by purchase, mortgage, lease, gift or otherwise either in his own name or in the name of any member of his family, of any immovable property;

  (ii) for the disposal of, by share, mortgage, gift or otherwise or the grant of any lease in respect of any immoveable property which was acquired or is held by him either in his own name or in the name of any member of his family.

19. Vindication of acts and character of Government servant

(1) No Government servant shall, except with the previous sanction of the Government, have recourse to any Court or to the press for the vindication of any official act which has been the subject-matter of adverse criticism or an attack of a defamatory character:

[Provided that if no such sanction is received by the Government servant within a period of three months from the date of receipt of his request by the Government, he shall be free to assume that the permission as sought for has been granted to him.]

(2) Nothing in this rule shall be deemed to prohibit a Government servant from vindicating his private character or any act done by him in his private capacity and where any action for vindicating his private character or any act done by him in private capacity is taken, the Government servant shall submit a report to the prescribe authority regarding such action.

20. Canvassing of non-official or other outside influence

No Government servant shall bring or attempt to bring any political or other outside influence to bear upon any superior authority to further his interests in respect of matters pertaining to his service under Government.

21. Restriction regarding marriage

(1) No Government servant shall enter into, or contract, a marriage with a person having a spouse living; and

(2) No Government servant having a spouse living, shall enter into, or contract, a marriage with any person:

Provided that the Central Government may permit a Government servant to enter into, or contract, any such marriage as is referred to in Clause (1) or Clause (2), if it is satisfied that:

(3) A Government servant who has married or marries a person other than of Indian nationality shall forthwith intimate the fact to the Government.
   (a) Such marriage is permissible under the personal law applicable to such Government servant and the other party to the marriage; and
   (b) There are other grounds for so doing.

22. Consumption of intoxicating drinks and drugs

A Government servant shall:

(a) Strictly abide by law relating to intoxicating drinks or drugs in force in any area in which he may happen to be for the time being;
(b) Not be under the influence of any intoxicating drink or drug during the course of his duty and shall also take due care that the performance of his duties at any time is not affected in any way by the influence of such drink or drug:
(bb) Refrain from consuming any intoxicating drink or drug in a public place:
(c) Not appear in a public place in a state of intoxication;
(d) Not use any intoxicating drink or drug to excess.

EXPLANATION-For the purpose of this rule 'public place' means any place or premises (including a conveyance) to which the public have, or are permitted to have, access, whether on payment or otherwise.

22-A. Prohibition regarding employment of children below 14 years of age

No Government servant shall employ to work any below the age of 14 years.

Annexure B

Code of Conduct for Ministers in the Government of India

In addition to the observance of the provisions of the Constitution, the Representation of the People Act, 1951, and any other law for the time being in force, a person immediately after entering office as a Minister, and in any case within a period of two months from the date of assumption of office, shall:

a) disclose to the Prime Minister, or the Chief Minister, as the case may be details of the assets and liabilities, and of business interests, of himself and of members of his family. The details to be disclosed shall consist of particulars of all immovable property and the total approximate value of (i) shares and debentures, (ii) cash holdings and (iii) jewellery. Such a Statement of assets and liabilities could be in respect of the financial year for which the income tax return has already been filed by the Minister;

b) sever all connections, short of divesting himself of the ownership, with the conduct and management of any business in which he was interested before his appointment as Minister; and

c) with regard to a business concern which supplies goods or services to the Government concerned or to undertakings of that Government (excepting in the usual course of trade or business and at standard or market rates) or whose business primarily depends on licenses, permits, quotas, leases, etc., received or to be received from the Government concerned, divest himself of all his interests in the said business and also of the management thereof.

Provided, however, that he may transfer in the case of (b) his interest in the management, and in the case of (c) both ownership and management, to any adult member of his family or adult relative, other than his wife (or husband, as the case may be), who was prior to his appointment as Minister associated with the conduct or management or ownership of the said business. The question of divesting himself his interests would not arise in case of holding of share in public limited companies except where the Prime Minister, or the Chief Minister, as the case may be, considers that the nature or extent of his holding is such that it is likely to embarrass him in the discharge of his official duties.

2. After taking office, and so long as he remains in office, the Minister shall:
   (a) furnish annually by the 31st August to the Prime Minister, or the Chief Minister, as the case may be, a declaration regarding his assets and liabilities for the previous financial year;
   (b) refrain from buying from or selling to, the Government any immovable property except where such property is compulsorily acquired by the Government in usual course;
   (c) refrain from starting, or joining, any business;
   (d) ensure that the members of his family do not start, or participate in, business concerns, engaged in supplying goods or services to that Government (excepting in the usual course of trade or business and at standard or market rates) or dependent primarily on grant of licenses, permits, quotas, leases, etc., from that Government; and
   (e) report the matter to the Prime Minister, or the Chief Minister as the case may be, if any member of his family sets up, or joins in the conduct and management of, any other business.
   (f) uphold the political impartiality of the civil services and not ask the civil servants to act in any way which would conflict with the duties and responsibilities of the civil servants

3.1 No Minister should :
   (a) personally, or through a member of his family, accept contribution for any purpose, whether political, charitable or otherwise. If any purse or cheque intended for a registered society, or a charitable body, or an institution recognised by

a public authority, or a political party is presented to him, he should pass it on as soon as possible to the organisation for which it is intended; and

(b) associate himself with the raising of funds except for the benefit of (i) a registered society, or a charitable body, or an institution recognised by a public authority and (ii) a political party. He should, however, ensure that such contributions are sent to a specified office bearer, etc. of the society or body or institution of party concerned and not to him. Nothing herein before shall prevent a Minister from being associated with the operation for disbursement of funds raised as above.

3.2 A Minister, including the Union Ministers, the Chief Ministers and other Ministers of State Governments/Union Territories, should not permit their spouse and dependents to accept employment under a Foreign Government, in India or abroad, or in a foreign organisation (including commercial concerns) without prior approval of the Prime Minister. Where the wife or a dependent of a Minister is already in such employment, the matter should be reported to the Prime Minister for decision whether the employment should or should not continue. As a general rule, there should be total prohibition on employment with a Foreign Mission.

4.1 A Minister should :

a) not accept valuable gifts except from close relatives, and he or members of his family should not accept any gifts at all from any person with whom he may have official dealings; and

b) not, nor permit a member of his family, contract debts of a nature likely to embarrass or influence him in the discharge of his official duties.

4.2 A Minister may receive gifts when he goes abroad or from foreign dignitaries in India. Such gifts fall into two categories. The first category will include gifts which are of symbolic nature, like a sword of honour, ceremonial robes etc. and which can be retained by the recipients. The second category of gifts would be those which are not of symbolic nature. If its value is less than Rs.5,000/- it can be retained by the Minister. If, however, there is any doubt about the estimated value of the gift, the matter should be referred to the Toshakhana for valuation. If the value of the gift, on assessment is found to be within the prescribed limit of Rs.5,000/- the gift will be returned to the Minister. If it exceeds

Rs.5,000/- the recipient will have the option to purchase it from the Toshakhana by paying the difference between the value as assessed by the Toshakhana and Rs.5,000/-. Only gifts of household goods which are retained by the Toshakhana, such as carpets, paintings, furniture etc. exceeding Rs.5,000/- in value, will be kept in Rashtrapati Bhavan, Prime Minister's House or Raj Bhavan as State property. (Note: The value of the gift refers to its approximate market value in the country of origin).

4.3 In case of grant of an award by any organisation to a Minister/a person holding the Minister's status/rank, the following procedure may be followed :

a) the credentials of the organisation giving award may be gone into;

b) if the credentials of the body giving the awards are unimpeachable, the award as such may be accepted but the cash part should not be accepted;

c) if the awards relate to the work done by the individual prior to his holding the office of Minister, such awards may be accepted but in all such cases specific approval of the Prime Minister or the Chief Minister as the case may be, should be obtained. The Chief Minister and other Ministers shall have to take permission of the Prime Minister and the Union Home Minister; and

d) those instances, where a Minister is to receive any award by any organisation which has connections with any Foreign Agencies/Organisations, such a Minister/ a person holding the Minister's status/rank, will have to seek prior approval of the Prime Minister of India.

4.4 A Minister should follow the instructions given from time to time by the Prime Minister in matters relating to attending functions arranged by foreign missions in India or abroad, and also for accepting the membership of any foreign trust, institution or organisation other than U.N. Organisations of which India is a Member.

5. A Minister should :

a) while on official tour, as far as practicable stay in accommodation belonging to himself or maintained by Government, Government undertakings, public bodies or institutions (such as circuit houses, dak bungalows etc.) or in recognised hotels; and

b) avoid attending, as far as possible, ostentatious or lavish parties given in his honour.

6. The authority for ensuring the observance of the Code of Conduct will be the Prime Minister in the case of Union Ministers, the Prime Minister and the Union Home Minister in the case of Chief Ministers, and the Chief Minister concerned in the case of State Ministers except where it is otherwise specified. The said authority would follow such procedure as it might deem fit, according to the facts and circumstances of each case, for dealing with or determining any alleged or suspected breach of this Code.

Explanation: In this code, a Minister's family shall include his wife (or husband, as the case may be) not legally separated from him (or her), minor children, and any other persons related by blood or marriage to, and wholly dependent on the Minister.

ANNEXURE C

Code of Conduct for Members of Parliament

The members of Rajya Sabha should acknowledge their responsibility to maintain the public trust reposed in them and should work diligently to discharge their mandate for the common good of the people. They must hold in high esteem the Constitution, the law, parliamentary institutions and above all the general public. They should constantly strive to translate the ideals laid down in the Preamble to the Constitution into a reality. The following are the principles which they should abide by in their dealings:

(i) Members must not do anything that brings disrepute to the Parliament and affects their credibility

(ii) Members must utilise their position as Members of Parliament to advance general well-being of the people.

(iii) In their dealings if members find that there is a conflict between their personal interests and the public trust which they hold, they should resolve such a conflict in a manner that their private interests are subordinated to the duty of their public office.

(iv) Members should always see that their private financial interests and those of the members of their immediate family* do not come in conflict with the public interest and if any such conflict ever arises, they should try to resolve such a conflict in a manner that the public interest is not jeopardised.

---

*Immediate family includes spouse, dependent daughters and dependents sons.

(v) Members should never expect or accept any fee, remuneration or benefit for a vote given or not given by them on the floor of the House, for introducing a Bill, for moving a resolution or desisting from moving a resolution, putting a question or abstaining from asking a question or participating in the deliberations of the House or a parliamentary committee.
(vi) Members should not take a gift which may interfere with honest and impartial discharge of their officials duties. They may, however, accept incidental gifts or inexpensive mementoes and customary hospitality.
(vii) Members holding public offices should use public resources in such a manner as may lead to public good.
(viii) If members are in possession of a confidential information owing to their being Members of Parliament or members of parliamentary committees, they should not disclose such information for advancing their personal interests.
(ix) Members should desist from giving certificates to individuals and institutions of which they have no personal knowledge and are not based on facts.
(x) Members should not lend ready support to any cause of which they have no or little knowledge.
(xi) Members should not misuse the facilities and amenities made available to them.
(xii) Members should not be disrespectful to any religion and work for the promotion of secular values.
(xiii) Members should keep uppermost in their mind the fundamental duties listed in part IV A of the Constitution.
(xiv) Members are expected to maintain high standards of morality, dignity, decency and values in public life.

Annexure D

The Right of Citizen for Time Bound Delivery of Goods and Services and Redressal of their Grievances

CHAPTER III
PUBLICATION OF CITIZENS CHARTER AND GRIEVANCE REDRESSAL OFFICER BY PUBLIC AUTHORITIES

4. Obligation of public authority to publish Citizens Charter

(*1*) Every public authority shall publish, within six months of the commencement of this Act, a Citizens Charter specifying therein all the category of goods supplied and services rendered by it, in respect of all services that are either quantifiable or amenable to timely delivery[14].

(*2*) Without prejudice to the generality of the provisions contained in sub-section (*1*), the Citizens Charter shall provide all or any of the following matters, namely:—

(a) the details of all the goods supplied and services rendered by the public authority and the name of person or agency through which such goods are supplied or services rendered

[14] Omitted "*the time within which such goods shall be supplied or services be rendered*" to restrict legal liability of public authority to create citizens charters only for those public goods and services that are amenable to it.

and timings during which such goods are supplied or services rendered;

(b) the conditions under which a person or organization becomes entitled for goods and services, the class of persons who are entitled to receive such goods and avail services, the process through which a person or organization can apply for such goods and services and the time within which such goods shall be supplied or services be rendered, the form in which the services that are rendered are going to be provided, the nature of assisted access available at the public authority for accessing electronic services[15];

(c) the quantitative and tangible parameters (including weight, size, frequency) of the goods and services available to the public;

(d) complaint redressal mechanism including the time within which the complaint be disposed of and the officer of the public authority to whom such complaint may be made;

(e) the name and addresses of individuals responsible for the delivery of goods or rendering of services as designated officer mentioned in (*a*) above;

(*f*)[16];

(fa) the person responsible for providing feedback forms and receiving the feedback or comments or suggestions offered by the citizens or organizations dealing with the respective public authority[17]

(fb) the month and year of next review of the charter[18].

(g) any other information relevant to delivery of goods or provision of services or such other information as may be prescribed;

(*3*) The appropriate Government may, by notification, make rules in relation to citizens charter and grievance redressal.

---

[15] Inserted to include mandatory elements of citizens charters and provisions of EDS bill.

[16] Omitted "*(f) any other functions, obligations, responsibility or duty of the public authority is required or reasonably expected to provide;*" as it is too broad to be amenable for Citizens Charters.

[17] Inserted to ensure that Citizens charters also contain information regarding the official responsible for receiving feedback.

[18] Inserted to ensure the process is institutionalized and conducted regularly.

5. Obligation of Head of the Department for updating and verifying the Citizens Charter:

(*1*) The Head of the Department in each public authority shall be responsible for updating and verifying the Citizens Charter every year and the accuracy of the contents thereof.

(*2*) It shall be the responsibility of the Head of the Department of every public authority to ensure that the Citizens Charter is widely disseminated to the public.

(*3*) It shall be the responsibility of the Head of the Department of every public authority to take steps in accordance with section 4 of the Right To Information Act, 2005 for providing relevant information to the public enabling them to exercise their rights mandated under this Act.

(*4*) Every Head of the Department shall ensure that all material be disseminated taking into consideration the local language and the most effective method of communication in that local area free of cost.

Explanation.—For the purposes of this section the expression "disseminated" means making known and communicating the information to the public through notice boards, newspapers, public announcements, media broadcasts, the internet or any other means, including inspection of offices of any public authority by any citizen.

(*5*) Every Head of the Department shall to the extent possible, ensure that the Citizens Charter is made available at the website of the public authority and in other electronic forms and shall be available free of cost.

(*6*) Every Head of the Department shall ensure that a copy of the Citizens Charter of the public authority duly certified by him is submitted to appropriate bodies, including appropriate Central and State Public Grievance Redress Commission, when it is published and subsequently, every time that it is modified, updated or amended.

(7) Every Head of the Department shall ensure that an appropriate feedback receiving mechanism is instituted and appropriate grievance prevention measures are taken to improve the delivery mechanisms of goods and services to the citizens[19].

(8) Every Head of the Department shall ensure that an appropriate stakeholder consultation process is carried out before the formulation and subsequent review of the Citizens Charter[20].

---

[19] Inserted to ensure that a feedback mechanism is put in place.

[20] Inserted to ensure that the concerned stakeholders are given a reasonable opportunity to express their preferences on standards of services available with the public authority.

CHAPTER IV
ESTABLISHMENT OF INFORMATION AND FACILITATION CENTRE

6. Establishment of Information and Facilitation Centre:

(*1*) Every public authority shall establish Information and Facilitation Centre for efficient and effective delivery of services and redressal of grievances, which may include establishment of customer care centre, call centre, help desk and people's support centre.

(*2*) Every Head of the Department of the public authority shall be responsible for the development, improvement, modernisation and reform in service delivery and redressal of grievance system and also include adoption of electronic modes, internet, etc.

(*3*) The appropriate Government may, by notification, make rules in relation to Information and Facilitation Centre.

CHAPTER V
APPOINTMENT AND OBLIGATION OF GRIEVANCE REDRESS OFFICERS BY PUBLIC AUTHORITY

7. Appointment and Obligations of Grievance Redress Officers, including for each municipality and Panchayat:

(*1*) Every public authority shall, within six months from the date of the coming into force of this Act, designate as many officers as may be necessary as Grievance Redress Officers in all administrative units or offices at the Central, State, district and sub-district levels, municipalities, Panchayats whereat supplies of goods or render services to receive, enquire into and redress any complaints from citizens in the manner as may be prescribed:

Provided that the Grievance Redress Officer so appointed shall be at least one level above and be deemed to have administrative control on the individual designated to deliver goods or render services as per the Citizens Charter as referred to in section 4.

(*2*) Every public authority shall, immediately on appointment or designation of a Grievance Redress Officer —

(*a*) give, through a public notice in a newspaper published in Hindi or English language and in a newspaper published in an Indian language in circulation in the area in which such service provider is providing services, indicating therein the name of the Grievance Redress Officer, his address and telephone number, e-mail address, facsimile number and other means of contacting him in respect of each area for which the Grievance Redress Officer has been appointed or designated and thereafter give such public notice at least once in twelve months in the same manner:

Provided that in case of change of the name of the Grievance Redress Officer, his address and telephone number, e-mail address, facsimile number and other means of contacting him shall be intimated by public notice, in the same manner specified in this clause;

(*b*) display, at its each office, Information and Facilitation Centre, call centre, customer care centre, help desk, People's Support Centre and at the sales outlets, website and at the office of the Grievance Redress Officer and the appellate authorities, the name of the Grievance Redress Officer, their addresses and telephone numbers, e-mail addresses, facsimile numbers and other means of contacting them, in respect of each area for which the Grievance Redress Officer have been appointed or designated.

(*3*) Every public authority shall appoint or designate such number of Grievance Redress Officer under sub-section (*1*) and for such areas, as may be considered by it necessary, for Grievance Redress Officer being easily accessible and available for redressal of grievance of the public.

(*4*) The Grievance Redress Officer shall provide all necessary assistance to citizens in filing complaints.

(*5*) Where a complainant is unable to make a complaint in writing, the Grievance Redress Officer shall render all reasonable assistance to the person making the request orally to reduce the same in writing.

8. Acknowledgement of complaint by receipt thereof:

All complaints shall, within two days of the making of the complaint, be acknowledged by a receipt, issued in writing or through electronic means or through text message or through telephone or through any other means as may be prescribed, specifying the date, time, place, unique complaint number and particulars of receiver of complaint along with the stipulated time frame in accordance with its Citizens Charter within which the complaint will be redressed.

Provided that where the complaint pertains to another public authority, the recipient shall refer the complainant to the appropriate authority[21].

---

[21] Inserted to ensure that citizens who are not aware of the appropriate authority are provided assistance.

9. Action to be taken by Grievance Redress Officer:

(*1*) Upon receipt of a complaint as defined in clause (*f*) of section 2, it shall be the duty of the concerned Grievance Redress Officer to ensure that,—

(*a*) the grievance is remedied in a time frame not exceeding three days in case of complaints relating to electronic services or goods/services which have no supply constraints, fifteen days in case of those complaints that warrant physical works, and sixty days in case of complaints related to violation of any law or rules or order pertaining to that public authority[22], from the date of receipt of the complaint;

Provided that an appeal of an urgent or immediate nature shall be disposed of within the same day of the receipt of the appeal or before the date on which the cause of action may cease to exist, which shall not be later than thirty days from the date of receipt of the appeal[23].

Provided further that the classification of goods/services into those that need to be delivered immediately or three days or fifteen days or sixty days shall be approved by the appropriate Grievance Redressal Commission[24].

(*b*) the reason for the occurrence of the grievance is identified and the responsibility of the defaulting office or individual is fixed and the grievance is redressed satisfactorily within thirty days from the date of receipt of the complaint by the Grievance Redress Officer;

(*c*) where the grievance has occurred as a result of a deficiency, negligence or malfeasance on the part of an office or individual then the action is taken in accordance with conduct rules and departmental procedures;

(*d*) where the Grievance Redress Officer is convinced that the individual responsible for the delivery of the goods and services has wilfully neglected to deliver the goods or services or there exist *prima facie* grounds for a case under the Prevention of Corruption Act, 1988, the Grievance Redress Officer can make an observation to that effect along with a

---

[22] Substituted for "*thirty days*" to include differentiated timeframes for different class of complaints.

[23] Inserted to keep this provision related to urgent complaints in sync with sub-section (7) of section 11 of this bill.

[24] Inserted to make the Commission the final authority on the classification of the services.

recommendation for the penalty, including compensation to the complainant, to be imposed, to the designated authority.

(*2*) The Grievance Redress Officer may seek the assistance of any other officer required for the proper discharge of his duties or may direct any other officer to take action to redress a complaint.

(*3*) Any officer, whose assistance has been sought under sub-section (*2*), shall render all assistance to the Grievance Redress Officer seeking his assistance and for the purposes of any contravention of the provisions of this Act, such other officer shall be deemed to be a Grievance Redress Officer for the purposes of this Act.

(*4*) The Grievance Redress Officer shall ensure that the complainant is informed in writing the manner in which the grievance is redressed and shall give him a report in the form of an action taken report.

10. Forwarding of details of non-redressal of complaints to designated authority:

The Grievance Redress Officer shall, immediately after the expiry of the period of thirty days, report every complaint which has not been redressed along with the details of the complainant, nature of complaint, and reasons for non-redressal of complaints to the designated authority.

CHAPTER VI
APPEAL TO THE DESIGNATED AUTHORITY

10A. Appointment of Designated Authority:

(1) The State Grievance Redressal Commission shall appoint an Ombudsman for each district and municipal corporation who shall not below the rank of district magistrate, in consultation with the State Government, to act as the Designated authority at the state level for purposes of this Act.

(2) The Central Grievance Redressal Commission shall appoint the Designated Authorities at the central level in consultation with the Central Government, who shall be an officer or authority outside the concerned public authority[25].

11. Appeal:

(*1*) Every complaint forwarded along with the details under section 10 shall be deemed to have been filed by way of an appeal to the designated authority.

---

[25] Inserted to appoint Ombudsmen at the state level at each district and municipal corporation. The mechanism for Centre has not been changed.

(*2*) Any individual aggrieved by a decision of the concerned Grievance Redress Officer or who has not received an action taken report in respect of a complaint filed by him, may, if he so desires, within thirty days from the expiry of such period or from the receipt of such decision, prefer an appeal to the designated authority:

Provided that the designated authority may admit the appeal after the expiry of thirty days if it is satisfied that the complainant was prevented by sufficient cause from filing the appeal in time.

(*3*) The receipt of the appeal under sub-section (*2*) shall be acknowledged by the office of the designated authority.

(*4*) The designated authority shall, for the purposes of its functions under this Act, have the same powers as are vested in a civil court under the Code of Civil Procedure, 1908 in respect of the following matters, namely:—

(*a*) summoning and enforcing the attendance of any person and examining him on oath;

(*b*) discovery and production of any document or other material object producible as evidence;

(*c*) receiving evidence on affidavits;

(*d*) requisitioning of any public record;

(*e*) issuing commission for the examination of witnesses;

(*f*) reviewing its decisions, directions and orders;

(*g*) any other matter which may be prescribed.

(*5*) The designated authority shall have original jurisdiction to adjudicate upon every application made to it under this section 11.

(*6*) The designated authority shall not be bound by the procedure laid down in the Code of Civil Procedure, 1908 but shall be guided by the principles of natural justice and subject to the other provisions of this Act and of any rules made thereunder, the Authority shall have the power to regulate its own procedure.

(*7*) Every appeal filed under this section or complaint deemed to be by way of an appeal shall be disposed of by the designated authority within three days in case of appeals relating to electronic services or goods/services which have no supply constraints, fifteen days in case of appeals that warrant physical works, and sixty days in case of appeals related to violation of any law or rules or order pertaining to that public authority[26], from the date of receipt of such appeal:

---

[26] Substituted for *"thirty days"* to include differentiated timeframes for different class of complaints.

Provided that an appeal of an urgent or immediate nature shall be disposed of within the same day of the receipt of the appeal or before the date on which the cause of action may cease to exist, which shall not be later than thirty days from the date of receipt of the appeal.

(*8*) The designated authority shall arrange to deliver copies of the decisions to the parties concerned within a period of five working days from the date of such decisions.

(*9*) The designated authority shall[27] impose penalty, including compensation to the complainant, in deciding an appeal against concerned officer for acting in a *mala fide* manner or having failed to discharge their duties without any sufficient and reasonable cause:

Provided that the concerned officers of the public authority shall be given a reasonable opportunity of being heard before any penalty is imposed on them.

(*10*) Where it appears to the designated authority that the grievance complained of is, *prima facie,* indicative or representative of a corrupt act or practice in terms of the Prevention of Corruption Act, 1988, on the part of the individual officer of the public authority complained against, then, it shall record in writing such evidence as may be found in support of such conclusion and shall initiate the proceedings or in writing refer the same to the appropriate authorities competent to take cognizance of such corrupt practice.

(*11*) The designated authority shall upon adjudication of a complaint have the powers to issue directions requiring the concerned officers of the public authority to take such steps as may be necessary to secure compliance with the provisions of Citizens Charter.

CHAPTER VII
ESTABLISHMENT OF STATE PUBLIC GRIEVANCE REDRESSAL COMMISSION

12. Appeal to State Commission:

(*1*) Any person who, does not receive a decision within the time specified in Chapter V, or is aggrieved by a decision of the designated authority, falling within the jurisdiction of the State

[27] Substituted for "*may*" to provide for mandatory penalties.

Government, may within thirty days from the expiry of such period or from the receipt of such a decision prefer an appeal to the State Public Grievance Redressal Commission:

Provided that the Commission may admit the appeal after the expiry of thirty days if it is satisfied that the complainant was prevented by sufficient cause from filing the appeal in time.

(*2*) The decision of the State Public Grievance Redressal Commission under this section shall be binding.

13. Constitution of State Public Grievance Redressal Commission:

The State Government shall constitute, by notification, a Commission to be known as "the State Public Grievance Redressal Commission" to exercise the jurisdiction, power and authority conferred under this Act:

Provided that the State Information Commission appointed under section 15 of the Right to Information Act, 2005 prior to the commencement of this Act shall function as the State Public Grievance Redressal Commission:

Provided further that henceforth the appointment of State Public Grievance Commissioners shall take place according to section 15 of this Act[28].

14. Composition of State Commission:

The State Public Grievance Redressal Commission shall consist of,—

(*a*) a Chief Commissioner; and

(*b*) such number of Commissioners, not exceeding ten, as may be prescribed, out of which at least one each shall be from amongst the Scheduled Castes, Scheduled Tribes and Women.

15. Selection Committee for Appointment of State Commissioners:

(*1*) The Chief Commissioner and Commissioners shall be appointed by the Governor on the recommendation of a Selection Committee consisting of,—

- (*a*) the Chief Minister, who shall be the Chairperson of the Committee;
- (*b*) the Leader of Opposition in the Legislative Assembly; and
- (*c*) a sitting judge of the High Court to be nominated by the Chief Justice of the State.

---

[28] Inserted to make Information Commission the Grievance Redressal Commission and the appointment prescribed in this Act is retained as it includes a judge in the Selection Panel as opposed to a Minister nominated by the Chief Minister.

(*2*) The selection committee shall select out of a panel of five eligible candidates for each vacancy which shall be finalised by a search committee consisting of such members as may be prescribed.

(*3*) Subject to the provisions of sub-sections (*1*) and (*2*), the Selection Committee may regulate its own procedure.

16. Qualifications for Appointment of State Commissioners:

A person shall not be qualified for appointment as a Chief Commissioner or a Commissioner of the State Public Grievance Redressal Commission unless,

(*a*) he is, or has been an officer of the State Government and has held the post in the rank of Secretary or the Principal Secretary to that Government; or

(*b*) he is or has been a District Judge for at least ten years; or

(*c*) he is or has been a Judge of the High Court of the State; or

(*d*) he is an eminent person recognised for his work towards public service in the area and who has worked for at least fifteen years in the social sector with a post-graduate degree in a relevant subject: Provided that the State Government may prescribe criteria in addition to the above for the appointment of the Chief Commissioner and Commissioners.

17. Terms of Office of Chief Commissioner and Other Commissioners:

(*1*) The Chief Commissioner and the Commissioners shall hold office for a term of five years from the date on which they enter upon office or until they attain the age of sixty-five years whichever is earlier.

(*2*) The Chief Commissioner and the Commissioners shall hold office for a term of five years from the date on which he enters upon his office and shall not be eligible for reappointment.

18. Staff, Salary and Allowances of State Commission:

(*1*) The State Government shall provide the State Public Grievance Redressal Commission with such officers and employees as may be required for the discharge of its functions under this Act.

(*2*) The officers and employees so appointed under sub-section (*1*) shall discharge their functions under the general superintendence of the Chief Commissioner.

(*3*) The salary and allowances payable to, and the other terms and conditions of service of,—

  (*a*) the Chief Commissioner shall be the same as that of an Election Commissioner;

(*b*) the Commissioners shall be the same as that of the Chief Secretary of the State:

Provided that if the Chief Commissioner or Commissioner, at the time of his appointment is, in receipt of a pension, other than a disability or wound pension in respect of any previous service under the Government of India or the Government of State, his salary in respect of the service as Chief Commissioner or Commissioner shall be reduced by the amount of that pension, including any portion of pension, which was commuted and pension equivalent of other forms of retirement benefits, excluding pension equivalent or retirement gratuity:

Provided further that where the Chief Commissioner or Commissioner, if at the time of his appointment, is in receipt of retirement benefits in respect of any previous service rendered in a Corporation established by or under any Central Act or State Act or a Government company owned or controlled by the Central Government or the State Government, his salary in respect of the service as a Chief Commissioner or the Commissioner shall be reduced by the amount of pension equivalent to the retirement benefits:

Provided also that neither the salary and allowances nor the other terms and conditions of service of the Chief Commissioner or Commissioner shall be varied to their disadvantage after appointment.

19. Filling up of Vacancies:

If, for any reason other than temporary absence, any vacancy occurs in the office of the State Public Grievance Redressal Commission then the Chief Commissioner shall appoint another person in accordance with the provisions of this Act to fill the vacancy and the proceedings may be continued before the Commission from the stage at which the vacancy is filled.

20. Resignation and Removal:

(*1*) Any member of the State Public Grievance Redressal Commission may, by notice in writing under his hand addressed to the Governor of the State with a copy to the Chief Commissioner, resign his office.

(*2*) Notwithstanding anything contained in sub-section (*1*), the Governor may by order remove from office the Chief Commissioner or any Commissioner if the Chief Commissioner or a Commissioner, as the case may be,—

- (*a*) is adjudged an insolvent; or
- (*b*) has been convicted of an offence which, in the opinion of the Governor, involves moral turpitude; or
- (*c*) engages during his term of office in any paid employment outside the duties of his office; or

(*d*) is, in the opinion of the Governor, unfit to continue in office by reason of infirmity of mind or body; or

(*e*) has acquired such financial or other interest as is likely to affect prejudicially his functions as the Chief Commissioner or as a Commissioner.

(*3*) The State Government may, by rules, regulate the procedure for the investigation of misbehaviour or incapacity of the aforesaid Chief Commissioner or Commissioners.

21. Powers of Commission and procedure before it:

(*1*) The State Public Grievance Redressal Commission shall, for the purposes of its functions under this Act, have the same powers as are vested in a civil court under the Code of Civil Procedure, 1908 in respect of the following matters, namely:—

(*a*) summoning and enforcing the attendance of any person and examining him on oath;

(*b*) discovery and production of any document or other material object producible as evidence;

(*c*) receiving evidence on affidavits;

(*d*) requisitioning of any public record;

(*e*) issuing commission for the examination of witnesses;

(*f*) reviewing its decisions, directions and orders;

(*g*) any other matter which may be prescribed.

(*2*) The State Public Grievance Redressal Commission shall not be bound by the procedure laid down in the Code of Civil Procedure, 1908 but shall be guided by the principles of natural justice and subject to the other provisions of this Act and of any rules made thereunder, the Commission shall have the power to regulate its own procedure.

22. Procedure of Adjudication by State Public Grievance Redressal Commission:

(*1*) The State Public Grievance Redressal Commission shall have original jurisdiction to decide every appeal made to it under section 12.

(*2*) The State Public Grievance Redressal Commission shall arrange to deliver copies of the decision to the parties concerned within a period of fifteen days from the date of such decision.

23. Proceedings before Commission to be Judicial Proceedings:

All proceedings before the State Public Grievance Redressal Commission shall be deemed to be judicial proceedings within the meaning of sections 193 and 228 of the Indian Penal Code and the

Commission shall be deemed to be a civil court for the purposes of sections 345 and 346 of the Code of Criminal Procedure, 1973.

24. Staff and Officers to be Public Servants:

The staff and officers of the State Public Grievance Redressal Commission shall be deemed to be public servants within the meaning of section 21 of the Indian Penal Code.

25. Time frame for Disposal of Appeals:

(*1*) An appeal under section 12 shall be disposed of within six days in case of appeals relating to electronic services or goods/services which have no supply constraints, thirty days in case of appeals that warrant physical works, and one hundred and twenty days in case of appeals related to violation of any law or rules or order pertaining to that public authority[29], from the date of receipt from the date of filing of the appeal:

Provided that an appeal of an urgent or immediate in nature shall be disposed of within the same day of the receipt of the appeal or before the date on which the cause of action may cease to exist, which shall not be later than fifteen days from the date of receipt of the appeal.

(*2*) The State Public Grievance Redressal Commission shall[30] impose penalty, including compensation to the complainant, while deciding an appeal against designated officer and Grievance Redress Officers for acting in a *mala fide* manner or having failed to discharge their duties without any sufficient and reasonable cause:

Provided that the concerned officers of the public authority shall be given a reasonable opportunity of being heard before any penalty is imposed on them under this section.

26. Power to Issue Directions and Exercise Original Jurisdiction:

(*1*) The State Public Grievance Redressal Commission shall, upon adjudication of a complaint, have the power to issue directions,—

(*a*) requiring the public authority to take such steps as may be necessary to secure compliance with the provisions of the Citizens Charter;

(*b*) requiring the timely creation, updation and wide dissemination of the Citizens Charter of the public authority.

---

[29] Substituted for "*sixty days*" to include differentiated timeframes for different class of complaints and increased in proportion to the time frame provided to the Grievance Redressal Officer and Designated Authority.

[30] Substituted for "*may*" to provide for mandatory penalties.

(2) It shall be the duty of the State Public Grievance Redressal Commission to receive and inquire into a complaint from any person,—
   (*a*) who has been unable to submit an appeal to the designated authority;
   (*b*) who has been refused redress of grievance under this Act;
   (*c*) whose complaint has not been disposed of within the time limit specified;
   (*d*) who has been denied access to the Citizens Charter of the public authority either because the Charter was not created by the public authority or is inadequate in any regard or it is not widely disseminated to make people aware of it;
   (*e*) in respect of any other matter relating to registering and redressing of a complaint or appeal under this Act.

(3) The State Public Grievance Redressal Commission may, *suo moto*, take notice of failure to deliver goods and services in accordance with the provisions of this Act and refer such cases for disposal to the Head of the Department of the Public Authority and in such cases, an action taken report shall be sent by the Head of the Department of the Public Authority to the State Commission within thirty days from the date of such reference.

(4) Where the State Public Grievance Redressal Commission, is satisfied that there are reasonable grounds to inquire into the matter, it may initiate an inquiry *suo motu* in respect thereof.

27. Burden of Poof to be on Grievance Redress Officer:

In any appeal proceedings, the burden of proof to establish that a non-redressal of complaint by the Grievance Redress Officer shall be on the Grievance Redress Officer who denied the request.

28. Where Grievance Complained of is a Result of Corrupt Practices:

Where it appears to the Commission that the grievance complained of is, *prima facie*, indicative of a corrupt act or practice in terms of the Prevention of Corruption Act, 1988, on the part of the responsible officer of the public authority complained against, then, it shall record such evidence as may be found in support of such conclusion and shall refer the same to the appropriate authorities.

CHAPTER VIII
ESTABLISHMENT OF THE CENTRAL PUBLIC GRIEVANCE REDRESSAL COMMISSION

29. Appeal to Central Commission:

(*1*) Any person who, does not receive a decision within the time specified in Chapter V, or is aggrieved by a decision of the designated authority falling within the jurisdiction of the Central Government, may within thirty days from the expiry of such period or from the receipt of such a decision prefer an appeal to the Central Public Grievance Redressal Commission:
Provided that the Commission may admit the appeal after the expiry of thirty days if it is satisfied that the complainant was prevented by sufficient cause from filing the appeal in time.

(*2*) The decision of the Central Public Grievance Redressal Commission under this section shall be binding.

30. Constitution of Central Public Grievance Redressal Commission:

The Central Government shall Constitute, by notification, a body to be known as "Central Public Grievance Redressal Commission" to exercise the jurisdiction, powers and authority conferred under this Act.

Provided that the Central Information Commission appointed under section 12 of the Right to Information Act, 2005 prior to the commencement of this Act shall function as the Central Public Grievance Redressal Commission:

Provided further that henceforth the appointment of Central Public Grievance Commissioners shall take place according to section 32 of this Act[31].

31. Composition of Central Commission:

The Central Public Grievance Redressal Commission shall consist of,—

(*a*) the Chief Public Grievance Redress Commissioner; and

(*b*) such number of Central Public Grievance Redress Commissioners, not exceeding ten, as may be prescribed out of which at least one each shall be from amongst Scheduled Castes, Scheduled Tribes and Women.

---

[31] Inserted to make Information Commission the Grievance Redressal Commission and the appointment prescribed in this Act is retained as it includes a judge in the Selection Panel as opposed to a Minister nominated by the Prime Minister.

32. Selection Committee for Appointment of Central Public Grievance Redress Commissioners:

(*1*) The Chief Public Grievance Redress Commissioner and Central Public Grievance Redress Commissioners shall be appointed by the President on the recommendation of a Committee consisting of,—

(*a*) the Prime Minister, who shall be the Chairperson of the committee;

(*b*) the Leader of Opposition in the Lok Sabha; and

(*c*) a sitting Judge of the Supreme Court to be nominated by the Chief Justice of India.

(*2*) The Selection Committee shall select out of a panel of five eligible candidates for each vacancy which shall be finalised by a search committee consisting of such members as may be prescribed.

(*3*) Subject to the provisions of sub-sections (*1*) and (*2*), the Selection Committee may regulate its own procedure.

33. Qualifications for Appointment of Central Public Grievance Redress Commissioners:

(*1*) A person shall not be qualified for appointment as a Chief Commissioner or Commissioners of Central Public Grievance Redressal Commission unless,—

(*a*) he is, or has been an officer of the Central Government and has held the post in the rank of Secretary to the Government of India; or

(*b*) he is, or has been a Chief Justice of a High Court or a Judge of the Supreme Court;

(*c*) he is, an eminent person recognised for his work towards public service in the area and who has worked for at least twenty years in the social sector with a post-graduate degree in a relevant subject:

Provided that the Central Government may prescribe criteria in addition to the above for the appointment of the Chief Commissioner and Commissioners.

34. Terms of Office of Central Grievance Redress Commissioners:

(*1*) The Chief Public Grievance Redress Commissioner and the Central Public Grievance Redress Commissioners shall hold officer for a term of five years from the date on which they enter upon the office or until the age of sixty-five years whichever is earlier[32].

---

[32] Inserted to include retirement age in line with terms of State Grievance Redressal Commission according to section 17 of this bill.

(2) The Chief Grievance Redress Commissioner and the Central Public Grievance Redress Commissioners[33] shall hold office for a term of five years from the date on which he enters upon his office and shall not be eligible for reappointment.

35. Staff, Salary and Allowances of Central Commission:

(*1*) The Central Government shall provide the Central Public Grievance Redressal Commission with such officers and employees as may be required for the discharge of its functions under this Act.

(*2*) The officers and employees so appointed under sub-section (*1*) shall discharge their functions under the general superintendence of the Chief Public Grievance Redress Commissioner.

(*3*) The salary and allowances payable to and the other terms and conditions of service of,—

(*a*) the Chief Public Grievance Redress Commissioner shall be the same as that of the Chief Election Commissioner; and

(*b*) the Central Public Grievance Redress Commissioner shall be the same as that of an Election Commissioner:

Provided that if the Chief Public Grievance Redress Commissioner or Central Public Grievance Redress Commissioner, at the time of his appointment is, in receipt of a pension, other than a disability or wound pension in respect of any previous service under the Government of India or the Government of State, his salary in respect of the service as Chief Public Grievance Redress Commissioner or Central Public Grievance Redress Commissioner shall be reduced by the amount of that pension, including any portion of pension, which was commuted and pension equivalent of other forms of retirement benefits, excluding pension equivalent or retirement gratuity:

Provided further that where the Chief Public Grievance Redress Commissioner or Central Public Grievance Redress Commissioner, if at the time of his appointment, is in receipt of retirement benefits in respect of any previous service rendered in a Corporation established by or under any Central Act or State Act or a Government company owned or controlled by the Central Government or the State Government, his salary in respect of the service as a Chief Public Grievance Redress Commissioner or the Central Public Grievance Redress Commissioner shall be reduced by the amount of pension equivalent to the retirement benefits:

[33] Inserted to restrict the term of Commissioners in line with those of State Grievance Redressal Commission as provided in section 17 of this bill.

Provided also that neither the salary and allowances nor the other terms and conditions of service of the members of the Central Public Grievance Redressal Commission shall be varied to their disadvantage after appointment.

36. Filling up of Vacancies:

If, for any reason other than temporary absence, any vacancy occurs in the office of the Central Public Grievance Redressal Commission then the Chief Public Grievance Redress Commissioner shall appoint another person in accordance with the provisions of this Act to fill the vacancy and the proceedings may be continued before the Commission from the stage at which the vacancy is filled.

37. Resignation and Removal:

(*1*) Any member of the Central Public Grievance Redressal Commission may, by notice in writing under his hand addressed to the President with a copy to the Chief Public Grievance Redress Commissioner, resign his office.

(*2*) Notwithstanding anything contained in sub-section (*1*), the President may by order remove from office the Chief Public Grievance Redress Commissioner or any Central Public Grievance Redress Commissioner if the Chief Public Grievance Redress Commissioner or the Central Public Grievance Redress Commissioner, as the case may be,—

- (*a*) is adjudged an insolvent; or
- (*b*) has been convicted of an offence which, in the opinion of the President, involves moral turpitude; or
- (*c*) engages during his term of office in any paid employment outside the duties of his office; or
- (*d*) is, in the opinion of the President, unfit to continue in office by reason of infirmity of mind or body; or
- (*e*) has acquired such financial or other interest as is likely to affect prejudicially his functions as the Chief Public Grievance Redress Commissioner or a Central Public Grievance Redress Commissioner.

(*3*) The Central Government may, by rules, regulate the procedure for the investigation of misbehaviour or incapacity of the aforesaid Chief Public Grievance Redress Commissioner or Central Public Grievance Redress Commissioners.

38. Powers of Central Commission and Procedure before it:

(*1*) The Central Public Grievance Redressal Commission shall, for the purposes of its functions under this Act, have the same powers as are vested in a civil court under the Code of Civil Procedure, 1908 in respect of the following matters, namely:—

(*a*) summoning and enforcing the attendance of any person and examining him on oath;

(*b*) discovery and production of any document or other material object producible as evidence;

(*c*) receiving evidence on affidavits;

(*d*) requisitioning of any public record;

(*e*) issuing commission for the examination of witnesses;

(*f*) reviewing its decisions, directions and orders;

(*g*) any other matter which may be prescribed.

(*2*) The Central Public Grievance Redressal Commission shall have original jurisdiction to adjudicate upon every appeal made to it under section 29.

(*3*) The Central Public Grievance Redressal Commission shall not be bound by the procedure laid down in the Code of Civil Procedure, 1908 but shall be guided by the principles of natural justice and subject to the other provisions of this Act and of any rules made thereunder, the Commission shall have the power to regulate its own procedure.

(*4*) The Central Public Grievance Redressal Commission shall arrange to deliver copies of the decision to the parties concerned within a period of fifteen days from the date of such decision.

39. Proceedings before Central Commission to be Judicial Proceedings:

All proceedings before the Central Public Grievance Redressal Commission shall be deemed to be judicial proceedings within the meaning of sections 193 and 228 of the Indian Penal Code and the Commission shall be deemed to be a civil court for the purposes of sections 345 and 346 of the Code of Criminal Procedure, 1973.

40. Burden of Proof to be on Grievance Redress Officer:

In any appeal proceedings, the burden of proof to establish that a non-redressal of complaint by the Grievance Redress Officer shall be on the Grievance Redress Officer who denied the request.

41. Staff and Officers to be Public Servants:

The staff and officers of the Central Public Grievance Redressal Commission shall be deemed to be public servants within the meaning of section 21 of the Indian Penal Code.

42. Time frame for Disposal of Appeals:

(*1*) An appeal under section 29 shall be disposed of within six days in case of appeals relating to electronic services or goods/services which have no supply constraints, thirty days in case of appeals that warrant physical works, and one hundred and twenty days in case of appeals related to violation of any law or rules or order pertaining to that public authority[34], from the date of filing of the appeal:
Provided that an appeal of an urgent or immediate in nature shall be disposed of within the same day of the receipt of the appeal or before the date on which the cause of action may cease to exist, which shall not be later than fifteen days from the date of receipt of the appeal.

(*2*) The Central Public Grievance Redressal Commission shall[35] impose penalty, including compensation to the complainant, in deciding an appeal against designated officers and Grievance Redress Officers for acting in a *mala fide* manner or having failed to discharge their duties without any sufficient and reasonable cause:
Provided that the concerned officers of the public authority shall be given a reasonable opportunity of being heard before any penalty is imposed on them.

43. Power to Issue Directions:

(*1*) The Central Public Grievance Redressal Commission shall, upon adjudication of a complaint, have the power to issue directions,—
  (*a*) requiring the public authority to take such steps as may be necessary to secure compliance with the provisions of the Citizens Charter;
  (*b*) requiring the timely creation, updation and wide dissemination of the Citizens Charter of the public authority

(*2*) It shall be the duty of the Central Public Grievance Redressal Commission to receive and inquire into a complaint from any person,—
  (*a*) who has been unable to submit an appeal to the designated authority;
  (*b*) who has been refused redress of grievance under this Act;
  (*c*) whose complaint has not been disposed of within the time limit specified;

---

[34] Substituted for "*sixty days*" to include differentiated timeframes for different class of complaints and increased in proportion to the time frame provided to the Grievance Redressal Officer and Designated Authority.

[35] Substituted for "*may*" to provide for mandatory penalties.

(*d*) who has been denied access to the Citizens Charter of the public authority either because the Charter was not created by the public authority or is inadequate in any regard or it is not widely disseminated to make people aware of it;

(*e*) in respect of any other matter relating to registering and redressing of a complaint or appeal under this Act.

(*3*) The Central Public Grievance Redressal Commission may, *suo motu*, take notice of failure to deliver goods and services in accordance with the provisions of this Act and refer such cases for disposal to the Head of the Department of the Public Authority and in such cases, an action taken report shall be sent by the Head of Department of the Public Authority to the Central Commission within thirty days from the date of such reference.

(*4*) Where the Central Public Grievance Redressal Commission, is satisfied that there are reasonable grounds to inquire into the matter, it may initiate an inquiry *suo motu* in respect thereof.

44. Where Grievance Complained of is a Result of Corrupt Practices:

Where it appears to the Central Public Grievance Redressal Commission that the grievance complained of is *prima facie* indicative of a corrupt act or practice in terms of the Prevention of Corruption Act, 1988, on the part of the responsible officer of the public authority complained against then it shall record such evidence as may be found in support of such conclusion and shall refer the same to the appropriate authorities.

CHAPTER IX
PENALTIES AND COMPENSATION

45. Penalty and Compensation for *Mala fide* Action:

(*1*) The designated authority, the State Public Grievance Redressal Commission or the Central Public Grievance Redressal Commission, as the case may be, shall[36] impose a penalty of two hundred and fifty rupees for each day of delay or[37] a lump sum penalty in the provision of goods and services, against designated official responsible for delivery of goods and services or Grievance Redress Officer for their failure to deliver goods or render services to which the applicant is entitled or Head of the Department for his

[36] Substituted for "*may*" to provide for mandatory penalties.

[37] Inserted to provide for imposing pro-rata penalties if the Commission deems fit.

failure to publish citizen charters in accordance to the provisions in sections 4 and 5 of this Act, as the case may be[38], which may extend up to fifty thousand rupees which shall be recovered from the salary of the official against whom penalty has been imposed.

(*2*) On imposition of the penalty under sub-section (*1*), the appellate authority shall[39], by order, direct that such[40] penalty imposed under the said section shall be awarded to the appellant, as compensation, as it may deem fit or in lieu of compensation, a written apology and an explanation of the steps being taken to ensure that such failures are not repeated shall be provided by the designated official to the appellant within a stipulated timeframe, if the appellant so desires[41]:
Provided that the amount of such compensation awarded shall not exceed the amount of penalty imposed under the said section.

(*3*) If any public servant is found guilty under sub-section (*1*), the disciplinary authority shall initiate the disciplinary proceedings against such officer of the public authority, who if proved to be guilty of a *mala fide* action in respect of any provision of this Act, shall be liable to such punishment including a penalty as the disciplinary authority may decide.

CHAPTER IXA
REWARDS FOR PERFORMANCE

45A Rewards for Better Performing Public Officials and Authorities:

(1) The Central Public Grievance Redressal Commission or the State Public Grievance Redressal Commission, as the case may be, shall

---

[38] Inserted to provide for imposing penalties on the Head of the Department if the Citizen Charters are not published.

[39] Substituted for "*may*" to provide for mandatory compensation to the appellants.

[40] Omitted "*portion of*" to provide for unambiguous compensation to be paid to the appellant.

[41] Inserted to provide for non-financial compensation for the appellant, if he so desires, as it is the minimum courtesy that is owed to him. Moreover the written explanation will lead to a reduction in such failures in the future. This provision is drawn from recommendations of a Parliamentary Select Committee of the United Kingdom. In fact, this committee goes to the extent of suggesting that the compensation to the complainant should be equivalent to restoring him to the position he would have been if the maladministration had not occurred. However, this might be too broad for the current Indian context. Presented in "Public Administration Public Administration Select Committee. (2008). *When Citizens Complain.* House of Commons, London".

design and implement a reward scheme with financial incentives for public authorities or their employees, who are fulfilling their duties better than the expected service levels laid down in the Citizens Charters in consultation with the Central Government or the State Government, as the case may be.

(2) The financial incentives to be provided in sub-section (1) would be drawn from a percentage of the fee collected from the citizens for the goods and services delivered [42].

CHAPTER IXB
SUPERVISORY FUNCTIONS AND POWERS OF THE GRIEVANCE REDRESSAL COMMISSION[43]

45B. Supervisory Functions and Powers of the Grievance Redressal Commission:

(1) The Central Grievance Redressal Commission or State Grievance Redressal Commission, as the case may be, shall monitor the implementation of this Act on a regular basis.

(2) Without prejudice to the provisions contained in sub-section (1), the supervisory functions and powers of the Central Grievance Redressal Commission or State Grievance Redressal Commission, as the case may be, shall, amongst other things, include the following, namely: —

- (a) directing the provision of services in electronic form within five years where feasible, except those services the Central Government or the State Government, notifies not to deliver electronically for the reasons to be specified in such notification [44];
- (b) monitoring the publication of services to be delivered in the citizens charters and adherence to the time schedule, manner of delivery and quality of service notified for delivery of public services by the Central Government or the State Government, as the case may be;

---

[42] Inserted to provide a reward scheme, which will complement the penalty mechanism proposed in this bill. Together they would orient the incentives of the public servants to strive towards better delivery of public services.

[43] Inserted a chapter to list out functions of Grievance Redressal Commission to incorporate functions envisaged for Electronic Service Delivery Commission in section 24 of EDS Bill, to incorporate feedback mechanisms, to disseminate good practices in public service delivery and other functions to improve the overall public service delivery.

[44] Inserted to incorporate the mandatory provisions listed in section 3 of the EDS Bill.

(c) acting as a unified dissemination centre for all the information pertaining to the citizens charters of all the public authorities in its jurisdiction by setting up a call centre for related enquiries and displaying this information on its website[45];

(d) monitoring the periodic progress made by the Central Government or the State Government or any public authority, as the case may be, towards achieving the delivery of all services in accordance with the provisions of this Act;

(e) monitoring the periodic progress made by the Central Government or the State Government or any public authority, as the case may be, towards compliance with the applicable electronic governance standards and make recommendations in respect thereof[46];

(f) recommending the simplification of processes and forms relating to delivery of goods and services by the Central Government or the State Government or any public authority, as the case may be and appropriate modifications to the Citizens Charters[47];

(g) recommending the simplification of processes and forms relating to delivery of services to be provided in electronic form;

(h) recommending the integration of delivery points through single window outlets such as common service centres[48];

(i) recommending the integration of Information and Facilitation Centres and Common Service Centres, where appropriate;

(j) conducting citizen awareness surveys of citizen charters and satisfaction surveys of citizens and organizations for the goods and services delivered by the public authorities[49];

(k) undertaking independent evaluations or performance audits of government schemes or programmes, when referred to by

---

45 Inserted to provide for a single window to get information related to any charter in the respective jurisdiction.

46 Inserted to provide for ease of inter-operability, harmonization and integration of different electronic services in accordance with the standards stipulated by the Central Government. This clause is in accordance with section 55 of this Bill, introduced in line with section 5 of the EDS Bill.

47 Inserted to ensure that Citizens Charters get reviewed from time to time. This will complement the obligations of the Head of the Department to review the Charters in accordance with section 5 of this Bill.

48 Inserted to provide for ease of transactions to the citizens or organizations.

49 Inserted to ensure that the dissemination of citizen charters is adequate. Surveys have shown that only 7% of the citizens knew about the existence of citizens charters that were launched as part of the reform initiatives in 1997. Presented in "Paul, S. (2008). India's Citizen's Charters: In Search of a Champion. *Economic and Political Weekly*, *43* (7), 67-73".

the Parliament or the Central Government or the State Government or the State Legislature, as the case may be[50];

(l) offering recommendations on design of new schemes or programmes, when referred to by the Parliament or the Central Government or the State Government or the State Legislature, as the case may be[51];

(m) compiling the best practices adopted in the process of delivery of goods and services including processes of e-governance, from the action taken reports sent by the Heads of the Departments or from any other source and organizing appropriate events such as training workshops or conferences etc., to disseminate and aid in adoption of such best practices[52];

(n) directing every public authority to take necessary steps to be Sevottam certified within five years of commencement of this Act;[53] and

(n) monitoring the progress made by the Central Government or the State Government or any public authority, as the case may be, in adopting the recommendations provided.

provided that the recommendations of the Central Grievance Redressal Commission or State Grievance Redressal Commission, as the case may be, shall be ordinarily implemented by the Central Government or the State Government or any public authority, as the case may be, in the specified time frame and reasons for any disagreement in implementation of these recommendations shall be provided to the appropriate Commission in writing [54].

[50] Inserted to leverage synergies in administration. This Commission would most likely have the data on grievances related to all the schemes and programmes of the Government and hence would have an advantage in taking up studies related to them.

[51] Inserted to leverage the experience of the Commission in the design of the schemes.

[52] Inserted to provide for the Commission to act as a nodal point in disseminating good practices in public service delivery.

[53] Inserted to ensure that every public authority becomes a citizen/client friendly organization as certified with a Sevottam standard developed by the Bureau of Indian Standards. Sevottam certification can be obtained if the process of instituting citizens charters, grievance redressal mechanism and developing adequate service delivery capacity are put in place.

[54] Inserted to strengthen the Commission to make binding recommendations to improve public service delivery, unless the Government gives reasons in writing the reasons for non-compliance. The flexibility for the Governments is provided, as ultimately the process of public service delivery is a policy issue and therefore an independent body ought not to have binding powers over the Government. This is also in sync with sections 37 and 38 of the EDS Bill, where the decision of the Government prevails over that of the Commission.

CHAPTER X
REPORTING OF REDRESSAL OF GRIEVANCES BY PUBLIC AUTHORITY

46. Reporting Requirements:

(*1*) Every public authority shall ensure that every Grievance Redress Officer keeps a record of complaints made to it or appeal therein and the decisions on such complaints and appeals.

(2) Every public authority shall publish on its website, by the 15th day of every month or at such shorter intervals, as may be prescribed, a report mentioning therein—

(a) the number of complaints received;

(b) the number of complaints pending;

(c) the number of complaints disposed of; and

(ca) the number of complaints upheld by the designated authority;

(cb) the number of complaints upheld by the Central Grievance Redressal Commission or the State Grievance Redressal Commission, as the case may be[55];

(d) such other particulars, as may be prescribed, for discharge of its functions under this Act.

(3) Every public authority shall furnish the following information to the Central Grievance Redressal Commission or the State Grievance Redressal Commission, as the case may be, namely[56]:

(a) information specified in sub-section (2);

(b) a compilation of the feedback received and an action taken report in pursuance thereof;

(c) action taken reports on the recommendations of the Commission in the stipulated time frame;

(d) the steps taken to enhance the services that are provided in electronic form;

(e) the steps taken to ensure availability of assisted access provided to the citizens to access electronic services;

(f) the steps taken to ensure compliance with the applicable electronic governance standards;

---

[55] Inserted to provide for this information to the public, as these indicators reflect the quality of grievance redressal by the Grievance Redressal Officer and the public display could induce performance improvements in the respective public authority.

[56] Inserted to incorporate provisions in section 25 of the EDS Bill and customized according to the broader objectives of this bill.

(g) the steps taken to simplify the processes and integrate delivery points of different goods and services;

(h) recommendations for further improvement of delivery of goods and services and the legal and policy interventions which may be required for this improvement;

(i) any other information, which the Commission seeks in relation to the provisions of this Act, from time to time.

Explanation:-For purposes of this section, the Head of the Department in the public authority shall be responsible for ensuring that the provisions are followed.

CHAPTER XA
ANNUAL REPORTS

46A. Annual Reports:

(1) It shall be the duty of the Central Grievance Redressal Commission or State Grievance Redressal Commission, as the case may be, to present annually to the President or the Governor, as appropriate, a report on the implementation of the provisions of this Act, the work done by the Commission and a memorandum explaining, in respects of the cases, if any, where the recommendations of the Commission was not complied with and the reasons given by the appropriate Government for such non-compliance [57].

(2) On receipt of such report, the President or Governor, as appropriate, shall cause a copy thereof, to be laid before each House of Parliament or the Legislative Assembly, as the case may be.

CHAPTER XI
MISCELLANEOUS

47. Appeal Against Decision of State Commission or Central Commission:

(*1*) Any person aggrieved by the decision of the Central Public Grievance Redressal Commission, which contains the findings relating to corruption under the Prevention of Corruption Act, 1988, may prefer an appeal to the Lokpal constituted under the Lokpal and Lokayuktas Act, 2011.

(*2*) Any person aggrieved by the decision of the State Public Grievance Redressal Commission, which contains the findings

[57] Inserted to incorporate sub-section 4 of section 25 of EDS Bill. Moreover these provisions could give the recommendations of the Commission a binding effect ordinarily. This provision will also result in constant updation of the processes in the public service delivery in terms of simplification, integration and ease of access for the citizens.

relating to corruption under the Prevention of Corruption Act, 1988, may prefer an appeal to the Lokayukta constituted under the Lokpal and Lokayuktas Act, 2011.

(*3*) The time within which and the manner in which the appeal may be filed under this section shall be such as may be prescribed by the appropriate Government.

48. Bar of Jurisdiction of Court:

No civil court shall have jurisdiction to settle, decide or deal with any question or to determine any matter which is by or under this Act required to be settled, decided or dealt with or to be determined by the Grievance Redress Officer or the designated authority or the State Public Grievance Redressal Commission or the Central Public Grievance Redressal Commission.

49. Enforcement of Orders by State Public Grievance Redressal Commission or the Central Public Grievance Redressal Commission:

Every order made by the State Public Grievance Redressal Commission or the Central Public Grievance Redressal Commission may be enforced by the State Public Grievance Redressal Commission or the Central Public Grievance Redressal Commission, as the case may be, in the same manner as if it were a decree or order made by a court in a suit pending therein and it shall be lawful for the State Public Grievance Redressal Commission or the Central Public Grievance Redressal Commission, as the case may be, to send, in the event of its inability to execute it, such order to the court within the local limits of whose jurisdiction,—

(*a*) in the case of a public authority not falling under clauses (*b*) and (*c*), the place at which the main office of such public authority is situated; or

(*b*) in the case of an order against a public authority being a company, the registered office of the company is situated; or

(*c*) in the case of an order against any other person, the place where the person concerned voluntarily resides or carries on business or personally works for gain is situated, and thereupon, the court to which the order is so sent, shall execute the orders as if it were a decree or order sent to it for execution.

50. Protection for Acts Done in Good Faith:

No suit, prosecution or other legal proceeding shall lie against any person or anything which is in good faith done or intended to be done under this Act or any rule made thereunder.

50A. Specification of Electronic Governance Standards[58]:

Any Department in the Government of India may, from time to time, notify, in such manner as may be prescribed, electronic governance standards, being not inconsistent with electronic governance standards notified by the Central Government, as may be necessary for ensuring inter-operability, integration, harmonisation and security of electronic services:

Provided that a State Government may prescribe such standards which had not been notified by the Central Government and the standards so notified by the State Government shall remain in force till such standards are notified by the Central Government.

51. Provisions to be in Addition to Existing Laws:

The provisions of this Act shall be in addition to and not in derogation of, any other law for the time being in force.

52. Power to Make Rules:

(*1*) The appropriate Government may, by notification, make rules for carrying out the provisions of this Act.

(*2*) In particular, and without prejudice to the generality of the foregoing power, such rules may provide for all or any of the following matters, namely:—

- (*a*) the officer or the authority to be designated as Designated Authority under clause(*h*) of section 2;
- (*b*) other information under clause (*g*) of sub-section (*2*) of section 4;
- (*c*) matters in relation to Citizens Charter under sub-section (*3*) of section 4;
- (*d*) matters in relation to the information and facilitation centre, under sub-section (*3*) of section 6;
- (*e*) the manner of inquiry into and redressal of grievance of the complaints received from citizens under sub-section (*1*) of section 7;
- (*f*) the other means by which complaints may be made under section 8;
- (*g*) the other matters for which the designated authority shall have power under clause (*g*) of sub-section (*4*) of section 11;
- (*h*) the number of Commissioners of the State Public Grievance Redressal Commission under clause (*b*) of section 14;
- (*i*) the members of the search committee under sub-section (*2*) of section 15;

[58] Inserted in line with section 5 of the EDS Bill.

(*j*) additional criteria in relation to selection of Chief Commissioner and the Commissioners of the State Public Grievance Redressal Commission under proviso to section 16;

(*k*) the procedure of investigation of misbehaviour or incapacity for removal of the Chief Commissioners and other Commissioners of, the State Public Grievance Redressal Commission under sub-section (*3*) of section 20;

(*l*) the other matters for which the State Public Grievance Redressal Commission shall have the powers under clause (*g*) of sub-section (*1*) of section 21;

(*m*) the number of Commissioners of the Central Public Grievance Redressal Commission under clause (*b*) of section 31;

(*n*) the members of the search committee under sub-section (*2*) of section 32;

(*o*) additional criteria in relation to selection of Chief Commissioner and the Commissioners of the Central Public Grievance Redressal Commission under proviso to section 33;

(*p*) the procedure of investigation of misbehaviour or incapacity for removal of the Chief Commissioner and other Commissioners of, the Central Public Grievance Redressal Commission under sub-section (*3*) of section 37;

(*q*) the other matters for which the Central Public Grievance Redressal Commission shall have the powers under clause (*g*) of sub-section (*1*) of section 38;

(*r*) the time within which the record of complaints to the public authority and the decisions on the complaints and appeals shall be published on the website and other particulars under subsection (*2*) of section 46;

(*s*) the time within which and the manner in which an appeal may be filed under sub-section(*3*) of section 47;

(*t*) any other matter which is required to be or may be prescribed under this Act.

53. Laying of Rules:

(*1*) Every rule made by the Central Government shall be laid, as soon as may be after it is made, before each House of Parliament, while it is in session, for a total period of thirty days which may be comprised in one session or in two or more successive sessions, and if before the expiry of the session immediately following the session or the successive sessions aforesaid, both Houses agree in making any modification in the rule or both Houses agree that the rule should not be made, the rule shall thereafter have effect only in such modified form or be of no effect, as the case may be; so, however, that any such modification or annulment shall be without prejudice to the validity of anything previously done under that rule.

(*2*) Every rule made by the State Government shall be laid, as soon as may be after it is made, before the State Legislature.

54. Power to Remove Difficulties:

(*1*) If any difficulty arises in giving effect to the provisions of this Act, the Central Government may, by order, published in the Official Gazette, make such provisions not inconsistent with the provisions of this Act as may appear to be necessary for removing the difficulty: Provided that no order shall be made under this section after the expiry of two years from the commencement of this Act.

(*2*) Every order made under this section shall be laid, as soon as may be after it is made, before each House of Parliament.

54A. Amendments to Other Acts:

The enactments specified in the Schedule shall be amended in the manner specified therein [59].

THE SCHEDULE

AMENDMENTS TO THE RIGHT TO INFORMATION ACT, 2005

No. 22 of 2005

1. In section 2, the following clause shall be inserted:
   (o) "Head of the Department" means an officer designated as such by the appropriate Government, as the head of the a Government Department or public authority[60];
2. In section 4, following shall be inserted:
   Explanation II:—For the purposes of this section, the Head of the Department shall be responsible for duties of the public authority listed in the sub-sections[61].
3. For section 12, the following section shall be substituted:
   12. The Central Public Grievance Commission established under section 30 of the Right of Citizens for Time Bound Delivery of

[59] Inserted to include amendments to Right to Information Act, 2005.

[60] Inserted a definition "*Head of the Department*" as mentioned in this bill.

[61] Inserted a definition to make the Head of the Department responsible for providing the information listed in section 4 of RTI Act.

Goods and Services and Redressal of their Grievances Act, 2011 shall function as the Central Information Commission[62].

4. For section 15, the following section shall be substituted:
15. The State Public Grievance Commission established under section 13 of the Right of Citizens for Time Bound Delivery of Goods and Services and Redressal of their Grievances Act, 2011 shall function as the State Information Commission[63].
5. Sections 13, 14, 16, and 17 shall be omitted[64].
6. In clause 18(1)(b), for the words "who has been refused access to any information requested under this Act" the words "who has been refused access to any information to be provided under section 4 of this Act or any information requested under this Act"[65];
7. The words "or sub-section (3)[66]" shall be inserted after "sub-section (1) or sub-section (2)" in sub-section 6 of section 19 of this Act.
8. In section 20, the following sub-section shall be inserted:
(3) Where the Central Information Commission or the State Information Commission, as the case may be, at the time of deciding any complaint or appeal is of the opinion that the Head of the Department of the concerned public authority, has, without any reasonable cause, failed to fulfill the functions under section 4 of this Act, it shall impose a lump sum penalty, which may extend to fifty thousand rupees:
Provided that the Head of the Department shall be given a reasonable opportunity of being heard before any penalty is imposed on him
Provided further that the burden of proving that he acted reasonably and diligently shall be on the Head of the Department[67].

[62] Substituted for Section 12 of RTI Act to make the Grievance Redressal Commission the Information Commission.

[63] Substituted for Section 12 of RTI Act to make the Grievance Redressal Commission the Information Commission

[64] Omitted sections relating to terms and conditions of Information Commissions as the terms and conditions mentioned in this bill shall take effect.

[65] Inserted to provide original jurisdiction for Information Commission on complaints regarding non-provision of information according to section 4 of the RTI Act.

[66] Inserted to provide for a stipulated timeframe in which the Information Commissions have to dispose of the appeals in line with that of the Public Information Officer.

[67] Inserted to provide for provisions to penalize the Head of the Department for non-provision of information according to section 4 in line with sub-section (1) and (2) of section 20 in the RTI Act.

ANNEXURE E

Ethics in Governance

Fourth Report of the Second Administrative Reforms Commission, 2007

Introduction

1.1 Ethics is a set of standards that society places on itself and which helps guide behaviour, choices and actions. The Commission is painfully aware that standards do not, by themselves, ensure ethical behaviour; that requires a robust culture of integrity. The crux of ethical behaviour does not lie in bold words and expressions enshrined as standards, but in their adoption in action, in sanctions against their violations, in putting in place competent disciplinary bodies to investigate allegations of violations and impose sanctions quickly and in promoting a culture of integrity.

1.2 Corruption is an important manifestation of the failure of ethics. The word 'corrupt' is derived from the Latin word *'corruptus'*, meaning 'to break or destroy'. The word 'ethics' is from the original Greek term *ethikos*, meaning 'arising from habit'. It is unfortunate that corruption has, for many, become a matter of habit, ranging from grand corruption involving persons in high places to retail corruption touching the everyday life of common people.

1.3 Anti-corruption interventions so far made are seen to be ineffectual and there is widespread public cynicism about them. The interventions are seen as mere posturing without any real intention to bring the corrupt to book. They are also seen as handy weapons for partisan, political use to harass opponents. Corruption is so deeply entrenched in the system that most people regard corruption as inevitable and any effort to fight it as futile. This cynicism is spreading so fast that it bodes ill for our democratic system itself.

1.4 There are two, somewhat contrary, approaches in dealing with corruption and abuse of office. The first is overemphasis on values and character. Many people lament the decline in values and the consequent rise in corruption. The implicit assumption is that until values are restored, nothing much can be done to improve the conduct of human beings. The second approach is based on the belief that most human beings are fundamentally decent and socially conscious, but there is always a small proportion of people, which cannot reconcile individual goals with the good of society. Such deviant people tend to pursue personal gain at the cost of public good and the purpose of organized government is to punish such deviant behaviour. If good behaviour is consistently rewarded and bad behaviour consistently punished, the bulk of the people follow the straight and narrow path. However, if good behaviour is not only not rewarded, but is actually fraught with difficulties and bad behaviour is not only not punished, but is often extravagantly rewarded, then the bulk of the people tend to stray from the honourable path.

1.5 In the real world, both values and institutions matter. Values are needed to serve as guiding stars, and they exist in abundance in our society. A sense of right and wrong is intrinsic to our culture and civilization. But values need to be sustained by institutions to be durable and to serve as an example to others. Values without institutional support will soon be weakened and dissipated. Institutions provide the container, which gives shape and content to values. This is the basis of all statecraft and laws and institutions. While incentives and institutions matter for all people, they are critical in dealing with the army of public servants elected or appointed – endowed with authority to make decisions and impact on human lives and exercising the power to determine allocation of resources. Public office and control over public purse offer enormous temptation and opportunity to promote private gain at public cost. Therefore, creation of institutions and designing of incentives are of utmost importance in promoting ethical conduct of public servants.

1.6 In our society, corruption and abuse of office has been aggravated by three factors. First, there is a colonial legacy of unchallenged authority and propensity to exercise power arbitrarily. In a society which worships power, it is easy for public officials to deviate from ethical conduct. Second, there is enormous asymmetry of power in our society. Nearly 90% of our people are in the unorganized sector. Quite a number of them lead a precarious existence, depending on subsistence wages with no job security. And nearly 70% of the organized workers with job security and regular monthly wage are employed by the state directly or through public sector undertakings. Almost all these employees are 'educated' in a largely illiterate and semiliterate society and economically even the lowliest of public servants are better off than most people in the country. What is more, their employment in government comes with all the trappings of power. Such asymmetry of power reduces societal pressure to conform to ethical behaviour and makes it easy to indulge in corruption.

1.7 Third, as a conscious choice, the Indian state in the early decades after Independence chose a set of policies whose unintended consequence was to put the citizen at the mercy of the State. Over regulation, severe restrictions on economic activity, excessive state control, near-monopoly of the government in many sectors and an economy of scarcity all created conditions conducive to unbridled corruption. In addition, many state subsidies and beneficiary-oriented programmes in a situation of asymmetry of power converted the public servant into patron and master and reduced most citizens into mendicants. This at once enhanced opportunities to indulge in corruption and reduced the citizens' capacity to resist extortionary demands.

1.8 The experience of the past six decades in our country and elsewhere offers us valuable lessons in curbing corruption. It is generally recognized that monopoly and discretion increase the propensity to corruption while competition and transparency reduce corruption. This has been dramatically witnessed in India in the wake of economic liberalization. As competition came in and choice expanded, corruption plummeted. Telephones, steel, cement, sugar and even two-wheelers are among the many sectors, which have seen enhanced supply and choice, reducing or even eliminating corruption. Similarly, wherever technology and transparency have been introduced, corruption has been significantly contained. Computerization and access to information have made many services from railway reservation to issuing of driving licenses increasingly free from corruption.

1.9 A factor which increases corruption is over-centralization. The more remotely power is exercised from the people, the greater is the distance between authority and accountability. The large number of functionaries between the citizen and final decision-makers makes accountability diffused and the temptation to abuse authority strong. For a large democracy, India probably has the smallest number of final decision makers. Local Government is not allowed to take root and power has been concentrated both horizontally and vertically in a few hands. The net results are weakened citizenry and mounting corruption.

1.10 It is well recognized that every democracy requires the empowerment of citizens in order to hold those in authority to account. Right to Information, effective citizens' charters, opportunity and incentives to promote proactive approach of citizens, stake-holders' involvement in delivery of public services, public consultation in decision making and social auditing are some of the instruments of accountability that dramatically curbed corruption and promoted integrity and quality of decision making.

1.11 In the ultimate analysis, the state and a system of laws exist in order to enforce compliance and promote desirable behaviour. Therefore, enforcement of rule of law and deterrent punishment against corruption are critical to build an ethically sound society. A detailed analysis of our anti-corruption mechanisms and the causes of their failure is necessary in order to strengthen the forces of law and deter the corrupt public servants.

1.12 Perhaps the most important determinant of the integrity of a society or the prevalence of corruption is the quality of politics. If politics attracts and rewards men and women of integrity, competence and passion for public good, then the society is safe and integrity is maintained. But if honesty is incompatible with survival in politics, and if public life attracts undesirable and corrupt elements seeking private gain, then abuse of authority and corruption become the norm. In such a political culture and climate, desirable initiatives will not yield adequate dividends. Competition and decentralization certainly reduce corruption in certain sectors. But if the demand for corruption is fuelled by inexhaustible appetite for illegitimate funds in politics, then other avenues of corruption will be forcibly opened up. As a result, even as corruption declines in certain areas, it shifts to other, sometimes more dangerous, areas in which competition cannot be introduced and the state exercises a natural monopoly. What is needed with liberalisation is corresponding political and governance reform to alter the incentives in politics and public office and to promote integrity and ethical conduct.

1.13 All forms of corruption are reprehensible and we need to promote a culture of zero-tolerance of corruption. But some forms of corruption are much more pernicious than others and deserve closer attention. In a vast majority of cases of bribery, the citizen is a victim of extortion and is compelled to pay a bribe in order to get a service to which he is entitled. Experience has taught most citizens that there is a vicious cycle of corruption operating and they often end up losing much more by resisting corruption. Delays, harassment, lost opportunity, loss of precious time and wages, uncertainty and, at times, potential danger of loss of life or limb could result from resistance to corruption and non-compliance with demands. In such cases, the citizen is an unwilling victim of coercive corruption. But there are several cases of collusion between the bribe giver and corrupt public servant. In such cases of collusive corruption, both parties benefit at immense cost to society. Awarding of contracts for public works and procurement of goods and services, recruitment of employees, evasion of taxes, substandard projects, collusive violation of regulations, adulteration of foods and drugs, obstruction of justice and concealing or doctoring evidence in investigation are all examples of such dangerous forms of corruption. As the economy is freed from state controls, extortionary corruption declines and collusive corruption tends to increase. We need to fashion strong and effective instruments to deal with this growing menace of collusive corruption, which is undermining the very foundations of our democracy and endangering society.

1.14 Corruption is a global phenomenon and has also become a serious global concern. The United Nations Convention against Corruption was adopted by the UN General Assembly in October 2003, providing an international instrument against corruption. The ADBOECD Anti-Corruption Action Plan, which has been signed by the Government of India, is a broad understanding to further the cause of inter-regional cooperation in the matter of prevention of corruption. The World Bank has also declared war against corruption by refusing to fund projects whose implementation is tainted by corrupt practices. At the annual meeting of the International Monetary Fund and the World Bank Group in Singapore in 2006, a joint statement was issued with major multilateral financial institutions agreeing on a framework for preventing and combating fraud and corruption in the activities and operations of their institutions.

1.15 In India, some recent anti-corruption initiatives are steps in the right direction. The Supreme Court has ruled that candidates contesting elections should file details regarding their wealth, educational qualifications and criminal antecedents along with their nomination papers. The Right to Information Act, which has recently been enacted, is a potent weapon to fight corruption. The introduction of information communication technologies, e-governance initiatives and automation of corruption prone processes in administration have succeeded in reducing corruption.

1.16 Much more remains to be done however, and beyond the realm of existing regulation. The escalating levels of corruption in various segments of our economy resulting in large-scale generation of black money, serious economic offences and fraud, and money laundering leading even to the funding of terrorist activities against the State, have created a grave situation which needs to be dealt with severely. Benami properties of corrupt public servants need to be forfeited, as also the assets illegally acquired from corrupt practices. Whistleblower legislation has to be put in place to protect informants against retribution. Also, we have to suitably strengthen the institutional framework for investigating corrupt practices and awarding exemplary punishment to the corrupt thereby raising the risk associated with corrupt behaviour.

1.17 Ethics in governance, however, has a much wider import than what happens in the different arms of the government. An across-the-board effort is needed to fight deviations from ethical norms. Such an effort needs to include corporate ethics and ethics in business; in fact, there should be a paradigm shift from the pejorative 'business ethics' to 'ethics in business'. There is need for ethics in every profession, voluntary organization and civil society structure as these entities are now vitally involved in the process of governance. Finally, there should be ethics in citizen behaviour because such behaviour impinges directly on ethics in government and administration.

1.18 One of the terms of reference of the Administrative Reforms Commission pertains to ethics in governance, specifically the following aspects:-

A. *Vigilance and Corruption:*

- *Strengthening pro-active vigilance to eliminate corruption and harassment to honest civil servants including, wherever necessary, limiting executive discretion.*
- *Addressing systemic deficiencies manifesting in reluctance to punish the corrupt.*
- *(a) Identify procedures, rules and regulations and factors which lead to corruption*

  (b) suggest measures to combat corruption and arbitrary decision making, and

  (c) suggest a framework for their periodical review in consultation with the stakeholders.

B. Relationship between Political Executive and Permanent Civil Service:

- *To suggest improvements in the institutional arrangements for smooth, efficient and harmonious relationship between civil service and the political executive.*

C. Code of Conduct for different organs of Government :

- *Political Executive, Civil Services, etc.*

1.19 While the Commission has examined items A & C in considerable detail in this Report; item B will be dealt with comprehensively in the ARC's report on Civil Services Reforms. The Commission has examined the relevant laws, codes and manuals, which deal with ethics and corruption. It has critically studied the institutional framework that investigates corruption and brings the corrupt to book. It has also looked at the corruption prone processes in government and examined the systems, rules and procedures, which govern these processes.

1.20 In order to ascertain views from different stakeholders on ethics in governance, the Commission organized a National Colloquium at the National Judicial Academy, Bhopal in September 2006. The Commission expresses its deep gratitude to the then Chief Justice of India, Mr. Justice Shri Y.K. Sabharwal who delivered the valedictory address[1], the Minister of State for Personnel Public Grievances & Pensions and Parliamentary Affairs Shri Suresh Pachouri who presided over the inaugural function[2] and to Mr. Justice S.B. Sinha for his valuable suggestions. The Chairman ARC addressed the gathering[3]. The list of participants at the National Colloquium organized by the Commission on the subject is at Annexure I(4). The recommendations of the Colloquium are at Annexure I(5). The questionnaire circulated to various stakeholders is at Annexure I(6).

1.21 The Commission would like to place on record its gratitude to the Lokayuktas, representatives of CVC and the state anti corruption wings, members of 'citizens' initiatives', officers of Government of India and the State Governments for their active participation in the workshop. The Commission also expresses its deep gratitude to Mr Justice J.S. Verma, former CJI; Mr Justice M.N. Venkatachaliah, former CJI; Mr. Justice Santosh Hegde, former Judge, Supreme Court; Mr Justice N. Venkatchala, former Lokayukta Karnataka; Shri Fali Nariman; Shri B.V. Acharya, former Advocate General, Karnataka; Shri K.R. Chamayya, former Law Secretary, Government of Karnataka; Shri K. Eshwara Bhat, former Law Secretary, Government

1. Speech at Annexure I(1)
2. Speech at Annexure I(3)
3. Speech at Annexure I(2)

of Karnataka and Admiral R.H. Tahiliani (Retd), Chairman, Transparency International, India, whose views and suggestions have been of immense help to the Commission in articulating its recommendations. The Commission expresses its appreciation for the valuable contribution made by Shri S K Das, Consultant ARC in drafting this Report.

1.22 As issues relating to ethics in governance cut across other terms of reference, an attempt has been made to deal with the major issues in this Report. The Report is organized in nine chapters dealing with different aspects of ethics in governance. The recommendations range from those seeking to change the legal framework to those which could be implemented through executive directions within a short time frame. Recommendations which could be implemented immediately through executive direction are identified by prefixing a symbol '*', in the Summary of Recommendations.

CONCLUSION

This report must end on a note of optimism. Indians have always valued a world beyond the material and have embraced spiritualism as a way of life. Instances abound in our epics of good behaviour, of the triumph of good over evil, of the wisdom of sages. Stories of the honesty, generosity and piety of legendry kings such as Vikramaditya, are told to our children even today. There is no reason why Ram Rajya cannot be attempted.

In modern India, poverty, insufficiency and class conflicts are slowly giving way to a confident, inclusive, empowered India. On the Transparency International's Corruption Index, India's position has improved significantly, and hopefully will continue to do so. The vigilance of our enlightened people will ensure this.

The Commission believes that this Report on Ethics in Governance is among the most important that this Commission has been called upon to write, because increased honesty in governance would have a major impact on the everyday lives of the people of India. When the recommendations in this report are implemented, greater efficiency in government work and accountability would be achieved, because more public servants would work not with a private agenda but for the larger public good. Equally importantly, a more corruption free regime would lead to a much higher rate of growth of our GDP, bring an overall improvement in the economy and lead to greater transparency in government actions in serving its people. All this, in turn, will lead to greater empowerment of the people – the core need of a vibrant democracy.

SUMMARY OF RECOMMENDATIONS

1. (2.1.3.1.6) Reform of Political Funding
   a. A system for partial state funding should be introduced in order to reduce the scope of illegitimate and unnecessary funding of expenditure for elections.
2. (2.1.3.2.4) Tightening of Anti-Defection Law
   a. The issue of disqualification of members on grounds of defection should be decided by the President/Governor on the advice of the Election Commission.
3. (2.1.3.3.2) Disqualification
   a. Section 8 of the Representation of the People Act, 1951 needs to be amended to disqualify all persons facing charges related to grave and heinous offences and corruption, with the modification suggested by the Election Commission.
4. (2.1.4.3) Coalition and Ethics
   a. The Constitution should be amended to ensure that if one or more parties in a coalition with a common programme mandated by the electorate either explicitly before the elections or implicitly while forming the government, realign midstream with one or more parties outside the coalition, then Members of that party or parties shall have to seek a fresh mandate from the electorate.
5. (2.1.5.4) Appointment of the Chief Election Commissioner/ Commissioners
   a. A collegium headed by the Prime Minister with the Speaker of the Lok Sabha, the Leader of Opposition in the Lok Sabha, the Law Minister and the Deputy Chairman of the Rajya Sabha as members; should make recommendations for the consideration of the President for appointment of the Chief Election Commissioner and the Election Commissioners.
6. (2.1.6.3) Expediting Disposal of Election Petitions
   a. Special Election Tribunals should be constituted at the regional level under Article 323B of the Constitution to ensure speedy disposal of election petitions and disputes within a stipulated period of six months. Each Tribunal should comprise a High Court Judge and a senior civil servant with at least 5 years of experience in the conduct of elections (not below the rank of an Additional Secretary to Government of India/Principal secretary of a State Government). Its mandate should be to ensure that all

election petitions are decided within a period of six months as provided by law. The Tribunals should normally be set up for a term of one year only, extendable for a period of 6 months in exceptional circumstances.

7. (2.1.7.3) Grounds of Disqualification for Membership
   a. Appropriate legislation may be enacted under Article 102(e) of the Constitution spelling out the conditions for disqualification of Membership of Parliament in an exhaustive manner. Similarly, the States may also legislate under Article 198(e).

8. (2.4.5) Ethical Framework for Ministers
   *a. In addition to the existing Code of Conduct for Ministers, there should be a Code of Ethics to provide guidance on how Ministers should uphold the highest standards of constitutional and ethical conduct in the performance of their duties.
   *b. Dedicated units should be set up in the offices of the Prime Minister and the Chief Ministers to monitor the observance of the Code of Ethics and the Code of Conduct. The unit should also be empowered to receive public complaints regarding violation of the Code of Conduct.
   *c. The Prime Minister or the Chief Minister should be duty bound to ensure the observance of the Code of Ethics and the Code of Conduct by Ministers. This would be applicable even in the case of coalition governments where the Ministers may belong to different parties.
   *d. An annual report with regard to the observance of these Codes should be submitted to the appropriate legislature. This report should include specific cases of violations, if any, and the action taken thereon.
   *e. The Code of Ethics should inter alia include broad principles of the Minister-civil servant relationship and the Code of Conduct should stipulate the details as illustrated in para 2.4.3.
   *f. The Code of Ethics, the Code of Conduct and the annual report should be put in the public domain.

9. (2.5.7.6) Enforcement of ethical norms in Legislatures
   *a. An Office of 'Ethics Commissioner' may be constituted by each House of Parliament. This Office, functioning under the Speaker/Chairman, would assist the Committee on Ethics in the discharge of its functions, and advise Members, when required, and maintain necessary records.
   *b. In respect of states, the Commission recommends the following:

(i) All State legislatures may adopt a Code of Ethics and a Code of Conduct for their Members.

(ii) Ethics Committees may be constituted with well defined procedures for sanctions in case of transgressions, to ensure the ethical conduct of legislators.

(iii) 'Registers of Members' Interests' may be maintained with the declaration of interests by Members of the State legislatures.

(iv) Annual Reports providing details including transgressions may be placed on the Table of the respective Houses.

(v) An Office of 'Ethics Commissioner' may be constituted by each House of the State legislatures. This Office would function under the Speaker/Chairman, on the same basis as suggested for Parliament.

1. (2.6.12) Office of Profit

a. The Law should be amended to define office of profit based on the following principles:

(i) All offices in purely advisory bodies where the experience, insights and expertise of a legislator would be inputs in governmental policy, shall not be treated as offices of profit, irrespective of the remuneration and perks associated with such an office.

(ii) All offices involving executive decision making and control of public funds, including positions on the governing boards of public undertakings and statutory and non-statutory authorities directly deciding policy or managing institutions or authorizing or approving expenditure shall be treated as offices of profit, and no legislator shall hold such offices.

(iii) If a serving Minister, by virtue of office, is a member or head of certain organizations like the Planning Commission, where close coordination and integration between the Council of Ministers and the organization or authority or committee is vital for the day-to-day functioning of government, it shall not be treated as office of profit.

(The use of discretionary funds at the disposal of legislators, the power to determine specific projects and schemes, or select the beneficiaries or authorize expenditure shall constitute discharge of executive functions and will invite disqualification under Articles 102 and 191, irrespective of whether or not a new office is notified and held.)

b. Schemes such as MPLADS and MLALADS should be abolished.

c. Members of Parliament and Members of State Legislatures should be declared as 'Public Authorities' under the Right to Information Act, except when they are discharging legislative functions.

11. (2.7.12) Code of Ethics for Civil Servants

*a. 'Public Service Values' towards which all public servants should aspire, should be defined and made applicable to all tiers of Government and parastatal organizations. Any transgression of these values should be treated as misconduct, inviting punishment.

*b. Conflict of interests should be comprehensively covered in the code of ethics and in the code of conduct for officers. Also, serving officials should not be nominated on the Boards of Public undertakings. This will, however, not apply to non-profit public institutions and advisory bodies.

12. (2.8.5) Code of Ethics for Regulators

a. A comprehensive and enforceable code of conduct should be prescribed for all professions with statutory backing.

13. (2.9.23) Ethical Framework for the Judiciary

a. A National Judicial Council should be constituted, in line with universally accepted principles where the appointment of members of the judiciary should be by a collegium having representation of the executive, legislature and judiciary. The Council should have the following composition:

- The Vice-President as Chairperson of the Council
- The Prime Minister
- The Speaker of the Lok Sabha
- The Chief Justice of India
- The Law Minister
- The Leader of the Opposition in the Lok Sabha
- The Leader of the Opposition in the Rajya Sabha

In matters relating to the appointment and oversight of High Court Judges, the Council will also include the following members:

- The Chief Minister of the concerned State
- The Chief Justice of the concerned High Court

b. The National Judicial Council should be authorized to lay down the code of conduct for judges, including the subordinate judiciary.

c. The National Judicial Council should be entrusted with the task of recommending appointments of Supreme Court and High Court Judges. It should also be entrusted the task of oversight of the judges, and should be empowered to enquire into alleged misconduct and impose minor penalties. It can also recommend removal of a judge if so warranted.

d. Based on the recommendations of the NJC, the President should have the powers to remove a Supreme Court or High Court Judge.

e. Article 124 of the Constitution may be amended to provide for the National Judicial Council. A similar change will have to be made to Article 217. Also, since the Council is to have the authority to oversee and discipline judges, further changes will need to be made to Article 217 (Clause 4).

f. A Judge of the Supreme Court should be designated as the Judicial Values Commissioner. He/she should be assigned the task of enforcing the code of conduct. Similar arrangement should also be made in the High Court.

14. (3.2.1.10) Defining Corruption

a. The following should be classified as offences under the Prevention of Corruption Act:
   - Gross perversion of the Constitution and democratic institutions amounting to wilful violation of oath of office.
   - Abuse of authority unduly favouring or harming someone.
   - Obstruction of justice.
   - Squandering public money.

15. (3.2.2.7) Collusive Bribery

a. Section 7 of the Prevention of Corruption Act needs to be amended to provide for a special offence of 'collusive bribery'. An Offence could be classified as 'collusive bribery' if the outcome or intended outcome of the transaction leads to a loss to the state, public or public interest;

b. In all such cases if it is established that the interest of the state or public has suffered because of an act of a public servant, then the court shall presume that the public servant and the beneficiary of the decision committed an offence of 'collusive bribery';

c. The punishment for all such cases of collusive bribery should be double that of other cases of bribery. The law may be suitably amended in this regard.

16. (3.2.3.2) Sanction for Prosecution
    a. Prior sanction should not be necessary for prosecuting a public servant who has been trapped red-handed or in cases of possessing assets disproportionate to the known sources of income.
    b. The Prevention of Corruption Act should be amended to ensure that sanctioning authorities are not summoned and instead the documents can be obtained and produced before the courts by the appropriate authority.
    c. The Presiding Officer of a House of Legislature should be designated as the sanctioning authority for MPs and MLAs respectively.
    d. The requirement of prior sanction for prosecution now applicable to serving public servants should also apply to retired public servants for acts performed while in service.
    e. In all cases where the Government of India is empowered to grant sanction for prosecution, this power should be delegated to an Empowered Committee comprising the Central Vigilance Commissioner and the Departmental Secretary to Government. In case of a difference of opinion between the two, the matter could be resolved by placing it before the full Central Vigilance Commission. In case, sanction is required against a Secretary to Government, then the Empowered Committee would comprise of Cabinet Secretary and the Central Vigilance Commissioner. Similar arrangements may also be made at the State level. In all cases the order granting sanction for prosecution or otherwise shall be issued within two months. In case of refusal, the reasons for refusal should be placed before the respective legislature annually.
17. (3.2.4.3) Liability of Corrupt Public Servants to Pay Damages
    a. In addition to the penalty in criminal cases the law should provide that public servants who cause loss to the state or citizens by their corrupt acts should be made liable to make good the loss caused and, in addition, be liable for damages. This could be done by inserting a chapter in the Prevention of Corruption Act.
18. (3.2.5.6) Speeding up Trials under the Prevention of Corruption Act:
    a. A legal provision needs to be introduced fixing a time limit for various stages of trial. This could be done by amendments to the CrPC.

b. Steps have to be taken to ensure that judges declared as Special Judges under the provisions of the Prevention of Corruption Act give primary attention to disposal of cases under the Act. Only if there is inadequate work under the Act, should the Special Judges be entrusted with other responsibilities.

c. It has to be ensured that the proceedings of courts trying cases under the Prevention of Corruption Act are held on a day-to-day basis, and no deviation is permitted.

d. The Supreme Court and the High Courts may lay down guidelines to preclude unwarranted adjournments and avoidable delays.

19. (3.3.7) Corruption Involving the Private Sector

a. The Prevention of Corruption Act should be suitably amended to include in its purview private sector providers of public utility services.

b. Non-Governmental agencies, which receive substantial funding, should be covered under the Prevention of Corruption Act. Norms should be laid down that any institution or body that has received more than 50% of its annual operating costs, or a sum equal to or greater than Rs 1 crore during any of the preceding 3 years should be deemed to have obtained 'substantial funding' for that period and purpose of such funding.

20. (3.4.10) Confiscation of Properties Illegally Acquired by Corrupt Means.

a. The Corrupt Public Servants (Forfeiture of Property) Bill as suggested by the Law Commission should be enacted without further delay.

21. (3.5.4) Prohibition of 'Benami'1 Transactions

a. Steps should be taken for immediate implementation of the Benami Transactions (Prohibition) Act 1988.

22. (3.6.4) Protection to Whistleblowers

a. Legislation should be enacted immediately to provide protection to whistleblowers on the following lines proposed by the Law Commission:

- Whistleblowers exposing false claims, fraud or corruption should be protected by ensuring confidentiality and anonymity, protection from victimization in career, and other administrative measures to prevent bodily harm and harassment.

- The legislation should cover corporate whistle-blowers unearthing fraud or serious damage to public interest by willful acts of omission or commission.
- Acts of harassment or victimization of or retaliation against, a whistleblower should be criminal offences with substantial penalty and sentence.

23. (3.7.19) Serious Economic Offences:
   a. A new law on 'Serious Economic Offences' should be enacted.
   b. A Serious Economic Offence may be defined as :
      (i) One which involves a sum exceeding Rs 10 crores; or
      (ii) is likely to give rise to widespread public concern; or
      (iii) its investigation and prosecution are likely to require highly specialized knowledge of the financial market or of the behaviour of banks or other financial institutions; or
      (iv) involves significant international dimensions; or
      (v) in the investigation of which there is requirement of legal, financial, investment and investigative skills to be brought together; or
      (vi) which appear to be complex to the Union Government, regulators, banks, or any financial institution.
   c. A Serious Frauds Office (SFO) should be set up (under the new law), to investigate and prosecute such offences. It should be attached to the Cabinet Secretariat. This office shall have powers to investigate and prosecute all such cases in Special Courts constituted for this purpose. The SFO should be staffed by experts from diverse disciplines such as the financial sector, capital and futures market, commodity markets, accountancy, direct and indirect taxation, forensic audit, investigation, criminal and company law and information technology. The SFO should have all powers of investigation as stated in the recommendation of the Mitra Committee. The existing SFIO should be subsumed in this.
   d. A Serious Frauds Monitoring Committee should be constituted to oversee the investigation and prosecution of such offences. This Committee, to be headed by the Cabinet Secretary, should have the Chief Vigilance Commissioner, Home Secretary, Finance Secretary, Secretary Banking/ Financial Sector, a Deputy Governor, RBI, Secretary, Department of Company Affairs, Law Secretary, Chairman SEBI etc as members.

e. In case of involvement of any public functionary in a serious fraud, the SFO shall send a report to the Rashtriya Lokayukta and shall follow the directions given by the Rashtriya Lokayukta (see para 4.3.15).

f. In all cases of serious frauds the Court shall presume the existence of mens rea of the accused, and the burden of proof regarding its non-existence, shall lie on the accused.

24. (3.8.5) Prior Concurrence for Registration of Cases: Section 6A of the Delhi Special Police Establishment Act, 1946

a. Permission to take up investigations under the present statutory arrangement should be given by the Central Vigilance Commissioner in consultation with the concerned Secretary. In case of investigation against a Secretary to Government, the permission should be given by a Committee comprising the Cabinet Secretary and the Central Vigilance Commissioner. This would require an amendment to the Delhi Special Police Establishment Act. In the interim the powers of the Union Government may be delegated to the Central Vigilance Commissioner, to be exercised in the manner stated above. A time limit of 30 days may be prescribed for processing this permission.

25. (3.9.4) Immunity Enjoyed by Legislators

a. The Commission, while endorsing the suggestion of the National Commission to Review the Working of the Constitution, recommends that suitable amendments be effected to Article 105(2) of the Constitution to provide that the immunity enjoyed by Members of Parliament does not cover corrupt acts committed by them in connection with their duties in the House or otherwise.

b. The Commission also recommends that similar amendments may be made in Article 194(2) of the Constitution in respect of members of the state legislatures.

26. (3.10.24) Constitutional Protection to Civil Servants – Article 311

a. Article 311 of the Constitution should be repealed.

b. Simultaneously Article 310 of the Constitution should also be repealed.

c. Suitable legislation to provide for all necessary terms and conditions of services should be provided under Article 309, to protect the bona fide action of public servants taken in public interest; this should be made applicable to the States.

d. Necessary protection to public servants against arbitrary action should be provided through such legislation under Article 309.

27. (4.3.15) The Lok Pal
   a. The Constitution should be amended to provide for a national ombudsman to be called the Rashtriya Lokayukta. The role and jurisdiction of the Rashtriya Lokayukta should be defined in the Constitution while the composition, mode of appointment and other details can be decided by Parliament through legislation.
   b. The jurisdiction of Rashtriya Lokayukta should extend to all Ministers of the Union (except the Prime Minister), all state Chief Ministers, all persons holding public office equivalent in rank to a Union Minister, and Members of Parliament. In case the enquiry against a public functionary establishes the involvement of any other public official along with the public functionary, the Rashtriya Lokayukta would have the power to enquire against such public servant(s) also.
   c. The Prime Minister should be kept out of the jurisdiction of the Rashtriya Lokayukta for the reasons stated in paras 4.3.7 to 4.3.11.
   d. The Rashtriya Lokayukta should consist of a serving or retired Judge of the Supreme Court as the Chairperson, an eminent jurist as Member and the Central Vigilance Commissioner as the ex-officio Member.
   e. The Chairperson of the Rashtriya Lokayukta should be selected from a panel of sitting Judges of the Supreme Court who have more than three years of service, by a Committee consisting of the Vice President of India, the Prime Minister, the Leader of the Opposition, the Speaker of the Lok Sabha and the Chief Justice of India. In case it is not possible to appoint a sitting Judge, the Committee may appoint a retired Supreme Court Judge. The same Committee may select the Member (i.e. an eminent jurist) of the Rashtriya Lokayukta. The Chairperson and Member of the Rashtriya Lokayukta should be appointed for only one term of three years and they should not hold any public office under government thereafter, the only exception being that they can become the Chief Justice of India, if their services are so required.
   f. The Rashtriya Lokayukta should also be entrusted with the task of undertaking a national campaign for raising the standards of ethics in public life.

28. (4.4.9) The Lokayukta :

a. The Constitution should be amended to incorporate a provision making it obligatory on the part of State Governments to establish the institution of Lokayukta and stipulate the general principles about its structure, power and functions.
b. The Lokayukta should be a multi-member body consisting of a judicial Member in the Chair, an eminent jurist or eminent administrator with impeccable credentials as Member and the head of the State Vigilance Commission {as referred in para 4.4.9(e) below} as ex-officio Member. The Chairperson of the Lokayukta should be selected from a panel of retired Supreme Court Judges or retired Chief Justices of High Court, by a Committee consisting of the Chief Minister, Chief Justice of the High Court and the Leader of the Opposition in the Legislative Assembly. The same Committee should select the second member from among eminent jurists/administrators. There is no need to have an Up-Lokayukta.
c. The jurisdiction of the Lokayukta would extend to only cases involving corruption. They should not look into general public grievances.
d. The Lokayukta should deal with cases of corruption against Ministers and MLAs.
e. Each State should constitute a State Vigilance Commission to look into cases of corruption against State Government officials. The Commission should have three Members and have functions similar to that of the Central Vigilance Commission.
f. The Anti Corruption Bureaus should be brought under the control of the State Vigilance Commission.
g. The Chairperson and Members of the Lokayukta should be appointed strictly for one term only and they should not hold any public office under government thereafter.
h. The Lokayukta should have its own machinery for investigation. Initially, it may take officers on deputation from the State Government, but over a period of five years, it should take steps to recruit its own cadre, and train them properly.
i. All cases of corruption should be referred to Rashtriya Lokayukta or Lokayukta and these should not be referred to any Commission of Inquiry.

29. (4.5.6)Ombudsman at the Local Levels

*a. A local bodies Ombudsman should be constituted for a group of districts to investigate cases against the functionaries of the local bodies. The State Panchayat Raj Acts and the Urban Local Bodies Act should be amended to include this provision.

*b. The local bodies Ombudsman should be empowered to investigate cases of corruption or maladministration by the functionaries of the local self governments, and submit reports to the competent authorities for taking action. The competent authorities should normally take action as recommended. In case they do not agree with the recommendations, they should give their reasons in writing and the reasons should be made public.

30. (4.6.6) Strengthening Investigation and Prosecution

*a. The State Vigilance Commissions/Lokayuktas may be empowered to supervise the prosecution of corruption related cases.

*b. The investigative agencies should acquire multi-disciplinary skills and should be thoroughly conversant with the working of various offices/ departments. They should draw officials from different wings of government.

*c. Modern techniques of investigation should also be deployed like electronic surveillance, video and audio recording of surprise inspections, traps, searches and seizures.

*d. A reasonable time limit for investigation of different types of cases should be fixed for the investigative agencies.

*e. There should be sustained step-up in the number of cases detected and investigated. The priorities need to be reoriented by focussing on 'big' cases of corruption.

*f. The prosecution of corruption cases should be conducted by a panel of lawyers prepared by the Attorney General or the Advocate General in consultation with Rashtriya Lokayukta or Lokayukta as the case may be.

*g. The anti-corruption agencies should conduct systematic surveys of departments with particular reference to highly corruption prone ones in order to gather intelligence and to target officers of questionable integrity.

*h. The economic offences unit of states need to be strengthened to effectively investigate cases and there should be better coordination amongst existing agencies.

31. (5.1.12) Citizens' Initiatives

*a. Citizens' Charters should be made effective by stipulating the service levels and also the remedy if these service levels are not met.

*b. Citizens may be involved in the assessment and maintenance of ethics in important government institutions and offices.

*c. Reward schemes should be introduced to incentivise citizen's initiatives.

*d. School awareness programmes should be introduced, highlighting the importance of ethics and how corruption can be combated.

32. (5.2.5) False Claims Act

a. Legislation on the lines of the US False Claims Act should be enacted, providing for citizens and civil society groups to seek legal relief against fraudulent claims against the government. This law should have the following elements:

i. Any citizen should be able to bring a suit against any person or agency for a false claim against the government.

ii. If the false claim is established in a court of law, then the person/ agency responsible shall be liable for penalty equal to five times the loss sustained by the exchequer or society.

iii. The loss sustained could be monetary or non-monetary as in the form of pollution or other social costs. In case of non-monetary loss, the court would have the authority to compute the loss in monetary terms.

iv. The person who brought the suit shall be suitably compensated out of the damages recovered.

33. (5.3.5) Role of Media

*a. It is necessary to evolve norms and practices requiring proper screening of all allegations/complaints by the media, and taking action to put them in the public domain.

*b. The electronic media should evolve a Code of Conduct and a self regulating mechanism in order to adhere to a Code of Conduct as a safeguard against malafide action.

*c. Government agencies can help the media in the fight against corruption by disclosing details about corruption cases regularly.

34. (5.4.2) Social Audit

*a. Operational guidelines of all developmental schemes and citizen centric programmes should provide for a social audit mechanism.

35. (6.2.5) Promoting Competition

*a. Every Ministry/Department may undertake an immediate exercise to identify areas where the existing 'monopoly of functions' can be tempered with competition. A similar exercise may be done at the level of State Governments and local bodies. This exercise may be carried out in a time bound manner, say in one year, and a road map laid down to reduce 'monopoly' of functions. The approach should be to introduce competition along with a mechanism for regulation to ensure performance as per prescribed standards so that public interest is not compromised.

*b. Some Centrally Sponsored schemes could be restructured so as to provide incentives to States that take steps to promote competition in service delivery.

*c. All new national policies on subjects having large public interface (and amendments to existing policies on such subjects) should invariably address the issue of engendering competition.

36. (6.3.5) Simplifying Transactions

*a. There is need to bring simplification of methods to the center-stage of administrative reforms. Leaving aside specific sectoral requirements, the broad 37. (6.4.7) Using Information Technology principles of such reforms must be: adoption of 'single window' approach, minimizing hierarchical tiers, stipulating time limits for disposal etc.

*b. The existing Departmental Manuals and Codes should be thoroughly reviewed and simplified with a responsibility on the Head of the Department to periodically update such documents and make available soft-copies on-line and hard copies for sale. These manuals must be written in very precise terms, and phrases like 'left to the discretion of', 'as far as possible', 'suitable decision may be taken' etc should be avoided. This should be followed for all rules and regulations governing issue of permissions, licenses etc.

*c. A system of rewards and incentives for simplification and streamlining of procedures may be introduced in each government organization.

*d. The principle of 'positive silence' should generally be used, though this principle cannot be used in all cases. Wherever permissions/licenses etc are to be issued, there should be a time limit for processing of the same after which permission, if not already given, should be deemed to have been granted. However, the rules should provide that for each such case the official responsible for the delay must be proceeded against.

37. (6.4.7) Using Information Technology

*a. Each Ministry/Department/Organization of Government should draw up a plan for use of IT to improve governance. In any government process, use of Information Technology should be made only after the existing procedures have been thoroughly re-engineered.

*b. The Ministry of Information and Technology needs to identify certain governmental processes and then take up a project of their computerization on a nationwide scale.

*c. For computerization to be successful, computer knowledge of departmental officers needs to be upgraded. Similarly, the NIC needs to be trained in department specific activities, so that they could appreciate each other's view point and also ensure that technology providers understand the anatomy of each department.

38. (6.6.4) Integrity Pacts

*a. The Commission recommends encouragement of the mechanism of 'integrity pacts'. The Ministry of Finance may constitute a Task Force with representatives from Ministries of Law and Personnel to identify the type of transactions requiring such pacts and to provide for a protocol for entering into such a pact. The Task Force may, in particular, recommend whether any amendment in the existing legal framework like the Indian Contract Act, and the Prevention of Corruption Act is required to make such agreements enforceable.

39. (6.7.3) Reducing discretion

*a. All government offices having public interface should undertake a review of their activities and list out those which involve use of discretion. In all such activities, attempt should be made to eliminate discretion. Where it is not possible to do so, well-defined regulations should attempt to 'bound' the discretion. Ministries and Departments should be asked to coordinate this task in their organizations/offices and complete it within one year.

*b. Decision-making on important matters should be assigned to a committee rather than individuals. Care has to be exercised, however, that this practice is not resorted to when prompt decisions are required.

*c. State Governments should take steps on similar lines, especially in local bodies and authorities, which have maximum 'public contact'.

40. (6.8.7) Supervision

*a. The supervisory role of officers needs to be re-emphasised. It bears reiteration that supervisory officers are primarily responsible for curbing corruption among their subordinates, and they should take all preventive measures for this purpose.

*b. Each supervisory officer should carefully analyze the activities in his/her organization/office, identify the activities which are vulnerable to corruption and then build up suitable preventive and vigilance measures. All major instances of loss caused to the government or to the public, by officials by their acts of omission or commission should be enquired into and responsibility fixed on the erring officer within a time-frame.

c. In the Annual Performance Report of each officer, there should be a column where the officer should indicate the measures he took to control corruption in his office and among subordinates. The reporting officer should then give his specific comments on this.

d. Supervisory officers who give clean certificates to subordinate corrupt officers in their Annual Performance Reports should be asked to explain their position in case the officer reported upon is charged with an offence under the Prevention of Corruption Act. In addition, the fact that they have not recorded adversely about the integrity of their subordinate corrupt officers should be recorded in their reports.

e. Supervisory officers should ensure that all offices under them pursue a policy of suo motu disclosure of information within the ambit of the Right to Information Act.

41. (6.9.4) Ensuring Accessibility and Responsiveness

*a. Service providers should converge their activities so that all services are delivered at a common point. Such common service points could also be outsourced to an agency, which may then be given the task of pursuing citizens, requests with concerned agencies.

*b. Tasks, which are prone to corruption, should be split up into different activities that can be entrusted to different persons.

*c. Public interaction should be limited to designated officers. A 'single window front office' for provision of information and services to the citizens with a file tracking system should be set up in all government departments.

42. (6.10.2) Monitoring Complaints

a. All offices having large public interface should have an online complaint tracking system. If possible, this task of complaint tracking should be outsourced.
b. There should be an external, periodic mechanism of 'audit' of complaints in offices having large public interface.
c. Apart from enquiring into each complaint and fixing responsibility for the lapses, if any, the complaint should also be used to analyse the systemic deficiencies so that remedial measures are taken.

43. (6.12.7) Risk Management for Preventive Vigilance
*a. Risk profiling of jobs needs to be done in a more systematic and institutionalised manner in all government organizations.
*b. Risk profiling of officers should be done by a committee of 'eminent persons' after the officer has completed ten years of service, and then once in every five years. The committee should use the following inputs in coming to a conclusion:
(i) The performance evaluation of the reported officer.
(ii) A self-assessment given by the reported officer focusing on the efforts he/she has made to prevent corruption in his/her career.
(iii) Reports from the vigilance organization.
(iv) A peer evaluation to be conducted confidentially by the committee through an evaluation form.

44. (6.13.2) Audit
*a. It should be prescribed that as soon as any major irregularity is detected or suspected by the audit team, it should be immediately taken note of by government. A suitable mechanism for this may be put in place. It shall be the responsibility of the head of the office to enquire into any such irregularity and initiate action.
*b. Audit teams should be imparted training in forensic audit.
*c. Each office should make an annual public statement regarding pending audit queries.

45. (6.14.3) Proactive vigilance on corruption
*a. Taking proactive vigilance measures should primarily be the responsibility of the head of the office. Some possible measures are indicated in para (6.14.2).

46. (6.15.2) Intelligence Gathering
*a. Supervisory officers should assess the integrity of his/her subordinates based on his/her handling of cases, complaints

and feedback from different sources. This could then become an important input for risk profiling of officers.

47. (6.16.2) Vigilance Network

*a. A national database containing the details of all corruption cases at all levels should be created. This database should be in the public domain. Identified authorities should be made responsible for updating the database regularly.

48. (7.9). Protecting the Honest Civil Servant

*a. Every allegation of corruption received through complaints or from sources cultivated by the investigating agency against a public servant must be examined in depth at the initial stage itself before initiating any enquiry. Every such allegation must be analyzed to assess whether the allegation is specific, whether it is credible and whether it is verifiable. Only when an allegation meets the requirements of these criteria, should it be recommended for verification, and the verification must be taken up after obtaining approval of the competent authority. The levels of competent authorities for authorizing verifications/enquiries must be fixed in the anti-corruption agencies for different levels of suspect officers.

*b. In matters relating to allegations of corruption, open enquiries should not be taken up straightaway on the basis of complaints/source information. When verification/secret enquiries are approved, it should be ensured that secrecy of such verifications is maintained and the verifications are done in such a manner that neither the suspect officer nor anybody else comes to know about it. Such secrecy is essential not only to protect the reputation of innocent and honest officials but also to ensure the effectiveness of an open criminal investigation. Such secrecy of verification/enquiry will ensure that in case the allegations are found to be incorrect, the matter can be closed without anyone having come to know of it. The Inquiry / Verification Officers should be in a position to appreciate the sensitivities involved in handling allegations of corruption.

*c. The evaluation of the results of verification/enquiries should be done in a competent and just manner. Much injustice can occur due to faulty evaluation of the facts and the evidence collected in support of such facts. Personnel handling this task should not only be competent and honest but also impartial and imbued with a sense of justice.

*d. Whenever an Inquiry Officer requires to consult an expert to understand technical / complex issues, he can do so, but the essential requirement of proper application of mind has to take place at every stage to ensure that no injustice is caused to the honest and the innocent.

*e. Capacity building in the anti-corruption agencies should be assured through training and by associating the required experts during enquiries/ investigations. Capacity building among public servants who are expected to take commercial / financial decisions should be built through suitable training programmes.

*f. The supervisory officers in the investigating agencies should ensure that only those public servants are prosecuted against whom the evidence is strong.

*g. There should be profiling of officers. The capabilities, professional competence, integrity and reputation of every government servant must be charted out and brought on record. Before proceeding against any government servant, reference should be made to the profile of the government servant concerned.

*h. A special investigation unit should be attached to the proposed Lokpal (Rashtriya Lokayukta)/State Lokayuktas/Vigilance Commission, to investigate allegations of corruption against investigative agencies. This unit should be multi-disciplinary and should also investigate cases of allegations of harassment against the investigating agency. Similar units should also be set up in States.

Bibliography

Aristotle. *The Ethics of Aristotle*, edited by J.A.K. Thomson. London: Penguin Books, University Press, 1958.

Arora, Ramesh K. ed. *Ethical Governance in Business and Government*. Jaipur: Aalekh Publishers, 2013.

——. *Ethics in Governance: Innovations, Issues and Instrumentalities*. Jaipur: Aalekh Publishers, 2008.

Bayles, Michael D. *Professional Ethics*, 2nd ed. Belmont, Calif.: Wadsworth, 1989.

Beauchamp, Tom L., ed. *Ethics and Public Policy*. Englewood Cliffs, N.J.: Prentice-Hall, 1975.

Benn, P. *Ethics*, London: Routledge, 2000.

Blackburn, S. *Being Good: A Short Introduction to Ethics*, Oxford: Oxford University Press, 2001.

Böhme, Gemot (translated by Edmund Jephcott). *Ethics in Context: The Art of Dealing with Serious Questions*, Cambridge: Polity, 2001.

Cahn, Steven M. (ed.), *Exploring Ethics: An Introductory Anthology*. New York: Oxford University Press, 2009.

Callahan, Daniel, and H. Tristram Englehardt. *The Roots of Ethics: Science, Religion, and Values*. New York: Plenum Press, 1981

Callahan, Daniel, and Sissela Bok, eds. *Ethics, the Social Sciences, and Policy Analysis*. New York: Plenum Press, 1983.

Corr, P.J. and G. Matthews (Eds.), *The Cambridge Handbook of Personality Psychology* Cambridge: Cambridge University Press 2009.

Denhardt, Katherine G. *The Ethics of Public Service: Resolving Moral Dilemmas in Public Organizations*. Westport, Conn.: Greenwood Press, 1988.

Eckel, Malcolm W. *The Ethics of Decision Making*. New York: Morehouse-Barlow, 1968.

Ewing, A.C. *Ethics*, New York: Free Press, 1953.

Frankena, W.K. *Ethics*, Englewood Cliffs NJ, Prentice-Hall, 1963

French, Peter A. *Ethics in Government*. Englewood Cliffs, N.J.: Prentice-Hall, 1983.

Ghuman, B.S., Anil Monga, Ramanjit Kaur Johal, eds. *Corruption and Quality of Governance*. Jaipur: Aalekh Publishers, 2012.

Giri, Ananta K., *Values, Ethics and Business: Challenges for Education and Management,* Jaipur: Rawat Publications, 1998.

Graham, Gordon. *Theories of Ethics: An Introduction to Moral Philosophy with a Selection of Classic Readings*. UK: Routledge, 2011.

Griffin, J. *Value Judgement: Improving our Ethical Beliefs*, Oxford: Oxford University Press, 1996.

Gupta, Ananda Das. *Ethics in Business: Concept, Cases and Context*. Jaipur: Rawat Publications, 2005.

Guttman, Amy, and Dennis Thompson. *Ethics and Politics*. Chicago: Nelson-Hall, 1984.

Harman, G. *The Nature of Morality: An Introduction to Ethics*. New York: Oxford University Press, 1977.

Hatcher, Tim. *Ethics and HRD: A New Approach to Leading Responsible Organizations*. Jaipur: Rawat Publications, 2007.

Hudson, W.D. *Modern Moral Philosophy*, Basingstoke: Macmillan, 1983.

Jacobs, J.A. *Ethics A-Z*, Edinburgh: Edinburgh University Press, 2005.

Jones, W.T. *Approaches to Ethics: Representative Selections from Classical Times to the Present*. 3rd ed. New York: McGraw-Hill, 1977.

Kerner, G.C. *Three Philosophical Moralists: Mill, Kant, and Sartre*, Oxford: Oxford University Press, 1990.

Leys, Wayne A.R. *Ethics and Social Policy*. New York: Prentice-hall, 1941.

MacIntyre, Alisdair. *A Short History of Ethics*. New York: Collier, 1966.

Mackie, J.L. *Ethics: Inventing Right and Wrong*, Harmondsworth: Penguin, 1977.

Murdoch, I. *The Sovereignty of the Good*, London: Ark, 1985.

Nagel, T. *Mortal Questions*. Cambridge: Cambridge University Press, 1979.

Nietzsche, F. *Beyond Good and Evil: Prelude to a Philosophy of the Future* (translated by R.J. Hollingdale with An Introduction by Michael Tanner). London and New York: Penguin, 1990.

Ramsey, Paul. *Ethics at the Edges of Life*. New Haven, Conn.: Yale University Press, 1978.

Raphael, D.D. *Moral Philosophy*, Oxford: Oxford University Press, 1981.

Rawls, J. *Theory of Justice*. Cambridge, Mass.: Harvard University Press, 1971.

Reamer, Frederic G. *Social Work Values and Ethics*. Jaipur: Rawat Publications, 2005.

Reid, T. *Practical Ethics* (edited by Knud Haakonssen). Edinburgh: Edinburgh University Press, 2007.

Richter, William L. et al. *Combatting Corruption: Encouraging Ethics – A Sourcebook for Public Service Ethics*. Washington, D.C.: American Society for Public Administration, 1990.

Sheeran, Patrick J. *Ethics in Public Administration: A Philosophical Approach*. Jaipur: Rawat Publications, 2006.

Singer, Marcus. *Generalizaton in Ethics*. New York: Alfred A. Knopf, 1961.

Thomson, J.A.K., ed. *The Ethics of Aristotle*. London: Penguin Books, 1955.

Warnock, G.J. *Contemporary Moral Philosophy*, London: Macmillan, 1967.

Warnock, M. *Ethics Since 1900*, Third edition, Oxford: Oxford University Press, 1978.

Williams, B. *Ethics and the Limits of Philosophy*, London: Fontana, 1985.

Index